ULTIMATES IN THE FAR EAST

Books by Hudson Strode

South by Thunderbird

Timeless Mexico

Now in Mexico

Sweden: Model for a World

Finland Forever

Denmark Is a Lovely Land

The Pageant of Cuba

The Story of Bermuda

Immortal Lyrics: An Anthology of English Lyric Poetry

Spring Harvest: A Collection of Stories from Alabama

Jefferson Davis: American Patriot

Jefferson Davis: Confederate President

Jefferson Davis: Tragic Hero

Jefferson Davis: Private Letters, 1823–1889

Hudson Strode

ULTIMATES IN THE FAR EAST

Travels in the Orient and India

Harcourt Brace Jovanovich, Inc.

New York

First edition
ISBN 0–15–192580–1
Library of Congress Catalog Card Number: 75–117576

Printed in the United States of America

The lines by Robert Frost quoted on page 243 are from "Stopping by Woods on a Snowy Evening," from The Poetry of Robert Frost, edited by Edward Connery Lathem, copyright 1923 by Holt, Rinehart and Winston, Inc., copyright 1951 by Robert Frost; reprinted by permission of Holt, Rinehart and Winston, Inc.

For Thérèse

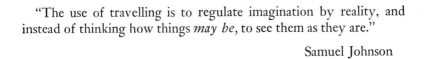

"The use of travelling is to regulate imagination by reality, and instead of thinking how things *may be*, to see them as they are."

Samuel Johnson

Contents

Foreword) *xiii*

Japan) *1*
  The Japanese Have a Word for It) *3*
  Green Belts and Tempura) *10*
  Autographs and Puppets) *19*
  Nikko: Gilded Tombs and Lordly Cedars) *26*
  A Buddhist Girl and a Literary Man) *37*
  To Hakone by Way of Kamakura) *46*
  Fuji with Snow) *54*
  Kyoto, "Capital of Tranquillity") *62*
  First Permanent Capital) *74*
  A Garden of Mosses and an Imperial Villa) *82*

Hong Kong) *91*
  Fragrant Harbor) *93*
  A Stroll and Charlie Mok) *97*
  Magic Casement) *102*
  The Legendary Tailors) *110*
  Holiday for Sweeping the Ancestors' Graves) *114*
  A Mine of Information) *118*
  Aberdeen and Repulse Bay) *123*
  Gloomy Thursday—and Fortunate Friday) *133*

Cambodia) 141
   The Khmers and Angkor Thom) 143
   "The Ultimate Expression of Khmer Culture") 158

Thailand) 165
   Sweet Day to Do Nothing) 167
   Another King and I) 176
   Siamese Phantasmagoria) 189
   Mystery of the Thai Silk King) 201
   Facts from a Happy Economist) 211
   Thirty-seven Golden Barges) 217
   Floating Markets and Fragrant Tokens) 223

India) 231
   Madame Pandit and Nehru's Museum) 233
   The Road to Agra) 244
   The Taj Mahal) 251
   To Jaipur) 265
   The Maharani of Jaipur) 274
   City Palace and Amber) 281
   "Think It Over") 289
   Heritage from Britain) 293
   Tiger Burning Bright) 298
   Old Delhi) 303
   Rajghat and the Place of Assassination) 309
   Stone's Embassy and an Alfresco Luncheon) 314
   Farewell, Delhi) 322

Acknowledgments) 327

Illustrations

Between pages 206 and 207

Shrine gateway, Toshogu Mausoleum, Nikko
Mount Fuji in winter
Aerial view of Horuyji Temple, Nara
Katsura Imperial Villa, Kyoto
A Chinese junk in Hong Kong Harbor
The fishing village of Aberdeen
Ruins of Angkor Thom
Temple of Angkor Wat
Her Majesty Queen Sirikit of Thailand
His Majesty King Bhumibol of Thailand
Chedis in the Royal Compound, Bangkok
Two of the golden barges in the Royal Barges Procession
The Taj Mahal, Agra
The Hawa Mahal, Jaipur
Palace at Amber
Chandni Chowk, Old Delhi

Foreword

The Elizabethan poet-soldier Sir Philip Sidney, on an early grand tour of the Continent, wrote to his brother: "A great many of us never thought in ourselves why we went, but a certain tickling humour to do as others have done." Travelers motivated merely by so plain an urge undoubtedly have their reward. Others go off to distant places for a richer recompense and are enticed by personal predilection to venture to this region or that. After a long life of travel and the publishing of eight books interpreting alien lands and cultures—from the green continent of South America to a kingdom as small as Denmark—I saved for the climax a voyage to the Orient and India.

This trip had been in my mind and on my heart ever since the time of my youthful enthusiasm for Joseph Conrad's books, which reflect some of his exotic sailings. I had been particularly enchanted by Bangkok in old Siam. For a score of reasons and after varied postponements, however, it was not until September, 1967, that I actually sailed with my wife, Thérèse, for the Far East to fulfill my youthful dream. In the words of Dr. Johnson, perhaps I went "to regulate imagination by reality," to see everything as it really was. Yet the reality surpassed my imagination.

In 1935, in the primitive days of air flight, I flew over the snow-encrusted Andes, and that flight remains in my memory as the ultimate in exciting beauty seen from the air. Once I spent a golden year in Italy and a February in Sicily, when the almond orchards were in bloom. I have enjoyed a week's cruise in and out of the Norwegian fjords to the North Cape in late June, when the sun shone at midnight. I have been thrilled by the skyline of Istanbul with its resplendent domes and minarets. I have reveled in the antiquities of Athens and Delphi and Crete. I have journeyed by bus in Finland from Rovaniemi on the Arctic Circle through that strange region of Lapps and reindeer to the Arctic Ocean. I have visited mosques and souks in Tunisia's once holy city of Kairouan and beheld the Sahara Desert below Biskra under the setting sun. But the climax of my journeys came in this recent voyage to the Far East.

The revolution in travel conditions in the East in one decade has been phenomenal. Today one does not have to endure the discomforts of the past. With transportation at the speed of sound and communication at the speed of light, far-distant travel has been touched with a kind of magic. Jet planes are commonplace in the air between the Asiatic cities. Luxury hotels have recently risen all over Japan, Southeast Asia, and India. Air conditioning is accepted as a component of modern living. Continental cuisine and uncontaminated water are assured in all the best hotels.

Because I have a strong affinity to the sea, my wife and I began the journey by water, sailing from San Francisco for Japan on the *President Cleveland*. We ended the tour by water, embarking from Naples on the *Leonardo da Vinci* in mid-December and reaching New York on Christmas Eve. The rest of the trip was by airplane, from Japan to Hong Kong, to Cambodia, to Thailand, to India, and thence to Rome. Our only train rides were in Japan, on her famous railways. Within countries we traveled sometimes by private car, with English-speaking drivers.

Since I was six I have enjoyed traveling, and I know how to travel economically. On my first trip to Europe I went steerage on a French liner. But in these later years, I have found it energy-saving to go first class and to stay in luxury hotels.

In India today one may journey by air-conditioned automobile, as well as by air-conditioned trains and buses. But it is still important to go in a good season, to avoid both the monsoon rains and the intolerable heat of late spring and summer. The fall is the best time, when the heat has abated even in the dank Cambodian jungle. The late spring, with cherry blossoms, is fine for Japan, but not good for Bangkok, New Delhi, and Agra, where the temperature soars. During the months of September, October, and November we found the weather salubrious.

Except for years of desultory reading of fiction and nonfiction about the Far East, I had little direct knowledge of the region. When we began to make our plans we knew personally only two individuals living in the entire area, a Thai girl named Wattanee, who was teaching accounting at Chulalongkorn University in Bangkok, and a former American student of mine, a girl now married to a British newspaper correspondent in Hong Kong. We knew no Indian, and no Japanese residing in Japan, although we had earlier been initiated into a Japanese tea ceremony and had seen a Noh drama. Back in October, 1939, a month after World War II had begun, when we were returning from Sweden on the last voyage of the *Gripsholm*, we had a table next to two Japanese gentlemen, one a millionaire paper manufacturer, the other his Harvard-educated secretary. They invited us to a tea ceremony performed with elegant and elaborate equipment, which they carried around the world with them. Of all unlikely places, we were initiated in the ritual of *chanoyu* with powdered emerald-colored tea at a corner table in a quiet room the ship's captain had provided. No charming little teahouse, set in a garden, was reached by steppingstones; we did not have to sit on the floor. Though we had rare caddies and bowls, known as *meibutsu*, which have been zealously preserved by the feudal aristocracy, instead of an ancient Japanese wall scroll for us to admire there was only the two-shaded blue horizon framed by a rectangular window. Yet we spent an hour in pleasure and instruction, and at the conclusion Mr. Fujihara's secretary, Mr. Fukukita, presented my wife with an inscribed copy of his book *Cha-no-yu, Tea Cult of Japan*, handsomely bound in pale-green silk. Long before 1967 Mr. Fujihara, who became a member of Japan's war cabinet, was dead. And I did not know how to locate the secretary, if he was indeed still alive.

In the early spring before our departure we had attended a performance of the leading Tokyo troop of Noh actors on their American tour. We met the performers at a party following the show, but not one, except the half-American manager, spoke English.

By blessed chance, however, only two months before we sailed, the Marchioness Chiye Hachisuka of Atami was brought to tea at our house by newcomers to our town, Ruth and Jack Shaver, who had lived for fourteen years in India and Japan. Madame Hachisuka became interested in our trip, suggested agreeable adjustments in our schedule, and wrote half a dozen prominent Japanese personages about our coming visit. Ruth Shaver happened to be godmother to the granddaughter of Madame Pandit, Nehru's sister, and she wrote the girl's mother, Rita Dar.

My friend Seymour Ziff, a New York business consultant with connections in Tokyo, telephoned to some men in a highly successful electronics concern. A former Japanese student of mine, Emiko Sakurai, now teaching Oriental literature at a branch of the University of Virginia, wrote to a literary friend in Tokyo.

These varied introductions proved delightful evidences of serendipity. Horace Walpole, who coined the word from those traveling princes of Serendip, defines "serendipity" as "the gift of finding valuable or agreeable things not naturally sought for." So we were to chance upon fascinating spots and memorable personalities—unheard of, undreamed of before we set out to circle the earth.

Our plans were emphatically eclectic: to see the glorious antiquities, like the magnificent temple of Angkor in Cambodia; the luminous, incomparable Taj Mahal in Agra; the Buddhist temple gardens of ancient Kyoto, still redolent of the enlightened consciences of their creative designers.

The pleasure journey turned out to be one of splendor and infinite variety. I was granted an audience with the charismatic young King Bhumibol of Thailand. We saw the rare water procession of thirty-seven golden barges on River Chao Phraya in Bangkok, the most spectacular pageant in the contemporary world. In Tokyo the day we arrived I was taken that evening to an international press party for the champion sumo wrestler, Taiho, chosen as Japan's man-of-the-year. In New Delhi our first lunch was with the distinguished Madame Pandit, who gave me a private tour through Nehru's home, Teen Murti, which is now a museum, with his personal effects left just as they were at the hour of his death. We were received by the Maharani of Jaipur, often called the world's most beautiful woman, who is a highly intelligent leader of the Conservative party. We were privileged to visit ex-Premier Shigeru Yoshida's garden in Oiso, where I first saw Fuji from his special rustic bench for viewing the volcano, and we were entertained at tea in his conservatory by his daughter. I talked with rich industrialists in Japan and with devout Buddhists. I learned much from Sikh chauffeurs in India. I got ideas from Japanese magazine editors, from tailors in Hong Kong, barbers in Thailand, room boys, shopkeepers, efficient

German hotel managers in Thailand and India, lovely women of the social world, and Connie Mangskau, the Thai-born friend who was with Jim Thompson, the Thai Silk King, when he disappeared during a house party in Malaya. Peculiarly rewarding were the perceptive and well-educated professional guides in various countries. The interesting variety of human contacts gave me much insight into the heart of matters. I found genuine warmth in the people of each country we visited. It was easy to form friendships. I have always enjoyed the foreign, the unfamiliar. We had no intention of judging by American standards, or "spying into abuses," to use Shakespeare's phrase, or criticizing the social orders in transition. What we did not understand, we respected.

"Tourists in the main are a very gloomy tribe," Aldous Huxley, an inveterate traveler himself, said to me when he was staying with us at our home in Tuscaloosa the year before he died. "I have seen brighter faces at a funeral than in the Piazza of St. Mark's."

"Ah, that was in sticky Venetian summer," I protested, "when you fight to get a seat at a café table in the square. In the spring and fall the faces are bright enough."

Huxley, wearing a handsome sports coat tailored in Hong Kong, grinned amiably, because I had caught him up. While we talked stretched out in long chairs in our garden with azaleas in full end-of-March bloom, he went on to say that for every traveler who has special tastes of his own the only useful guidebook will be the one that he has written himself. "Others often mark with stars works of art that he finds dull. Occasionally he is enticed to travel long disagreeable miles to see a pile of rubbish."

Many excellent books on Japan and India are to be enjoyed, and there is Malcolm MacDonald's valuable *Angkor*. But I know of no book that depicts travel in Japan, Hong Kong, Cambodia, Thailand, and India in a single volume. So I have set down this account of an unflurried journey for the benefit of those who plan to travel in the East, to make green again memories of those who have visited the Far East, and to evoke for those who travel by armchair the golden realms.

While I think I saw everything with clear vision, I must confess to being enthusiastic. Yet I have described events just as they happened and recorded conversations as they occurred. That redoubtable Thomas Carlyle, who can hardly be accused of sentimentality, once wrote: "If a book comes from the heart it will contrive to reach other hearts. All art and authorcraft are of small account to that." It is my hope that my feeling for these alien lands and peoples may communicate with my readers.

HUDSON STRODE

Cherokee Road
Tuscaloosa, Alabama
May 27, 1970

JAPAN

The Japanese Have a Word for It

As a writer of books "interpreting" foreign lands, and consequently a traveler, I feel somewhat as St. Augustine did fifteen centuries ago when he said, "The world is a book, and those who do not travel read only one page." Now that I have been up and down and around the world I cannot believe that there is a more fascinating page for the alien than Japan. What makes it unique is its utterly different ambience; it is not suggestive of any other spot in Europe, Africa, or the Western Hemisphere. Richly endowed at the primal creation, it has been cultivated by the world's most gifted gardeners. Japan's infinite variety of contrasting topography—jagged mountains, wildly cascading waterfalls, green fields spread serenely in cultivated terraces, sand beaches adorned with wind-sculptured rock, and thatched cottages along winding, flowery lanes—offers continual delights under the twelve-winded sky. An evanescence, caused by a capricious sun and enchanting mists, keeps the charm from becoming too familiar. At one and the same time I was to find the Japanese landscapes "peaceful and exciting," as Gertrude Stein found Paris.

The *President Cleveland* docked at the port of Yokohama around ten on a Thursday morning. An English-speaking representative of the Japan Travel Bureau came on board to assist us during entrance procedures. A pleasant, highly intelligent young matron in a Western-style suit was to be our guide. She asked us to call her by her first name, Kiyoka, as her married name was long. A private car was waiting to take us to our hotel in Tokyo. There is nothing of significant interest on the traffic-congested way from Yokohama to Tokyo. It is merely low-keyed Japanese in architecture, advertising signs, and kimonos on village streets. What struck us particularly was that pine trees in the vicinity of factories were dying at the top. "The pines are weak to the gas," our guide explained, unconsciously using a very apt phrase. Ordinarily, Kiyoka, a university graduate, spoke very good English with scarcely a trace of accent. The Japanese were seriously concerned about the damage to trees from industrial air pollution, she told us, but because of the necessity of swift economic comeback from the war's devastation, so far little had been done, though strong measures were under consideration. In a small town through which we passed, the main street was lined with flourishing gingko trees, which were not nearly so "weak to the gas" as the lofty pines. The gingkos were approaching the end of their summer green. Soon their fan-shaped leaves would turn a glorious gold, Kiyoka said. "The gingko tree is long-lived and is considered a good omen. You will see many gingkos in the grounds of your hotel, the Okura, and the distinctive gingko leaf, unlike any other, has been utilized in single-leaf pattern generously by decorators throughout the hotel." Then she added rather wistfully, "The Japanese have always regarded the pine as the symbol of stability and strength, but, alas, it finds industrial modernity hard to cope with."

In the sprawling largest city in the world with more than eleven million citizens, much of Tokyo looked brand new. A mighty building boom was in progress ever since the war's end, when a third of the city lay in rubble. Tokyo is by no means beautiful, but some of the new buildings in the modern style are pleasing enough. And altogether, except for the increased traffic, it is much more attractive than it was before the bombs fell.

We swirled around the façade of the handsome United States Chancellery, built in Hoover's time, up a short steep street and into the grounds of the Okura Hotel, which had a private museum set like an enormous summerhouse in the front garden. The front rooms of the hotel faced across the street the trees that embowered the American Embassy.

The Japanese have "a word for it": "*shibui.*" Among its meanings are "mellowed, understated richness," or "the acme of good taste," "intrinsic good quality, both sober and rich at the same time," and "simple beauty undefiled." On our noontime arrival at the Okura, poised in the portico was the personification of the word. She was tall and slender, in her middle thirties, exquisitely groomed, and wearing a kimono of rich silvery-gray silk with some simple stylized design woven into the material in colors of wheat and bronze. She wore no jewelry. The delicate bone structure of her face, the distinction of her features, stamped her beauty as aristocratic. As she stood in an expectant attitude, her lovely head held high, at once cool and alert, she seemed unaware of the comings and goings swirling about her. When her limousine drew up, she stepped in with unaffected grace, very sure-footed. Behind her lingered no expensive aroma of French perfume, but a wisp of inimitable glamour. In sheer admiration I paused until her charming image dissolved in the throng of cars. "*Shibui,*" I said to my wife. "Absolutely," she agreed, as we entered the Okura lobby with its own quiet elegance.

I took a quick glance at the spacious, high-ceilinged proportions of the striking lounge beyond the lobby, the harmony of the soft dove colors, the gingko leaf stamped in platinum on draperies, the upholstered wide modern chairs—black, deep gold, or cream-colored—arranged about round low black lacquered tables in fives like the petals of a lotus flower. Pale yellow hexahedral lamps were strung from the ceiling perpendicularly in series of fives and hung in clusters of six. "Yes," Thérèse said, "*shibui!*"

When I had finished registering, Kiyoka said, "Mr. Nohara is on his way to greet you. He's the J.T.B. head executive in charge of independent tours. Shall we await him in the lounge?"

We had just found chairs about a table when Mr. Nohara appeared. He was not tall, but he was the handsomest Japanese male we had ever seen. He looked like a movie star of the matinee-idol type. He had enormous dark eyes and perfectly molded features; he reminded me of a calm, slightly Oriental Lord Byron. With utmost urbanity and delicacy he had really come to be paid in advance for the varied services the Japan Travel Bureau was to render us between this last day of September and October 13.

First, he presented us with two booklets attractively bound in blue cloth with stitched decorations in stylized bands. Within was the Strode itinerary, day by day, for sight-seeing in Tokyo, for train trips to Nikko and to Kyoto, and private cars to Kamakura, Hakone National Park, and Nara. There were maps of the cities we were to visit, instructions on how to stay at a Japanese inn, useful phrases in Japanese, information on flower arrangements, on Japanese gardens, on population, on religion, and, surprisingly, the location and telephone numbers of leading Catholic and Protestant churches, including the Christian Science church. One item in the little book struck my special interest: "Water from the tap is safe in any city or town throughout Japan."

Mr. Nohara also presented us with two decks of playing cards artistically encased in burgundy-colored velour and stamped "*Ukiyo-E*" in gold. "*Ukiyo-E*" is the Japanese term for prints of genre pictures of the Edo period. The subjects were chiefly active figures and profiles of Kabuki actors and girls at their toilettes or walking under parasols in the rain. Each of the fifty-two cards was different, and all were beautifully reproduced.

The cordial amenities óbserved in some ten agreeable minutes, I felt that the moment had arrived for me to draw out my checkbook. "Don't you think I might as well pay J.T.B. now for all the services to come?" Almost as if deprecating such a gesture, Mr. Nohara said, "Perhaps—if it is entirely convenient." So I made out a draft on the First National Bank of Tuscaloosa, Alabama, which he accepted with a faint bow. After a promise to secure permission from the Royal Household for us to visit the Katsura Detached Imperial Villa at Kyoto, he was gone.

"In a moving picture he could play Genji, if he could act," Thérèse said to Kiyoka. Lady Murasaki's *Tale of Genji* was one of her favorite books, and Genji was something like a beau ideal among the heroes of world literature.

My first introduction to a Japanese business transaction conducted with suavity and grace was followed late that afternoon by a totally unexpected business affair with rare hospitality as a bonus. A strongly British-accented voice on the telephone announced himself as John Ishizaki, managing editor of the magazine *This is Japan*. Our mutual friend Madame Hachisuka had written him from San Francisco and asked him to call. Down in the lounge a smiling Japanese with a decidedly Western aura was awaiting me with a lovely young Japanese woman, one of his assistant editors. He had brought a copy of the last issue of his magazine—a handsome, heavy, ten-by-thirteen volume got up in best Japanese style and published once a year by the great newspaper *Asahi Shimbun*. "It is printed in English and goes to seventy different countries about the world," Mr. Ishizaki said. "We hope you will do an article for us for *This is Japan*, 1969. Whatever you care to write about—any phase of Japan. See, Lin Yutang has the lead article in this number. Men of various nations write for us, as well as our Japanese authors." Before I could say yea or nay or protest that I had only been in Tokyo a few hours, a staff photographer had his camera poised and took six shots of me. Mr. Ishizaki told me he would give me top rates. "It's not as much as you would get from *Holiday*, say, but it's the best we can afford." Agreed. I would think about a special subject as we traveled. "And now," Mr. Ishizaki said with a flashing smile, "Mrs. Shimomura and I want to take you and your wife to a cocktail party at the Overseas Press Club honoring the man of the year, Taiho, the world champion sumo wrestler. It will be a good introduction to cosmopolitan Japan. We shall return for you in a couple of hours. And do call me John."

"My name is Mitsuko, but please call me Mitzi," said the lovely girl. "Everyone does."

It was all so quick and so dynamic, so warm and cordial that I was slightly carried away. I had only time to ask one question of the girl. "Are you a Buddhist?"

"Indeed I am, and my engineer father is a Zen Buddhist teacher at Kamakura." We parted with bows and handshakes, to meet again in two hours.

"The East and the West have met," I said to Thérèse back in our room, "and we are more one than twain. The Japanese are briskly efficient. Their charm seems to match their vitality. And already I have found a real Buddhist for you—a delightful young woman you will like. She promises to come to tea one afternoon."

Later, in the front seat of John's small car, we three sat cozily as he drove with remarkable skill through the traffic. (Thérèse had elected to stay in the room and do some drip-dry washing.) Mitzi pointed out the vast outer walls of the moated Imperial Palace in the center of the business district as we sped past. "Almost everywhere you go in Tokyo you will pass on one side of the Imperial Palace," she said.

In the Press Club the first man John introduced to me was the correspondent for the *Manchester Guardian*, who had masterminded and mostly written the excellent article signed by Prime Minister Shigeru Yoshida in the 1967 edition of Encyclopaedia Britannica's *Book of the Year*. Ishizaki seemed to know everybody, and when he went to the bar to get me a Scotch-and-water, Mitzi introduced me to several journalists of European papers, some youngish Japanese, and several men from the diplomatic corps. When John brought my drink I was enjoying conversation with an interesting attaché of the Saudi Arabian Embassy. The card he handed me said that his name was Bashir Kurdi. Just as the Saudi Arabian was offering to show me some of Tokyo one day, there was a stir and then a hush as the champion in his huge magnificence entered the reception room. He was wearing a black satin kimono. I set down my glass to join in the applause. I had expected a sumo wrestler to be massive in girth, but hardly to be six feet three in this nation of rather short men.

Taiho had good-looking features in his round face and a well-scrubbed, pink-and-white complexion. He was the cleanest-looking man imaginable. His black hair was drawn back from his high, wide forehead into a topknot in wrestler fashion. People clustered about enthusiastically, some reaching for his hand, as the popular idol made his way to stand behind a broad table at the far end of the room, on which sat an ink pot and brush and small sheets of paper. Someone brought him a soft drink. Taiho did not drink anything alcoholic, any more than did the Buddhist girl at my side, who sipped orange juice.

"Taiho comes from the far north in Hokkaido," Mitzi explained. "His mother is Japanese, but his father was Russian. He is only twenty-seven. The professional name he took, Taiho, means 'the best,' 'the ultimate.' He has already bettered past records in the number of individual matches won. His toughest adversary is now himself," Mitzi said, "—to keep himself in prime condition for the duration of the next five grueling fifteen-day tournaments."

Taiho, whose real name is Koki Naya, was born in 1940. As a little boy he had an exceptional physique and phenomenal physical strength. In primary school he peddled fermented soybeans on the street and delivered newspapers, getting up at four in the morning in the freezing temperature of Hokkaido. He was number one in every sport, from baseball to table tennis. When he finished junior high school at fifteen, he stood more than six feet tall. Now, at six feet three, he weighed 314 pounds. At sixteen he had entered his first wrestling tournament and won seven out of eight matches. Altogether, he had won the tournament twenty-five times, with total victories of 548 matches. "Taiho," Mitzi said, "is an inspiration to Japanese youth, for he proclaims that 'a genius is one who strives more than anybody.' "

When John Ishizaki took me over to present me, he handed Taiho the stiff thick program sheet, turned it over on the unlettered side, and asked for his autograph in both Japanese and English. With deft strokes Taiho obliged in distinguished calligraphy. As I put out my hand to accept it, John, noting the contrast in the size of our hands, impulsively reached for Taiho's and then mine and put them palm to palm. Since Taiho's well-shaped, well-manicured hand was massive and I come of two families with small hands, the sizable difference drew a broad grin from the amiable champion, who spoke no English.

I safely stowed the calligraphic autograph with my hat before giving myself over to the cosmopolitan evening and the buffet supper. Taiho's double autograph is framed in black and decorates a wall in my studio like a small Japanese scroll.

When Ishizaki and Mitzi brought me back to my hotel, I felt that my first day in Japan with its pleasant surprises had given me significant insight into a race very different from the Anglo-Saxon. Within the borders of exotic lands one is supposed to meet profound differences. But except for the language I felt surprisingly little strangeness in the Japanese themselves. If they spoke English, I would find myself forgetting that they were "Japanese." Barriers dissolved in the first smile, bow, American handshake. Friendly relations were quickly established—at least with those under forty. Many of the Japanese, who are the travelers among the Orientals, have developed a distinct aura of the cosmopolite.

From talking with younger men at the party I had quickly gathered that this present generation of Japanese has no militaristic yearnings. They re-echo the words of the late Shigeru Yoshida when he declared as prime minister that he absolutely opposed the rearming of Japan. The money saved on armaments hastened the economic resurgence that has amazed the world, and flooded Japan with consumer goods and unaccustomed luxuries. Today's young men have no notion of being drawn from their new amenities into foreign fights. As palpable as is their country's need for more arable land, few young Japanese would lift a rifle for territorial expansion. Japan's boys are pleased to stay on home soil, however crowded, and enjoy their motor bikes and new cars and grow an inch or two taller than their fathers on the regular meats and sweetmeats that many of their parents tasted only on festival days. The young men like their Western-style clothes, smart or sloppy, their pocket money for girls and shows, their seaside vacations and sports of all kinds, from karate and mountain climbing to the fantastically popular American baseball. The youths strive to take advantage of the seventy-three colleges and universities in Tokyo alone that are open today to the cleverest among them. The young Japanese licks his current bowl of butter with a grin, and he has no itch to finger a gun except for duck or deer shooting.

Green Belts and Tempura

We did not need the services of our J.T.B. guide the next two days, because Seymour Ziff, a New York friend, who had a consultant's interest in the Tokyo Electron Laboratories, had arranged matters for our pleasure. The firm's president, Mr. Endo, who was not using his car on those days, put it at our disposal. With his chauffeur came a sweet, pretty Japanese girl, who had accompanied the Ziffs on some of their excursions. She was one of the secretaries of Mr. T. Kubo, the general manager of the concern. Her name was Yasuko. She was a modern Japanese in a Western suit, but she had lost none of her countrywomen's traditional deprecating appeal. She welcomed the opportunity to practice her English, though she confessed with a giggle to odd deficiencies and to having told Rita Ziff that the National Diet Building, the impressive seat of Japan's Parliament, was the National Banquet Hall.

Yasuko reminded us at starting that there are more people in Tokyo than can be properly handled, that there was inadequate housing, and that there were far too many motor vehicles for comfort. Tokyo is where all the members of the imperial family live. Here the national government functions and the Supreme Court and various other traditional offices are established. Here are located the foreign embassies and the headquarters of foreign firms. Thousands of foreigners at a time pour into the capital for international conventions. A tour through the Marunouchi, the chief business district, with its high buildings bearing names of well-known American firms, gives vivid evidence that Tokyo leads in industrial production, embracing huge plants and distributing organizations. Tokyo is something like a New York, Washington, and Detroit merged into one supermegalopolis, though still remaining racially homogeneous.

The crowded conditions of the world's most densely populated metropolis, with its time-devouring traffic congestions, are made bearable by numerous spacious parks and "green belts." In the city's very heart spreads a 250-acre oasis, the grounds of the Imperial Palace.

As we approached the plaza before the estate's great eastern gates, Yasuko said, "There are only two days when the public is allowed inside the palace garden. These fall on January 2, the New Year's Festival, and on April 29, the Emperor's birthday. Though the Emperor is no longer worshiped as a god, no modern monarch has such complete privacy."

Because Tokyo was first called Edo, the Imperial Palace was originally called Edo Castle. It was built by a war lord named Ota-Dokun in 1457. Then for centuries Edo was the administrative center of Japan under the Tokugawa shogunate.

When the Imperial Court was transferred from Kyoto to Tokyo in 1868 by the powerful Emperor Meiji, the palace was rebuilt, the slanting masonry walls of the moat were strengthened, and the periodic corner towers were heightened and reinforced. Pine trees were ordered planted so that their roots would bind the soil and prevent erosion of the embankments. The willow-fringed feudal moat that encloses the royal estate has romantic overtones. To many a foreign visitor it is the capital's outstanding attraction. When Paul Claudel, the French poet, was ambassador to Japan from 1921 to 1926, he declared that the most beautiful place in Tokyo was the moat surrounding the Imperial Palace grounds. The extensive plaza before the main gate has pleasant stretches of pine-studded turf on either side of the graveled open space. It is a favorite meeting place of the Japanese people. As Yasuko said, "The Imperial Palace Plaza is to Tokyo what Hyde Park is to London."

When Emperor Hirohito broadcast his dramatic surrender message, citizens by the thousands converged on the plaza, prostrated themselves in grief, and wept for their Emperor and the nation. Some officers and common soldiers stained the ground with their blood by committing hara-kiri unrestrained. Now with the new democratic ways, since the American occupation, young couples "going together" occupy the benches and court, almost, as it were, in the Emperor's presence, irreverent and unabashed.

"Turn around," Yasuko suggested, "and you can see a new Tokyo." There across the enormously wide boulevard rose the silhouette of the Marunouchi, the district of the waxing industrial economy. "A few of the bolder greedy ones," she said, "would like to buy up this open plaza before the palace gates to erect more high buildings, and in time even get hold of the palace grounds."

"As it has been suggested," I interpolated, "that that sublime square of San Marco would make a fine parking lot for tourist automobiles in Venice."

Yasuko drew in her breath in shock, and then said, "With Tokyo land in this vicinity selling for eighteen million dollars an acre—more, I read, than in Manhattan—perhaps the idea is tempting, but the *people* of Japan aren't that depraved—yet."

To get a better perspective I asked that we drive entirely around the walls and moat of the Imperial Palace. During our October visit the sloping turf embankments were lushly verdant and the west side was dotted with naturalized white lilies. Scores of old peasant women, brought into the city in trucks, were working in diagonal rows across one area of turf at a time, plucking weeds from about the flowers and stuffing them into trailing sacks. With their head-rags and tucked-up skirts, their stooping bodies made an arresting animated frieze.

After circumnavigating the vastness of the Imperial Palace grounds we wanted to visit Meiji Park, with its three hundred open acres. The park and Meiji Shrine commemorate that Emperor Meiji who brought about Japan's real debut into the modern world, mightily stimulated by Commodore Perry's famous two visits with his steam frigates in 1853 and 1854, which resulted in opening the doors of Japan to American trade. The outer garden of 120 acres includes: the ultramodern Olympic Stadium, built in 1963; a 60,000-seat baseball park; a Rugby football ground; two enormous swimming pools; and a vast auditorium. All of these postwar facilities are architecturally good in themselves and enjoyed with gusto by the intensely sports-minded Japanese, according to their skills and enthusiasms. But we were chiefly interested in the Inner Garden, a beautiful wooded park of 180 acres, holding at its climax a Shinto sanctuary dedicated to the Emperor.

This memorial park has more than 100,000 trees presented by municipalities from all over the nation. On the long, broad winding road, where no vehicles are permitted, one passes under four rust-reddish torii gateways with towering pillars forty feet high and four feet in diameter, each made of Formosan cypress logs, said to be 1,700 years old. Even with the treading streams of Japanese sight-seers and school children in regulated batches with teachers holding aloft rallying identification banners, the great oaks of the forest on either side created a palpable sense of peace.

"In June the garden is particularly beautiful when the water lilies of the pond blossom and a hundred varieties of iris are in bloom," Yasuko told us, while we strolled happily under the arch of spreading branches that met overhead. "The original shrine, which was completed only in 1925, was partially destroyed by bombs on April 1, 1945," Yasuko said. "This shook the people's faith in the imperial divinity. Until then the Japanese believed that the Meiji Shrine and the Imperial Palace were invulnerable to American bombs, even though a great part of Tokyo lay in rubble. But the restoration was made in 1958, and men have begun to come again not only for recreation, but to pray."

When we arrived at the shrine, I took my place with Japanese supplicants in Western business suits. I threw some coins into the wire-netted pit, clapped my hands to attract the presiding deity's attention, and breathed a prayer that the rest of our sojourn in Japan would be as pleasant as our first twenty-four hours had been.

On our way back to the old Imperial Hotel, we circled the 125 landscaped acres of Tokyo National University. This, Yasuko told us, was *the* university of Japan. Those young people accepted as students have exceptional minds and abilities. Altogether, some 16,000 are enrolled. They sit before the nation's most eminent professors and lecturers. Admission is so fervently sought that each year several aspirants who have failed the stiff entrance examinations kill themselves for causing their parents disappointment. Even though there are seventy-two other colleges in Tokyo where they might receive a good education, they prefer death. Tokyo National University is a government institution and has arisen on what was once the feudal estate of the wealthy Maeda family. The botanical gardens of the university are much admired, because of their rare trees and shrubs. In 1890, the Crown Prince, who later assumed the throne as Emperor Taisho, set a patron's example by planting some trees himself, which have grown to maturity and are marked with identification.

The morning's drive and walks had given us the assurance of the love of the Japanese for open spaces and green growing things even in a city bursting at the seams with human beings and where every square foot of earth is at a constantly increasing premium. We thought it a pity that so many foreign visitors do not venture far from the so-called fabulous Ginza with its posh department stores and dance halls and the mere excitement of crowds by day and by night.

The old Imperial Hotel, where we were to be the absent Seymour Ziff's guests at lunch in the famous Prunier's Restaurant, had been built solidly by Frank Lloyd Wright to withstand earthquakes. We were among the last to eat there, for the old building, once so admired for its architectural design, was shortly to be torn down. Though it had acquired fame as one of the world's outstanding hotels, to us it seemed excessively heavy with its interior stonework —much of it imported from Stone Mountain in Georgia—and now rather dingy. Not having stayed at the Imperial in its heyday I had no sentimental qualms about its destruction, as so many senior Americans did. Its annex across the parking space was already flourishing with the modern luxuries.

At Prunier's, named for its Paris counterpart, seafood is the specialty, so we lunched on lobster chosen from its bed of ice in a glass case. The restaurant tables were almost completely occupied by smartly tailored Japanese businessmen who exuded an aura of recently acquired wealth.

That evening we dined with Mr. T. Kubo, general manager of Tokyo Electron Laboratories, at a very different style of restaurant, pure Japanese and for us something "out of this world." The place stands out as a rare treat for discriminating foreigners who want a distinct flavor of Japan. The Inagiku Tempura Restaurant is smallish, expensive, and set in a tree-shaded, lantern-lit court, on a side street in the retail business district. Though Mr. Kubo spoke fluent English, he brought Yasuko along, not to interpret but to act as hostess.

We were greeted by graceful kimonoed girls in the vestibule, who knelt to remove our shoes and put soft slippers on our feet. In a parlor or smoking room we paused in comfortable chairs for an appetizer and were presented with tightly rolled hot wet cloths in wicker baskets.

Over a small glass of sake, Kubo gave an inadvertent sigh and grinned slightly, as he began to relax from the business tensions of a hard day. We knew little about the man except that Seymour Ziff had said that he was an absolute whizz in business affairs, with a sixth sense and a genius for organization. Kubo had done us the courtesy of paying us a brief call at the Okura the afternoon of our arrival, just before John Ishizaki came. He had sent his card to our room. It was engraved "T. Kubo." Beneath it was his title: General Manager, Tokyo Electron Laboratories. Like the Norwegians, many Japanese do not care to reveal their first names and use only the initials. When I pointedly asked him what the T. stood for, he confessed it was Tokuo. "But in New York," he said, "my bosses and friends called me Tom."

When Kubo had been offering his services and inquiring into our special interests, I felt that his penetrating eyes were unobtrusively sizing us up. He was unusually long-limbed for a Japanese. His six feet towered above all the rest of his countrymen in the hotel lounge. Decidedly unhandsome, with irregular features and small eyes, he was yet vibrantly attractive. His aura, however, was sympathetic, anything but hard-boiled. He came from Kyushu, that island province at the south end of Japan. As soon as he finished college he had boldly ventured to New York, where he had got his first business training in various jobs in Wall Street. Returning to Japan just as the gross national product began to surge, with his training in American business dealings he had risen rapidly. Now in his mid-thirties, he was obviously what is called a marked success.

At the Inagiku, as he relaxed more and more—for he did not find our company a strain—Kubo told about his business trip the previous week to Bangkok, where we were going shortly. He had succeeded in accomplishing his mission, but there had been high-powered, strenuous sessions. To recharge his batteries he had hired a private launch to take him on a trip along the klongs to the famous floating markets across the river.

"When I first saw those natives along the klongs," Kubo said, "existing in such poverty on their little boats or in their stilted shacks, I was appalled, and I pitied them. Then as our motor launch proceeded through jungle-like scenery, I came to discern their contentment, their actual joy in living, their utter freedom from care or worry—for they had abundant food. And I said to myself, 'Why, those happy poor people would not exchange lots with me for anything.' Don't you suppose they even felt a bit sorry for me and my tense-nerved kind?"

A strange wistfulness seemed to transform his features. A girl came to ask if we were ready to be served dinner in an adjoining room. Then with the smile of a host he rose and said brightly, "Well, I suppose one must follow his destiny."

Three weeks later at our meeting with Seymour Ziff in Hong Kong, when I spoke of this wistfulness in Kubo and his experience on the Thai klongs, he was astonished. He had seen only the business-genius side of this rangy Japanese. And he was amazed that we felt—of all things—affection for him.

In the dining room we were seated at a circular counter with contrivances of electrical cooking equipment. The chef, rotund and jolly, ascended from a lower floor on a round elevator platform. One cook served six persons at a time. A New Zealander and an Australian sat on the other side of our circle. "The largest number that can be served at one banquet is fifty," Yasuko said. "It is in another room."

Tempura is the name of special batter in which the delicacies are fried. First an egg yolk is well mixed with water, then some flour is lightly added. The ingredients, fish or fresh green vegetables, are thoroughly coated with the batter and cooked in a vegetable oil made of sesame, olive, and camellia oils. Prawns are the favorite shellfish, and they are never so delicious as in tempura, not even those wonderful Yugoslavian *scampi* served at Harry's Bar in Venice. Bits of various fish in season are served from the Inagiku's own fish preserves. One piping-hot morsel after another was placed on our plates, while a maid from behind our chair stools kept the sake cup replenished. Nobuo Asona, master in the big hall, declares that every morning for the last thirty years he has offered a thirty-minute prayer, "freeing his mind from earthly thoughts," and desiring only that he cook a tempura that his guests will enjoy with keen relish. One wonders if the promised ambrosia of paradise would measure up to Inagiku shrimp in tempura.

When we had eaten so much with such tempting flavors, we implored the chef to desist. So, smiling, he touched a button, gave an appreciative bow and a farewell wave, as the whole center complex dropped completely out of sight into a lower floor like a bit of magic.

Returning to a small parlor, and again being presented with hot wet cloths, we were served fruit for dessert, luscious large white grapes and those crunchy pale Japanese pears, shaped strangely like apples. On departing came the ritual of shoes and shoehorn by beguiling Cho-Cho-Sans, who at the last shyly pressed into our hands gifts of special chopsticks and boxes containing two little curved ceramic fish designed as chopstick rests. The car, which had been parked in the lantern-lit, flowery patio, was right at the door. We had had a very special Japanese dinner never to be forgotten, and when we drove on into the garish, night-bedizened Ginza, we thought we wanted absolutely none of that.

On sudden impulse, however, I suggested that we leave the car and walk down the neon-blazing Ginza for a few blocks with the chauffeur trailing us. And in that most unlikely setting for serious conversation, at the relatively uncrowded evening hour of half past nine, I saw into the heart of the matter of the trauma of Japan's defeat and the phenomenal recovery that has surpassed anything of its kind in world history.

In answer to a question, as we strolled and glanced desultorily into the glittering windows of famous department stores, Mr. Kubo spoke softly. But his words were incised on my mind.

"Our recent ancestors," he said, "set their goals on acquiring extra territories. In 1905 they defeated Czarist Russia. Then they began annexing hunks of earth like Manchuria, Okinawa, Korea, Formosa, and smaller islands here and there, just as Britain did so lavishly in the nineteenth century. During the economic crisis created by the world depression of the 1930's, Japan's nationalism hit a new high. With it came a fervent revival of the mythology of the emperor's divine ancestry and the glorification of the warrior class. Through brisk trade we gained a kind of economic dominance in various Asiatic countries. Then by miscalculation, by seeking too much and striking at Pearl Harbor, we lost every square foot of our acquisitions in the twentieth century. And the emperor-god myth died irrevocably.

"Along with losing the war and outlying possessions, the majority of our people also lost their religious beliefs. We had actually been taught in school that Emperor Hirohito was a god and that the Japanese people were invincible. Even when the war was going very badly for us we still believed in ultimate victory. And then one day over the wireless—I was just eleven—the Emperor admitted utter defeat and said in so many words, 'Submit to the conqueror on his terms.' We were stunned and aghast. Scales dropped from the eyes of Japanese youth along with the stinging tears, and we no longer believed in anything. We were left in a vacuum."

We paused at a street crossing. I realized that perhaps no country in history has ever been more touched to the quick by defeat than Japan. I had heard from others that pride went into the ash cans and that the unstrung Japanese virtually wallowed in the misery of humiliation. Some begged on the streets; others involved themselves in shady deals. Some well-brought-up girls painted their faces blatantly, acquired a vulgar walk, and asked for chewing gum and often a night's custom.

We went over to the next curb and continued our stroll. Kubo resumed his thoughtful explanation. "Crushed and confused, betrayed by heaven and the military leaders, after a while we turned within and found a reserve of resilience that began to work like yeast. We gradually shook off the neurosis of defeat by laboring with a will to rebuild and to produce—in peace."

Kubo saw that he held our complete and sincere interest and talked on. We heard directly from his Japanese lips much of what we knew from recent reading. In a few short years, starting again from scratch, Japan became the number-one shipbuilder of the world, and also first in the production of motorcycles and radio and TV sets. She had risen to second place in the production of cameras, watches, and spun rayon, and third in steel and cotton fabric. And because daily labor is cheaper than in America and Europe, new markets open weekly around the globe. Trade continues to escalate. In these last fifteen years Japan has achieved an annual average economic growth of almost 10 per cent a year, a record unsurpassed by any great power. According to economic experts the gross national product of Japan passed the hundred-billion-dollar mark in 1967 and put Japan in fourth place among nations, after the U.S.A., the U.S.S.R., and West Germany. In 1969 it was to rank third.

"So Japanese prestige is steadily rising," Kubo said, "as less advanced countries are assisted with investment and loan programs on stipulation that the goods and services bought with the money should be of Japanese make. Our electrical engineers, chemists, agricultural experts, bankers, executives of industries are to be seen in the best Eastern hotels unobtrusively looking over situations for trade expansion. Her financiers and trading groups seek investments, not only in the East, but also in South America and far-flung regions like Africa's Zambia, where they look to buy up copper facilities."

We had strolled three long blocks when the car came up alongside and we got in. It had been an enlightening as well as a delightful evening. Mr. Kubo's restrained, quiet explanation of the shock and resulting neuroses of Japan's paralyzing defeat was felt in the innards as much as in the brain.

When he let us out at our hotel the evening was not over for him. He had to catch a train for his surburban home. He would be back at his office at half past eight. Yasuko also lived in suburbs, in a different direction. She caught a seven-thirty train on most evenings and was generally at her office desk by eight in the morning. The Japanese worked not only hard at whatever they did, but for long hours as well. This was a large part of the reason for the country's phenomenal rise. The demoralization after the war lasted only a few horrid years. Then self-discipline, which is a keynote of the Japanese character, began to reassert itself and the traditional virtues were again admired and pursued.

Autographs and Puppets

Yasuko arrived at our hotel the next morning at ten, fresh as a daisy, although she had risen at six, taken a jammed commuters' train, and put in two hours of early-morning office work. She bore a gift to Thérèse from Mr. Imamichi, chairman of the board of Tokyo Electron. It was a handsome outsize book called *Japanese Gardens for Today*, with hundreds of illustrations of garden details, both in color and in black and white. The author was David H. Engel, a young American garden-maker, who had spent four years in Japan studying models, and who is becoming more noted year by year. "This is Mr. Kubo's prompting," I said, recalling his brief visit the afternoon of our arrival. When he had asked what we were principally interested in seeing in his country, Thérèse had impulsively said, "Gardens." Kubo had replied, "You will see the best of those in Kyoto." But he had remembered, and now here was this unexpected beautiful gift.

"Mr. Imamichi," Yasuko said, "regrets that he is indisposed at his country estate, but Mr. Endo, the president of the company, is expecting us for luncheon." Mr. Imamichi, who was a passionate garden lover, hoped that we would care to see his garden "hanging under the sky" on the sixth floor of the Tokyo Broadcasting Station's Kaikan Building outside the board room's wall of glass.

It had begun to rain as we drove off in Mr. Endo's car to Ueno Park with its collection of first-rate museums, art galleries, and a noted zoological garden. Because of weather reports forecasting rain we had brought raincoats and umbrellas, although the car itself carried two rolled umbrellas against emergencies. The Japanese forget nothing.

This was not the right day for even a quick tramp through the park to the menagerie of foreign and native animals and birds. So we concentrated on our chief objective, the Tokyo National Museum, a vast structure covering four acres. This is the largest museum in Japan and houses the most extensive collection of Japanese archaeology and art in the world. It also contains priceless collections of Chinese and Korean art. Protected by umbrellas and overshoes we wound around puddles in the paved courtyard and entered the massive door.

We passed through the Japanese archaeological section, which contains over 36,000 individual items, pausing only to admire the most striking pieces of sculpture. Many of the splendid Buddhist statues on view were on long-term loan from various temples. We had glimpses of Jomon pottery and rare masks and figurines, Yokin bronze mirrors, and Kofu metal works of swords, helmets, and horse trappings. We admired Chinese paintings dating to the eighth century, together with some exquisite Chinese ceramics.

We must have overstayed our time, for when we got held up in an unexpected traffic jam partly caused by the rain, Yasuko jumped from the car to call from a street-corner telephone booth that we would be about ten minutes late. Though in the residential district, where street names and numbers are baffling and sometimes incomprehensible, a Japanese host is prepared for late arrivals, in the business district punctuality is as essential an amenity as in Sweden. The rain had ceased by the time we reached the gleaming modern Kaikan Building. We went by elevator to one of the upper floors to Mr. Kubo's office, passing through an enormous room where hundreds of typewriters were clicking. Kubo met us at the door and led us to a small reception room where three youngish executives received us. Chilled orange juice was served immediately. Then Kubo excused himself. He could not join us for luncheon, for he was about to close a deal with a big United States firm whose representative was even then in his office studying charts.

On the wall facing me I spied four framed single-page letters of most unlikely dead celebrities: Turgenev, Shelley, Bismarck, and Edgar Allan Poe. As my eyes widened in delighted amazement one of the young men said, "Autograph letters of famous personages is Mr. Imamichi's other hobby, besides gardens. Would you like to see other letters in the room across the corridor?"

In the great rectangular reception room six large square wooden pillars of polished wood supported the high paneled ceiling. At comfortable eye level on each of the twenty-four faces hung a framed holograph letter from a person of world renown. The wonder grew as I went from pillar to pillar, reading the signatures of Goethe, Byron, Darwin, Jefferson, Lincoln, Verdi, Baudelaire, Sarah Bernhardt, Anatole France, Dumas *père*, Whitman, and others. Fascinated, I asked, "How on earth did Mr. Imamichi collect these treasures?" The answer was that a Princeton professor friend of his had got most of them from dealers in autographs and that Mr. Imamichi himself picked up a few in Paris and London.

From the letters and the wall cabinets of priceless artifacts we turned to the long glass wall with sliding doors. Outside lay the garden under a blue sky that had suddenly cleared. It utilized the roof of a wing of the building. Obviously Japanese, it was yet smartly modern. There was no turf, only a ground cover of large white pebbles about the size of pigeon eggs glistening with the wetness like enormous pearls. Dwarf pines, now enhanced by water drops, were set with calculated artistry here and there. Some small-leafed vines adorned the oyster-white masonry walls that surrounded three sides. A smaller-than-life-size green bronze statue, modern in conception, but not contorted, stood on a stone pedestal in the garden's center. The garden was severely tailored, with no stream, no bridge, no lantern, no flowering shrub generally found in the traditional Japanese garden. It was all pearly white and green, striking, if austere. As we stood silent, gazing, one of the men volunteered the information that this recently designed garden was quite different from the extensive "stroll" garden at Mr. Imamichi's place in the country. "But if one is pressed with anxiety over some deal or contract," another said, "he can slide the doors back and step out under the sky and take a turn or two among the dwarf pines to clear his thinking."

I confessed that I liked this modern conception of a garden, because it was just as he implied, so "clarifying."

The luncheon was in a front private room of a French restaurant on the ground floor of the building. Along the corridor red-and-white-striped awnings over tables simulated sidewalk cafés in Paris. The chef, we were told, was French and had been Prime Minister Yoshida's chef when he was ambassador to Great Britain. The food and the wines had been chosen with expert care. The Japanese take quickly to cosmopolitan ways, even though underneath is that residue of centuries of distinctive culture that no contacts with the new Western civilization will dislodge.

Mr. Endo proved to be a chubby, shortish man, who radiated such infectious good humor that he might have been created by Dickens. He had very light skin and ruddy cheeks. For all his business acumen, which had thrust him into a significant presidency, he smiled as if his achievement were a bagatelle. A jolly Japanese is anything but typical, and Mr. Endo was one of those rare viscerotonic Japanese who seems to take life cheerfully, no matter how hard he works or what things go wrong. It was a gay and pleasant meal; all talk of business was as taboo as at a tea ceremony.

Yasuko looked in her purse to be sure she had the tickets for the Bunraku matinee. When Kubo had asked us if we wanted to see a Noh drama, a Kabuki performance, or a glittering girlie show something like the Folies-Bergère, I had said that we would much like to see one of the famous Japanese puppet shows.

Because of the matinee and the fact that the men had to get to their work, the luncheon ended without ceremony, though without any sense of haste. We went back up to the executive offices with Mr. Endo. Thérèse and I wanted, if possible, to say good-by to Mr. Kubo and thank him for all his thoughtful courtesies. When he came out from his inner sanctum, I said, "I trust that you got the contract just as you wanted it."

He grinned at me slowly in a way that seemed both frank and sly, and, as if taking me into his secret, said, "*As* usual." Not cocky, not boastful, hardly smug, yet his simple statement had such a positive ring that I almost trembled at his colossal assurance.

Comfortably seated in the theater a few minutes later we noted that the audience was about 95 per cent Japanese and that a goodly percentage of the patrons were in kimonos. Yasuko said these people came again and again, year after year, to see the same plays.

The puppet show in Japan—the Bunraku—is undoubtedly the best of its kind in the world. The artistry of manipulation of the three-foot-high dolls is amazing. The movements and the expressions of the figures are guided by the expert hands of stone-faced puppeteers, who often have inherited their jobs from generations of ancestors. The audience shares in the excitement as they see the puppets "laugh, weep, make love, fight, dance, seduce, kill." The dramatic reader we heard was little short of superb. He sits traditionally to the side of the stage and nearer to the audience, as if in an unroofed royal box, turning the pages of the oversized parchment text with studied effect. He speaks the lines of all the puppet actors. This man had both a magnificent presence and a splendid voice, which he could make roar or coo. His mobile face with darting eyebrows changed to the emotion of the moment. Whatever the program provides, the impression of a Bunraku performance is like an enduring seal on wax. No foreigner should miss the puppet show in Tokyo.

Because we had somehow gathered that Yasuko had an appointment with a suitor when she was done with us, we did not stay for a second puppet performance. Four or five different plays are presented, one following another. Many in the repertoire are classics and have played to generations. The one we had just seen had a vivid plot line with suspense to the very end, and it ran a veritable gamut of emotions. As we came out into the lobby, Yasuko excused herself to call her "boy friend" (her word), for she would be free sooner than she had expected. Then she gave the order to the chauffeur to take us back to our hotel.

When Mr. Kubo had said that Seymour Ziff wondered if we would like a geisha party, I had answered with an emphatic "No, thank you." I knew that a dinner in a geisha house was terribly expensive, and though such parties given by businessmen were tax-deductible on expense accounts, it seemed for us a waste of money. Besides, I had read that many executives were now patronizing high-priced night clubs with glittering floor shows, finding them more exciting than the geisha's traditional entertainment and playing on the monotonous three-stringed samisen. Now suddenly I realized that we had had for two days the refreshing services of a young lady who was really like a highly intelligent geisha, at little cost to anyone. Yasuko had made the most amiable of geishas, though without costly kimono, elaborate lacquered wig, and clown-white painted face. She had been fresh, charming, and well-informed, with natural, not studied, sweetness, and with a delightful rippling little giggle which I doubted the most accomplished geisha in Tokyo could surpass. It was her mission to please, as well as to be our guide, and she had pleased us utterly. Making her living in the new world of business, she had yet lost none of that shy grace that goes with the world's conception of the Japanese woman.

That evening we met a Japanese lady who gave not the faintest indication of being the subservient wife of folklore and literature. Her husband was Shimichiro Kudo, head of the Manichi newspapers. At the suggestion of our mutual friend, Madame Hachisuka, Mrs. Kudo had telephoned us and asked us to dine with her and her husband. She had also arranged with Mrs. Takakichi Aso, the daughter of ex-Prime Minister Yoshida, for us to visit his garden in the seaside town of Oiso on our way to Hakone the following week. Mrs. Kudo, pure Japanese, was born in Seattle, where her father had extensive business connections. Part of her upbringing had been in the States.

When we joined the Kudos in the Okura lobby there was obviously an aura of the American woman about the wife. She was as direct as she was gracious, and I felt that a kimono would be hampering to her. Her husband was essentially Japanese. The two words that sprang to mind were "courtly" and "sophisticated." Though his well-groomed, wavy hair was iron-gray, his face was youngish. He was extraordinarily handsome, with chiseled features of aristocratic distinction. Mrs. Kudo said that, to give us a change, she was taking us to the best and most popular Chinese restaurant in the city. She said that she had left the car on a side street by the Okura and led the three of us out the entrance into a night drizzle. She herself took the wheel, for it was the chauffeur's evening off.

At the garish restaurant's entrance, strung with colored lights and Chinese banners, she gave the car over to an attendant to park and led us up broad stairs to a semiprivate dining room on the second floor. She had already ordered the food by telephone, merely telling the headwaiter to serve us his very best menu. When the excellent, exotic dinner, which began with shark-fin soup and duck, was over, the lady paid the bill. Her amiable husband seemed pleased to let his wife handle all the details, for she did it with such ease and competence. We noticed that Mr. Kudo ate most sparingly, barely tasting of each delicacy. I got the idea that he was exercising care in maintaining his slim, lithe figure, of which his wife was as proud as he.

It is often said that while Japanese wives are reticent in public, they are supreme matriarchs in their households, until the husbands get home in the evening. We had heard that a Japanese man generally gives his wife the household money to handle. We did not inquire into the intimacies, but we judged from three hours that Mrs. Kudo saved her husband diurnal energy that he put to good advantage in his management of one of the world's most-read newspapers.

I questioned Mr. Kudo about the role I assumed that Japan might play in the near future, and he replied with modest candor. "In many Oriental countries there is increased discussion of those contributions Japan could make to the stability and prosperity of Southeast Asia in general. While the Japanese have no immediate desire to take on the 'protection' of disturbed Eastern nations, if Communism, stemming from either Red China or Russia, becomes too offensive and invasive, Japan may feel forced to take up arms again. And whether the younger generation likes it or not, capable Japan, as the foremost capitalistic nation of the East, may feel impelled to assume certain responsibilities and obligations, particularly when the United States withdraws from Vietnam."

"Will it not be hard to rouse contemporary youth to put on military uniforms?" I asked. "From what I have gathered in our few days in Japan, the sons and nephews of those gallant kamikazes, who volunteered for suicide air missions in the Pacific war, seem too satisfied with their prosperous ways ever to make such heroic gestures."

Mr. Kudo's smile was by no means inscrutable. "As we have both seen patently in our time, propaganda can do almost anything. After this interval of bountiful peace for us, it may not be easy to stir Japanese youth to military ambitions. It will take most extraordinary and dynamic propaganda. Even now, without propaganda, the young men are clamoring for the United States to return Okinawa to Japan immediately, though the American bases there are serving to protect us in Japan, and Okinawans relish the American cash that flows in. The occasional youth riots in Tokyo are for peace, for noninvolvement. But, as I say, a turn in events could create a potent new propaganda."

The only student riot that occurred while we were in Japan happened the very next morning and resulted in the first fatality. Thousands of organized youths were protesting against involving alliances and aiming to prevent Prime Minister Sato from being lured into any pact with the United States that would ship a Japanese to fight on some alien soil.

Nikko: Gilded Tombs and Lordly Cedars

A popular Japanese saying runs: "Do not speak of splendor until you have seen Nikko." One of Japan's chief centers of pilgrimage and sight-seeing, Nikko is visited by ten million tourists annually, including hundreds of thousands of foreigners. A Japanese guide-book declares that Nikko is considered by many foreigners the most interesting spot in Japan. Some persons will suggest to the newly arrived visitor that he leave Nikko for last, lest every other attraction seem anticlimactic. But even before we had been to Kyoto we felt that the climax lay there in that ancient capital, with its thousand Buddhist temples.

Though the majority of tourists do the Nikko trip in one day, it is tiring, with three or four hours spent on trains. We had arranged to stay the night at the Kanaya Hotel to give two days to the area.

Our guide, Kiyoka, came for us at eight. We left from the Asakusa Station by the comfortable Tobu Electrical Railway. In less than two hours we were in the cool, invigorating atmosphere of Nikko, ninety-one miles north of Tokyo. The town lies at the edge of the Nikko National Park, with its spectacular assortment of mountain peaks, clear blue lakes, tumbling cascades, and idyllic small farms.

The picture window of our second-floor room in the Kanaya Hotel gave upon a noble prospect. Just beyond the edge of the garden, spanning the narrow Daiya River, was the famous Sacred Bridge with its brilliant vermilion lacquer glowing despite the drizzle that had begun to fall. The rapids of the swift river threw silvery veils of foam over the rocks. The bridge, originally placed in the seventeenth century and rebuilt later, commemorates the spot where in the ninth century two accommodating serpents miraculously appeared to take over the water a holy man, who placed a foot on the back of each reptile. Beyond the gracefully humped bridge, which may be crossed only by priests, lay the shadowy incline leading up to the Temple Grove surrounding the Toshogu Mausoleum and various shrines. Trees rose to towering heights and hid the religious structures from our view. Scores of pilgrims and tourists were negotiating the upward path leading to the sanctuaries. Under a scattering of raised umbrellas, the women, for the most part, wore kimonos, but some of these were obscured by raincoats.

The green garden just beneath us, with a stone Buddha meditating under a tree, was spread with inviting deck chairs, deserted now in the dampness. In the original fountain of the pool, water gushed up from and spilled over a large moss-covered hollow cypress stump.

After an early luncheon, to avoid the rain we did not approach the shrines like the pilgrims, but drove a long way around and into a parking space surrounded by lofty cedars. Kiyoka told us that it is believed that some Shinto shrine was established in Nikko as early as the fourth century. It is historically known that a Buddhist temple was founded in 767 by a noted priest named Shodo Shonin. She reminded us that the Japanese often practiced without any disharmony both the ancient Shintoism and Buddhism, which had been brought in from Korea in the sixth century.

The elaborate complex of gateways, mausoleums, temples, shrines, pagodas, reliquaries, armories, and stables for the sacred horses was created as a memorial to the most illustrious of Japan's shoguns, the redoubtable Ieyasu Tokugawa, who died in 1616, the same year as Shakespeare.

"Shogun" was the title of military governors of Japan who usurped power. "The word is equivalent to 'generalissimo,' " Kiyoka said, "and also has much the same significance as 'tycoon,' from the Japanese *taikun*, meaning 'great lord.' "

During the last half of the sixteenth century Japan was wracked by terrific feudal struggles. Ieyasu Tokugawa, born in 1542, as able as he was ruthless, possessed political genius. Playing one powerful war lord against another, by 1600 he became virtual dictator of Japan. In 1603 Ieyasu made his headquarters at Edo, which was to be renamed Tokyo only in 1868. The Tokugawa shogunate Ieyasu established lasted for 265 years.

It was the third Tokugawa shogun, Iemitsu, who sought to glorify his grandsire and himself by creating all the grandeur spread out on terraces rising before us. Though there are some writers whose enthusiasm for Nikko is decidedly tepid, the site is considered one of the Orient's most splendid monuments after that of India's Mumtaz Mahal, who has the incomparable Taj Mahal for her tomb. In 1626, Iemitsu employed thousands of the Orient's finest artists and workers, who labored for a full decade and completed the monument in 1636, the very year in which Mumtaz died.

The craftsmanship of the Japanese buildings with the dazzling glitter of gold leaf and lacquer is undoubtedly brilliant. But the whole spectacular complex did not stir us as did those lordly cedars of Nikko, enormous with age and infinitely more grand than the cedars of Lebanon ever were. They rise in the wondrous grove, protectively, all about the fanciful temples, keeping a respectful distance, but unobtrusively bearing witness that what the mighty shogun created with thousands of artisans cannot surpass certain masterpieces of nature. When heavy contributions for the shrine's construction were levied on Japan's daimio—feudal lords—those of small means could only afford to set out thirty miles of parallel cedar saplings—15,000 in all—to line the approach to Nikko. And today, after three centuries, these least gifts have, to me, become the greater glory.

For a few moments we turned our backs on the architectural achievements we had come to see and gazed captivated down the avenue of cedars leading off toward Tokyo. Then we turned and joined the throng of umbrellas, kimonos, and school children ascending the broad stairs to the elaborate gold-and-red Yomeimon Gate. The treads of steps were narrow, and in the wetness one had to make sure of his footing. Known as the Gate of Sunlight, with its ornate carving and its dazzling colors, it is said to be the most magnificent gateway in the East.

Within the courtyard to the left rose a five-storied Buddhist pagoda bright with red lacquer and the zodiac's twelve signs carved on its walls. The Rinnoji Temple, Kiyoka told us, stands on the very site of the first Buddhist temple in Nikko. It bears the imperial family's chrysanthemum crest on its doors. Within presides a thousand-handed Kannon, goddess of compassion, almost thirty feet high.

The ashes of Ieyasu lie in the elaborate Toshogu Mausoleum on the paved terrace separating the Yomeimon Gate and Karamon or Chinese Gate. The smaller gateway before the mausoleum itself is notable for the kitten napping in a bed of peonies, an odd decoration for the tomb of a fierce samurai, and yet appropriate enough when one considers that the Tokugawas brought a peace to Japan that lasted two and a half centuries. The Karamon Gate is richly decorated with a mythological beast carved in bronze and a medley of dragons, mountain birds, apricots, peonies, and chrysanthemums.

The "sacred" stables evidence the old Japanese superstition that monkeys carved on stalls protect horses from disease. Over the lintel of the main door in pastel-colored bas-relief are the world-famed three monkeys, one with paws over ears, one with paws over mouth, and a third with paws over eyes, to hear no evil, speak no evil, see no evil. Tourists are amazed to find the familiar figures here in Nikko.

Iemitsu has his own special mausoleum called the Daiyuin. It stands on a hill and is reached by four gates all aglitter with florid gold carvings.

Thérèse, surveying the whole refulgent complex, remarked, "There's a tang of the *nouveau riche* about all this display."

"Well," Kiyoka replied laconically, "the Tokugawas, you know, were not exactly aristocrats." Then she pointed to an umbrella pine outside the Oratory, which priests claimed had been planted in the eighth century.

It was not a good day for removing one's shoes, but we did once, and paused for a few minutes in a small Shinto chapel to watch an elaborate service in progress, which was meaningless to us.

After leaving the chapel I noticed an open space behind the crowded complex and sought to investigate. It was about half an acre of mossy ground with scores of antique stone lanterns set in artistic groupings. Rising shoulder-high, they resembled a gigantic breed of mushroom. Kiyoka said that in a hundred visits to Nikko she had never been in this spot before. Its feeling of simplicity and utter peace was pleasing after all the ornamental superfluities. At the far end of the open space stood a low wooden house. A lamp was burning behind a shaded window. I imagined it to be the home of some Buddhist monk, though I was puzzled by the prone bicycle on the small veranda and the sandals neatly placed beside the vehicle. I had heard that Buddhist monks were not permitted to own bikes. Perhaps this was some caller seeking consolation or a messenger or an old friend having a cup of tea.

Feeling somewhat like intruders we crept away with the remembrance of this serene garden of unlit lanterns, which touched us more than the magnificent accumulations of Chinese lacquer and gold.

"May 18 is the date of Nikko's major festival," Kiyoka felt it her duty to tell us, though she was careful never to give too much information unless questioned. "It is extremely colorful, with a thousand marching men in authentic samurai armor. The portable shrines are borne on shoulders and paraded down through the town. Priests pass over the Sacred Bridge. Special rituals are performed and a religious dance is enacted. It is fantastic, but fascinating. The trouble is in battling the tremendous crowds that come from all over Japan to see the ceremonials. A few of the people are devout religious pilgrims, but naturally most of them are mere sight-seers."

Our chauffeur had seen us coming slowly down the wet slippery staircase and brought the car sharply around to its base. I asked to be driven some miles down the avenue of three-hundred-year-old cedars.

Since the rain had stopped altogether now, Kiyoka suggested that we might like to leave the car and walk a short distance down the old royal way between Edo and Nikko. She said that the car would go ahead by the parallel modern paved highway and pick us up in about the distance of three blocks. "As you can hear, the main traffic is over there."

The historic dirt road overgrown with moss seemed to have sunk several feet during the years. The depression made the gigantic cedars on opposite banks tower the higher. It was as peaceful as the garden of unlit lanterns behind the ornate mausoleums. The magnitude and height and age of the trees made one feel humble. In the dark-green branches that formed their high choir lofts, birds were singing softly after the rain's cessation. There was something so noble about these majestic cedars that seemed to stretch on to infinity that they suggested Wagnerian trees set to lead heroes to Valhalla.

After we got back into the car, Kiyoka asked if we would care to visit a little farm about five miles farther on. "Remember," she cautioned us, when we pulled into a kind of rough courtyard, "it is no show place. The proprietor and his two sons work hard for a living. They specialize in chickens, eggs, and mushrooms."

The old farmer immediately came out of the wooden cottage and greeted Kiyoka affably. His day's work was done. We were very welcome. His sons had gone to arrange for transport of products to Tokyo's markets.

The farmer, who spoke no English, invited us into his front room. We paused just inside the threshold and were disinclined to go farther. We did not want to disturb his wife and her guests. Four middle-aged-to-old peasants, two male and two female, were sitting on floor mats around a table sunk in a square depression in the center of the floor. The ends of a blue-and-white-checked table cover were drawn up over their knees. Concealed in the square hole was a charcoal brazier for keeping lower extremities warm. All four persons turned as if by some slow clockwork mechanism, regarded us briefly, nodded vaguely, and returned to viewing a television program on a tiny set in a corner. "The neighbors don't have television," Kiyoka interpreted for us, "and they have come to enjoy it here." In the dusky atmosphere of the room without windows I recall no other piece of furniture except that small television set. The blue-and-white table cover was the focal spot of the scene. The four lumpish figures in black or dull-gray kimonos, turned in diagonals to view the screen, would have made an original composition for some Japanese Rembrandt.

With the farmer I visited his henhouse and poultry run, where the last-to-bed hens were still pecking at random grains. The breed surprised me: the hardy smallish white Leghorn, originally from the Mediterranean, and a most popular egg-producer in the States.

While Thérèse and Kiyoka were admiring a primitive small Buddha, half-concealed in the unpruned garden, I went with the farmer to his grove of skyward-stretching bamboo. I had never seen such enormous bamboo. Some individual stalks were of such a thickness that my two hands could not encircle them. In the shadowy atmosphere they seemed to extend to the gray canopy of sky. But what interested me more were the elongated mounds of rich loam under the bamboos. The orderly rows were all sprouting mushrooms. I had never imagined bamboo serving as a nursery for the edible fungi. But here the mushrooms were incubated to make delicacies for Tokyo's gourmets. Gathered and packed at dawn, they were sent by truck to the capital.

I came to learn that bamboo was one of Japan's double dowries, of economical value as well as aesthetic. The stalks or poles cut into proper lengths make stout and attractive fences, utilitarian gutters, drainpipes, and even a builder's sturdy scaffolding stories high, as we were to observe later in Hong Kong. In Japan's gardens short bamboo is arranged most effectively as decorative screens.

Driving away, Kiyoka reminded us of a change in Japanese husbandry. "The Japanese are losing their nostalgia for bucolic yesteryears. The young are drifting from farms to factories. The old people cannot blame them. They do not forget their days of gnawing fear—of bad weather, of hunger in crop failures, of unsympathetic landlords. Those who idealize the joys of rural life in Japan never endured the hardships of small-farm life, especially in winter. So our cities become more congested—like the rest of the world's."

That evening on our way to dinner in the hotel we stopped in the Red Bar for a Martini. The youthful bartender did not look up until I tapped twice on the counter. He was deeply absorbed in reading a paperback book. When he finally did look up, his expression was far-off. "Did you care for something?" he asked, a bit disgruntled.

"I'm sorry to disturb your literary pursuits," I said, "but we would like a Martini, not too dry, just three to one."

The young man rose lethargically, laid down his book carefully open at the place where he had left off, and went about his mixing. Suddenly I realized that with a hotel full of guests we were the only patrons in the bar. Perhaps they had all already gone in to dinner. But the barman's frosty indifference was certainly not conducive to a convivial atmosphere. I thought of the young William Faulkner as the local Oxford, Mississippi, postmaster disinclined to stir to sell stamps until he had finished the chapter he was reading.

In the brightly lighted, spacious dining room the atmosphere was quite different. The headwaiter, a tall, spare Japanese with refined features, received us like honored guests, as he did everyone. The service was swift and expert. When the headwaiter noticed that Thérèse was having difficulty with her mountain trout, ingratiatingly, with the deftest manipulation, he showed her how to lay by the fillets. I questioned him about himself. For at least seven recorded generations, he said, his ancestors had resided in Nikko. "But we believe that we were here long before the Tokugawas," he added with a modest smile. "I think it fitting for a family to content itself with one locality. Though I learned my trade in de luxe city restaurants and have traveled to some extent, I desired to put roots down here where I was born and where the air seems purer. To me, pure air is better than wealth. The idea that a man should live and die in the house where he was born is fast losing favor in Japan, as I read it is in England." He took in the occupied tables at a glance. "Nikko people don't really need to travel to see the world. Eventually the world comes to Nikko." He gave us a charming smile, and went to greet some late-arriving patrons. It was refreshing to see a man who was not disturbed by the new driving restlessness that gripped many other Japanese. Apparently he was not plagued by ambition or a yearning for materialistic betterment. A soothing calm emanated from him, an unwonted quality indeed in a maître d'hôtel of an ever-crowded hotel.

After dinner I went with Thérèse to an exhibition performance of ikebana in the hotel's auditorium with about forty Americans and a spattering of European tourists. Naturally, we had read much of the Japanese art in arranging flowers and seen countless colored pictures of specimen creations. I knew that all well-brought-up girls were schooled in ikebana, just as late-Victorian young ladies were taught china painting. I anticipated a pretty young Japanese in a pastel kimono performing with practiced grace, in which each body bend and flutter of delicate hands would be an aesthetic treat, as she dropped a spray here or placed a single blossom just so, there. I conceived the coming show to be something like visiting a geisha house free.

On a small stage before us stood a sturdy kitchen table with various empty bowls and vases and a full glass water pitcher. Two boy attendants brought out jars of varied blossoms and greenery, setting some on the floor and some on the table. For another full two minutes we waited for the Japanese lovely to appear and make magic with the flowers. At last a side door was flung open. The audience became still in alert attention. Then a purposeful, heavy-set, past-middle-age matron in a dull black kimono stalked deliberately to center stage front. Wearing steel-rimmed spectacles she half glared at the respectfully waiting boys and cast a critical glance at the receptacles and utensils on the table and at the jars on the floor. She wrinkled her nose and sniffed. Then grimly she grasped a formidable pair of shears in one hand and stooped to seize a long-stemmed flower from a jar. Taking measurements with her eye, she whacked off the bottom two inches with a vengeance and stuck the blossom in a bowl.

"I think she must come of a long line of Tokugawa executioners," I said *sotto voce* to the French lady at my other side. The process of whacking and sticking went on, workmanlike, as the eager faces of the audience began to lose luster. The woman kept measuring with a cold eye and hacking away at stems. Finally placing one last small blossom securely into the arrangement, she gave it a long stare. Then wiping her hands together briskly like an unrepentant Lady Macbeth, she looked her audience in the eye for the first time. Nodding curtly she bared her gold teeth in a half-grin, as if to announce "the deed is done." It was the signal for applause. We all clapped, though without any excessive fervor. Undoubtedly, it was a very creditable and pleasing arrangement. But I had had enough. My dream of ultimate grace in the performer had been rudely shattered. We excused ourselves to the French lady and slipped into a side aisle. Three American men in the back were already stealing away ahead of us.

The sun shone golden the next morning when we took the drive to Lake Chuzenji, lying more than 4,000 feet above sea level and eleven miles north of Nikko. The well-paved road is exciting in its curves and dizzying heights. But its construction is such a skillful feat of engineering and the experienced Japanese drivers are so assured that one feels safe. The climax is the thrilling ride up the Irohazako Drive with its thirty sharp hairpin turns. I thought of Italy's spectacular Amalfi with its solar-plexus-catching twists and turns. But the Amalfi Drive has the pounding sea below while the Irohazako has cascades tumbling from on high.

From the level where vehicles can go no farther, we left the car to survey the awesome Kegon Waterfall plunging over a sheer lava cliff down 330 feet into a boulder-studded basin. Then in an elevator jam-packed with tourists, mostly Japanese, we descended the equivalent of four stories. From a wet concrete platform, protected by stout iron railings, we gazed far up the tempestuous spill and looked down into the roiling waters, which many romantics chose as the scene of their suicides.

The Kegon Waterfall is magnificent, but it is not lovely like the narrow Ryuzu Cascade, which we next drove to see. Here the falls seem feminine in contrast to the warriorlike masculinity of the bold Kegon. The glistening white-silver liquid of the Ryuzu lurches and zigzags in such a manner that the Duchamp painting "Nude Descending a Staircase" came to my mind. The slender

Ryuzu, almost three hundred feet tall, is bordered by small maples, leaning gracefully over the perpendicular stream. Already they were half-turned to burnished gold. An extraordinarily appealing cascade, for some ineffable reason, like Fuji, it seems peculiarly Japanese and a subject for a Buddhist artist.

Lake Chuzenji stretches four miles long and is almost two miles wide. The color of the Chuzenji's water is a luminous blue, which, Kiyoka said, came from its great depth. The surrounding area is dotted with hot-spring spas. Many well-to-do Japanese and representatives of American and European firms have summer cottages in the region, because the weather never gets unpleasantly hot. Quantities of trout, salmon, and carp make the lake a happy fishing ground for anglers. Boating is a popular pastime in the warm months. In winter skaters and skiers abound.

"Chuzenji has always seemed such a happy place to me," Kiyoka remarked. "Harassed citizens of Tokyo shed their cares as soon as they get here. There is a clarifying quality in the atmosphere. In another fortnight, when all the maples have turned, there won't be a spare room in the region. And in the late spring, when the cherries have finished blooming around Tokyo, the fresh blossoms here draw people like magnets."

Returning by a different scenic route we made a last halt at the Nikko Trout Hatcheries. I have visited many interesting fish hatcheries in Europe, particularly those for salmon in Finland and Sweden. But this layout seemed peculiarly enchanting in its criss-crossing of narrow crystal canals overlaid with wooden bridges. The thick shadows of tall trees made a gloaming at noontime and created a kind of never-never-land atmosphere. The aquarium, spread out below ground level, was like a maze. But signs identified the varied species in the unglassed runnels.

What made the hatcheries particularly memorable, however, was a special breed of luminous pale silver-gold trout that looked almost transparent. As the white peacock is perhaps the most decorative specimen of the bird kingdom and the rare white tiger of India is undoubtedly the most magnificent of animals, so this gracefully slender, foot-long trout of translucent gold is the most exquisite of the finny tribes. They are so prized in Japan that they are raised only for their aesthetic value. "No Japanese would think of eating anything so beautiful," a local guide told us in mock

horror, when I asked if they could possibly be of finer flavor than
rainbow trout.

"They might be the fish of paradise," I observed in extravagant
admiration, after my *faux pas.*

"Perhaps," he agreed with a grin. "But they could never have
existed in the Garden of Eden, because these trout flourish only
in very cold streams."

We had not expected jewel-like fish so sacrosanct as a bonus
to a trip to the grand Tokugawa memorials. On the train ride back
to Tokyo late that afternoon we thought more of the extra attractions—the orderly rows of mushrooms under the tall bamboos, the
stirring waterfalls, and that superb avenue of venerable cedars—
than we did of the lacquered gates and gilded mausoleums. As
Sterne wrote that digressions were the soul of literature, so we
were to discover that digressions in Far Eastern travels brought
rich dividends.

A Buddhist Girl and a Literary Man

The next afternoon in Tokyo the young woman of the editorial staff of *This is Japan,* who had accompanied John Ishizaki
and me to the Overseas Press Club party for Taiho, came to call
on Thérèse. Mitsuko Shimomura was our first living proof of the
deep activity of Zen Buddhism in Japan.

Thérèse knew something of Buddhism. She possessed a Buddhist
Bible edited by Dwight Goddard, and some works of Dr. D. T.
Suzuki and Ruth Fuller Sazaki, among others. But she had never
actually met but one practicing Buddhist, a Thai girl studying
accounting at the University of Alabama.

Mitzi was awaiting us in the Okura lobby. She was one of the
very few Japanese women who look especially well in Western-
style clothes. She had the height to carry off the style of a smart
dark-blue suit. Her grace was the same as if she had been wearing
a kimono. She was naturally pretty without make-up, and there

was an illumination about her that made her appealing. Thérèse was immediately charmed.

I suggested that we have tea on the terrace of the hotel's backgarden restaurant four floors below the lobby level. The restaurant faced green lawns, with a rivulet at the foot of the landscaped hill. A diminutive waterfall dropped between rocks and flowering shrubs. Wide steppingstones climbed on an angle to a gate at street level above.

Though Mitzi, as a busy editor, knew seven of the Okura's restaurants, she said that she had never seen this quiet garden spot before. "This must have been a part of Baron Okura's stroll garden! All this uneven plot of ground where the hotel now stands belonged to the estate of the late Baron Kishichiro Okura. The conception and construction of the hotel took four full years. It was opened for guests in May, 1962. I was here. I remember the director saying, 'We felt that we had to build a hotel exemplifying the artistic genius of Japan.' Every detail of design in the decoration and furnishings was submitted to first-rate artists."

We expressed enthusiastic admiration for the result. Then Thérèse said, "You mentioned 'stroll' garden."

"There are hill gardens and flat gardens. The flat gardens are generally for viewing from a room or veranda. The hill gardens are for walking about in, for strolling," Mitzi explained. "One walks along paths or on skillfully laid steppingstones that wind to nooks or ascend to a pavilion. Stroll gardens have a therapeutic value for both the man-of-affairs and his wife. An early-morning walk in a secluded garden can clear the head for business palaver. A late-afternoon stroll can soothe nerves taut from office grind and maddening traffic congestion."

We ordered tea. Mitzi took from her bag a book she had brought Thérèse. It was called *The Three Pillars of Zen: Teaching, Practice, Enlightenment*, edited by Philip Kapleau. It had been inscribed to her father, Kyozo Yamada, "in warm friendship and deep respect." Mitzi now inscribed it to Thérèse. "But will your father not miss this book?"

"No, he gave it to me. He more or less knows everything in it. You see, he is himself a lay Buddhist teacher in Kamakura. He conducts regular classes in Zen. But he's a highly trained electrical engineer. He does not find conflict in the two professions. Perhaps he may eventually become a full-fledged priest."

"My husband told me that you are a practicing Buddhist," Thérèse said. "Are all the members of your family?"

Mitzi smiled. "My mother is a medical doctor, but she meditates every morning before she goes to her office. My husband, who works in a bank, and I meditate each morning. And my young brother voluntarily took his meditation cushion with him to Harvard; from his letters it seems he practices his religion in Cambridge."

Mitzi told us that she herself had studied Zen at a monastery for some weeks and submitted to the disciplines. Thérèse asked what it was like in a monastery.

"Well, it was very simple, austere, even primitive," she said. "But comfortable enough. One paid no attention to food, though it was adequate."

When Thérèse said that she did not believe she could take blows from a Zen stick, Mitzi was horrified. She explained that the Zen master's use of the stick was greatly misunderstood. It was not meant to punish, only to alert those whose attention wandered in meditation, those who needed it, those who even asked for it. But the masters were very perceptive and knew who was too sensitive to receive even a light blow across the shoulders. "The masters treat each individual differently," she said, "according to his needs and temperament. They are really gentle, sympathetic, and seemingly all-knowing."

As we drank tea, it did not seem at all strange to hear this sophisticated girl say—she did it so naturally—"My master says . . ." or "When my father attained enlightenment . . ."

"Just what is *satori?*" I asked.

"It is hard to define. It's a kind of transcendental or fourth-dimensional consciousness, a spiritual discernment, that faculty which discerns what the mind cannot hear, see, taste, smell, or touch."

"Was your father in a monastery when he realized enlightenment?"

A smile broke over Mitzi's lovely face. "You will hardly believe it," she said. "He was on the train going from Tokyo back to Kamakura. One never knows when or where it will strike. You will recall that the Buddha got enlightenment sitting under a bodhi tree. One long-seeking old Japanese fell off a cliff and broke his leg and *satori* came to him that moment. Some earnest seekers never attain it, though their lives are better for the disciplines." We urged her to talk on. "Zen, as you know, is a meditative Buddhist religion or philosophy that has its greatest strength in Japan. In Zen one does not gain salvation by intellectual effort, good deeds, or any performance of rituals. One only finds it by an inward look into one's heart. The Japanese monk Eisai, returning from China, introduced the Rinzai sect of Zen in 1191."

After a pause, noting our attentive interest, Mitzi continued to enlighten us. Zen's stress on personal character and discipline made it a dominant religion among the feudal samurai families. Enlightenment was to be achieved through understanding the self and self-reliance. All Zen sects emphasized the direct personal transmission of truth from teacher to disciple and an austere discipline as preparation for rigorous meditation.

In the fourteenth to the sixteenth centuries the Buddhist monasteries of Kyoto and Nara housed the foremost scholars, writers, and artists of the age. In these monasteries was developed the style of art which even today more or less dominates contemporary Japanese taste. In China, Zen, called Ch'an, laid emphasis on nature and rusticity. "The cultivation of the little" was a chief tenet. That ideal marked Japanese painting and poetry, which combine nature and intuition. Painting took on what might be called a spiritual inwardness, an evanescent radiance from the mystic attitude. The great nature paintings of the Zen artist Sesshu came in the last half of the fifteenth century. The Zen gardens that utilized rock and sand and water were created in this age. The tea ceremony, still practiced extensively today, originated with Zen monks, and also the art of flower arrangement. "Regardless of the mass of unbelievers since the Pacific war," Mitzi said, "the Japanese realize that their culture is tremendously indebted to Buddhist influence."

"Would it be farfetched," I ventured to ask, "to think that the spirit of Buddhism may prove a solvent to some of the 'troubles' of Japan's new rampant economy?"

"Not at all," Mitzi answered thoughtfully. "Buddhism does indeed have a salubrious influence. I know a few millionaires who go to remote mountain monasteries for a fortnight to refresh themselves in the austere atmosphere. The tenets of Zen unobtrusively have a quieting influence on many men deeply involved in the too-muchness of the world."

After a pause, she smiled and said, "For the determined non-religious in this wild pace of production, Japanese culture has other age-old traditions for relaxing the tired businessman. The loose kimono when he gets home; the self-effacing wife to minister to his comforts; the occasional tea ceremony, where commerce is a taboo subject; the rarer geisha parties; and, best of all, the secluded private garden, where a kind of balm emanates from rocks and mosses and trickling streams. One of the best ends to merging the self with the infinite is a garden. A garden is really more important to the student of Zen than a mass of religious texts. That is why the garden plays such an important role in Japanese culture."

Mitzi glanced for some moments at the brook meandering along the base of the rise opposite us. Her manner changed perceptibly. "In the long-ago days when every man of breeding was something of a poet," she said brightly, "there was a quaint custom where guests were seated at intervals along the bank of a narrow stream and provided with a small jug of sake and an inkpot and a writing brush. The honored guest at one end would select the subject of the poem and write a stanza of poetry on a long strip of fine Chinese paper. Then he would send the poem being composed downstream in a little boat. When it reached the second guest, the amateur would add a stanza bearing on the chosen theme and send the boat on its way to the third man, who had been steadily sipping sake, as had they all. And so on to the host at the end, who would provide the final verse. Then the company would gather for a feast and the completed poem would be read. By the time the little boat got to the last men before the host, they were rather high with sake. Sometimes the intoxication showed up in the verses and created merriment."

A tall young waiter answered the phone ringing on a buffet near us. He glanced about, then came up to me, since I was the only American man on the terrace. "There is a gentleman waiting for you in the lobby, sir."

"Yes, of course. I am expecting him, thank you." I had told the office where I was to be found. The man was Yokichi Miyamoto, a lecturer in Tokyo National University and the translator of Hemingway, Malamud, and John Updike. A former Japanese girl student of mine, Emiko Sakurai from Nagasaki, had written him about our visit, and he had offered to be of service. I excused myself, and left Thérèse and Mitzi to continue their talk.

The waiter who had delivered the message preceded me to the door of the corridor and politely opened it for me. Then he went to punch the elevator "up" button. I glanced at him closely. About six feet two, he was taller than any Japanese I had seen except Taiho, the wrestler. Though his hair and eyes were dark-brown, his skin was white with a pink flush in his cheeks. His handsome sensitive features suggested American blue blood. "Are you Japanese?" I asked.

He gave me a kind of confiding smile, both frank and wistful, and answered with one word, "Half." I wondered about his soldier father. If he could have seen the charming issue of his indiscretion he should undoubtedly have been proud. The elevator came and I never saw the young man again, but I remembered him as a rare exhibit resulting from those passing love affairs between two alien races in wartime. Some of these offspring had been brought to the States and fitted well enough into the present social order. In Japan others had had a rough time, because the Japanese, a most homogeneous people, are generally inclined to frown heavily on miscegenation. For more than a thousand years they have kept their ethnic blood relatively pure. However, when the children of an American-Japanese alliance turn out to be attractive, there is small penalty. But those half-caste children whose G.I. fathers were Negroes have suffered much. They are held in such contempt, Kiyoka had told us, that they are relegated to certain ghettolike districts and are discountenanced on the main thoroughfares.

In the lobby Yokichi Miyamoto and I recognized each other easily. He was a man in his mid-thirties, with a good-looking, broad face and large kind eyes. My first impression was that he was highly intelligent and essentially compassionate. Our mutual friend had written, "Though very clever, he is truly as humble a man as you may want to find." I understood that she meant modest about his achievements.

Miyamoto had not been able to bring his friend, the writer

Yukio Mishima, along, as I had hopefully suggested by letter. Mishima had left for India only the previous week. "I certainly hope that he will write a book on India," I said. "I would like to see India through his perceptive eyes."

I had read five of Mishima's novels and my enthusiasm was high. I knew that in his twenties he had established himself as a writer of top rank with his first two novels, *The Sound of Waves* and *The Confessions of a Mask*. Now with a dozen novels to his credit, he is generally recognized as one of the world's most gifted living authors. A brilliant scholar, with top honors from Tokyo National University, he is deeply read in both classic and modern literature. Yet Mishima is as modern as the latest electronic device. His imagination is so outreaching that he can create anything from a tender idyll of young love to a dramatic tale dealing with unconscionable inversion, and from middle-aged amours and the corruption of politicians to a psychological study of a deranged Buddhist monk. Mishima illuminates everyday commonplaces with such incandescence that they remain fixed in the mind. He is a master of unpredictable surprises, which are yet completely credible. Peculiarly endowed with that sixth sense that speaks most eloquently between the lines, he is so subtle that I get the feeling that those sentences costing him the most labor are those the casual reader may think cost him none. Yukio Mishima, to me, is something of a paradox—like Japan herself—where a profound appreciation of beauty is yoked with clear-sighted, diamond-hard materialism. I spoke of my opinion to Miyamoto to get his reaction. "I could not agree with you more," he said sincerely.

"Yukio just now is somewhat obsessed with *kendo*, the sword discipline, a kind of Japanese fencing," Miyamoto added. "He goes in vigorously for athletics, and is an expert swimmer. He has been spoken of as the Japanese Hemingway, though two men could hardly be more unlike in physique. Hemingway was huge and beefy. Yuko is lean, lithe, and muscular."

Miyamoto ventured to ask how much I knew of Japanese literature. I told him that I had a smattering from Donald Keene's *Anthology of Japanese Literature*, published in 1956, with selections of some hundred authors of prose and poetry from the eighth century to today. Lady Murasaki's *Tale of Genji* was an all-time favorite of mine and certainly one of the world's most delightful works. I said that I regarded Murasaki as the first important woman writer to follow the Grecian poet Sappho. I told him that I owned four volumes of well-translated haiku, five novels of Mishima, and two by Yasunari Kawabata.

"Do you know Junichiro Tanizaki's work?" Miyamoto asked.

"Only small selections translated by Edward Seidensticker."

"Tanizaki, born in 1886, is one of the tops of this century. There were rumors that he was to receive the Nobel Prize. But then he died. Now there is some stir among the literary in several countries in favor of Mishima, who was born only in 1925 and is rather young for such an honor."

I told him that I had dined with an international Japanese businessman who said people rather expected the next Nobel to go to Mishima.

"Well, that would be fine, and it would not spoil Yukio. He is a dedicated worker. He can write good Noh dramas and regular plays and poetry, as well as novels and short stories."

"The present century," Miyamoto continued, "has been peculiarly rich in Japanese prose writers. You will recall that strange young genius Ryunosuke Akutagawa, who wrote *Rashomon,* which was made into a world-famous motion picture. Then, of course, there are Tanizaki, Mishima, and Kawabata, who is our most subtle interpreter of women. Tanizaki's number-one position as Japan's foremost literary figure at his death has now been assumed by Mishima, for Kawabata has not written anything for years. And Kawabata frankly states that Mishima is the foremost Japanese writer producing today. Kawabata is not so popular in Japan as Mishima, who is little more than half his age, but he is ranked extremely high by critics for his carefully selected words and his sharp eyes that catch the most delicate beauty. Mishima himself likes Kawabata's stories most among living Japanese writers."*

I told Miyamoto that I enjoyed the Japanese haiku of seventeen syllables as a delicate and graceful poetry form. I said I had read that the Emperor himself occasionally published a haiku of his own composition. "Is the haiku still popular in this second half of the twentieth century?"

* Yasunari Kawabata was awarded the Nobel Prize in 1968. A letter to me from Miyamoto said that when the news was received in Tokyo, "Mishima rushed to Kamakura to bless him."

"In a way, quite, though not as much in vogue as in the eighteenth century. Few are up to the standard of Basho, Issa, or Buson. Still, it is estimated that a million new haiku are printed in various Japanese magazines each year. Do you have a favorite among haiku?" I said that perhaps I had, and then I quoted one by Ryota as translated by Peter Beilenson.

"Angry I strode home . . .
But stooping in my garden
Calm old willow tree."

"Yes," Miyamoto said with an approving smile. "It does have a soothing effect. It is particularly good in Japanese."

I asked him if there were any outstanding modern haiku poets.

"There are several good ones born in the first decade of this century. I like Kusatao Nakamura. A rather sly one of his shows that he knows the Adam and Eve story.

"The sky is the blue
Of the world's beginning . . . from my wife
I accept an apple."

After a grin of appreciation, I asked about American authors who are liked by the Japanese.

"Well, it is much as you might expect. Of the classic writers, Poe stands very high. Both Akutagawa and Tanizaki admired his stories. Melville's *Moby Dick* is still widely read, and Hawthorne's *The Scarlet Letter*. Emerson has always been a favorite of the Japanese intellectuals, perhaps because of his understanding of Buddhism. Hemingway, Faulkner, and Steinbeck are quite popular. But J. D. Salinger's *Catcher in the Rye*, Mailer's *The Naked and the Dead*, and John Updike's *Rabbit, Run* sold well. Capote's *In Cold Blood* is selling extremely well."

Miyamoto reached into his briefcase and brought out a recent copy of the *University of Chicago Quarterly*. "I also occasionally translate Japanese prose into English. Here is my latest publication in English. It is a short story from western Japan. You may keep the magazine." He began gently to push his chair back. "Now, alas, I'm afraid this time I have to run. I came straight here from the university. I seem to stay maddeningly busy. The Japanese communications media demand so much time from writers and professors. I speak on television early this evening. On another day I won't be so pushed. I do hope that you may let me fetch you and your wife so that we may entertain you in our little house and my two children can meet you. I have a little car and I would be glad to drive you about."

I thanked him warmly for his courtesy, but since we were leaving for Hakone the next morning there would be no time. "Perhaps you will be returning to the States as an exchange professor," I said, walking to the door with him. "Then you could come to see us in Alabama."

In 1969 Miyamoto was to write that he was busier than ever and quite exhausted, for he had been asked to negotiate with university students on strike who were clamoring for what they called "democracy," and "wanting to tear down school buildings to get it." The world student rebellion reached Japan months after it had upset the United States and Europe. It seemed so out of place in such a well-disciplined society as that of the Japanese.

I quote from a letter Miyamoto wrote me on December 1, 1969—after the revolting student situation was under control. "At the peak seventy universities were 'occupied' by radical students. Since this October most of the universities were operated normally with the help of police. The newspaper reports you have seen have not been exaggerated. But now things are quiet. It is one of the aspects of the Japanese to flare hot and then cool down almost immediately. Perhaps the students will forget the 1969 summer riots. I surely hope so."

To Hakone by Way of Kamakura

All the way from Tokyo to Yokohama the four-lane highway was jammed with trucks, carts, automobiles of every size and make, and phalanxes of motor bikes. Getting through Yokohama was a trying, nerve-testing business. And even after we had left its factory chimneys behind, the road was still impeded by a plethora of vehicles. Eventually we slowed to a crawl and crept at about five miles an hour because a huge Tokyo-bound lorry had got itself turned over between two lanes, causing a formidable bottleneck. But at some hamlet we branched off for Kamakura and then reached the coast road, where driving was agreeable. Kiyoka assured us that a superior parallel road from Tokyo to the coast was under construction and that by the 1970 Exposition in Osaka the way to that city from Tokyo would be easy transit.

Kamakura gave its name to a period in Japanese history that lasted from 1185 to 1333. Late in the twelfth century the first of the shoguns, Minamoto Yoritomo, chose to make this fishing village on Sagami Bay the seat of military government. He did the real ruling and left the Emperor and his court to a curtailed existence at Kyoto, two hundred miles away. The historical period dating from 1185 marked the end of the brilliant Heian era at Kyoto. Court life lost its luster. The manners and stern realities of warriors supplanted the subtle refinements, soft luxuries, and whispered intrigues of the court. However, the Buddhist monks' disciplines and devotion to an ideal found response in the Kamakura warriors, as did "their pointing directly at the heart of man," without the paraphernalia of sacred treatises.

A new period of sculpture and painting eventually flourished in Kamakura, which gradually became more splendid. Today many well-known and aspiring artists live in the same district where ancient artists made their homes. Kawabata, the novelist who was to win the Nobel Prize in 1969, lives there. Since the Pacific war, development has been rapid and building construction has increased enormously. Yet Kamakura is regarded chiefly as a popular seaside resort, with sandy beaches stretching for miles. The attraction that draws foreign tourists is the world-famous massive bronze statue of the Buddha, cast in the year 1252. At the beginning the image was housed in a shedlike temple. The building was blown down in 1369 and reconstructed more substantially. However, an unprecedented tidal wave completely devastated the second structure in 1495. Since that date the Buddha has sat serenely exposed to the elements on a high terraced platform approached by broad stone steps. The hands of this sloe-eyed Buddha lie in his lap with palms up and finger tips touching. For the religious this is the reassuring pose of absolute faith and fidelity.

Though strikingly impressive as outdoor sculpture and weighing more than a hundred tons, this Amida Buddha is not an appealing piece of work or of the highest artistic merit, yet it does have repose, and is better done than the colossus at Nara, which is the largest Buddha in Japan and is housed in the largest wooden building in the land.

In the vicinity of the Buddha are temples, shrines, and museums, but we passed up these and started driving west toward Oiso, the home town of the former prime minister Shigeru Yoshida. In the evergreen hills above Kamakura the well-to-do have vacation cottages and villas. Many professional and business men prefer to live here the year round or in neighboring towns and commute to Tokyo by electric train. At a noted seaside resort hotel we stopped for a good lunch. The cheerful dining room was not crowded in mid-October, but during the summer season it does a tremendous business.

A few miles west of Kamakura on the way to Oiso we reached the famous Tokaido Road, the highway that for centuries linked Kyoto, where the emperor resided, with Edo (Tokyo), where the Tokugawa shoguns had their seat of government. The Tokaido was Japan's strategic road of history. On this road court officials and feudal lords traveled in high style in litters and sedan chairs or rode on gaily caparisoned horses with scores of colorfully dressed outriders and attendants on foot. Here in two-way traffic passed a conglomeration of samurai, men of wealth, pilgrims, actors, artists, wrestlers, vagabonds, nuns, and priests. Along the way inns and teahouses sprang up and shrines and brothels of varied categories.

On October 5 the air of the Tokaido was invigorating, with a fresh salty tang. Tall twisted pines lined both sides of the road in places, with glimpses of the sea on our left and charming old thatch-roofed houses on our right. While driving along the beautiful scenic coast I glanced from time to time toward the north, eager to catch a glimpse of Fuji. Though the sky over the sea to the south was a pellucid turquoise, clouds curtained Japan's foremost attraction. However one may employ his time in his first days in Japan, the famous profile of Fuji hovers in the back of his mind along with apprehension that inclement weather may prevent his seeing it. Fuji, some Japanese declare, is feminine. She wraps herself in misty veils and reveals her full beauty to the moon and mortal men only now and again. In our first week in Japan, according to the papers, Fuji had remained in concealment.

To cheer us, Kiyoka said, "We have a consolation haiku, written three centuries ago by the master Basho when he took a long, hard trip to visit Fuji, and it rained and rained and vapors covered the cone.

> "Though Fuji is hidden
> In the mist and rain of winter
> On such a day, too,
> There is joy."

"Thank you," I said. "It's a lovely poem. But I shall not be consoled if I spend three weeks in Japan and don't see Fuji."

Concerned about a view of Fujiyama I was also not entirely at ease about our appointment to see Prime Minister Yoshida's garden. The arrangements had been made through Mrs. Kudo, who telephoned us that her friend Mrs. Aso, Yoshida's daughter, would be expecting us sometime this early afternoon. But we had had no direct contact with the lady herself.

Finally we reached the pretty seaside town of Oiso with its walled estates. The chauffeur inquired the way to the Prime Minister's place. Three security guards were standing outside the closed gate when we reached the oval space before high stone walls. I got out and approached them in a most affable and assured manner, saying that Mrs. Aso was expecting us. Kiyoka, visibly nervous, left the car to interpret. The plain-clothes men looked at us steadily, noncommittally. They glanced at Thérèse within the car. I said that we were American friends of Madame Hachisuka of Atami, and that she had written Mrs. Aso. The men spoke to each other in low-toned Japanese. "But the Prime Minister is ill," they repeated. I said that we knew he was ill, and we only hoped to see the garden. "Mrs. Aso is not at home just now," one of the men said. "But we were expected," I insisted, nevertheless feeling doubtful. The guards exchanged glances and then stared down the street. Disappointed, I had turned away toward our car when a limousine driven by a liveried chauffeur drew up. "Here is Mrs. Aso now." A lovely lady in a smart Western suit got out. I approached and introduced myself and said that Mrs. Kudo had telephoned about our coming and that we were friends of Chiye Hachisuka. "Ah," Mrs. Aso said, "my maid took Mrs. Kudo's call, and it was a bit confused. Chiye did write about your visit to Japan. I had to run down to the village on an errand for my father. You want to see the garden. Of course, do come in, please." I helped Thérèse out of the car and presented her and Kiyoka. The big gates were swung open, and we entered. I inquired about the Prime Minister's health.

"My father has been confined to his bed for almost a fortnight now, since a too-lively celebration on his eighty-ninth birthday in late September." She smiled, as if to minimize his condition. "He loves to have people about him. Too many friends came to pay their respects."

Mrs. Aso spoke perfect upper-class English. She had learned from the best people in England, when her father was ambassador there. The aura of an English country gentlewoman emanated from her. Her manner was charming, gracious, and reserved at the same time. We strolled through the garden in front of the villa. The usual layout, a small pond with water lilies, decorative bridges, huge rare rocks placed artistically, flowering shrubs, antique stone lanterns, but all marked by an individual pattern and design. In one strategic spot of the garden was a small Shinto shrine and in another a Buddhist shrine, neither of which we entered.

We went up through a pine thicket carpeted with bronze-colored needles and on to a winding path built of small rectangular wooden blocks. Mrs. Aso explained that of course the path to the cleared crest should have been pebbled. But since her father declined in his late eighties, the pebbles hurt his sandaled feet, so the wooden walkway had been laid.

Above the fragrant pines bent by sea winds we came upon a rustic bench with a panoramic view. "May I sit?" I asked.

"Do, please," Mrs. Aso urged. "This is my father's special outdoor seat for viewing Fuji. He has another special window in his study. He is very fond of Fuji."

I sat, and as my eyes began to sweep the horizon, there straight before me, without a filament of mist, was Mount Fuji, illuminated by the midafternoon sun. "But look, Fuji!" I exclaimed, not daring to move, as the three women grouped themselves behind me. Surprised and quite pleased, Mrs. Aso said, "And Fuji has not shown herself for ten days. You are indeed fortunate."

We all gazed in silence.

I have seen flaming Mount Etna from Taormina in February, with almond orchards in full flower about her feet and climbing decoratively up her flanks, while the winter snow made the volcano a sparkling crown of diamonds against a blue Sicilian sky. And Etna is magnificent. But the sight of Mount Fuji somehow touches the heart in a more subtle way. The symmetry, the etched delicacy against an autumnal sky, and the utter serenity give the peak transcending appeal. "Fuji, I think," Mrs. Aso said, "is still more beautiful with snow."

When we at last broke away from the enchantment, Mrs. Aso invited us to have tea in the semidetached oval-roofed conservatory of glass and gleaming copper, amid exotic ferns, fuchsias, and trickling water. This was her father's favorite part of the house, our hostess said. He had got his idea of the conservatory in England from one of the notable Edwardian houses, she told us. Her manner of pouring tea made her seem even more like a British noblewoman than a Japanese lady. Just as she finished filling her own cup, a doctor from Kamakura arrived to see the Premier. Mrs. Aso rose to excuse herself, but she pressed us to have a look at her father's walled rose garden and his collection of bonsai trees before we left. A pastry cake was brought in by a handsome young butler, who was obviously only half Japanese. His manner was both charming and shy as he knelt on one knee to serve the delicacy to each of us. The cake had a frozen fruit mousse inside and was as delicious as any pastry I have ever tasted, even at Demel's in Vienna.

After visiting the rose garden, I reflected on this ideal retreat in which a senior statesman might end his days of accomplishment. Yoshida had been the essential man for his nation when it lay devastated, confused, and prostrate at the end of the Pacific war. Late in 1944 he had been jailed for championing peace, but in 1945 he had returned to the government. He became head of the Liberal party and was made premier five times. It was he who had masterminded Japan's phenomenal recovery.

From afar I had admired this towering figure of Japanese postwar history. And now I had come almost within touching distance of the great statesman. From his rustic bench on the hillock I had had my first sight of Fuji. Yoshida was to die three weeks later, when we were in Thailand. A Bangkok paper was to compare his death to "the falling of a giant star."

Despite its formidable population density, in a land that is over 80 per cent uninhabitable, Japan does not sacrifice its precious park areas for housing projects. What is designated as the Fuji-Hakone-Izu National Park covers in its combined area some 235,000 acres. The region of Hakone itself has been called the garden spot of Japan. The chief objective of most foreign tourists is the justly famed Hotel Fujiya in the little town of Miyanoshita. From this hub one ranges on excellent roads to the varied scenic delights, including divers spots for the viewing of Fuji. The best way to reach the Hakone region from Tokyo is through the pretty town of Odawara, dominated by its elaborate old castle. It is to Odawara on Sagami Bay that thousands of Tokyo pilgrims come for the unfolding of spring plum blossoms. I once had a letter from a young American friend teaching in Tokyo describing his trip in February from the freezing capital to Odawara to behold the first plum blossoms. In Odawara he said his feet were warm for the first time since mid-November.

After Odawara the road begins to climb to the mountain town of Miyanoshita, which, because of its altitude of 1,300 feet, remains cool in summer while Tokyo swelters in humid heat, though the two places are only sixty-five miles apart.

The Fujiya is one of those rare old-fashioned hotels with all the modern luxuries. It spreads out in wings and courts through several levels of gardens. The various segments have names like Flower Palace and Forest Lodge. In the former an Edwardian atmosphere pervades. The new, four-story Forest Lodge is ultramodern, with blond woods one might expect to find in Sweden. We preferred to stay in a modern room, which was extra large and where the picture window that extended along an entire wall gave upon the peak of Mount Myojo, more than 3,000 feet in altitude. Below us were flower gardens, and we could see glimpses of town shops across the street.

Attractive kimonos for a man and a woman, decorated with prints of arrow feathers, lay across the foot of the beds. Sandals sat neatly in pairs on the floor. But instead of descending to any of the special mineral baths on lower floors—the Mermaid Bath, the Roman Aquarium, the Gold Fish Bath, the Dream Pool, or the Bath of Eternal Youth and Perpetual Spring—we merely drew the steaming mineral water from the tap in our bathtub and soaked away the tensions of the ride from Tokyo. The therapeutic water of Miyano-shita is good for rheumatism and all sorts of ailments. And one drinks the hot water for stomach and intestinal difficulties, and gargles it for sore throat.

At length, dressed for dinner, we stood a long time before the wide window, fascinated by the mists that coursed the face of the mountain. They came in tenuous filaments and then in sheets or heavy folds like those of an opera-house curtain.

On our way to dinner we observed the spaciousness of the Fujiya. Its library was stocked with books that foreign guests had been leaving for many decades, besides the volumes purchased for it. There was a ballroom and a long shopping arcade where quality wares were displayed. Along a ground-floor corridor ran a floor-to-ceiling aquarium where iridescent fish sported and aquatic plants waved gently. I looked in vain for those pale silver-gold trout of Nikko, but was told later that even the mountain streams of Hakone were not cold enough for them.

A tall, clean-cut, blond young American stopped beside us to admire the sparkling activities in the aquarium. We spoke together. Since he was traveling alone we asked if he would care to join us for dinner. He turned out to be the son of a well-known West Coast travel agent. His name was Kennedy, and, oddly, he looked as if he might be a brother of the Massachusetts Kennedys. He said he had often been told of the resemblance. At dinner, to our surprise, we learned that he was seriously interested in Buddhism and often went to the Buddhist temple in Los Angeles. He told us something that we had not discovered. Hotels he had stayed in on this "inspection" trip to Japan had small Buddhist texts as well as Gideon Bibles in bedside table drawers. He said he carried one of the slim Buddhist texts in his bag and often read it on trains. He confessed that he found spiritual nourishment in the philosophy of Buddha. "I like Buddha's psychological idea that all that happens to us is fundamentally determined by our thoughts," he said. "Buddha's teaching on karma," he said, "involves a hopeful and positive aspect, rather than the fatalistic or predetermined ones of some Christian churches. I believe that our thoughts are subject to control and that the mental attitude toward everyday life makes that life."

During a well-served, well-prepared Continental dinner in the chandelier-lit Japanese dining room we listened with interest to this athletic-looking young American, the father of two children, talk to us about his pleasant experiences with Buddhism.

Kennedy also had a very practical streak. He had come to inspect and categorize hotels all through Japan for the family tourist business. He told us that one of the first things he examined in a hotel bedroom was the carpet. If it was pure wool, well and good, but if it was some product of nylon, it gave the place a less good name. Nylon carpets could not easily be kept clean, he said, and they wore badly in spots. "If you are ever in an American motel, look at the carpet, and you can tell much about the place's classification."

Kennedy was flying the next day to Hokkaido, that far-northern island province and most sparsely settled part of Japan. It was fast becoming a popular international ski resort. New hotels had sprung up so fast, he said, that travel agencies could hardly keep up with them.

When we got back to our room I immediately pulled out the drawer of the table between our beds. But there was neither Buddhist text nor gift of the Gideon society. Perhaps guests had snitched them. However, we were to find both books two days later at the Miyako Hotel in Kyoto.

Fuji with Snow

In the Hakone region there are no monuments or places of historic significance to visit, only picturesque scenery, highlighted by Fuji and blue Lake Hakone, which the Japanese call Ashi, or Reed Lake. We set off at nine in a different car with a new chauffeur to admire the mountain scenery, with the ardent hope of beholding

Fuji again. Some tourists choose the Skyline Course and glide by ropeway to the top of Mount Komagatake for panoramic scenes of both Fuji and the lake. But I had noticed in the booklet of the Japan Travel Bureau that the words "weather permitting" were invariably inserted after anything pertaining to Fuji. I had met persons who had been transported up the ropeways to find every view from the uppermost heights blanked out by clouds.

Japan is a land richly endowed with forests. She has been as scrupulously careful to preserve the beauty of her woods as have the Germans of Baden their famed Black Forest. Though Japan's civilization is founded on wood and paper—used in houses, doors, windows, umbrellas, even holy shrines—she has been discriminating in the cutting of trees. Being a national park of vast area, the mountainous Hakone region is handsomely wooded. Pristine nature's arrangements of contours and folds, of valleys and peaks, of passes and gorges delight the eye. The deciduous trees, the conifers, the cryptomerias—special cedars that grow only in Japan—and the stands of feathery bamboo seem arranged by a master gardener.

We drove as directly as the circuitous road permitted along the Nagoa Pass to a cleared place on a craggy eminence. It was marked by a small Oriental-roofed pavilion with a seat to accommodate about six persons. And there was Fuji, base to summit, with its cone glistening under a mantle of new-fallen snow! It was incomparably beautiful. The morning paper, Kiyoka said, had announced that the first snow of the season had fallen on Fuji in the night. She had not told us, for she wanted it to be a surprise. Snow crowning the symmetry of the elegant and perfect cone of the volcano did greatly enhance its beauty, as Mrs. Aso had declared.

We had Fujiyama all to ourselves and could gaze in silence. The tourist buses from Miyanoshita and Odawara took different routes and left this sublime view of Fuji for the climax. Far down in the valleys lay green farms and thatched villages that could be only dimly seen from our height. There was nothing directly between us and the mountain but crystal-clear air. A supernatural arrow shot straight from our pavilion would have pierced the heart of Fuji, just about where the snow line ended. An intense quiet prevailed, while we four looked across the valleys to the "god-mountain." This is the silence of the gods, I thought. I could understand why some

Japanese say that in the presence of snow-capped Fuji mere man so closely touches the divine nature that his own independent thinking processes are lost sight of in his contemplation of Spirit.

"Undoubtedly this is an ultimate among the world's most glorious scenes," I said at last, breaking the spell of intense silence.

"The Japanese," Kiyoka remarked, "speak of Fuji as 'that which is without equal.' "

"The epithet is perfect," I said. "It is natural that Fuji should inspire countless poems."

"Thousands during the ages. One of the earliest by the poet Mushimaro expresses Fuji well, I think. His poem begins: 'Lo! There towers the lofty peak of Fuji!' It ends:

> "The snows quench the burning fires,
> The fires consume the falling snow.
> It baffles the tongue, it cannot be named.
> It is a god mysterious."

"Fuji is often spoken of as Fujiyama, because '*yama*' means 'mountain.' But we generally call it Fuji-san or Lord Fuji."

I turned in astonishment. The words came from the soft-spoken masculine voice of our chauffeur, whom I had presumed neither understood nor spoke English.

"Where did you learn English?" I asked.

"I speak only tourist English." He smiled. "I listen to tourist talk."

I observed him closely. He was another of those rarely handsome Japanese males, who are certainly not plentiful. He called to my mind the young Johnnie Mack Brown, the Alabama football hero of the late twenties, later leading man to such diverse movie stars as Mary Pickford, Greta Garbo, and Mae West, and finally the cowboy star of countless westerns. Thérèse saw the resemblance instantly. Johnnie Mack had been a lifelong friend of ours. As we walked back to the car, I asked the driver his name and where he lived. His name was Kato. He was thirty years old. He lived in Odawara, in sight of the castle. He had a plum tree by his door. His two children were learning English.

Curving around a mountain we came to a place called Owaku Dani or Big Boiling Valley and sometimes Big Hell. We parked amid hundreds of cars, got out and looked down at a gaping gorge, where water boiled up and sulphurous gases rose. Japanese sight-seers were thick, snapping pictures excitedly.

For lunch we stopped at a spa hotel called the Hakone Kanko, on Lake Hakone. It, too, commands a view of Fuji. It seemed a delight-ful hotel and good for a relaxing fortnight's stay. The dining room was full when we arrived. Something had gone amiss about our luncheon reservations. But the headwaiter deftly had a table spread for us in one of the drawing rooms by a floor-to-ceiling window giving on the water and away from dining-room chatter.

We were so imbued with the spell of Fuji reflected in the lake that we were only vaguely aware of the sight-seeing launch ride we later took across the water to join Kato and the car at some other shore.

We had changed our day's schedule arranged by J.T.B. and done the sight-seeing trip in the morning instead of the afternoon. We had been scheduled "to spend the morning at leisure strolling through the Fujiya gardens, shopping, or taking one of the hot-springs baths." Partly to let Kiyoka return by train to her Tokyo household, we had switched the afternoon's activities to morning. It was fortunate that we had. For by the time we returned to the Fujiya phantomlike mists were drifting across Mount Myojo, which faced our room.

From our picture-window vantage point we had another spec-tacular view of those eerie, evocative mists that have inspired poets. Peculiar to Japan, the mists are like ghostly pageants, where one ethereal, fantastic formation is followed closely by another. Poeti-cally beautiful as the floating clouds are, they obliterate the solid natural scenery. Unlucky persons who took the Hakone scenic trip that afternoon were dismal in the evening. "We have seen nothing, absolutely nothing, only fog!" a New York couple bewailed to us on the way to dinner. "Not a glimpse of Fuji!" Weather in Japan, one learns, is a big gamble.

We spent the afternoon hours admiring the stroll garden and window-shopping on the quaint slanting street across from the entrance to the hotel. Outside one shop Thérèse found a meditating Buddha in stone bas-relief. It seemed quite fitting for the base of an oak on our back terrace. Its price was surprisingly low, only twenty-five dollars in American currency; it would cost another fifty to send it to Alabama. We hesitated, and began to think we might find a full figure we liked better in Thailand. In the end we passed up this bargain and have not ceased to regret it.

At the shop of M. Ishii & Sons a few doors away we were struck by the beauty of an enameled ceramic bowl displayed on a black velvet stand in the window. "*Shibui*," murmured Thérèse. We went into the shop to examine it closely. It was a lovely piece of Kutani ware in silver-gray, dull gold, and pearl-white, with a large white chrysanthemum edged with gold on the front and another similar flower in the bottom of the interior. Looking long at it I was moved to quote Keats: "O Attic shape!" It was so skillfully proportioned that though it looked taller than it was wide, when I put a tape measure to it, the diameter of the rim was ten inches, and the actual height, tapering inward toward the base, was only nine inches.

The shop manager, a slight little man with melancholy eyes, instantly inspired confidence. He told us that all Kutani pieces were done by hand and that this especially lovely bowl was among the last by the master himself. Mr. Kutani would probably do no more, for he was approaching eighty. He also said that because this was an original work of art it would come into the States duty-free—which it did. The price was 28,000 yen, or eighty dollars. Yes, he accepted American Express credit cards. I handed him mine. He made the necessary arrangements and gave me a receipt. We were so delighted with our acquisition that we also bought trays in gold lacquer and in red lacquer, each decorated with sprays of bamboo. That evening after dinner we visited the Ishii shop in the Fujiya's arcade and bought a samurai horse in whitish iron, a fine copy of an ancient masterpiece. Everything had arrived, expertly packed, by the time we reached home at New Year's.

The next morning we were to catch the eleven-thirty train for Kyoto at Atami, Japan's most popular hot-springs resort. Our roundabout route from the Fujiya lay over the Ten Province Pass, where we might possibly get another panoramic view of Mount Fuji. I had asked the J.T.B. branch office located in the Fujiya garden that Kato be our chauffeur. I said that we did not need a special guide, that Kato spoke enough English for our purposes. We liked him and felt very safe with his driving. He was at the Fujiya promptly at nine o'clock.

When we came down into the lobby the manager, Mr. Ishii (no relation to the shop manager), and the personable young man who had married the daughter of the hotel's owner, were in the lobby to bid us godspeed. They showed us photographs of scores of notable Europeans who had been the Fujiya's guests. Among them was King Gustaf VI Adolf of Sweden, who had stayed there with his first wife when he was crown prince forty years before. The list was impressive.

The morning was bright and clear. "I think you see Fuji-san again," Kato said, with his warming smile. And see it we did, after about a half-hour's drive through more picturesque mountain scenery and vistas of neat, terraced farms. Fuji was glistening with what seemed to be fresh snow. The snow line appeared to be lower on the cone. "Did it snow on Fuji again last night?" I asked. Kato grinned and made a joke. "I don't know, sir. I was asleep in Odawara. I haven't seen a morning paper. But it sure looks like it did."

"Do you sleep in a Western-style bed," I asked, "or on the floor?"

"I'd be afraid to sleep on a bed," he said in mock dismay. "I might roll off. And my wife would no more let the little children sleep on a bed than on the edge of Fuji's big hole."

"Have you ever climbed Fuji?"

"No, sir. It's too cold at the top. But once my brother did. The mountain is open to climbers from the first of July to the last day of August. There are stone shelter huts along the trails. Thousands of people climb it every summer."

Though Atami, on the boasted Riviera of Japan, is only twenty-three miles from Miyanoshita, we consumed almost two roundabout hours in getting there. The schedule was purposely arranged by J.T.B. to give us the pleasure of fresh series of spectacular scenes. At the end Kato drove us a distance on a high coast road with magnificent rock formations in arches and columns suggesting ruined cathedrals. Then we coursed the road along the sandy beaches and plunged into the city proper.

The Atami hot-springs baths, indoor and outdoor, are plenteous and of numerous categories. There are comfortable Western-style hotels, but far more Japanese inns, for Atami is a center for Japanese tourists and draws honeymooners from all over the country. In summer Atami boasts of being ten degrees cooler than Tokyo, and in winter ten degrees warmer. The garden villas high above the town domicile old families like the Hachisukas, who were there before Atami was. I asked about finding Madame Hachisuka's estate, but Kato feared we might be caught in a traffic jam near the station and was reluctant. He was right. We were caught in the terrific density of cars three blocks from the station. In the milling crowd, as we approached the station, the J.T.B. man, awaiting us, pushed his way out to meet us. He had been assigned to conduct us to our seats, Number 113 A, on the limited express "Kodama" (Echo). It was all spelled out for us in our blue cloth schedule book. This higher-up was a brisk, keen, smartly dressed chap of obvious good birth, whose middle name might have been efficiency. Modern as they come, he was quite a contrast to the *simpatico* Kato with his irresistible smile and gentle aura.

We parted with Kato as if we were saying good-by to Johnnie Mack Brown. To boost his prospects with J.T.B. I told the young official that we had needed no other guide, that Kato had enough English to tell us everything we wanted to know on that morning's motor trip. Impulsively, I said that my wife and I had become very fond of Kato. The young man stared at me in amused astonishment, as if to say, "Do you really mean that individuals can make any difference to you, if they do their work well?"

When I protested that the undersized, bandy-legged, gray-haired porter whom he had engaged to handle our luggage was too old to carry the heavy pieces, the impersonal guide scoffed, though not impolitely. "Old Japanese are stronger than young ones," he declared. But with a slightly cynical expression on his cool, impersonal face, he took my hint and carried Thérèse's tote bag, when I insisted on carrying my own small bag. We walked up the broad stairs to an upper platform and left the old porter to wrestle the two heavy suitcases onto the escalator.

On the platform, our companion pointed to a dressed-up young couple just ahead of us. The man was carrying both suitcases. "You may be sure they are honeymooners," he said. "You see the male is carrying the bags. In Japan, we say that the husband carries the bags for the first two weeks after the wedding. For the rest of their lives *she* will carry the bags *and* the bundles."

We laughed. But I thought to myself, You are probably the kind who would like periodically to beat your wife, like Premier Sato, whose wife told a newspaper correspondent her husband did indeed often beat her during their early years of marriage. But this young man's wife was probably too modern to stand for anything so old-fashioned as a beating.

Japanese families with children were crowding the many platforms. "Contrary to what I have read," I said, "the husbands seem to take their wives on vacations with them."

The guide slanted his eyes at me. "*Only* to hot-springs resorts— *occasionally,*" he emphasized. "You won't find a city man including his wife in any of his nightly recreation plans."

We were walked to an exact spot on the platform just before the train rushed in. The old porter was Johnny-on-the-spot with the luggage. The door to our carriage opened precisely where we stood. As our new friend led us to our seats he instructed us, "Now when the train gets to Kyoto, just sit still. A J.T.B. official there knows exactly where you will be seated. He has your number, 113 A. He will come and fetch you and conduct you to the Miyako Hotel."

Such efficiency I had never experienced in foreign travel before. We shook hands briefly. I looked directly into the bright, cold, smiling eyes of the new age. But I liked this fellow. He was so perfectly adjusted to whatever the future held. "That chap is made to survive," I observed to Thérèse, as his straight back disappeared down the aisle.

"But at least let's be glad," Thérèse said, "there are some Mitzis and some Katos left, with all their natural sweetness."

After a week in Japan I had been convinced that there were no more efficient people in the world than the Japanese. Not even the Swedes or the Germans, to whom the palm for efficiency goes in Europe, surpass them. "The Japanese worker is unique: he needs no supervision." A plump Pakistani electrical engineer made this arresting pronouncement to me on this Kyoto-bound train, skimming past a heron-graced lake at ninety miles an hour. I had moved over into the vacant seat beside him for a better view of the white birds. He came every year from East Pakistan, he said, to buy railway rolling stock and electrical products for his government. "A Japanese worker catches on to his job with celerity and then he never has to be told again," he observed. "To do a shoddy job or to malinger seems in general repugnant to the Japanese nature."

But I also found that the high-powered executive head often drives himself more than the worker, partly, perhaps, to prove by results superior qualities in the national make-up. He is aggressive, shrewd, extra-polite, and far-seeing. He is game and will take chances. Poker-faced, he has a peculiar talent for reading his opposite number's mind. "Don't ever think," the Pakistani bore me out, "that you can outdo a Jap in a business deal."

At precisely 2:15 P.M., according to schedule, the train came to a stop in the Kyoto station. Almost instantly a young J.T.B. official was at our side with a wide welcoming smile. He, too, was an up-and-coming modern, but he retained some of the traditional Japanese charm.

Kyoto, "Capital of Tranquillity"

Though for us Kyoto was to prove one of the most fascinating and rewarding cities in the world, when we stepped out of the station we experienced a shock of disappointment. The square before us was, as in Tokyo, crowded with tramcars, buses, motorcars, swarms of people. The borders of the square were outlined with dull, characterless modern buildings, with an ugly white tower rearing up just ahead. Was this the venerated heart of Japan, the imperial capital for a thousand years, the center of Buddhist religion, with its 1,500 temples and its 200 pavilions? Except for a great torii gate here and the curved roof of an ancient temple far over there, little was reassuring in the taxi ride to the Miyako Hotel. Perhaps I had forgotten that Kyoto had become an industrial center, as well as Japan's prime cultural center, and that its population numbered almost a million and a half.

I refrained from asking the amiable J.T.B. man, "Is *this* Kyoto?" as we drove through business blocks. Sensing our initial disappointment, he spoke of history. "When, in 805, the Emperor Kwammu actually moved his capital to what is now Kyoto, it was first called Heian-kyo, 'capital of peace and tranquillity.' This was the name given to the Heian period of history, from 794 to 1185. But the city has more frequently been known as Miyako or Kyoto, words of

Chinese origin, both meaning 'capital.' " He paused, smiled encouragingly, and continued. "Once Kyoto was noted for its fine brocades and other silks, for lacquer ware, ceramics, and handsome books. The city had a long tradition of producing art goods and materials of highest quality for the superior taste of the imperial court. We still make those high-class products. But since 1950 the expanding industries include chemicals and machinery and, above all, textiles, to take care of the needs of the increasing population."

When we drove up into the grounds of the Miyako Hotel, nestled in a wooded hillside, our escort said, "I have assigned you one of our very best guides for your stay here. He is a knowledgeable young man and a university graduate. I think you will like him. His name is the equivalent of 'hill walker' in Japanese, and his professional cards are often so printed. If you need anything special, I shall be at your service. I am the Bureau's head here. My telephone number is in the blue book Mr. Nohara gave you in Tokyo."

The Miyako sits at the eastern edge of Kyoto, away from the hurly-burly of the city's new modernity. A nearby public park extends to the north of the hotel and another to the south. Besides greenery, there is little to be seen from upper terraces except the National Museum in Ozakazi Park and two or three curving roofs of shrines or temples behind protective trees. The hills that surround Kyoto are known by romantic names like the Mount of Wisdom, which rises to almost 3,000 feet. It holds dark, mysterious forests, in which are hidden temples and monasteries. The men who so placed the Miyako were inspired by the custom of Buddhist temples to half conceal themselves at the foot of a mountain. One did not have to look out upon walls and other windows at the Miyako. Our fifth-floor balconied bedroom faced the far western mountains, giving a distant view refreshing to the eyes.

We were aware from translations of Japanese literature that from ancient days the Japanese set great store on moon-viewing and that the architects of villas designed special rooms and galleries for enjoying the seasonal risings of the moon. Here at the Miyako from our beds, which faced the picture window on the west, we had an ideal situation for viewing sunsets.

As the sun began to lower to a distant peak, I pressed the "immediate" service bell and tea was brought in. On our twin beds, propped against pillows at our backs and sipping tea, we reveled in the phantasmagoria of dazzling colors that illuminated the western sky. It was as if a score of volcanoes had burst into simultaneous eruption beyond the picturesque mountains. We were to make a ritual of sunset-gazing after each day of temple-hopping.

When traveling in exotic lands the stranger comes to realize the importance of his guide's personality. There is always a slight apprehension at the moment before meeting. He will click with you or he will not. He may enhance or diminish the pleasure of sightseeing. The next morning at nine in the lobby a young man in his late twenties approached and presented his card. On one side it read Hirooka Hajime, on the other, Hajime Hillwalker. He was small, very neat, very dignified, undistinguished-looking, a low-keyed personality. Later we learned that he was an omnivorous reader, and he turned out to be sensitively discriminating. He liked all the best things, and seemed to divine our tastes and predilections. Thérèse and I became fond of him.

This bright day and the two days following were to be the climax of our meeting with Japan. For all of Japan's superlative bestowals of nature, her *gloria in excelsis* is the man-made temple gardens of Kyoto and Nara, those ancient capitals now, alas, tinctured with modernity. Yet in these hectic decades even after centuries the ordered beauty of the gardens seems to be as much appreciated as it was in those halcyon times when Lady Murasaki strolled the scented paths of Kyoto and recorded her enchanting tale of Genji.

Like fine brandy, a garden, with savor and that mysterious power to stir the imagination, should be old. In the temple gardens of Japan, antiquity and the aristocratic tradition are fundamental, blended with Buddhist inspiration and devoted daily care. Created at intervals from the seventh century through the seventeenth, these are among the world's oldest gardens and the top exhibit in Japan's perennial exposition.

Hillwalker proved most agreeable to varying, according to our inclination, the schedule in the J.T.B. book. Though it was not set down for this morning, we asked to see first, above everything, the most unusual garden in the region, the Ryoanji Temple Garden of rock and sand. It lay to the northwest, just beyond Kyoto and across a river.

We were lucky to arrive before the crowds thronged the Ryoanji. Fewer than thirty people were already there. Within the temple we sat on bleacherlike wooden steps in stockinged feet and contemplated what lay before us. Rocks become starkly mystical in this abstract fifteenth-century garden. This rectangular garden is made up of nothing but raked white sand and fifteen odd-shaped barren rocks, big and little, strategically placed in five groups of two, three, or five stones. The whole is framed by three ancient earthwork walls smeared with lichen. Some moss grows at the base of the larger rocks. Ornament is absolutely excluded. The assymetrical equilibrium is pronounced. The artist, Soami, who created this garden in 1499, here expressed his understanding of Zen enlightenment. The mind of the beholder, stained with mortality, is supposed to be purified by the beholding. For some foreigners the garden does create a kind of spell; for others, mere bemusement at Zen simplicity. As we sat quietly gazing on beauty pure and simple, a tangible silence engulfed us. The mystique of serenity I cannot explain, but I certainly felt it.

When at last we pulled ourselves away from the magnetizing spirit of this "Zen poem in minerals and light," crowds began to pour in at the entrance to the arcade. Many of the people were obviously peasants. "To the simple folk of Japan," Hillwalker said, "the effect of a monastic order concentrating on the act of living is of great impact. Here in this odd garden it is said that you see Zen as a kind of shock-treatment therapy of the spirit, which stirs men out of their intellectual pretensions."

On our way to our next objective, the famed Golden Pavilion, we drove along the banks of a river. The river, named Tenji, was striped with color as if rainbows had lain down on the cooling water. The dyers of Kyoto's silks were setting the colors of their fabrics in the clear flowing river.

The Golden Pavilion, the Kinkakuji, was originally built as a villa for a fourteenth-century nobleman and later taken over and elaborated by the Shogun Yoshimitsu as a retirement house. A hereditary shogun at the tender age of nine, Yoshimitsu lived an able, stressful, warrior's life until he was forty. Then, having had his fill of the world, he retired to this pavilion covered in gold leaf and crowned with a bronze phoenix bird, all reflected in the garden pond. He turned to religion, and decreed that at his death his last earthly home should be transformed into a Buddhist temple. For centuries the Golden Pavilion survived as one of the loveliest relics of ancient days. Then in 1950 a half-demented monk of meager abilities, but with a burning desire to distinguish himself, turned arsonist. One of the prides of Japan went up in smoke in less than an hour. However, luckily, Yoshimitsu's architectural plan had been preserved, and with the aid of photographs the temple was rebuilt in 1955.

As we drove to the edge of the garden we could see the three-storied pavilion glittering in its coating of gold. The garden, the pond, the stream, and the arrangement of trees, Hillwalker told us, had hardly been changed since the sixteenth century. A great camellia bush in the front garden was claimed to be over three hundred years old.

But where we might have expected stillness there was constant movement, not only of sight-seers, but also of priests and monks busying about in ceremonial garb. Distracting bright silk banners hung from the three delicately carved balustrades. To us, it seemed some sort of religious celebration day. But Hillwalker said it might just possibly be a silk merchants' convention for displaying their creations. "Religious orders do not receive help from the state since the war," he added, "and on rare occasions some abbots let their temples for conventions. Our temples are largely dependent on tourists' fees now to keep their gardens." Because of the human jam we did not go inside the temple. But we could imagine the delicate beauty on a less festive day before the crowds surged in.

The elaborate Nijo Castle, officially called the Nijo Detached Palace, was built in 1603 as a town house for the Shogun Ieyasu Tokugawa, who lies entombed in splendor in Nikko. The castle is near the geographical center of the city, about nine blocks to the west of the Kamo River, which runs through Kyoto. It is set in seventy acres of gardens, with a cascade and water garden among the artfully arranged rocks and trees. A high stout masonry wall surrounds the property. The four thick corner towers remind one that the town house was also a fortress, erected in treacherous times.

Five separate buildings within the enclosure compose the palace and are connected by wooden galleries. In those seventeenth-century days of intrigue and betrayal the most powerful man in the land did not consider himself safe from an assassin's dagger. Confronted with five houses, a potential killer could not be sure where to find the shogun. A most ingenious system of supplementary protection was devised in the wooden boards of the flooring in the galleries. They were designed to sound as much like the warbling of a nightingale as possible. When the nightingale sang out, the royal guards were on the alert. The boards still squeak today. As we went along the galleries with other tourists a muted chorus of plaintive bird calls marked our footsteps.

Hillwalker called our attention to the artistic carvings and the paintings of the dividing panels between the rooms. The murals on wood and the ceilings are elaborate. In one large audience chamber, life-size wax figures embody a scene of the shogun receiving homage from some twenty kneeling vassal lords. They are dressed in richest-colored silks. The extraordinary thing is that all the men's skirts have trailing trains several yards long. "Why?" I asked. Hillwalker grinned. "The shogun devised this obligatory court attire to hamper the movements of the vassals. The trains made it difficult for them to turn and run. And if a man with murderous intent started to rush forward to slash the shogun's throat, a guard or some loyal lord could halt him in his tracks by stepping on his train."

Nijo Castle should not be missed, because it has a solemn grandeur hardly surpassed in Japan. But the most memorable and distinct feature of Nijo Castle is the walk along the galleries, where you make a squeaky music even on tiptoe.

Our last stop of a morning full of contrasting interest was at the Temple of Sanjusangendo, not far from the Municipal Museum. Erected to the glory of Kannon, the Buddhist goddess of compassion, the present structure dates from 1266. Its main hall is like no other in the world. One thousand standing statues of the goddess, approximately life-size, painted gold, stand on tiers in the long, darkish nave. The expressions of no two faces are exactly alike, though similar. The sculptors have carved their individual interpretations of gentle mercy. A single colossal figure of Kannon stands in the midst of the thousand replicas, but this heroic one has a thousand arms and hands that radiate like rays of the sun to suggest that her compassion flows out in all directions. Not in China, where she is revered under the name of Kuan Yin, has the goddess been more honored. Not in Christendom is there any such multiple manifestation of the holy mother of Jesus. The effect of the Sanjusangendo is haunting, almost forbidding. Bizarre rather than beautiful, it is yet unforgettable.

In our first morning of sight-seeing we had visited three temples
and a palace, and we could have taken in no more. At our rate, with
its 1,500 temples and two hundred pavilions—of which more than
750 are said to be really worth-while—it would take a man a full two
years to do justice to the treasured places, each of which has its distinctive features. We still had to save for another day what we came
to consider our three favorite gardens in Kyoto: the Kokedera or
Moss Garden, the Samboin, and that of the Detached Imperial Villa
called Katsura, for which permission must be obtained from the
Royal Household.

In the afternoon, however, we visited a small subtemple made to
accommodate only sixteen in meditation at a time. It was loosely
connected with a huge Zen temple complex, the Daitokuji, founded
in 1324, which is one of the seven headquarters of the Rinzai sect of
Zen. It had been built by a well-known American, the widow of a
Japanese priest, Sokei-an Sasaki, who had founded the First Zen
Institute of America in New York City in 1930 for the purpose of
instructing American students in Zen. Ruth Fuller Sasaki was a rich
Chicago-born lady, whose photograph in *Time* in 1958 had shown
her to be beautiful and serene. She was known as the only foreign-
born Zen priestess in Asia. I recalled one statement Mrs. Sasaki had
made to *Time*'s interviewer: "The practice of Zen does not prevent
one from enjoying grand opera or an occasional glass of champagne." Years after the death of her husband, whose brother had
been chief abbot of the Daitokuji Monastery, she had established a
school called the First Zen Institute of America in Japan for teaching the disciplines and meditative practices to Americans and Europeans in Kyoto. Through Helen Wolff in New York I had secured
a letter of introduction. Mrs. Sasaki and I had exchanged letters. At
the time of our arrival she herself was in New York on Zen business, but she had invited us to see her house and garden and the
detached temple.

I telephoned Mrs. Sasaki's home. A pleasant-voiced young man
with an upper-class New England accent and a distinguished American family name answered. He acted as Mrs. Sasaki's secretary. He
would be happy to receive us at four, he said.

Addresses in Japanese cities are often the plain devil to find—
even when the hotel porter writes them in both Japanese and

English on a card for the taxi driver. The address Mrs. Sasaki had on her letterhead looked complicated:

> Ryosen-an 107 Daitokujicho
> Murasaskino, Kita-ku
> Kyoto-shi, Japan

However, my letters so addressed had reached her. But Hillwalker looked distressed when I handed him the address. "It's far toward the northwest, I know," he said reflectively. The chauffeur shook his puzzled head. Hillwalker consulted two other J.T.B. guides standing nearby. A light broke over one. He spoke in rapid Japanese and made gestures left and right and straight ahead, but without convincing assurance. We got into the car uncertainly. "If we can't find it," Hillwalker said, "the nearest police station will direct us."

Lost foreigners are advised in handbooks to go to the nearest police station for directions. But how can one who can't speak Japanese find a police station? It is said that if you are invited to a private home for dinner in Tokyo the host may expect you to be about an hour late. It is hard to understand why the clever Japanese, with all their remarkable efficiency, do not get some simpler system of street names and house numbers.

It was a long ride. After passing avenues and under various torii gates we went down streets like alleys, trying for a short cut. Behind a university in just such a narrow passage we encountered scores of students leaving for their homes. We had to wait until they had cleared from the alley. Several bicycles were parked at random along one wall. Our car could not squeeze past. The chauffeur got out and replaced the bicycles slap against the masonry. Then we crept by with hardly an inch to spare on either side. At last we came to the end of the three-block-long alleyway. Then we rode smoothly for a while, but in the end we had to seek the precinct police station. Hillwalker made inquiries. Eventually we arrived at the Sasaki gate in a high white plaster wall.

An elderly, shabby-looking Japanese stood there, as if guarding it. At first he seemed disinclined to let us pass. I explained our mission. Hillwalker translated. Hearing the talk, the young secretary, in casual clothes and sandals without socks, appeared and opened up the gate. He was blond and ingratiating. He conducted us down a walk with shrubbery and through a wide tile-roofed inner entrance gate. Before the house lay one of those perfect miniature formal gardens laid out with pebbles and green turf and dominated by a gnarled, twisted dwarf pine. In one corner stood a neck-high ancient stone lantern, beside a pruned camellia bush so old that its woody trunk was as thick as that of a tree. In the entrance hall of the house to the left of the door a tokonoma or kind of shrine held a black-and-white framed photograph of the late Mr. Sasaki, and on the wall was a long hanging scroll in ancient calligraphy. Mrs. Sasaki had studied Rinzai Zen since 1932. Her husband had been her teacher in the States. She had married him during the war to secure his release from a concentration camp when he was seriously ill. But he had not survived 1945. The widow re-established the Zen Institute in New York. Later she went to Japan for special study in the *koan* at the Daitokuji Monastery in Kyoto. The authorities permitted her to rehabilitate at her expense an old house at the edge of the property for her residence. After she had rebuilt a detached subtemple, she had to be consecrated a priestess to continue living on the property. Her house was furnished partly with American, partly with old Japanese pieces, all quite harmonious. The fireplace for logs added special cheer to the drawing room.

"The main house was in a dreadful state of repair," the disciple said, "when Mrs. Sasaki was granted permission to rehabilitate it. Everything is virtually new, including, of course, the two bathrooms. The dining room has an American table and American chairs, so guests do not have to sit on the floor. Would you like to see the library and the *zendo*—the meditation hall?"

To the east of the director's residence stood the library and the meditation hall. Gardens separated the three buildings, some in pure Japanese style, some showing Western influence. There was a small water garden, an azalea garden, and a bamboo garden—all simple and natural, giving an intimate sense of solitude. In one place a spreading weeping cherry was supported by a complex of trellises. Mrs. Sasaki, who was the author of several books herself, had collected a large reference library, which was stacked, shelf after shelf, with books in Japanese, many very old, and priceless old parchment manuscripts in Chinese. Volumes in English, French, and German on religious and philosophical subjects stood beside classics. There was also an excellent selection of first-rate modern novels. In one alcove stood Mrs. Sasaki's desk and typewriter. In the study room there were other desks and typewriters, filing cabinets, and a commodious American fireplace with a long davenport and two armchairs before it. Here everything was made comfortable for the scholars doing translations of Zen texts from the Chinese and Japanese into English.

"A research staff of three distinguished Japanese scholars and one American works here from time to time," the young man said. "The students have access to the library at all times."

Outside again, we followed a winding path of steppingstones to the temple. It was a steep-roofed wooden building in rectangular shape. We removed our shoes at the threshold and entered in stocking feet. The young man, who had kicked off his sandals when we had entered the residence, was already barefooted.

The series of large windows was set high in the walls, so that one could not easily see out and be distracted while meditating. Parallel platforms, about two feet high from the black tiled floor, lined opposite walls. Spread at intervals were wide square cushions for cross-legged meditation, eight cushions to a side. At the end of the room, facing the entrance door, was a kind of altar-lectern with Buddhist texts and two pointerlike sticks, one with a much heavier end than the other. "The heavier one is for winter," the disciple told us, "when the meditators wear thick padded garments." Then, noting Thérèse's recoil at actually seeing the famous rods, he explained, as Mitzi had, but with an amused smile, "The sticks are not used for punishment by the master, but to make the students take a better posture or to arouse the drowsy. Proper posture and breathing are deemed essential in Zen meditation. Group meditation is held from seven to nine each evening under direction of Japanese or Westerners trained in the art of *sazen*. But the hall is open from early morning every day for individual practice. One may come at any free hour and meditate—away from household or rooming-house distractions. After *sazen* has been mastered, the student is ready to study the *koan* with a special master."

"I have read a book on the subject," I said, "but I don't understand the *koan*."

The young disciple smiled, regarding me with a kind of transcendental look. "You aren't supposed to," he said cryptically. We let it go at that.

Then he added in his soft voice. "Zen is difficult to talk about. How can one speak of what is not communicable in words? The nature of enlightenment is inherently not communicable. He who has not experienced it knows nothing about it; he who has experienced it cannot describe it."

"Have you attained *satori?*" I looked directly into the young man's blue eyes.

"Not absolutely—yet. But I have had glimpses."

Thérèse asked about the nationality of the current students. There were eight Americans, two Scandinavians, and some twenty Japanese enrolled. All of the Japanese worked, and six of the Americans held some kind of a job.

"Where do the students reside?" I asked.

"In different lodgings, according to their tastes and pocketbooks. There is no dormitory connected with Ryosen-an. I myself live about a mile from here and come daily by bike. I like the ride."

I was interested in noting the changing expression on the face of the doubting Hillwalker, as he looked searchingly at everything and listened with keen interest to the disciple's explanations. Brought up in Osaka in the harsh aftermath of the war, he had never been much touched by religious feeling. To our surprise, as we were leaving, he quietly asked, "Could anyone enroll for a course in Zen here? Myself, for instance?"

The young American turned his pale eyes upon Hillwalker with a look that might have been both metaphysical and clinical. "If he were sincerely interested."

"I am by profession a guide," Hillwalker interjected, "but I like to read and have some scholarly inclinations."

"Zen need not interfere with one's profession," our host said. Then, as he walked with us to our waiting car, he added cheerfully a final word. "Despite its seeming obscurities, the essence of Zen is simple. It is freedom; it is actuality; it is action; it is daily life."

While we were driving back to our hotel along a broad avenue, I asked Hillwalker if he had been at all serious in considering taking up the study of Zen.

"Who knows?" he answered earnestly. "One tries new things— in these restless, unsatisfactory times. Zen has been a blessing to several persons I know."

At a stop light we had a good look at two pretty girls in elaborate hairdos and sumptuous kimonos. "They are geishas," Hillwalker said, "going early to their evening work. Kyoto is renowned for its geisha schools, the best in the land. Attractive and talented girls from the country are rigorously trained in the graces, in the art of make-up, in playing the samisen, in pleasing men. The most excitingly lovely geishas in Tokyo are trained in Kyoto. The two most renowned training schools are on opposite sides of the Kamo River. At certain festivals in the spring the girls perform for the general public. The word 'geisha' is written with two ideograms, *'gei'* meaning 'culture' and *'sha'* meaning 'person.' So the term implies nothing wicked or salacious, but merely 'an accomplished person.' A *maiko* or apprentice geisha submits to approximately a two-year training course. The prices of a geisha party are so exorbitant that now only big businessmen with company expense accounts can afford them. It is said that every breath one draws in an A-1 geisha house costs a fortune. And as for the price of pillow service! . . ."

Hillwalker raised his hands in an eloquent gesture. Then he continued. "People also say that the average Kyoto girls in their daily life reflect some of the charm of the geisha houses in their carriage, the tilt of their heads, their manners. Have you noticed? I don't know myself, because I am rather afraid of girls."

"Afraid?"

"Well, timid. Would you believe that most Japanese men are inherently shy around women? Perhaps it is because for centuries our marriages were all arranged for us by our parents. The custom has been changing fast since the war. I refused to let my parents arrange a marriage for me. And so far I have been too timid to make advances for myself.

"Because Kyoto is the head of many sects of Buddhism, don't think that all its citizens are pious," Hillwalker changed the subject. "There are some ten different districts in Kyoto given over almost entirely to night life. I am told that it is like Rome, where the shadow of the Vatican falls upon blocks that are anything but holy. Each district in Kyoto has its own peculiar character, atmosphere, and widely varying prices."

About four blocks from the Miyako we learned of a unique facet of Japanese mores. As we drove by a respectable-looking hotel, Hillwalker told us it had housed the young Prince Edward of Wales when he came to see Kyoto's temples. "It was the best in the city then," he said. "Now it is rated 'a dubious hotel.' "

"Dubious?"

"It's where you take a girl for the night, no luggage necessary, no questions asked. They are all over Japan—of various standards. Husbands and wives, too, find them quite convenient. There is little privacy in a Japanese house. Walls are of paper, you know, and, besides, sometimes the children sleep between the parents. So for an uninterrupted night of love—why, the dubious hotel."

At the Miyako I found the best masseur I have ever encountered, better than any in the Scandinavian countries or Germany or India. He came to our room at call after we had watched the sun set. Small, neat, wiry, dark-skinned, and fixedly unsmiling, this little fellow went about relaxing my muscles with the assurance and inspiration of a virtuoso pianist attacking a difficult concerto. Since he spoke no English I could compliment him on his performance only by calling him Taiho, the name of the grand champion sumo wrestler. Because the gigantic Taiho was about four times his size, this amused him and brought forth a grin. He knew that I was calling him the best.

First Permanent Capital

Leaving three of the best-prized places around Kyoto to be seen on our last day, we set off on an eight-hour excursion to Nara, the first permanent capital of Japan, from 710 to 784. It lies only twenty-five miles west of Kyoto.

The main highway goes through the legendary and profitable tea plantations of Uji, where peasants in picturesque costumes and broad hats were engaged in their various chores. By each thatch-roofed cottage stood a Japanese persimmon tree heavy with globes of burnt-orange-colored fruit. "The sight of the ripening persimmons never fails to give me a thrill," Hillwalker remarked. "Since I was a tiny tot, the persimmon has been my favorite fruit."

We were delighted with the orderliness of the tea plantations and the geometrical spacing of the bushes. "According to the best authority," Hillwalker said, "tea was introduced from China by a Buddhist priest in 805. He set out the first tea plants on the slopes of Mount Hiei near Kyoto. Tea had a pleasant, relaxing effect on the nerves of those bored with the sameness of a monastic regime. And the drink was supposed to be beneficial to studious eyes. In the beginning tea was taken only by the priests, then by the aristocrats. After six centuries tea drinking became a custom of the people. The tea ceremony, which at first had the elements of a religious practice, was indulged in by those who could afford tea-houses in their gardens. It was practiced to induce serenity of mind and heart. And then it was indulged in to cultivate good manners."

Although Nara today has something like a population of 140,000 and some conventional modern buildings in its business district, it still retains much of the charm of an ancient small town. The city lies among green hills, with a river irregularly bisecting it. A vast park of 1,250 acres is spread out in its center, the largest municipal park in Japan, made distinctive by hundreds of tame deer roaming at will. Near the city rises wooded Mount Kasuga, the traditional home of the Japanese gods; no trees are ever cut here. A few of the ancient temples may be seen from the broad highway.

"You get the feeling in Nara," Hillwalker remarked, "that it is much much older than Kyoto. Some of the best shrines go back to the eighth century, during the period when Nara was Japan's capital. But the glory lasted only seven decades."

Though Nara produces some exquisite lacquer work, in general it is blessed with the absence of factories. The town lives almost entirely on pilgrims and tourists. Nara was much as I had expected Kyoto to be.

Without stopping in Nara we went straight through the town out into the country, a half-hour's drive to the southwest, to get to the Horyuji, Temple of the Flourishing Now, the oldest Buddhist temple in the land. We hoped to see it before tourist buses from Kyoto reached there. We were fortunate; few visitors had arrived.

The Horyuji is not romantically situated at the foot of a mountain or by a stream or atop a hill. It stands in flat green fields that reminded me of Denmark's smiling landscape. Far away from a town the air is salubrious. One drives up a tree-bordered avenue and sees the temple's calm curved roofs, which came from Chinese inspiration. At the left of the great gateway inside the compound a graceful five-storied pagoda soars into the air.

"The first Buddhist missionary priests arrived in 552 with the religion that had taken powerful hold in China," Hillwalker said. "The temple was begun by the regent prince, Shotoku, an ardent convert, in the year 607. It contains the grave of Jimmu, Japan's first emperor."

Doubtless a deal of the wood has been replaced in thirteen centuries, but experts believe that the original designs have held firm. The temple is the oldest wooden building in the world. It is the "longest-to-survive" temple in Japan. Fire, tempest, and war have destroyed other sanctuaries, though most of them have been rebuilt. But the Horyuji has stood, its original self, since the seventh century, despite one fire in 1949 that damaged interior walls where some restoration work was being done.

Chinese ideas are embodied in the arrangement of halls and pavilions around a huge square cloister. Simplicity is the keynote in the decoration outside and inside. But the most memorable thing is the beauty of ancient woods, particularly the columns of the long arcades, which had never been painted, but polished with cloths in the loving hands of monks and novices throughout centuries.

The Horyuji is world-famous for its statues of the Amida Buddha, the gentle healing Buddha. Perhaps the most notable of all the temple treasures are the frescoes on the walls of the *kondo* or main hall. Though the date of their creation and the identity of the artists are unknown, some connoisseurs consider them the finest work of their kind in the Orient. It is believed from scant historical evidence that the work was done by seventh-century painters from China who became naturalized Japanese.

"Ironically," Hillwalker said, "after standing for thirteen centuries, the temple was almost lost in 1949. Still more ironic was the accidental cause of the fire. As insurance against some future destruction, a first-class artist was employed to copy the murals in miniature so that they might be replaced, if ever damaged. In the chill early morning of January 26, the electrically heated cushion on which the man warmed his seat while he worked short-circuited. A disastrous fire broke out, a large portion of the priceless murals was totally destroyed and many walls were smudged with smoke.

"The newspaper *Asahi Shimbun* underwrote the restoration of the frescoes and contributed twenty million yen to the project. Businessmen and philanthropists made up the rest of the hundred-million-yen cost. There were in existence many colored photographs to serve as models, as well as the copying done by painters. Four groups of artists who possessed a thorough knowledge of the original frescoes were set to work on March 1, 1967. They are kept busy from nine to five every day. The work will be completed in February, 1968. Come back another year and the copies will all be in place."

The Horyuji museums, Hillwalker told us, were loaded with treasures. Though we could spend a profitable full day examining works of art conserved through the ages, he said that if we wanted to see Nara we could not tarry long.

Regretfully we left the peace and the aged beauty of the polished wooden columns of the cloister. Although it was longer than any of those beautiful fluted colonnades of monasteries in Portugal and was absolutely without adornment, it gave one much the same feeling.

Nara Park is one of the most charming parks in the world. It has character and flavor: green meadows, gentle hills, and rich woodlands are its components. The Sarusawa Pond, fringed with weeping willows, lies near the entrance and reflects a five-tiered pagoda built in 1426 and rising to a height of 165 feet. Its foremost distinctions are its tame deer and the thousands of commemoratory lanterns of aged stone or bronze, higher than a man's head and set on embankments along an upward-inclining road. Out from among the trees and the lanterns emerge spotted deer to nuzzle the visitor and beg for the flat rice cakes, shaped like New Orleans pralines, that may be bought at the park's entrance. Hillwalker provided each of us with a cellophane pack of cakes. We had not gone far when the first deer approached shyly, politely, with nostrils aquiver at the scent of the cakes. A few would submit their graceful necks to be caressed, but most of them retreated a short way into the woods after their first cake was swallowed.

Grown men, Western and Oriental, were taking as much delight in feeding the pretty spotted creatures as little children. From the array of smiling faces it seemed everyone felt it a privilege if the deer would accept his tribute. One of the fawns that I tried to make friends with hesitated to come out into the open from its shelter between a tree and a bush, so I had to scramble up to it and offer a cake.

"The deer are very content with their living arrangements," Hillwalker observed. "They have no urge to roam far from their woods. At nightfall, when a special Japanese taps is sounded, the 150 animals line up in orderly procession and proceed to their sleeping quarters, where each knows his own soft alcove."

Besides the spotted deer and the impressive lines of lanterns, our objective was the Kasuga shrine sitting on a rise at the end of the road. With the stately lines of tall lanterns, which have stood there for hundreds of years, and the flashes of emerging and retiring live deer, the approach is superb. "On February 3," Hillwalker said, "at the festival of Setsubun, all the lanterns are lighted. The effect is spectacular and awe-inspiring. Maidens perform a sacred dance in one of the halls of the shrine."

At the top of the rise spreads the Shinto shrine that was an eighth-century gift of the powerful Fujiwara family. Four ornate buildings in brilliant vermilion lacquer are connected by galleries. The Kasuga may be starred in guidebooks, and it is undoubtedly impressive, but I was not drawn to it. I found the polished plain wood of the simple Horyuji more to my taste. I had the tactlessness to say aloud that I did not care much for the Kasuga. Hillwalker looked surprised and disappointed. As we started away he paused, turned back, knelt before an altar, placed his hands together in prayer, moved his lips, and left some coins. Walking down through the north side of the complex on a path, he said he had asked the god of the shrine to forgive me for my criticism so that he might not cast an unfortunate spell on me. We could not be sure how serious he was, but I thanked him for his thoughtful precaution.

During this one October week the bucks can become extremely disgruntled—when their antlers are removed. In a rude amphitheater spectators buy tickets as to a bullfight to watch the painless amputations with electric saws, deemed necessary for the peace of the deer community. Hillwalker asked if he should get tickets for us. But we did not care to witness the indignities. However, we stopped to commiserate with one old stag who had already been shorn of his glory. Alone, couchant, motionless on a jutting slab of rock in full sun, he looked for all the world like a model for some heraldic device. He cast one disdainful eye on me and, still in high dudgeon, sullenly ignored the last sweet-smelling rice cake I sympathetically laid as near to his nose as I thought respectful.

Doubtless we might have appreciated the Kasuga shrine more if we had been fresher. And perhaps we were so under the spell of the long approach with that magnificent royal guard of ancient lanterns and spotted deer that the purported climax seemed an anticlimax. We were glad to freshen up at the Nara Hotel and have luncheon at a window giving on green lawns and a groomed garden that descended to a river as pretty and evocative as the Avon.

On our departure from Nara we made a stop at the Todaiji Temple, founded in 745 at the city's eastern edge. It is the largest wooden building in the world. The huge temple has stood there since the twelfth century, though several times it was destroyed by fire or storm. The present structure dates from the year 1708. The enormous Daibutsu or "Great Buddha," the chief object of worship, is the largest bronze statue in the world.

Hillwalker told us that formidable difficulties were encountered in the casting of anything so mammoth. After several failures, the image was successfully cast in 749. It weighs some five hundred metric tons. The statue, seated on a ten-foot pedestal, is just over fifty-three feet in height. The face itself is sixteen feet in length. Back of the figure a huge gilt halo radiates light.

The Kegon sect of Buddhism, Hillwalker said, uses the Todaiji as its "cathedral" and the general headquarters of the order. But we did not find this stupendous bronze image particularly pleasing aesthetically. It is less sympathetic than the open-air statue at Kamakura. But we did greatly admire the octagonal eighth-century lantern that stands thirteen feet high before the great hall.

We left Nara with a sense of enriching memories of the antiquity of Japan, and with a profound appreciation of the talent and dedication of those early Buddhists.

We had been warned before leaving the States that the monastery gardens created by monks for solitude and to induce meditation might be crowded with Japanese school children, but that they would be quiet and well-disciplined. "You will not have solitude," we were told, "but you will have quiet." On the way back to Kyoto, at Ugi, we ran into hordes of these young sight-seers at the pavilionlike Byodoin Temple or Phoenix Hall. It was a graceful building with a roof like a great bird's wings and verandas running around the entire structure. It had been built only a few yards from a clear running river. The Byodoin, Hillwalker told us, had once been the country villa of an ancient prime minister named Genji, but since he lived some two centuries after the tenth-century romantic hero of Murasaki he could not have been that beau-ideal character. Yet because this was precisely the perfect setting for that legendary figure, people came to speak of this garden estate as Genji's. Placed in the center of the great pavilion sat a Buddha in meditation. However, the dark-blue cloud of school children's uniforms made it impossible to get close enough to note sculptured details. The verandas, too, were jammed, as were the bridges and the lawns. The thought occurred to me that one could drown in a sea of teen-agers. And here they were anything but respectfully silent. There was babbling, murmuration, and even whooping as they snapped pictures. The world-wide lack of reverence in school children had at last struck scrupulously disciplined Japan. It was not easy to extricate ourselves from the kids in uniform. Finally we reached the narrow entrance-exit gate and ran into an oncoming stampede of other noisy youngsters eager to push through into the grounds. For a while we waited politely. But seeing no end to the surging file, I boldly barred the way. "Just a second!" I commanded in a strong voice. By sheer authority I stemmed the tide, as at Thermopolae pass, long enough for Thérèse and Hillwalker to slip through the gate. One jut-jawed youngster scowled threateningly and shook his fist at me. "The Japanese didn't accept the pill soon enough," I muttered aloud to the air, "or perhaps it wasn't invented soon enough." Then to Hillwalker directly I said, "It is fine and commendable to have excursions of school children come in buses from all over the land to see their historical landmarks. But could there not be some regulation, so that the boys and girls from a dozen distant prefectures would not converge at one spot at the same time? Or could there not be special hours for children, when all foreign visitors would be requested to stay away?"

"That is all being considered," Hillwalker said dubiously. "The school kids make it hard on Japanese sight-seers, too, and particularly on our guides. Timing is a gamble. Let's hope we shall be lucky at the Samboin. Incidentally, they don't encourage children at the Samboin, and the priests forbid all cameras. A Japanese boy would rather go sight-seeing without his pants than without his camera."

The long day's excursion ended most happily. After passing again through miles of those agreeable tea plantations of Uji we arrived shortly before sunset at the Samboin Temple in Daigo at the western edge of Kyoto. A blessed peace and quiet prevailed. There were not more than a dozen visitors, all Japanese, sitting silent on the veranda floor admiring the garden.

Favorites among Japanese gardens vary with the taste and sensitivity of the beholder. But our most treasured memory is definitely that of the ineffably lovely one adjoining the Samboin Temple, a miniature in perfection, designed and created in the sixteenth century.

In the reception room of the temple, backed by delicate Buddhist wall paintings, stood a priest in a white robe. He was the only priest in Japan to whom we were actually introduced. Plump and, naturally, head-shaven, he glistened with radiant health and inviolable serenity. Obviously, he had attained *satori* and could live in this mortal world with a kind of blissful detachment. But he had a most friendly smile. On a white cardboard placard placed on something like a music stand I spied the word "*taiho*," which means "the greatest," and pointed it out to Hillwalker. For some reason Hillwalker told the priest that I had met Taiho, the wrestling idol. The man regarded me with bright-eyed interest and laughed pleasurably, as if a smidgen of Taiho's triumph and charisma had rubbed off on me. So even in the monasteries and the temples the monks kept up with the world's ups and downs.

The garden, which has been preserved in its original state, should be viewed from the rooms or verandas of the temple and the appendages of teahouses. The pond contains not one, but several, small islands, which are connected by various bridges of different kinds. Each rock in this garden facing the temple was selected with special care for its pleasing shape and texture. The Japanese say that the Samboin garden is without equal in the wealth of stones utilized. The sheared azaleas and hollies are shaped into molded forms, but they are planted in the irregular patterns of nature. The pond both divides and links the cultivated areas of the buildings with the naturalistic plantings on the other side of the garden and its crowning background hill of maples.

One of the attractive features of the Samboin is that the pond water flows under the very floor of one of the three tea pavilions. A stone water basin providing water for the guests to rinse their hands stands in the water. As one bends to wet his hands he sees his face reflected in the pond. This sight is supposed to induce a feeling of humility before one stoops under the low portal to enter the teahouse. An unusual bridge is formed by planks upended and lashed together linking the two banks of the pond inlet. On either side clipped azalea bushes give a softening effect even when they are not in bloom.

Except for its famous weeping cherries that lean Narcissus-like over the limpid pond, the Samboin is made of the same components as other gardens: water, small islands, arched bridges, bamboo, azaleas, feathery pines, stone lanterns, steppingstones, and alluring pathways. Yet the innate subjectivity of its inspired creator breathes out after four centuries. Though perishable, the garden seems a far more suitable monument to the gentle Buddha than those bronze colossi at Kamakura and Nara that depict his image boldly. The Samboin's appeal seeps in the heart to stay there. And, for us, it is perhaps the most magnetic single loadstone to draw us back to Japan. We long to see it in the springtime when the weeping cherries are in flower.

A Garden of Mosses and an Imperial Villa

For the last full day in Kyoto our schedule listed among other attractions two of its superlative gems. In the morning we were to see the unique Moss Garden of the Saihoji Temple, and in the afternoon precisely at two by appointment we were privileged to visit the famous Detached Imperial Villa called Katsura, ranked by many experts as the nonpareil among the gardens in Japan.

It was a long drive to the Saihoji, with the mountains rising in the background. But the day was perfect with that richness of blue sky that comes with the Japanese humidity. In the vast stroll garden of the Saihoji, nature and art met six centuries ago. A luxurious carpet of rare mosses of scores of varieties brought from faraway places spreads out under shade trees whose lower limbs have been cut away. The trees are principally evergreen oaks, pines, cypresses, and cryptomerias, with occasional clumps of bamboo. The pines have been given a light and feathery appearance by the discreet plucking of their needles, partly to keep the needles from falling on the soft green moss and partly to let in an abundance of filtered light. As trees died with age during the centuries, other similar trees were planted precisely in their places. So a feeling of continuity has been preserved. From the high overhead limbs a dappled golden light sifts down to the ground, providing just the right degree of shadow for the health of the different mosses. This moss ground cover of various shades of green—avocado, olive, lime—has fanned out from rocks placed on the banks of the large pond and other stones set artistically along the alluring paths. With boulders rising here and there in eerie effect, the garden gives the impression of an enchanted woodland. One has to be reminded that the garden is a creation of a religious man named Muso-Kokushi, who lived six hundred years ago.

The shore line of the pond juts out irregularly here and there, and is accented with flowering shrubs and slender flowering trees that create a series of planes of dappled light to enhance the sense of mystery. In the large irregular pond huge old rocks rear up above the water. We were told that they were "symbolic islands where mariners may rest during long sea voyages." One lone skiff was moored in a tiny bay, not to be used for sport but for tidying the rocks in the pond if leaves or branches were blown on them.

Our leisurely aesthetic strolling in this storybook principality of mosses was not to last long. Suddenly a thousand chattering school-girls in dark-blue middy-blouse uniforms appeared behind us. They had been disgorged from holiday buses from some far-distant school districts, and they were expecting to see as many notable spots as possible in one day. The children were almost on the run in their eagerness to get to the next place. We stepped aside from the path onto a patch of precious moss to let them surge past us to the temple rising on its hill at the north end of the garden. I recall nothing of the temple or monastery except long wooden verandas facing the garden and more priests and monks about than I had noticed at other sacred places. Was their function disciplinary, to slow down the rushing of the uniforms? Ah, well, we had had some twenty quiet minutes among the exotic mosses.

"You may be sure," Hillwalker said that afternoon, "that you will see the Katsura in perfect peace. Only about fourteen are admitted at a time for the hour's tour."

We had been fortunate, for Mr. Nohara had secured passes for us, after my two requests to the Royal Household in Tokyo, spaced by months, had remained unanswered. Mrs. Kudo, the wife of the head of the Manichi newspapers, had told us she had never yet seen the Katsura herself, though she was on the almost endless quota list, and that she hoped to visit the villa before she died.

According to one story, toward the end of the sixteenth century the warrior shogun Hideyoshi ordered the villa built for Prince Toshihito, a nephew of the Emperor. Somewhat in the way of the imperial Romans this rude man of the people, who has been called Japan's Napoleon, "adopted" the Prince, presumably for two reasons. He wanted to lay some claim to relationship with the aristocracy, and he wanted to keep the adherents of the Emperor pacified, since they had been shorn of power. Prince Toshihito was reckoned to be one of the most cultivated men in the land. He had been tutored by foremost scholars and poets. He wrote poetry. He collected treasures of old manuscripts. Among other gems he possessed was the original of Murasaki's *Tale of Genji*. The Prince is believed to have got some of his best ideas for a garden from Lady Murasaki's description of gardens and villas in that Heian heyday of the eleventh century. Though Toshihito had suggestions of what he would like embodied in the garden and the villa, the actual architectural work and final design was the creation of Kobori Enshu, a noted Zen tea master of the time. Hillwalker told us that legend says Kobori demanded three conditions on undertaking the work of years: that he be allowed all the money and all the workmen he deemed necessary, that he never be hurried, and that no one see the work before everything was finished to Kobori's satisfaction. The work was completed in the first decade of the seventeenth century.

As we waited with the eager knot of fortunate American tourists outside a high gate of polished bamboo, Hillwalker said that there had been some sort of villa standing on the west bank of the sparkling Katsura River since the early part of the eighth century, when the area first became noted for moon-viewing. "When the present estate was landscaped, Kobori had the model of the Samboin to animate him. The Zen Buddhist influence pervades in the Katsura, though the Imperial Villa was designed for royal princes and not for humble monks."

After we were admitted, a few yards along the way Hillwalker and other Japanese guides stopped at a small pavilion with a roof and seats for waiting. It was as far as outside guides were permitted. We were taken in charge by an amiable middle-aged Japanese, who spoke English in such soft tones that only those very close to him could hear his explanations. Within three minutes after following the resident guide along a gravelly path, I knew that I could never do justice to the Katsura with any description. First, I noticed the elegant restraint. Focal places on the eastern side of the villa are arranged for viewing the rising moon beyond segments of lovely landscaping and distant hills. To no people on earth do moonrise, sunset, and dawn seem to mean so much aesthetically as to the Japanese.

The irregular main building is much more extensive in area than all the other eight buildings together. The Japanese purity of design is obviously at its best in the large villa. Its material is chiefly hand-polished wood and paper. Nothing grand or pompous looms up, nothing fantastic or artificial. The villa is a spreading, many-angled, one-story building, standing on piles about three feet high, against a possible overflow of the river. The overhanging roof is made of tiny cypress shingles arranged artfully to form a rough surface that curves slightly. The roofs are without gutters. The rain drips or pours from the eaves onto a catch of pebbles and sand. The wide doors are of beautiful aged wood, and the shoji is of paper.

Removing our shoes we stepped onto the tatami of one of the reception rooms. We admired the faded delicate paintings on the walls, the metal handles or indentations on the sliding doors in the form of wisteria blossoms or chrysanthemums. Some of the cedar doors are the more beautiful for being unstained. One bears stylized cocks in pale red and yellow. In the Spear Room and the Hearth Room samurai taste had been maintained. Delicate Indian landscapes by the three famous Kamo brothers add distinction to one of the apartments. The best Japanese painting has what might be called a spiritual inwardness, an evanescent radiance of the mystic attitude. The music room looks out upon a green stretch of turf. On its broad veranda, half wood, half tatami, guests once sat to watch exhibitions of archery and horsemanship. In another room a great window shaped like a lady's comb gives upon a woodland scene.

While the building represents purity of design at its best, the house is mainly a place from which to observe the garden, to let the garden flow, as it were, into the rooms themselves. The gardens are far more important than the buildings. The villa and teahouses fit so unobtrusively into the landscape as to seem to be a part of it. From each room we had vistas of water. More or less in the center of the nineteen-acre estate lies a very large irregular pond with five islands of various shapes and sizes. Here at the Katsura is that perfect fusion of building and garden, which is inexorably asymmetrical.

Following the guide out into the garden, we made a tour of pavilions and teahouses. The pavilions have poetic names like Waves of Moonlight, Flower Delight, Cheerful Heart, Murmur of the Pines. The adventure is the stroll in getting to them on the stepping-stones along the way. Nowhere are steppingstones laid with more artistic care than in Japan. The bridges to islands in the pond are all different in character, and different bridges lead away from the islands. Set here and there strategically are ancient stone lanterns, squat or tall, classical or comic. A notable style of lantern at the Katsura is called firefly on water, which casts its night reflection on the pond in summer. Another series of snow-lighting lanterns are artistically arranged for illuminating the snow on winter lawns.

"The Japanese ideal in lanterns," the soft-spoken guide said in a side remark, "is about 40 per cent used for light and 60 per cent used for appearance." When we came upon a wisteria arbor not now in bloom, he remarked that wisteria was most highly regarded in Japan. "In ancient Kyoto a wisteria festival was held annually within the imperial court."

The "crouching door" on the Miyaki Path in a muted red plaster wall has been the surprise of many a tall foreigner who has banged his forehead on the lintel. It happened now to a tall blond man from Ohio, who was dazed for a few moments.

I recall a mass of things: little canals and a boathouse, one teahouse on an island that can be reached only by boat, a square hand basin of stone sitting by a single low lantern, a wide branching pine tree standing alone on a promontory. I recall a "footwear stone" for depositing one's shoes before entering a teahouse, the small blackish river stones of certain paths and gates of polished bamboo. But the most notable cachet of the cultivated Japanese garden is the dwarf pine. In the Katsura the dwarf pine—twisted, bent, pruned, and plucked by an artisan's skillful hand—dramatizes the entrance to a bridge, the curve of a pond, a jutting peninsula of pale moss.

In the time of Murasaki a profusion of flowers bloomed in the colorful court gardens. But it is not so today; form is the important factor. The cutting garden for fresh blossoms is often concealed. Do not expect to see flower beds with annuals in the best Japanese gardens. Japanese iris may grow in clumps along the shore line of a pond, and azaleas in season and weeping cherries. Dwarf maples turn to flame and gold in the autumn. But generally there is little color besides green and the gray of rock.

We were told that each teahouse, as well as many facets of the villa, had one side or window designed to face the rising moon. Nooks for moon-gazing are also appropriate for catching the cool breezes in summer and trapping the sun's rays in winter.

With all its multiplicity of details, the Katsura estate has surprisingly been described by one Japanese expert as being "refreshingly lucid." Though I had been warned that the manifold different effects could produce aesthetic indigestion, I found it aesthetically harmonious. Two ideas were incised on my mind. Although the Imperial Villa and garden have withstood three and a half centuries of natural wear and tear, if the prince who first lived there were to return to earth, he would feel about as much at home as if he had just come back from a three months' visit to China. And as Hillwalker later quoted from his wide reading, the fact that the elaborate mausoleums of Nikko were built only a few years after the Katsura gives some idea of "the heights and depths between which Japanese art has been capable of moving during the centuries."

One is struck by the fact that Japanese gardens are utterly different in character from those splendid formal gardens of both France and Italy. The word that most nearly expresses their character is "natural." But they are by no means copies of nature. They are artful reminders of nature, or deep appreciations of nature. With a few carefully selected simple materials the maker of a garden suggests and hints. Though the garden-maker of today has a free hand to create according to his inspiration, he has tradition at his elbow to guide him and the example and experience of centuries. While Nikko represents the acme of elaborate display in architecture, wealth, lavish gold, and vermilion lacquer, the Katsura Imperial Villa, presumably financed by an upstart, was executed by an aristocrat and represents the aristocratic tradition of restrained beauty, yet it seems freshly modern. The young Frank Lloyd Wright is said to have been so stirred and influenced by the Katsura buildings that he incorporated into his revolutionary modern designs something of the spirit of ancient Japanese architecture at its simplest.

After the Katsura we did not care to see anything else on this visit to Japan. Something more might have dimmed or befogged impressions. We were sure which were our favorites besides the Imperial Villa garden. The Samboin headed the list. The others were the Moss Garden and the oldest temple of all, the Horyuji, beyond Nara. The transcending glory of Kyoto and Nara was evolved by the patient work of inspired meditative priests and monks.

The return to Tokyo on the superexpress train via the new Tokaido Line the next morning served as an exclamation point to mark the modernity, the efficiency, and the comfort to be had in Japan today. Still euphoric in the spell of the beauty, the antiquity, the distinction of those incomparable temple gardens of Kyoto, we could now enjoy the variety in the landscape on both sides of the roadbed. We passed historic Nagoya, the largest industrial city in central Japan; Hamamatsu, where the best musical instruments are made; Shizuoka, noted for its green-tea production; and Atami, that most popular seaside hot-springs resort. At the Tokyo station Kiyoka was waiting outside the door of our railway coach with a stout porter. When we arrived at the Okura it was strange to feel as if we were coming home, even though we went *down* in the elevator this time to a lower-floor room in a wing facing the stroll garden.

A message signal was flashing as we entered. The American Embassy was calling. "We have great news for you," a pleasant feminine voice said. "A cable has just come from Bangkok asking us to get in touch with you. You are to be received by Their Majesties, the King and Queen of Thailand, on Tuesday, October 24, at eleven o'clock in the morning. Another item: Mrs. Alexis Johnson, the Ambassador's wife, would like the Strodes to come to tea at four-thirty. You know, it's just across the street from the Okura. Unfortunately, Ambassador Johnson is away on official duties in another part of Japan."

I was mightily pleased about this firm promise of an audience with King Bhumibol. Thérèse still maintained that she preferred not to go through a royal audience, as I had written to Senator Lister Hill, who had made the overtures.

The American Embassy in Tokyo, built in the time of President Hoover at a then phenomenal cost, spreads handsomely and attractively at the end of a beautiful garden. With our embassies in Rome and in London, which I knew, and the one in New Delhi, which we were to see, it is among the top four in which Americans may take special pride.

Besides the Ambassador's lady, there were only three persons of the staff present, until the lady who had given me the verbal message about the Thailand cable came in a bit late. The tea that was served in the library was the best I had had in Japan, along with that offered us in Prime Minister Yoshida's conservatory. The company impressed upon me how singularly fortunate we were to be received by Their Majesties in Bangkok. "My wife isn't going," I confessed. "She thinks it would be too great a strain and she wouldn't know what to wear in the morning in a hot country."

Mrs. Johnson, who was a very pretty golden blonde, looked a bit nonplused. "Then I can assure you," she said with soft emphasis, "if your wife does not accompany you, the Queen will not appear. Mark my words. The Queen will not appear."

When Kiyoka came for us at ten the next morning to take us to the Tokyo International Airport I thought how rich our sixteen days in Japan had been. We had only sampled the country but the samples were of the best and peculiarly rewarding. Our experiences might have been different and still more varied if we had had the energy of twenty or thirty years earlier. But we could not have been more satisfied with those facets of culture that we had seen.

If one does miss by accident or design those special advertised features that guidebooks vaunt, one need not bewail. For Japan offers a plenitude of memorable attractions and aesthetic satisfactions besides costly geisha or *chanoyu*, that prolonged tea ceremony which definitely has its very special charm, but which painfully cramps middle-aged legs unaccustomed to floor-sitting. To appreciate Japan one does not need to take lessons in flower arrangement or pretend to delight in the tiresome "lion dance" of the Kabuki or to sleep on a pallet or to eat raw fish and seaweed or to scald one's self in a neck-deep bath, even though the velvety feeling of aged wood is a luxurious sensation; nor does one need to get smashed in a neon-lit crowd on the Ginza on his way to a strip-tease show.

When we flew away from this fascinating, beautiful, and paradoxical Japan I thought of the line of Enobarbus to Marc Antony on supposing that he had missed meeting Cleopatra. "O, sir, you had then left unseen a wonderful piece of work, which not to have been blest withal would have discredited your travel."

HONG KONG

Fragrant Harbor

As our Japan Air Lines jet winged over a stretch of blue Pacific before reaching the still-bluer South China Sea, I leafed through an American magazine the pretty stewardess had offered me. We had just sipped Cherry Heering after an excellent lunch with the renowned supertender Kobe beef as the entrée. Settled back in the deep and roomy seat in a relaxed kind of euphoria, I was arrested by a wood engraving of Benjamin Franklin among the advertisements. In large type a quotation from the sage occupied a quarter page: "I have not yet, indeed, thought of a remedy for luxury." Beneath in finer print he elucidated: "Suppose we include in the definition of luxury all unnecessary expense, and then let us consider whether laws to prevent such expense are possible to be executed in a great country, and whether, if they could be executed, our people generally would be happier *or even richer*." I read on to the end of the ad. "Is not the hope of being one day able to purchase and enjoy luxuries, a great spur to labor and industry? May not luxury, therefore, produce more than it consumes, if, without such a spur, people would be, as they are naturally enough inclined to be, lazy and indolent?"

We had just left one intensely industrious country, which had waxed sudden rich, partially by providing an abundance of new luxuries for the masses at home and abroad. And shortly we would reach the tiny British Crown Colony called Hong Kong, where 98 per cent of the population is Chinese, and where its people work, with a skill and diligence that rival those of the Japanese and for even longer hours, to meet the export demand, principally.

In Hong Kong, indeed, the global desire for nonessentials—from lacquered chests, carved jade, and beaded bags to transistor radios and smart tailoring—nourishes the very lifeblood of the Colony. Careful work helps make it possible for the two million refugees from Red China to sustain existence.

Because Hong Kong is a free port, shopping for bargains from the world's top marts, as well as for local quality products, is a stronger lure for tourists than the spectacular beauty of its exotic harbor. I have known persons—even in our own Alabama—who rationalize that by taking recurrent vacations in Hong Kong on the other side of the globe they are economizing because they get three years' family tailoring done, refurnish a house, or replace lost watches and valuable photographic equipment. Swiss watches and French perfumes are considerably less expensive in Hong Kong than in Geneva or Paris.

The couple from Argentina across from us on the aisle said frankly that they were chiefly interested in the shopping. He was an aging Norwegian-blooded industrialist, and his youngish golden-haired wife was of Spanish blood. They had been many times to Hong Kong, they said, and delighted in it more on each visit. The Japanese steward had brought them trays of rings and bracelets for their inspection, but I got the feeling that they merely wished to compare the prices of the free port of the air with those to come in the free port of Hong Kong. Indeed, the lady assured us that we could buy the best Mikimoto pearls of Japan much cheaper in Hong Kong than in Tokyo—which, I confess, we precisely looked forward to doing.

The captain announced the approach to the Kai Tak Airport. The stewardesses had changed to flatteringly graceful kimonos. In my alertness at the arrival a slight shiver of apprehension ran through me. The headlines in the Tokyo morning paper had announced another bombing in the Colony by Communist agents. Would we really be met by a representative of the Mandarin, as I had been assured by the English manager, Anthony Ross, that we would?

These scare tactics had been going on for two or three months to frighten the British to make some kowtowing gesture to Mao. On this street corner and in that alley bombs had killed or maimed innocent citizens. In July, Red China had cut down and threatened to cut off entirely the Colony's fresh-water supply from the mainland. The grandson of the President of the Confederacy, Jefferson Hayes-Davis, a banker in Colorado Springs and my longtime friend, had written urging us to skip the Hong Kong visit. "Why do you want to expose yourselves to dirty water and bombing?" But we had had reassurances from an American friend living in Hong Kong.

So we decided to chance uprisings and sporadic bombings—in which no white persons had been killed, only unfortunate Chinese. Our jet seemed to be skimming the water like an amphibian. However, I knew that a runway had been fabricated of dredged earth and thrust more than a mile out into sea water. The Kai Tak International Airport, which serves twenty-three international airlines, has an 8,354-foot runway extending into Kowloon Bay as an artificial bund or quay. Completed in 1962, the terminal itself is capable of handling 550 passengers an hour.

In the airport we were met and greeted affably by a Londoner with a Cockney accent and conducted to a waiting car. He was apparently the welcomer and dispatcher for Mandarin guests. "Mr. Ross has sent his own chauffeur to fetch you," he told us. Cheerily, a thin, tall, dignified old Chinese with benign patchworks of wrinkles, opened the door of a Rolls-Royce with an ingratiating smile. Though his manner was winningly reassuring, I instinctively remarked that I hoped the street bombings had stopped completely. "Well," he said in a sweet voice, "almost, but not absolutely. A bit of trouble on the road this afternoon, but we shall be quite all right. Have no qualms."

I was thinking that the make of our car might be a tempting target for a proletarian zealot, when our driver made a sudden stop. We had not gone more than a few hundred yards beyond the airport property. In front of us several police officers were waving warningly and pointing to a newly posted detour sign. We distinctly saw a gaping hole in the asphalt, with broken stones or slabs of concrete lying behind a rope cordon. Knots of silent Chinese stood as close as they dared. "I fear they have been at it again," the chauffeur observed with a philosophic smile, clucking his tongue at the shame of it.

When we came out into a kind of plaza before the vehicle-ferry entrance of Kowloon, our car was again halted. Police were chasing a man who had just emerged in flight from the ferry building. A curious crowd looked on as the fellow was apprehended and hustled into a waiting police car. "What's he done?" I asked. The chauffeur turned and smiled sweetly. "Communist," he said, and shrugged. We rolled onto the ferry.

So the American press had not exaggerated too much in its sensational reports in the spring and summer. We had not expected to come so close to actual trouble in October.

Soon we were on the water for the trip across the harbor from Kowloon to Victoria, the capital city, on Hong Kong Island. To the right and left, before and aft of the ferry, were hundreds of ships: junks, sampans, water motor taxis called walla wallas, lighters loading or unloading goods from freighters of China and countries on the other side of the globe. A lone woman in a canoelike craft bearing fresh fish manipulated it with ingenious skill and complete assurance. These water people had got their living on the sea for untold generations, and they were almost as native to the element as the very fish they caught.

"Hong Kong," the chauffeur was saying, "means 'Fragrant Harbor,' though some interpret it as 'Isle of Fragrant Waters.' "

The sea smell was salt and fresh and good. A pleasant breeze stirred. I looked to Hong Kong, where the latest in modern skyscrapers dot the reclaimed shore road, and up to the towering majesty of Victoria Peak, which rises a precipitous 1,800 feet, its greenery studded with villas of the affluent. The backdrop of sky was a stunning cobalt blue. One long glimpse of beauty was enough just now, for the ferry was berthed. We sped along the shore boulevard without further incident into Connaught Street and up to the portal of the Mandarin.

The two doormen in crimson silks who greeted us were turbaned, bearded Sikhs from North India. The porter, named Mr. Nichols, suavely, kindly, dependably, and indubitably English, and a Londoner, saw us to our rooms. This one time on the round-the-world journey we had engaged a suite. There are special occasions in life when extra luxuries seem particularly desirable. Partly because I delight in harbor views by night, as well as by day, I wanted the extra room into which I could slip at any wakeful hour without disturbing Thérèse and let my eyes luxuriate at will. On the seventeenth floor our two individual balconies afforded a sweeping panorama of the harbor and the city of Kowloon, backed in the distance by eight misty mountainous peaks called the Dragons. The sitting room was harmonious and even elegant in an off-white and a soft blue that Thérèse called Nattier blue after the French painter. The strikingly beautiful lamps were copied from ancient Chinese works of art.

In Japan we had often been told that the Okura was the best hotel in that country, but that Hong Kong's Mandarin topped all in the East. In a 1967 article called "Imperturbable Oases in a Clamorous World," in *Fortune* Magazine, the Mandarin, although only four years old, was ranked among the eleven great hotels of the world. "Imperturbability" was the criterion by which the author, Arthur Beardwood, distinguished the truly great hotels from the merely very good ones. "The Great Hotels," he wrote, "are able to make an extraordinary task seem routine, to solve problems urbanely, and to be imperturbable in the face of adversity."

A murmur of adversity suddenly sounded from the bedroom. One of the porters discovered that the lock on Thérèse's large suitcase had been smashed in transit. It was a moment of despair for us. How could the Chinese mend an American lock? Mr. Nichols, who was still with us, showing us how to work the air-conditioning adjustments and indicating the three-legged green ice bucket, examined the damage with "imperturbable" aplomb. "Oh, we can remedy that," he said, with most genteel reassurance. "We have our own locksmiths. We can put on a new lock exactly like the broken one."

The contents of the suitcase were piled upon one of the beds, and the damaged luggage was borne off "urbanely." What had appeared to us as an impossible task had been made to seem routine. When we returned from a look-about stroll that afternoon, the suitcase, with a brand-new lock, stronger than the original, sat there in something like smug triumph.

A Stroll and Charlie Mok

Architecturally, the city of Victoria is a mélange of a few British-type buildings of past decades and modern soaring skyscrapers. The post office, the Supreme Court building, and one of the best men's clubs suggest the early 1900's. The chief square, which faces the harbor on one side, is full of blossoming shrubs and flower beds. On three sides it is punctuated by impressive banks, among them the massive Hong Kong and Shanghai Banking Building and its neighbor, the seventeen-story Bank of China, in which millions are cleared into and out of Red China. Interspersed between the banks and great insurance companies are stylish shops and restaurants of repute. A stream of people moves along on the sidewalks around and through the plaza. Slim-hipped women in their *cheonsangs*, those tight-fitting, high-necked silk outfits with a slit in the narrow skirt far up the thigh, slip in and out of the predominately male crowd with swift and easy grace. Both men and women carry on bamboo poles over their shoulders their stocks in trade, which may be silks, dried fish, sugar cane, hot chestnuts, or the latest editions of newspapers. Weary shoppers rest on convenient stone benches, as do tourists and some pathetically poor recent escapees from China. And down at the shore's edge a block away from the square is the new ultramodern City Hall with its concert hall and other auditoriums.

The municipality called Hong Kong, though really named Victoria, has only a few broad boulevards, but scores of steep-rising "ladder" streets climb the hills. The streets are crammed with houses and shops emblazoned with bold painted vertical signs in Chinese symbols hanging from bamboo poles. In the Chinese section the poorer people seem to go about their daily routine as if they had never been touched by Western ways.

At the junction of Tai Ping Shan Street and Pound are four Chinese temples. One of the temples, called Pak Shing or the Temple of the Hundred Names, with its Broad Blessings Shrine, dates from 1851, when a committee of residents petitioned the British governor for a grant of land. This temple is one in which are placed tablets commemorating dead persons, often called soul tablets. Some Chinese hold the belief that one of the three souls people possess resides spiritually in the tablet to receive proper filial attentions, which will make the ghost comfortable and happy in the spiritual existence. Commemorative tablets of enlarged photographs of the deceased relative or friend may be put up by anyone who pays the price, which varies according to the prominence of location. A space in the central portion behind the altar costs five times as much as a side position. Across the top in Chinese calligraphy an inscription reads: "Let the descendants prosper in the manner of young flowers in bloom."

Though occasionally pockets have been picked in Hong Kong, one feels relatively safe in walking along the crowded Chinese streets. Yet at the front door of jewelry stores a guard stands with shotgun in hand to blast the daring thief. Some guards are armed with nothing more lethal than heavy hockey sticks, but these are as handy for bashing a dishonest head as for driving a rubber puck to the goal. One may be surprised to see coffins being made before the public gaze at the Virtue and Long Life Coffin Shop. We noticed billboards flaunting current offerings at the cinemas. The majority were of Hong Kong make or Japanese, and carried Chinese titles. But Elizabeth Taylor and Richard Burton in *The Taming of the Shrew* seemed to command top billing and were said to be drawing crowds of Chinese as well as local Britishers and tourists.

In our first afternoon stroll it was not the handsome glass-and-aluminum bank buildings or the inviting flowery plaza that made the most impression, but a high-rise building in construction across a side street west of the Mandarin. Framing it like a gigantic cocoon was a network of bamboo scaffolding, pole upon pole of flimsy-looking bamboo laid upon crisscrossing lateral poles. The men at the top looked like diminutive puppets employing mechanical toy tools. The sight brought to mind Jack's fairy-tale bean pole. One could well wonder if the airy, yellow-green complex might crumple into the street at any moment. In Japan, however, I had learned the tensile strength of the deceptively fragile-looking bamboo. I was told that this inexpensive native product had been employed throughout Hong Kong's magic decade of rising skyscrapers. Yet I was never able to pass this construction work without marveling at this peek-a-boo embroidery shooting thirteen stories up into the air.

A discreet knock at the door came just after our return to our room. Then a smiling Chinese in a black sateen jumper entered with his master key, announcing himself as our room boy, Charlie Mok. Later we learned his full name was Charles Shu Fan Mok. He, like a dozen other persons we met around the world, possessed that engaging quality that might be called instant charm. He was a handsome fellow, slightly under middle height, with smooth complexion the color of whipping cream and large black eyes that could become deeply thoughtful, even melancholy. He had come to make sure that everything was to our satisfaction. As he helped us unpack for our week's sojourn and laid by certain garments to be pressed and some pieces for the laundry, I engaged him in conversation. When he saw that I was really interested in him as a person he was a ready and agreeable talker. He had learned his English in King's College, he said, one of the best secondary schools in Hong Kong. He had finished the form equivalent to the American ninth grade. He was not Hong Kong-born. His "auntie" had escaped with him out of China when he was a lad. The British Colony government was generous about helping to educate the hordes of refugees. Now he was thirty-three, and he had been married for two years. No children; the world was still too unsettled.

Charlie said that he had been working in the Mandarin since the hotel opened in October, 1963. He had charge of sixteen rooms on the seventeenth floor. Oh yes, he had an assistant room boy, nearly twice his age, and two helpers to do the bathrooms twice a day.

"When I stopped school I worked in an uncle's stationery shop as a clerk. But I went into hotel service for the better pay. Because I couldn't go on with my education, I'm now only a room boy."

"To be a room boy at the Mandarin is not to be scorned," I said. "But why didn't you go on with your education?"

His lower lip turned down involuntarily. "I fluffed one question out of five on my final examination. I knew the causes of the French Revolution and I could trace Napoleon's movements after his return from Russia, and I answered two other questions. But I got all mixed up on the Crimean War, who fought who and who won what. I went down in defeat, and so"—he made a deprecating gesture—"I am a room boy."

"Four out of five questions seems a good batting average to me."

"Ah, but the competition here to get a higher education is really stiff. Only the very smartest can go on. I think I was naturally bright enough, but I wasn't as studious as I should have been. I have accepted my present lot, and I am reasonably content. I find it a pleasure to make people comfortable. I meet such nice people from all over the globe. I particularly like Americans because of their pleasant and relaxed manner. I am so vastly much better off than tens of thousands of other escapees from China. A few are so pitiful the sight of them hurts your heart. They have left or lost everything. A man can bear up over the death of a father, but the loss of an inheritance can drive him to black despair. Some refugees look so frightened and so hopeless and so skeleton-thin. They make me think of a Hindu proverb we were taught in school: 'If you hate a man, don't kill him, let him live.' "

The hanging up of the clothes in the twin closets was finished and Charlie was about to move off. He paused at the ice bucket to see that the cubes were still in firm form.

"Tell me about this three-legged ice bucket," I said. "It's most original." The body and exterior were made of some heavy nonferrous alloy. The antique finish was a chalky dull green. The inside was a luminous light-green plastic that resembled porcelain.

"It's a reproduction of a covered urn of the Shang dynasty, which lasted from 1766 B.C. to 1122 B.C. The official tale goes that it was originally used by emperors for cooking tidbits after successful game hunts. Its decorative cryptograms represent animals for which the Chinese have special admiration. The body of the urn, you see, bears motifs of the elephant, which in ancient China was the symbol of greatness, peace, and good will. The surface of the lid displays features of the water buffalo, which represents the highest sacrifices. The handle is two fishes out of water. With the Chinese the fish is a symbol of freedom, fighting spirit, and happiness. Mr. Ross imports these ice buckets from a firm in Taipeh, Taiwan."

Charlie gave me a knowing look. "Maybe it's a more pleasant story about a cookpot for an emperor. But, I tell you confidentially, I think those ancient urns were used to hold ashes of the dead."

"What an excellent idea!" I said to Thérèse. "You could stow me right in here."

Charlie laughed and turned, indicating the two breakfast order slips hanging on the doorknob. "You know, of course, that you are to check the items you want for breakfast and hang this card outside the door when you retire. Be sure to indicate the hour you want breakfast—and it will be here—exactly." With a slight bow and a winning smile he was gone. "His smile is irresistible," Thérèse said. "He himself is quite irresistible." I could only agree. "Too bad about the Crimean War," I said. "But then we would have missed Charlie Mok. Let's go out on the balcony and have another long look at Hong Kong's irresistible harbor."

Magic Casement

Ten minutes before breakfast was due to arrive in the sitting room I pressed a button by my bedside table and the heavy Thai silk curtains at the wide window were drawn back as if by invisible hands. Golden sunlight flooded the room. Slipping on a dressing gown, I went to the window to look across to Kowloon and down onto the harbor. In a flurry of purposed movement, vessels of a score of categories were going about their business, each illuminated by slanting shafts from the sun. It is impossible to describe the impact of Hong Kong Harbor. A feeling of excitement and exhilaration catches one. Perhaps, in my case, it was somewhat motivated by my lifelong attraction to moving ships, tinged with romantic teen-age readings of sailings to far-off exotic harbors. At any rate, I am stirred by the sight of boats on salt water, blue, green, or gray, particularly foreign boats of unfamiliar shapes and alien flags.

Hong Kong's importance and prosperity stem from its excellent harbor. Hong Kong is the only safe deep-sea anchorage between Shanghai and what was once called Indochina. It can accommodate vessels of up to 40,000 tons. Here world freighters bring their cargoes to be unloaded, broken up into smaller units and transshipped by coastal steamers and diesel junks to various spots in the Far East. But the mere depth of a harbor does not make it a great modern port. Hong Kong has the necessary facilities for mooring, berthing, discharging and loading cargo, warehousing, repairing, bunkering, provisioning, and watering. The charges are all decidedly reasonable, as the world's shippers freely attest.

Hong Kong Harbor ranks with those of Rio de Janeiro and San Francisco as one of the foremost natural harbors in the world. It varies in width from one to three miles and has a total area of seventeen square miles. I know both Rio and San Francisco well, and they are top favorites of mine as cities as well as harbors. Rio with its Sugar Loaf and other peaks is the most spectacular and beautiful of all cities, as approached by ship or plane. But from front windows of hotels one can only look out on water. In Hong Kong one looks upon water, moving craft, and beyond to the city of Kowloon and the brooding hills of Red China in the background. By night, the lights of Kowloon's hotels and tall buildings illuminate the landscape and are reflected in black-blue water. From Kowloon, if one stays on the mainland side, the panorama of Hong Kong Island with the great Victoria Peak is perhaps even more picturesque. The ceaseless activity of small boats, the strung incandescence that outlines the silhouette of naval ships of Britain and the U.S.A., and the faithful lighted ferries carrying people back and forth every few minutes, altogether make for a fascination beyond that of the more magnificent Rio.

With all the swirling activity in Hong Kong it may seem odd that so many tourists say they find it a restful place. It is because one never needs to visit some historical building, cathedral, or museum, for there is nothing important of the kind there. For the Western world the history of Hong Kong begins in the 1840's, when only clustering fishermen's shacks existed.

Before 1841 Hong Kong had virtually no history. The earliest settlers, it is believed, came from rugged, icy North China on their way to the Philippines or Borneo about 2000 B.C. A few stayed to make habitation. Around A.D. 500 some Cantonese appeared. Today Canton blood is the principal strain found in Hong Kong citizens. In A.D. 964 about 8,000 troops of the Sung dynasty were stationed at Tai Po, in what is now the New Territories, to protect the pearl industry for the Emperor. In the thirteenth century the last Sung monarch fled to the Kowloon region and died there. In a small way Hong Kong was one of the bloody scenes as the fading, once great Ming dynasty succumbed to the upstart

Manchus in the middle of the seventeenth century. Through the ensuing years only a small fishing population lived on in Hong Kong, augmented after 1700 by Chinese pirates, who would take refuge in its protective coves.

Strange are the results of minor historical events. Here we were, dwelling temporarily in this Mandarin luxury and gazing upon the shifting magic of harbor delights, because from 1839 to 1841 Great Britain had been so determined to profit by smuggling Indian opium into China that she created a war. Opium was contraband in China's customs offices, and the Emperor strove to keep the stuff from his subjects. But the Chinese navy suffered defeat off the mainland. Hong Kong itself was formally occupied by a British naval party on January 26, 1841. Its leader, Captain Charles Elliot, R.N., proclaimed the island a British Colony. By the treaty of Nanking, shortly thereafter, Hong Kong, the thirty-nine-square-mile island, was ceded in perpetuity to the British Crown, "it being obviously necessary and desirable that British subjects should have some port whereat they may careen and refit their ships."

Lord Palmerston, the British Foreign Secretary, sneered at the new property as "a barren island with hardly a house on it." And in the next year, 1842, he made one of the most erroneous predictions in history when he declared publicly: "Hong Kong will never be a mart for trade." In June, 1843, after the treaty had been ratified by both China and Britain, the name "Victoria" was conferred upon the rude village settlement that was to become the Colony's capital. In an editorial of December 17, 1844, the *Times* of London complained sourly: "The site of the town is most objectionable, there being scarcely level ground enough for the requisite buildings." The editorial was right enough in 1844, but the writer did not reckon on the resourcefulness and the engineering talents of the British. Queen Victoria was delighted with this new tiny acquisition to her waxing empire and proud that the capital city destined to stretch along the island's north shore and climb the hills behind should be named for her. Prince Albert, however, twitted her about being the "Empress of Hong Kong." As far as I have read, Victoria had no pricks and stings of conscience about her traders thrusting opium upon the Chinese. She saw only the advantage of having another haven and base for her British ships on the far side of the globe.

In 1860 another controversy over opium trade flared between China and Britain, with France now as Britain's ally. By the Convention of Peking (1860), the Kowloon Peninsula and Stonecutters Island were ceded to the British Crown, again in perpetuity. At the close of this second, briefer "Opium War," China finally agreed to legalize the import of the drug from India, and, as a kind of self-defense to outwit British dope pushers, the Emperor permitted the cultivation of the opium poppy on his own soil. Whatever the original contention, Britain had gained by opening the ports of China to world trade, and Hong Kong from the first was declared a free port.

As to Lord Palmerston's prediction, the Crown Colony's *raison d'être* and its magnetism as a star tourist attraction lie in the fact that Hong Kong is an alluring trade mart.

In 1898, because China feared French and Russian ambitions, she leased to Britain for ninety-nine years a hunk of mainland adjoining Kowloon on the north, together with 235 islands in the vicinity. By this Convention of Peking, the area of Hong Kong was extended to 398 square miles.

When I turned back from the window, breakfast was laid out on the coffee table and a folded morning paper lay neatly by the chair set for me. Thérèse appeared, to preside on the davenport, after an admiring look at the glorious harbor view. While she poured the coffee I glanced at the front page of the Hong Kong *Standard* of Saturday, October 14. The news was not quieting. The first three-column spread carried the headlines: BOMB KILLS POLICEMAN IN WAVE OF NEW TERROR.

"We shall have to walk warily," I said, dabbing Dundee marmalade on a piece of toast. "Last night a police constable was killed by a bomb in Gloucester Road—wherever that is. Listen! According to the paper, it seems that bombs were set all over the Colony to greet Lord Shepherd, Britain's State Minister for Commonwealth Affairs, who arrived yesterday. Several bomb throwers were caught and will be charged with attempted murder."

The bomb talk did not interfere in the least with our enjoyment of breakfast, mine hearty and English, with bacon and a three-minute egg. Thérèse stuck to coffee and toast, though there were delicious croissants.

A messenger delivered a note. It was from Mr. Ross, the manager, with whom I had corresponded. He invited us to have an apéritif with him in the lounge of the Roof Garden at twelve. He regretted that he had a business-luncheon engagement. I had seen pictures of Anthony Ross—good-looking, plump, and jolly, a Roman of the viscerotonic type, who likes good food and drink and conversation. He had been manager of the Mid-Ocean Club in Bermuda, where we had lived in a Paget cottage for three years.

When we emerged at noon from the elevator on the twenty-fifth-floor Roof Garden, I thought I instantly spied Ross, sitting in the bar lounge at a table by a grand piano. A graceful Chinese girl in a smart, miniskirted outfit approached us, called our name with only a faint question, and introduced herself in very British English as Kai-Lin Lo, public relations. We learned later that she had a degree from Cambridge. She led us to Mr. Ross, who, though exceedingly genial, had just got out of a private hospital for a few days' interval and expected to return again. "I have asked one of our resident decorators, Theresa Kwa, to join us. She is a very talented lady, who paints, writes excellent Chinese calligraphy, and also is manager of a shop selling fine Chinese embroidery. Miss Kwa designed several of our suites." We complimented him on our own charming suite and on the magic efficiency of Mr. Nichols, the head porter, who had made the extraordinary task of getting a new lock put on Thérèse's suitcase seem routine.

"Ah, that! But, of course, that's what we aim for."

A tallish, slim woman, who looked only partially Chinese, arrived at the table. Four of us took Bristol Cream sherry. Miss Lo asked for a more sophisticated Campari-and-soda and sipped only a third of it. Ross and Thérèse and I spoke first of mutual friends in Bermuda. Then I brought up the bombings. The disturbance had hurt tourist trade slightly in June, Ross said. Since August, the hotel had been more heavily booked than usual. "Despite the flurry yesterday and last night, the trouble will splutter out," Ross assured us. "Of course, Mao could take over Hong Kong in a day. But he is too bright to strangle the golden goose. He badly needs the trade that is transshipped here."

I said that in May we had been more concerned about the water Mao threatened to cut off from the mainland. "In the Mandarin that need not have bothered you," Ross said. "We have our own desalinization plant and purifier, the first of its kind in any Far East hotel."

Thérèse was asking Miss Kwa about silk brocades to cover our long davenport at home. "I could get you superb stuff," said the decorator. "But the brocades come from Red China and you could not take in the material or send it to the States. You have to have a bona fide certificate of origin. America does not permit entry of any products made in China. Your customs officers are vigilant and strict about this."*

I wanted advice on tailors. We had had so many recommendations of different tailors from friends at home and from ship's officers on the *Cleveland*. One thing I knew was that, since we were on Hong Kong Island, we were not going to ferry over to Kowloon and then take a romantic rickshaw to tailors, however reputable, on the other side of the water. So Thérèse asked Miss Lo directly the name of her personal tailor. "Celia Chen," she replied promptly. "Her main establishment is in Kowloon, but there is a branch on the Mandarin mezzanine. The ladies' tailors here are all men. The one who does the measuring and fitting is called Johnny Yee, and I don't know a better one. He's a refugee from Shanghai."

"And who is your tailor?" I asked Anthony Ross.

"His name is Chui Cheong Kai, of the firm of A-Man Hing Cheong. I think he's the best—certainly for me, for with my bulk I am not easy to fit. His shop is in this building, but it is at Number 3 Ice House Street, and you have to go outside the front entrance and around the corner. Tell Cheong that I sent you."

We noted the advice, and in that minute had already selected our respective tailors.

In answer to my questions I learned that the Mandarin had 650 guest rooms and that the cost of construction and interior decoration was twelve million dollars in U.S. money. The general interior design was the work of Don Ashton of Hong Kong, a designer of international repute. He was the first to blend successfully the color and fascination of exotic Chinese traditional designs with

---

* In July, 1969, a law was passed permitting an American to bring in one hundred dollars' worth of stuff made in Red China.

the modern comfort of the West. "The gold temple carvings in the main lobby," said Miss Kwa, "have started a craze for these works of art."

"I wonder if we could see some of your de luxe suites?" I put the question to the three of them. They exchanged glances, and the two women agreed at the same time. Miss Lo went to telephone for a boy to bring the keys to three that were unoccupied.

After Mr. Ross excused himself to go to his luncheon engagement, Thérèse and I, with Miss Kwa, took a swift survey of the vast Roof Garden, which was encased in walls of glass. It was like an enormous observation tower on the grandest scale. "On clear days," Miss Kwa said, "you can see into China. And, look, you can now! Beyond those Dragon Hills what you see is Red territory."

At the elevators we joined Miss Lo and the boy bearing the keys. A handsome door on the twenty-fourth floor was marked with a name plate: Mandarin Suite. "We'll show you our special pride first," said Miss Lo. "Those in the so-called aristocratic mold, or those who like to fancy themselves so, would be especially attracted to this suite, I think," she said. "It reflects the opulence of the ancient Chinese court and yet has every modern comfort." In dull gold and pale gold, with chairs upholstered in rich blue silk, it was indeed elegant. "When King Baudouin and Queen Fabiola of the Belgians occupied this two-bedroom suite," she continued, "we converted an adjoining room into a private chapel, so that they could attend Mass every morning. The Queen was so delighted with the wastepaper baskets—which are, in fact, nineteenth-century Japanese flowerpots—that Mr. Ross presented her with one for the Palais Laken."

"Charlotte Horstmann designed this Mandarin Suite," Miss Kwa said. "She was born in Berlin of a Chinese mother and a German father and she married a German. She came here as a refugee from Shanghai, and she has her own swank decorating shop in Hong Kong today. Charlotte put to use her belief that classic Chinese furniture is quite adaptable to modern interiors."

"We learned that in Sweden and Denmark," I observed.

In the luxurious sitting room one of the striking pieces was a large nineteenth-century Shansi lacquer chest decorated with delicate paintings of court scenes. The wardrobes of the two bedrooms were two full-sized Ming copies in teak. "The gold mosaic shower tiles of the bath came from Italy," Miss Kwa said. "When Mrs. Horstmann could not find a Chinese material to suit her creation, she drew upon Thailand, India, Japan, and Italy."

"The Henry Fords also occupied this suite when they were here," said Miss Lo. "Christina Ford, the beauteous Italian second wife, got a great deal of good out of it, for she rarely rose before mid-afternoon. Mr. Ford did all of his shopping in this sitting room. He had all sorts of lovely things from the mezzanine shops brought to the suite to make his selections. He bought pearls for all his secretaries."

"Who else in the so-called big-name world has stayed in this suite?" I wanted to know.

"Well, let's see. The Giovanni Agnellis of Turin, the handsome Fiat man, then the very handsome Prince Raimondo Orsini, the Phillipe Rothschilds, the Archduke and Archduchess von Hapsburg, and Prince Juan Carlos of Spain, Clare Boothe Luce, Doris Duke, and others. Among the various movie stars who have occupied other suites are Peter O'Toole, Marlon Brando, Gina Lollobrigida, and Geraldine Chaplin. Among writers, I particularly recall your John Steinbeck and Italy's Alberto Moravia."

We moved to the Scheherazade Suite, which Miss Kwa had designed and decorated. It was rich in the traditional Arabian Nights style, with deep-piled carpets and soft cushions in strong Persian reds, blues, and purples, and with ornamental hanging lamps of pewter and brass. "When Prince Adonreza Pahlevi of Iran and his Princess were here, they naturally occupied this suite," Miss Lo said. Miss Kwa glanced at her watch, said she had an appointment in her shop, offered to help Thérèse in any way she could at any time, and left us.

"All of our suites done by men seem to be occupied," Miss Lo said. There was only one other suite free at the moment. It was called the Magnolia. Thérèse fell in love with it at sight. It was in delicate blue and white. The wall behind the beds was painted in enormous sprays of white Japanese magnolias on a soft-blue ground. The tall lamp bases were of pale-blue ceramic with white silk shades. It was cool, fresh, original, and, as Thérèse said, "exquisite and delicately harmonious." This, too, had been created by the Berlin-born Charlotte Horstmann.

"I should think this suite would be the ultimate for honeymooners," I said. "It is lyrical—and virginal."

"I can't recall what Peter O'Toole thought of it," said Miss Lo with an odd twist to the corner of her lip.

We laughed.

"This pleasant little tour in modernity is better than traipsing through a museum," I said in thanking Miss Lo. "I'm rather glad that Hong Kong has so little history. We look forward to the ancient glories of Angkor, Thailand, and India. It's nice to have a free-as-a-bird interlude in Hong Kong."

The Legendary Tailors

Chinese tailors are legendary for their swiftness of execution and their remarkable ability to copy exactly a used suit or a picture in a book. Art Buchwald once wrote a humorous piece about having had a Hong Kong tailor take his measurements in his cabin as soon as his ship landed and then, when he had finally got through immigration and customs and had registered at his hotel, finding the finished suit hanging in the clothes closet.

Dr. W. C. Baty, retired rear admiral turned Tuscaloosa county health officer, who gave us our inoculations against Far Eastern diseases, had shown us a handsome topcoat made overnight on a Hong Kong stopover thirteen years earlier. Measurements had been taken at nine in the evening, and the next morning at nine— twelve hours later—the finished garment was delivered to his hotel room. He was still wearing the coat proudly.

A French friend of mine had told me of an experience he had had in 1935. A white silk suit was made for him while his ship between Singapore and Cherbourg lay over for twenty-four hours in Hong Kong. He had given the tailor a used silk suit and told him to copy it exactly. A half hour before his ship sailed the tailor brought the suit. It was a beauty and fitted perfectly. But there was a strange gray-black stain the size of an American nickel over a breast pocket. "What is this?" demanded my friend. "That," said the Chinese, "really caused us more trouble than all the cutting and tailoring." "But it looks like the ink spot on the old suit." He compared them. "Exactly," said the grinning Chinese. "That is what you ordered—'exactly like the used suit.' That is what you ordered, that is what you have." The Frenchman did not yell "Idiot!" He merely said, "Extraordinary," paid the man, and gave him a tip.

Some tailors in Hong Kong today will, if it is necessary, turn out a suit in twenty-four hours. But they prefer to be given two days, or three. Thérèse and I allowed our tailors three and four, and left some garments to be finished and sent after our departure.

Celia Chen's tiny shop on the Mandarin mezzanine does a flourishing, if somewhat exclusive, business. The middle-aged fitter, Johnny Yee, takes the measurements, notes defects, and makes cryptic marks. The manager of the shop is a lisping, wispy, sharp-eyed young man in his middle twenties named Jimmy Lok. Though he does not design, I came to dub him the Yves Saint-Laurent of Hong Kong. Let no one be put off by Jimmy's lisp. He knows precisely what he is doing and what to advise. He seems to have impeccable taste. He cannot bear to see a patron err in color or style for her type. He may speak tactfully, but he will stick to being frank and honest.

Before him on the glass counter were spread the latest fashion magazines from France, Italy, Spain, and Germany. Jimmy will help a lady pick a model that will do the most for her. Celia Chen's people can copy anything from a picture. If you bring your material with you—say, a stunning piece of silk from Thailand—they will make it into an afternoon dress; or if it is some exquisite cashmere you could not resist in Edinburgh, Celia Chen will turn out a suit that might easily pass for a Balenciaga.

Ceiling-high shelves behind Jimmy are stocked with bolts of carefully selected fabrics at much less per yard than one could find in the land of their origin. And across the narrow room from the counter hang a few dozen cocktail dresses, street dresses, suits, and topcoats made up as distinctive models; something more substantial than a photograph. A customer may try them on. Johnny —as well as Jimmy—will offer his opinion. Jimmy, too, is an émigré from Shanghai and has generations of tailoring in the blood.

When I asked Jimmy about the safety of mail transport to Alabama, he assured me that all packages were registered and insured, and that outfits from Celia Chen went to many states in the Union. He picked up an airmail letter that had obviously come in that morning's post. It was stamped from Macon, Georgia, where, coincidentally, my grandfather Hudson had been born. The lady began, "I was absolutely thrilled," and went on to say that both costumes fit "absolutely perfectly." They had been made from measurements taken at Celia Chen's two years previously. I decided that we need not worry about safe delivery.

Thérèse wanted a light wool suit. While she was looking at a model on the rack, my eye swiftly ran over the bolts of soft tweed fabrics on display. "There it is," I said, and a third boy pulled it out. It was an off-white with a subtle design in mauve and charcoal, distinctive and smart. Thérèse agreed at once. The bolt was laid by. Thérèse also wanted a black silk suit for dress occasions. She found one on the rack done up in Italian raw silk with the jacket lined with a black-and-white printed Thai silk, which formed the lapels and cuffs, and had a sleeveless blouse of the same material. It turned out to be elegant and slimming when Johnny finally fitted it to *his* satisfaction two days later.

Thérèse went with Johnny into the cubbyhole behind the blue curtains for the measuring, and Johnny began calling out measurements in Chinese like some abracadabra to the third Chinese boy, who had also entered the sanctum with pad and pencil ready. I heard Thérèse mentioning what she thought were her defects of figure, though a size ten rarely had to be altered for her except in the skirt. Johnny gently murmured pooh-poohs and assured her that any real or imagined defect would be concealed in the finished product.

The curtains were finally parted, and Thérèse and the two Chinese emerged in smiles. The deed was done. A messenger boy was called and dispatched with the materials, designs, and measurements to the cutters across the harbor in Kowloon. It had all been competent, swift, and easy.

But the fittings were to come in two days. And then Thérèse was to be kept standing for almost two hours while Johnny ripped out seam after seam, made new chalk marks, adjusted here and there. Johnny Yee was a perfectionist. The process was so long

I finally went behind the curtain to watch and sat in a low padded chair, while Thérèse grew pale and weak with standing. What seemed quite right enough to her, Johnny would not have. "Don't dispute with an artist," I said to her encouragingly. Thérèse broke out in perspiration. Finally Johnny smiled with satisfaction. The finished garments would be ready the next day. Bows were exchanged and hands shaken. "I think I must go to our room before luncheon," Thérèse said in a faint voice.

When we got into the bedroom and she began to change for luncheon, we saw she had broken out in hives around her middle. Though minor, the welts were quite visible. "I have never had hives in my life," Thérèse exclaimed, "not from strawberries or shellfish or anything, but a perfectionist Chinese tailor made me break out." I whooped with laughter, but I urged her to lie down for half an hour. I called room service for a luncheon menu. The discomfort seemed to disappear after she had some delicious seafood.

The afternoon of our first morning at Celia Chen's I had a four o'clock appointment with Mr. Cheong of A-Man Hing Cheong Company, at Number 3 Ice House Street on the ground floor of the Mandarin building. I was lucky to find him free, though two other customers were being fitted and one was being measured. Mr. Cheong came from behind a desk where he presided. I introduced myself as the friend of Anthony Ross, who had telephoned. I got a pleasant smile. Mr. Cheong was a well-built man with a strong, broad Chinese face and penetrating eyes. I trusted him at once. "Mr. Ross tells me that you make suits for most of the Establishment here," I said, "and for many of the United Kingdom officials who turn up."

"We are an old firm," he said modestly, "the oldest tailoring business in Hong Kong. My father and one of his close friends founded this concern of A-Man Hing Cheong in 1898. I happen to be the manager now. I am Hong Kong-born and brought up in tailoring. I've had more than thirty years' experience."

"My first need," I told Mr. Cheong, "is a dinner jacket in off-white Italian raw silk. Then a sports coat of British cashmere in some modified hound's-tooth pattern."

With extraordinary perception as to my taste, Mr. Cheong pulled out two bolts of materials and gave them a couple of flips to reveal a yard or so of cloth. I looked upon the shelves to see if there was something that pleased me better. I preferred his first offerings. Together we selected the style of each jacket from some London fashion sheets. With expert alacrity he laid his tape measure across my frame here and there and called out Chinese numbers to his agile assistant.

When he had finished with the jacket measurements, I said that I wanted a good-looking business suit in his best gray worsted, but no flannel. Again Mr. Cheong found material that hit me just right, and took trouser measurements. I asked that the dinner jacket and the sports coat be made first, because I needed them to take with me on the rest of the way around the world. The other suit could be sent to Alabama.

The two separate jackets were ready for fittings late the next afternoon. The white was perfect. Mr. Cheong made a few adjustments in the cashmere. And, incidentally, the handsome dinner jacket cost about forty dollars, while the ten-year-old one I was discarding, bought from a rack in one of New York's best shops, had cost one hundred and twenty-five.

Holiday for Sweeping the Ancestors' Graves

Next morning we received a telephone call from Seymour and Rita Ziff, who had arrived from Cambodia and were staying at the Peninsula in Kowloon, across the harbor. They wanted us to lunch with them at Gaddi's Restaurant in their hotel. Rita asked where we were located in the Mandarin. I said in a front room on the seventeenth floor, facing Kowloon. "Look out from your balcony," Rita said. "Seymour is waving a light-blue pajama top from our fourth-floor room." As soon as I hung up, I imagined I saw the greeting signal. At any rate, I waved my dark-blue pajama jacket back at him.

At noon we took our first ride on the Star Ferry. The Mandarin's northeast corner is hardly more than a Joe Namath forward pass from the ferry terminal. But it is reached by a broad lighted tunnel under Connaught Road. The round-trip ticket amounts to about four cents.

Inside the boat we sat by a well-dressed, prosperous-looking, youngish Chinese gentleman, who was holding a large bouquet of red roses a bit self-consciously. "I am taking them to a sick friend in Kowloon," he said. I told him that we were going to lunch with friends at the Peninsula. I admired a handsome and expensive-looking watch on his wrist, and coveted one like it. The gentleman said that he was the Hong Kong agent for this particular Swiss watch, which was reputed to be the finest in the world.

I spoke of the swift convenience of the double-deck ferries as we passed one in mid-harbor going from Kowloon to Victoria. "Yes, we would be rather lost without our faithful ferries," he said. "More than 100,000 persons are carried daily."

I asked if the ferries were government-owned. "With the exception of the railway," the man said, "all public transportation in the Colony—ferries, trams, taxies, rickshaws—is operated by private enterprise. But the government retains some power in order to ensure efficient operation. Two large companies have monopolies to operate ferry services on specified routes across the harbor. The Star Ferry, for passengers between Victoria and the tip of the Kowloon Peninsula, uses ten vessels, each with a passenger capacity of 5,500. They run every few minutes."

As the three of us stepped off the ferry together I said I thought we would walk to the Peninsula. The gentleman glanced at Thérèse and signaled a taxi. "It is farther to the hotel than you may think. I would be happy to drop you there. It is not at all out of my way."

I accepted the favor. When the car stopped at the hotel entrance our friend got out and assisted Thérèse to alight. For a moment he fingered a rosebud as if to take it from its companions to give her. We thanked him warmly, and went up the short flight of steps. At the door I turned and saw his taxi sweep around the curving drive and begin retracing the route we had come. "This *was* out of his way," I said. We had experienced an old-world Chinese courtesy.

There in the direct center of the lobby was the beaming Seymour Ziff, who had acquired a ruddy color hopping temples in the sun of Angkor. The Ziffs had also been to Ceylon considering business investments, but the Rothschilds had everything pretty well tied up there, Seymour said. It had been terribly hot everywhere, Rita said when she came up. "We could have sent our entire suitcases to the cleaners without bothering to unpack. But this Hong Kong weather seems perfect." The Ziffs had been to Hong Kong several times before—Seymour had an interest in some business there—and they generally stayed in the same rooms at the Peninsula.

Before lunch we wanted to do a little shopping on the hotel's mezzanine. I particularly desired some pajamas made by Dynasty, which had boutiques in the Peninsula and the Hilton, but not yet in the Mandarin. Once on a cruise I had bought some good Dynasty pajamas from Cavanaugh's in the Virgin Islands. We four traced the high-ceilinged corridors of the regal old hotel and at the very end of the mezzanine reached the glass doors of the spreading Dynasty shop.

"Closed for the Holiday," a large printed placard announced. "What holiday?" I wanted to know. The Ziffs could not imagine. Then we noticed that more than half of the shops were closed. We entered one of the open shops, which specializes in folding beaded bags. "What is the holiday?" I asked in outraged disappointment. The Chinese proprietor all but grinned with amusement. "It is the holiday for sweeping the graves of the ancestors," he informed me. "Most shops are closed today."

"Are you serious?"

"Oh, but yes. Go to any of the many Chinese cemeteries today and you will see thousands with brooms and brushes and clippers tidying their ancestors' graves."

"But then what are you doing open?"

He grinned broadly, revealing some gold teeth. "I do not have any ancestors buried in Hong Kong. Mine lie in Shanghai."

We bought half a dozen beaded bags, two white on white, two midnight blue, and two gold on red. We gave the man the names and addresses of relatives and friends for mailings. Then I asked the price of a dozen S monogram linen handkerchiefs I saw on display. He quoted me seventy-five American cents apiece. "That's too much," Rita interposed quickly. "Take them for sixty-five cents," the man replied instantly. I pulled out my checkbook. "Will you take my personal check on an Alabama bank? Here is my name and address stamped at the top. I am a retired university professor." He glanced at the check, then at me. "But of course." So I added a pair of burgundy silk lounging pajamas to be sent to me as a gift from my wife. A tall, white-haired industrialist from Joliet, Illinois, said that he had just ordered six pairs of lounging pajamas in the six different colors.

Gaddi's Restaurant on the ground floor of the Peninsula is generally considered to be the finest in Hong Kong. It is elegant and chic, with an old-world quiet and impeccable service. The food is superb, about as good as you can find in the best spots in Paris, and expensive, but far less expensive than in Paris. One of the dishes we had was a delectable concoction of crabmeat.

During lunch we talked first of the Ziffs' Japanese friends who had been so hospitable, and then mostly of Angkor. For the Ziffs, Angkor Wat was the ultimate among world wonders, as we expected it to be for us. "We have engaged our guide for you," Seymour said, "for next Saturday and Sunday. I gave him a generous tip so that he will assuredly be reserved for you. He's a personable Cambodian of about twenty-two or -three with the funny name of Huot Samoeun. He couldn't be better. You will both love him. I also took the liberty of changing your room reservation at the Auberge des Temples to the one we had, right in the convenient center of things, facing the courtyard, halfway between the office and the garden restaurant. The Auberge spreads far and wide in L's in this and that direction, and they're adding more rooms. You will be exhausted from walking among the temples, and from your room you won't have to walk much more. The management is looking out for you."

The Ziffs promised to lunch with us on the Mandarin Roof Garden the next day.

And the next day as we were taking our plates along the buffet tables laden with delicacies of cuisines of France, Sweden, and China, and even with English rare roast beef with Yorkshire pudding, an explosion stopped everybody in his tracks. Patrons, with outstretched plates, held various attitudes, as in the old children's game of statues. "That was close," Rita said quietly. "Indeed it was," agreed the Chinese servitor on the other side of the table opposite her, holding his utensils momentarily suspended.

Before we had finished dessert of delicious chocolate mousse, which might have been done by a licensed Cordon Bleu chef, a waiter I knew brought word to our table. "It was the Supreme

Court Building just across the square. Someone placed a bomb on
one of the inner window ledges. Several windows were shattered.
But no one was hurt. Fortunately, it was the lunch hour."

But that was the only bomb we were actually to hear. And, because the British had refused to scare or offer the faintest nod of
obeisance to Mao, before Christmas the silly gestures of terrorism
were to cease altogether.

A Mine of Information

When we prepared for our round-the-world jaunt, we knew only
one person in Hong Kong, the wife of John Hughes, the chief Far
East correspondent of the *Christian Science Monitor,* who had just
won a Pulitzer Prize in April for his reportage on Indonesia. At
the University of Alabama Libby Pockman had made top grades in
my Shakespeare course and been the star of several stage produc-
tions. Later in Boston she had married Hughes, a Welshman. After
a few years of reporting in East Africa, he had been sent by the
Monitor to Hong Kong. We had looked forward to meeting him
and having Libby show us the Colony. But as chance had it, the
Hugheses were to be in England on vacation at the very time of our
scheduled visit. Libby wrote that she was asking a family friend to
"look after" us.

A gentleman named Ronald McLaren telephoned to say that Mrs.
Hughes had asked him to be of service to us. He would be glad to
furnish me with any information about the Crown Colony that I
desired. We invited him to tea in our sitting room that afternoon.
He turned out to be the best possible person to answer my queries,
because he was the head of Government Information Services.
McLaren was a soft-spoken Londoner of Scotch ancestry, of pleasant mien and medium stature. He had lived in Hong Kong for many
years and, though he owned a cottage in Sussex, where he and his
small family vacationed every two years, he enjoyed life in the
Colony—away from England's damp winters. Here were his British

club, the race track, numerous playing fields, and some English families who had lived on the island since the nineteenth century. Persons of international interest came and went. Living was not only pleasant, but remarkably inexpensive—and with plenty of good servants.

"As you know," Mr. McLaren said, "wherever Englishmen have gone in their imperialistic or missionary endeavors they have taken their tea, their tennis rackets, and their brand of culture with them. Ten years after the founding of the Crown Colony, cricket was being played on one of the few flat areas. Today, near the center of Victoria's stirring business district, the Hong Kong Cricket Club has its green lawn where matches are enthusiastically attended. About every known British sport, except fox hunting, has been introduced here. We have no foxes and no proper fences for jumping, only cliffs to jump over. Hong Kong is tremendously popular with American soldiers on recreation leave from South Vietnam."

Over a real English tea with scones and strawberry jam, at my request Mr. McLaren, who has an extraordinary memory, gave us desultory résumés and figures. But he had also thoughtfully brought along the latest Hong Kong yearbook and some pamphlets and fact sheets, which he gave us.

I wanted to know what he considered the Colony's chief "problems."

"Accelerating population, inadequate housing, and ever-increasing need for fresh water," came his quick reply. "And, of course," he added with a grin, "abutment on Red China."

"I would like to know something about the growth in population and the proportion of Chinese to British."

After two sips of tea and a moment of reflection, McLaren said: "Well, as you know, this British-ruled colony is about 98 per cent Chinese. The first official report to reach England after Hong Kong became a Crown Colony in 1842 gave the total citizenry as 23,817, of whom 595 were Europeans, 362 Indians, and almost 23,000 Chinese. By 1861 the population had risen to 119,000, of whom 116,000 were Chinese. This pattern and proportion has been more or less repeated through the years. After the Colony was 'liberated' from the Japanese by British troops on August 31, 1945, the population increased threefold in two years. When the Communists began to rout the forces of Chiang Kai-shek in 1948, refugees from the mainland

began pouring into Hong Kong by the scores of thousands. They
have never stopped coming. Some still slip across the border at
night. Some are smuggled in by boat from the Portuguese island of
Macao. The census of 1966 reported a population of 3,716,400. The
total is moving up fast to four million."

"And your government has to feed all these refugees?"

"Not only feed them, but also try to provide some kind of shelter.
Building has gone on at a furious pace since 1950. Blocks of low-
rent apartment houses go up almost overnight. In a district where
there is palpable need for more flat building surfaces, the authorities
will cut off the top of a hill and tip the dirt into the edges of bays."

We learned that almost 1,200,000 people, most of them refugees,
have been rehoused in twenty-odd resettlement estates and nine
low-cost housing estates. Almost a million more will have been rehoused by 1974. In the New Territories, two new whole industrial
towns, Kwan Tong and Tsuen Wan, have been created out of reclaimed soil brought down from the hills into the sea. A half-million
persons have already moved into new efficiency apartments. When
these two towns are finally completed they will have a total population of a million and a half.

Mr. McLaren paused to compliment the strawberry jam. "It
tastes as fresh as Devon."

"What about health conditions and hospitals?" I asked. We had
already noted enormous hospitals rising high and spreading over
acres.

"The British look after the citizens' health, too. There are thirty-
two government-run or -aided hospitals with more than 12,000 beds.
Eleven private hospitals maintain another 1,600 beds. The number of
private nursing homes runs to seventy-seven. Altogether, the hospitals of the Colony can efficiently take care of some 15,000 ailing
persons at a time."

I next asked about labor and wages.

"Hong Kong knows no labor shortage, because of the continuing
flow of refugees from Red China," Mr. McLaren said. "However,
wages, by British or American standards, are quite low, little more
than an American dollar to two dollars a day. Unskilled workers
are grateful to earn anything they can."

I had expected to find that wages were low, but I was surprised to learn that the small Colony had more than three hundred registered unions, over 250 for workers and fifty different employers' associations. "The labor unions have a membership of some 165,000," Mr. McLaren said. "The majority of the Chinese workmen, however, choose to remain independent to produce by the piece in their own way and time."

"What are the principal products manufactured?"

"The textile industry dominates Hong Kong economy, accounting for 60 per cent of its domestic exports and employing 42 per cent of its industrial labor force. The production of garments within the industry is the largest sector. Embroidered blouses, beaded cardigans, brocaded evening wraps, men's pajama suits have a world-wide popularity. The value of exports in clothing amounts today to approximately five hundred million American dollars annually. The rapid growth in plastics and electronics, television sets, transistor radios, and the like show how alert Hong Kong is to modern consumer demands."

"What of your water supply now?"

"As you know, like Bermuda, Hong Kong depends chiefly on rain from heaven. The rain falls chiefly in summer, from mid-May to mid-September, and is caught on spreading concrete spills and stored for the year's supply. The provision of adequate water has always posed problems, because the Colony has no springs and no stream of any size. In 1963 an enormous reservoir on long Lantau Island, eight miles from Hong Kong, was perfected, and its water reaches Hong Kong by a submarine pipeline.

"But with all these innovations and provisions water must also be brought from the China mainland. Hong Kong has been purchasing from Kwangtung Province 15,000 million gallons during the nine drier months. When Mao, using intimidation tactics, cut off this supply in the spring, the sensational news was carried in the world press. Then, after some weeks, he relented, and the water from China's Pearl River came again. I am happy to say that our water-supply worries are virtually over. A vast six-hundred-million-dollar catchment complex, called the Plover Cove Reservoir, will soon be in operation. Its 37,000-million-gallon capacity more than trebles the water supply previously available. It is by far the most impressive project ever undertaken by the government."

As Mr. McLaren accepted from Thérèse a second cup of tea, I said, "Besides the full economy of your superb harbor, how important is marine fishing?"

"The Hong Kong fishing fleet is perhaps the largest in the British Commonwealth," he said. "It includes some 7,000 junks of various sizes and designs, of which 5,000 are mechanized. Salt-water fish is really our chief natural product. In volume, Hong Kong handles more fish than any other British colony. Fish from Hong Kong is exported to numerous Far East countries and to the United States. Hong Kong profits well, too, from its ship-repair yards. And we have some twenty shipbuilding establishments."

"Does agriculture amount to anything significant?"

"Of course, Hong Kong can't feed itself—except on fish. But in the New Territories almost every foot of the flat land is cultivated intensively, and even the hanging valleys contain villages with terraced patches of cultivation. Most of the inhabitants are small farmers, who still wear the characteristic sun hats of the mainland districts from which their ancestors came. The Chinese farmers are so industrious that they raise several crops of vegetables a year, as well as quantities of rice. The area of land under market gardening has increased from 2,250 acres in 1954 to more than 8,800 acres today."

"You've been invaluable in acquainting me with the aspects of Hong Kong that I want to understand. I hope I haven't exhausted you," I said.

McLaren made a slight gesture of waving away my concern. "But information is my business."

"Then I have one last query. What about schools and education in general?"

McLaren gave me a long, steady look. "You may be surprised with my direct answer. You can find it on the first page of the yearbook's chapter on education. I quote: 'Primary education in Hong Kong is neither free nor compulsory.'" Then, allowing a moment for the statement to sink in, he added, "But the government gives all sorts of grants to schools and remits fees in primary schools in cases of genuine hardship, and it buys the books for the needy."

Thérèse poured each of us a third cup of tea. McLaren proceeded. "Education has really taken giant steps since 1945, when there were barely 4,000 children altogether in the schools. Now there are some

600,000, without enforced school attendance. More than half of the schools are private. English is taught in all the schools, as a first or second language."

He told us, too, that the University of Hong Kong was established in 1911 and that the standard of teaching is high. In late 1963 the new Chinese University was inaugurated. It already has an enrollment of about 3,000. The Technical College has an enrollment of more than 16,000 and offers one hundred different courses. Almost 2,000 Hong Kong students go on scholarships to the United States for further study.

When McLaren rose to go to another appointment before a dinner engagement, Thérèse asked him what was the quality he admired most in the Chinese people.

He did not need to ponder. "Their extraordinary adaptability in constantly changing conditions," he answered. Then he added, "They seem to know from babyhood that 'patience is the best remedy for every trouble,' as Plautus wrote two hundred years before Christ."

Mr. McLaren said that if we were free the next afternoon he would take us to places we might like to see.

"Would you drive us over the mountain through some of the best residential districts and to Repulse Bay? We could have tea at the old hotel there."

Nothing would give him greater pleasure, he said. "Libby's car really needs exercise. I promised to keep it in good running order for her while she is in England."

Aberdeen and Repulse Bay

Tourists speak zestfully of the glitter and "go" of Hong Kong, but on the other side of the island behind the Peak to the south, far from the sound of ships' sirens, automobile tootings, and the metallic construction noises, lie placid spots with silvery beaches and enchanting seascapes. The winding drive over the mountainous roads and down to Repulse Bay is an experience not to be missed. Repulse Bay can be comfortably reached from the Mandarin by taxi in twenty minutes. We were fortunate in having a more lingering drive.

Mr. McLaren came to fetch us in Libby Hughes's compact cream-colored 1000 MG, peculiarly adept in hill-climbing. Hong Kong Island is something like a steeper San Francisco, with hardly a straight street. The roads are a series of winding curves, some of them sharper than those above Amalfi on the way to Ravello. McLaren said he was saving the top of the Peak for the end of the afternoon, on our return from Repulse Bay.

Before we were quite out of Victoria, I asked about a white pagoda rising nine tiers high to the left.

"It belongs to the Tiger Balm Gardens, which some call an Oriental Disneyland. The pleasure park was a gift to Hong Kong by the late Aw Boon Haw, a rags-to-riches chap, who started life without even the proverbial penny and became fantastically rich manufacturing cure-all patent medicines, chief of which is an ointment called Tiger Balm. This panacea is claimed to cure almost everything, from flat feet and falling hair to skin rashes, stomach-ache, and venereal diseases. Whatever its merits, many intelligent persons swear by its effectiveness. This Boon Haw had a brother named Aw Boon Par, whom he took into a business partnership, which expanded into newspaper complexes, a tremendous insurance business, and other profitable ventures. The brothers' jade collection in Singapore is said to be the finest in the world. When they turned to philanthropy, they built pleasure gardens in various Far Eastern cities for the people and their children. The grotesque sculptures, representing scenes in Chinese mythology, are a bit too grotesque, but children and tourists seem fascinated. Want to go?"

"Thank you, no," we said together, as the car began a steeper climb.

I commented on the abundance and variety of trees along the way. "Because of a scientific program of restoration," McLaren said, "Hong Kong is well wooded with acacia, eucalyptus, banyan, various conifers, mangoes, and palm and olive trees. The Urban Council continues to plant tens of thousands of seedling trees, shrubs, and seasonal flowers during the year."

Here and there on the twisting road McLaren indicated the residences of several of the Colony dignitaries, including the Governor's mansion. The residence of the American Consul General was up so high that it almost seemed to be suspended from the sky. I had a letter to the Consul from Senator Hill in my suitcase, but I had no need to disturb him, after we had met McLaren.

Some of the palatial houses belong to wealthy Chinese who had managed to escape from Red China with a sizable part of their capital in foreign securities. A deal of ingenious engineering has gone into the landscaping, and much thought and labor have produced the velvety lawns and brilliant flower beds. Happily, gardeners are easy to come by in Hong Kong.

One natural amphitheater after another seems designed by nature for enjoying the sea view and the sunsets behind the distant islands rising from the deep-blue water. Yet the scenic beauty holds nothing man-created that is outstandingly interesting, except for a vast and ancient Chinese cemetery, where the odd headstones climb the terraced hills. "You see," McLaren observed, "the graves are in the pink of condition, because they have just been swept."

When we came down to sea level and nearer the famous fishing village of Aberdeen, McLaren put the car into a crawl. Opposite the land hamlet, the watery area was a forest of masts, yards, booms, gaffs, and canopies, with occasional planks laid from junk to junk, sampan to sampan, houseboat to houseboat for communicable sociability. Thousands of vessels were "at rest" because of a morning warning of a likely typhoon. Daily life proceeded in accustomed rhythms. Cooking was being done, nets were being mended, washed clothes were being hung on lines, babies were being nursed, mahjong was being played. Tradesmen's sampans came alongside this or that boat with supplies, so that shopping could be done at the rail.

"This fishing village, named for the Marquis of Aberdeen and Scotland's city on the North Sea, was originally called Pai Wan," McLaren told us. "It was a notorious haunt of Chinese pirates from the time of the Mongol dynasty. The British chased most of them away in the middle of the nineteenth century. A principal vehicle of destructive vengeance was the British battleship H.M.S. *Repulse,* after which our loveliest region gets its name, 'Repulse Bay.'"

McLaren stopped the car to give us a better view. "Hong Kong's oldest residents do not live on the island," he said, "but prefer to stay on boats in the surrounding waters. These Tanka people have been in the region since time unknown and are still the principal seafaring people and fishermen of South China. They live much as they have for centuries, crowded into flat-bottomed junks and sampans. Other thousands are based in the Yan Ma Tei typhoon shelter in Victoria Harbor.

"The majority of these fisherfolk," our friend continued, "belong to tribes that migrated to the delta area of the Pearl River near Canton. They have kept their own dialect and customs, and they are not related to those speaking Cantonese or Mandarin, who form the bulk of Hong Kong's residents today. They are still defiantly individualistic and indomitably cheerful. They prefer their slum poverty and the freedom of the sea to any land existence. Of Hong Kong's four million inhabitants, about 140,000 are strictly water people. Some 80,000 live on the fishing boats that make a livelihood from the sea. An estimated 20,000 live close to shore on small houseboats.

"Many of those junks," McLaren added, "serve as the interstate or intercountry trucks. From Red China they bring back meats and vegetables for the Hong Kong markets, bricks and other building materials, elaborate brocades, and often smuggled refugees."

"In this modern age doesn't work in the city attract the young folks?"

"Yes, to a degree. However, to the Hong Kong Chinese the 'boat folk' have always been considered people apart. Laws once forbade them from settling on the shore, to marry with landowners, or to stand for the government examinations. Recently, the discriminations have been removed. Today, some of the water people work on the cargo lighters, loading and unloading foreign freighters. Some work in the shipyards and the repair yards that line the harbor shore. During the last few years a number of the young men and young women have been lured to take factory jobs. A few make their living operating walla wallas and sampans to take night passengers across the harbor after the ferries have stopped running. But the great majority of these Dragon People remain determined fishermen. And when they go out to catch fish, their homes, their wives, their children, and their pets go with them. For centuries these water people have lived their lives almost entirely on calm or turbulent seas. They have been born aboard ship, been nurtured, grown to adulthood, had their love life, raised their families, grown old, and died with scarcely ever setting their sandaled feet on dry land. They are unique. It's their way, and who is to reform them? However, we do send medical boats among them, with doctors and nurses' aides and medicines, and school boats with teachers to give primary instruction."

The vital shoreside village of Aberdeen facing the forest of masts was not a place to linger in long, though it was colorful, with its gay perpendicular streamers in bold calligraphy. Piles of drying fish near the water's edge gave off an odor almost as strong as that of those sardine-canning towns in Brittany.

We resumed our drive, and the smell followed us to the famed floating restaurants, Tai Pak and the Sea Palace. They loomed up garishly on the skyline, though the strings of electric lights were not yet lit. These double-decked eating halls, somewhat resembling old Mississippi "floating-palace riverboats," are a popular tourist attraction. Blue-canopied sampans, with straw-hatted women acting as taxi drivers, scull patrons from the shore to the boat landings. One may select his own live fish from huge glass tanks and even watch it being cooked. The food is reputed to be consistently good. Princess Margaret and her spouse made headlines by dining in one of the floating restaurants, just as most tourists do. But a fishy smell so pervades the gaudy atmosphere that we were not tempted to indulge. Right in the Mandarin there were too many excellent restaurants for us to bother to take a taxi to eat in Aberdeen. And, personally, there was nothing cozier than dining in our own sitting room facing the great window that gave on the harbor lights. We could order sent up the best of seafood: Macao sole, Golden Thread, or delectable large prawns.

After Aberdeen, we came upon the settlement known as Stanley, with its attractive beaches and pleasant residential area, where many of the "smart set" lived. Then we passed Deep Water Bay, another fashionable residential subdivision, affording a view of another sand beach and other seascapes.

At last we drove into the landscaped grounds of the very British Repulse Bay Hotel, steeped in tradition. There could hardly be a sharper contrast than between bustling, vehicle-and-people-jammed streets of dynamic Victoria and this tranquil haven with its green open spaces, tropical trees, and the gently lapping water on the crescent moon of a white beach. An amiable Chinese attendant came to park our car. We stepped out into a fragrant flowery atmosphere. Instinctively we lowered our voices as we moved leisurely up a broad garden path to the spreading white hotel. It had inviting terraces and a wide veranda for taking in the sea view. I neglected to ask the year the Repulse Bay Hotel was built, but it had a definite Edwardian tang, outside and in, and I knew that it had been a favorite luxury hotel with the British for decades. Like the Hassler in Rome, it seemed to be run for discriminating, well-bred people who had had fair means for a long time. And now, understandably, its somewhat old-fashioned amenities were reveled in by weary American army officers on leave from the bloody hurly-burly of fetid Vietnam.

On the veranda, in a moderately secluded spot, we found a table ideal for gazing at the softly stirring sea and the distant islands, whose contours brought Rio de Janeiro nostalgically to my mind. A Chinese waiter came to take our order. We all wanted Earl Grey tea and toast with Dundee marmalade. "What a charming, relaxing spot," Thérèse exclaimed. "It is so—so stabilizing." We seemed actually to breathe more gently than in the city, which so fascinated us.

It is not easy to set down in words the effect of the calm beauty of Repulse Bay. One might think of the faraway tall islands land-locking the bay into a sanctuary as being designed by an artist's hand. But pristine nature had surpassed any work of art in the way the islands folded gently upon each other in such placid harmony. With any change in degree or intensity of the refulgent light from the sky, the velvety greens and soft shades of chamois shifted so subtly that the islands actually seemed to breathe.

At half past five of the mid-October afternoon all the bathers had departed. The pearly beach had repossessed itself and lay accepting the caresses of the waves as it might have done some thousand years ago. On the water not a sail was visible. I, who doted on harbors and moving ships, was satisfied to look upon a sea that was one clear expanse of gently pulsing blue, clean to the edge of islands that blocked the horizon.

"This place," Thérèse said, "would have made a fit setting for some monastery of a contemplative order."

While we drank in the view, the soft-treading waiter began

setting out the tea things. During tea, Mr. McLaren told us something of Hong Kong piracy and its grisly end in 1898.

"As you know, piracy was endemic on the South China Coast for centuries. Successive emperors failed in their efforts to eradicate the evil. Some of the brigands were outstandingly notorious. One pirate chief named Ching Yik was reputed to have a fleet of six hundred sail. And when he was washed overboard in a typhoon in 1807, his wife became commander and directed the piratical operations for several years.

"From time to time fortune-hunting Europeans threw in their lot with the rascals. Eli Boggs, an American adventurer, joined a Chinese piracy gang that masqueraded as simple traders. It was his job to kill the officers of the clippers. The brother of Jane Austen, the novelist, Rear Admiral Charles Austen, wrote about this Boggs, who escaped hanging because all the witnesses were dead. One Britisher named Daniel Caldwell, who held the high position of the Colony's register general, became a partner of a local rich Chinese in a shady shipping venture in 1861. The next year the Chinese was found guilty of piracy and deported, and Caldwell was dismissed from office.

"The last notorious case of piracy occurred on December 10, 1890, when the steamer *Namoa* of the Douglas Steamship Company left Hong Kong for Swatow with a few saloon passengers and 220 Chinese deck passengers, including about forty pirates simulating innocent travelers. The majority of the Chinese were returning home from San Francisco with their life's savings and all their newly acquired possessions. When the ship passed the island of Ping Hoi, while the captain and first-class passengers were at lunch, forty pirates, armed with cutlasses and revolvers, suddenly appeared. They first made an attack on the saloon, the officers' quarters, and the bridge. Captain Pocock was shot fatally in the right breast. The attack was so sudden that resistance was out of the question. When the pirates got full control, the ship was headed out to sea, and the returning Chinese were systematically robbed of their valuables. The pirates then brought the vessel to her original position of capture, where six junks waited to receive the loot and take on the robbers. With damaged gear the ship made its handicapped way back to Hong Kong to report the tragic outrage. British ships set out on a fruitless search. Then officials in China took action, and many of the pirates were run down. On April 17, 1891, on a beach near Kowloon, where the airport now stands, thirteen of these pirates involved in the *Namoa* affair were publicly beheaded, and on May 11 fifteen more lost their heads on the same spot. The publicized executions seem to have given the final deathblow to piracy in the region."

During McLaren's tales of piracy we had been enjoying the view of the far-out mountainous islands while the lowering sun drenched them in a kind of golden shower of light.

"Now that Chinese piracy in Hong Kong waters has been 'out' for seventy years," I said, "are there still any opium dens here?"

"Oh, don't speak of dens," McLaren exclaimed in mock remonstrance. "They are called opium 'divans.' It is said that one may be visited if the visit is arranged with the police. The divans are generally found in squatters' tin-roofed shacks. It is estimated that we have more than 100,000 addicts. With so many ships arriving daily, dope smuggling is hard to control."

At that psychological moment I recognized a former student of mine coming out the lobby entrance far down the veranda, followed by a bellboy with his bag. I knew him to be an Air Force intelligence officer. He had been based in Saigon for nine months. I excused myself and hastily went to speak to him. "What are you doing here?" I called to him. He greeted me with surprised pleasure.

"I'm just off to emplane for Vietnam. I'm not here for rest and recreation." I walked with him down to his waiting car. "I've completed a two days' assignment, helping the Hong Kong police ferret out and catch five gold smugglers." He spoke with a touch of modest pride.

Hong Kong is a strategic center of gold smuggling between Red China and Zurich, he explained. Mao's agents generally get first to Macao and then to Hong Kong by boat or plane. From Hong Kong they can fly to Zurich with only two stops. Mao, in pressing need of cash to nourish subversive elements in small countries, is melting down priceless gold artifacts and figurines into kilo-weight slabs the size and shape of a cigarette case. The smugglers wear special undershirts of heavy linen fashioned with rows of pockets each to hold snugly the slabs of pure gold. Because they are hard to detect under regular shirts and jackets, a man may carry on his person hundreds of thousands of dollars' worth of gold. The garments are uncomfortable, but the metal slabs do not clank. However, if a gold-laden man fell into the water, he would sink, though an expert swimmer, because of the dense weight of the metal.

With the keen co-operation of the Hong Kong police force, five smugglers had been caught between their separate lodgings or hotels and the airport. It is necessary to apprehend the smuggler with the gold on his person. Two of these arrested Mao agents were Swiss; two, French; and one, American. Three-fifths of the confiscated gold was to be sent to the Bank of England. Two-fifths was to be kept by the Colony administration to be used in welfare work. Since these particular smugglers could be of no further use to Mao, they were to be released to follow their own inclinations.

"I'm dreadfully sorry I can't stay over another day," the young captain said, when he had told his story in about two minutes. "But now, alas, I must really fly—back to Vietnam. And they say a typhoon is in the offing here." His last words were: "Isn't this Repulse Bay the loveliest of places?"

When I got back to the table I had my own tale to tell. Then we made ready for the homeward trip by way of the top of the Peak.

The flame-colored ball of the setting sun had barely alighted on the rim of the topmost hill when we drove out of the hotel grounds, to return by a different route of climbing whirls. We passed new apartment houses perched near the edge of cliffs, facing the south or west, with superlative views of the sea and islands. McLaren lived in one of those on Albany Road. We wound up around and up again until we came to the top of the Peak. At 1,800 feet the air was fresh and exhilarating. The temperature is claimed to be ten degrees cooler than that of Hong Kong at sea level.

In the railed observation area McLaren parked the car not far from the topside of the steepest funicular railway in the world. Yet from the business center of Victoria below, it takes only eight minutes to reach the top. We arrived just as a trainload of commuters got out. To avoid the crowds, tourists are urged to make the ascent after nine and before five. I remarked the stout cables and listened to the assured humming of the machinery, and it all seemed quite safe. The cars are drawn by nearly two miles of steel cable. The present haulage system, McLaren told us, has been in use since 1925, and not one accident has yet occurred.

Since there were no tourists in the late afternoon we had the railed observation area almost to ourselves. To the north, we could look down on Hong Kong Harbor, where the few vessels now to be seen seemed as small as a child's plastic toys in a bathtub. We could see beyond Kowloon to the Dragon Hills. We took a long look northward and then turned to face the west, and I saw one of the most thrilling sunsets in my remembrance.

The great globe had dropped entirely out of sight now behind the ramparts of the offshore islands. The whole expanse of the western heavens was radiant with apricot-colored light. The islands themselves seemed to be streaming cascades of molten gold from the top ridges down into the water of the bay. I had noticed in Kyoto only a few days earlier how distant mountains enhance the setting sun's luminosity. But here there was no intense vermilion in the sky as at Kyoto, only effulgent apricot and gold, with occasional streaks of lemon or tangerine. Once in Dresden at a performance of Verdi's *Otello* I had seen an apple-green stage sunset. Although it was excitingly lovely, I had said, "There is no such thing in nature." Only three weeks later in Rome I had actually seen, from the Pincio Gardens, an all-green sunset beyond St. Peter's. And several years later I had beheld another green sunset in Montevideo. Both were eerily beautiful and incredible, yet visibly real. But I cannot recall any sunset more luminescent or altogether more splendorous than this apricot one in Hong Kong seen from the top of Victoria Peak.

Such a strong wind had sprung up while we gazed westward that we hardly demurred about leaving evanescent beauty and taking refuge in the MG. As we began the curving, breath-taking descent down to the realities of city life, Thérèse asked McLaren if he thought the typhoon would really strike.

"We can never say for sure. Often at the last hour there's some beneficent change in direction."

"I suppose all planes stop running if the wind becomes too fierce."

"All ferries, too. You couldn't get across the harbor to Kowloon to take a plane."

For a moment a blackish veil seemed to drop down over Angkor, where we were due on Friday afternoon. "Pray for us," I said. "To have to miss Angkor Wat, the sight of sights, would be hard to take."

"Well," McLaren said cheerily, "though the papers cry typhoon and people are already beginning to batten down, the Star Ferry's storm warning wasn't flying when we left your hotel."

As we rounded a curve in nearing the city's center we noted the plain outlines of the Star Ferry Terminal. A minute later we saw that a red flag was flying above it, and somewhat wildly in the increasingly aggressive wind. "What does that mean?" I asked, apprehension clutching at my innards.

McLaren smiled a somewhat grave smile. "The red flag means that ferries may stop running at any moment. But the situation is by no means hopeless. If the blue flag goes up, it means that the ferries *have* stopped."

We drew up before the entrance to the Mandarin. A solemn, turbaned Sikh opened the car door for us. "Remember," McLaren said in parting, "hurricanes are given feminine names because they are whimsical and often change their minds. This Carla may switch herself off to the northeast of us."

We invited him in for a drink, but he did not drink, and he had to hasten back to his place on Albany Road to prepare for emergencies.

"Well," I said to Thérèse, rationalizing, "a typhoon in Hong Kong would be something to experience. But let's cross our fingers and hope to fly on Friday."

In our sitting room I walked to the window and looked down on choppy leaden-gray water. Except for one steadfast ferryboat, there was no other vessel of any size or description in sight. The only color I noted was the warning red of Star Ferry's flapping flag.

Gloomy Thursday—and Fortunate Friday

At breakfast I glanced quickly at the front page of Thursday's Hong Kong *Standard*. According to the paper, "thousands of boats were already in their typhoon shelters, squatters were fastening down their meager possessions, and in more prosperous homes servants were bolting windows and pulling in laundry lines." When the paper went to press Typhoon Carla was centered about 190 miles southeast of Hong Kong and was moving west-northwest at ten knots an hour. In the night winds over Hong Kong it had increased in speed with gusts of up to sixty-three knots recorded in some spots. The number-two typhoon signal, the blue flag, had been hoisted late in the night, and aircraft had stopped landing at the airport. The temperature had dropped rapidly. The weather forecast for Thursday said "continuing cool." I walked to the window. Yes, there on the Star Ferry roof flapped the ominous blue flag. All ferries had definitely stopped running. Now it looked as though we were not going to get our Friday plane to Cambodia. The imminent typhoon caused us far sharper anxiety than had the bombings.

It was an eerie experience to look out upon the miles of empty harbor to east and west. The luxury liners had departed. The United States naval ships had gone out into the open sea. The glittering kaleidoscope of colorful activity had become like a blank sheet of wavy gray glass.

With a sense of adventure I donned my raincoat. Braving the wind, with head down and thrust forward, I went out the front door of the Mandarin and around the side to the office of Air France, which acted as agent for Royal Air Cambodge. At first I could not find it, though I knew exactly where it was. The great plate-glass windows were concealed behind walls of rough boards. It was so with all the shop fronts. There was nothing but slabs of planks to be seen. I looked up directly across the street to the top of the thirteen-story cocoon of bamboo scaffolding. The yellow-green poles, lashed together vertically and horizontally, appeared extremely vulnerable and defenseless.

In the Air France office the solicitous Chinese staff could say nothing for sure about our Royal Air Cambodge flight the next afternoon. They were just preparing to close and try to make it to their respective homes before the typhoon struck. No, no Air France flights had been allowed to land this day. "The typhoon might come any hour now," one man behind the counter said, "but then sometimes it just misses the island." "If it misses us," the sympathetic young lady clerk said, attempting an optimistic smile, "your plane will fly tomorrow. Your reservation is in perfect order. Let us hope."

I pushed my windy way homeward past the boarded-up shops and offices as if I were fighting undertow. To keep my raincoat from being ripped from my back, I buttoned it to the last top button. I must confess that though darkly apprehensive about the next day's plane flight, I was perversely enjoying this sense of adventure and uncertainty. I walked a half block to the south, turned to the left and eventually came in the back entrance of the Mandarin. I passed through the mezzanine glancing in the display windows. The boutiques were deserted except for the salespeople.

I reported to Thérèse that I had come safely through, that the streets were virtually empty, that no rickshaw and only two or three taxis were to be seen. I said I had stopped at a shopwindow and had seen something she might like—if we and the hotel were here tomorrow.

When I attempted to go out on the balcony for a wider panoramic look, the wind pushed its fist hard against the outside of the door, stronger than my hand and body. So I just stared through the glass at that flapping blue bunting warning of danger. In the unnatural light the hotels and office buildings of Kowloon across the harbor seemed to have hunkered down as a passenger is taught to bend his head between his knees when there is about to be a forced landing or a crash.

A sophisticated buzz at the door startled me. I turned to see a bobbed-haired Chinese girl in a man's brown sweater two sizes too big for her enter briskly with an armload of evening dresses. She announced herself in a hearty baritone that was the nearest thing to corn-fed Middle West an English-speaking Chinese girl could manage. "I brought these up to your room to let your wife decide at her convenience."

I recognized her as a saleswoman from the mezzanine boutique called Royal Fashions. One was a white cocktail dress with ice-blue pear-shaped glass globules hanging in pendants among the white sequins of the bodice. It had caught my eye in passing. I had thought it striking and rather lovely. This girl had rushed out of the shop and almost pounced on me as the spider did the fly, calling, "Come in! Come in!" I protested that I did not have time, but I thought that my wife might just want that very dress.

"We have many lovely others," she said seductively in a loud voice. Like a magnet she drew me within, to the amused smiles of two male Chinese who watched her bold salesmanship tactics. She held up a simple pink taffeta. "This is a little beauty for informal parties and only nineteen American dollars. We have it in black, too. A lady can slip in and out of all kinds of places, you know, in black."

Almost before I knew it, she had the number of our room. "Perhaps I'll bring my wife in tomorrow," I said, making my escape.

But that direct, tomboyish salesgirl was not to be eluded, even though a typhoon was about to strike. Here she was in our suite dangling three cocktail dresses before Thérèse's eyes.

Thérèse was pleased with all three, especially the white Italian raw silk with the glass pendants. "But I don't need so many," she protested.

"You'll never find such bargains," I prompted.

She tried on one after the other, while the gusts of wind beat menacingly against the window glass. "Yes, yes," the girl muttered huskily to everything. The white and the black seemed perfect. But the pink wasn't quite right, though the girl first insisted loudly that it was, and then reluctantly admitted a defect. "We can remedy this tonight."

"How can your boy get across the harbor to Kowloon?"

"I don't even know how I can get home to my husband tonight, but we have expert adjusters right in our shop. You will see tomorrow morning." The girl left two of the dresses and took the shell-pink one away over her incongruously oversized and dowdy sweater sleeve.

"She's a little typhoon in herself," I said. "I didn't dream there were such hearty types among Chinese females. But she's a good-enough girl, just a bit loud and pushy. Her salary is probably just a pittance, and she lives on commissions."

Even in an oncoming typhoon we had been able to shop.

The next morning when I pressed the bedside button and the curtains were drawn back, the sun was miraculously shining. The Hong Kong *Standard* of this Friday, October 20, announced happily: "Typhoon Carla passed Hong Kong in the night without leaving a trail of serious destruction behind." But, it said, the strong winds did cause a high-rise bamboo scaffolding to collapse into the street at 70–72 Queen's Road West. This was not the scaffolding across the street from the Mandarin that I had marveled at. The paper went on to say that the howling winds "kept most of the bomb planters behind closed doors." But the Communist-inspired zeal of one group was ardent enough to brave the gale to plant bombs in Kuntong Road. The police spotted the bombers and gave "chase through the screeching wind." One man was seized and jailed. The others got away. Of the seven "objects" planted by the group, two turned out to be real explosives. They were deactivated by the police.

On Thursday, the paper stated, at the Kai Tak Airport forty planes had not been allowed to take off, and the unlucky ticket-holders of those canceled flights had had a "most uncomfortable time." Fifteen planes had been forbidden to land at Hong Kong and were forced to seek other fields in other countries. We were singularly fortunate that our plane reservations were for this day instead of yesterday. On the telephone I was assured by Air France that our plane for Phnom Penh was scheduled to fly.

And on the front page under the caption "A Million Homes" it was announced that the Hong Kong government had accepted a recommendation "to build one million low-cost housing units over a six-year period." The date set for completion was March 31, 1972. So, unintimidated by the Red-instigated bombing, the British Colony was going ahead improving the condition of its Chinese poor.

I had hoped to see Tex McCrary's son, who was teaching at Hong Kong University. His father in New York had asked me to call on him and had told me that Michael was delighted with his life there. But the morning was so crowded with this and that and packing that the best I could manage was a good chat over the telephone. He was reaffirming his enthusiasm for Hong Kong living when the sweater girl from Royal Fashions breezed in with Thérèse's altered pink silk. No, she had not been able to get to her home in Kowloon last night. And the alteration had been done in the back of the shop. She began to praise the perfection of the fit before Thérèse had adjusted the tie around the waist. I went down with her to the shop to write a personal check for the manager. His native city was Shanghai, he said. He was obviously a Chinese gentleman who had seen better days. He was one of the thousands of cultured background and means who had had to make a fresh start in the British Colony. One had to admire the resilience and courage of these displaced persons.

After lunch Thérèse and I went out on the bedroom balcony to take a last sweeping look at the harbor, now as calm and blue as if the word "typhoon" had no meaning in Hong Kong. The ferries were coming and going in their accustomed lanes. From their discreet hiding the junks had emerged like joyous butterflies following a shower. Their varicolored ribbed sails—rust, orange, avocado green, maroon, and dull gold—were puffed out in the invigorating breeze.

Charlie Mok, whom I had rung for, glided in. "I hope," said he, "that you and Madam will not forget us, that you carry away pleasant memories. We have a Chinese proverb that says, 'That which enters the eye will never leave the heart.'"

"You don't think that we could ever forget this view of your harbor. It is one of the world's prime sights."

In the bedroom Charlie helped professionally with the packing. I laid my old cream-colored dinner jacket across his arm. "This is for you to get whatever you can for it. Or you may have it cut down to your size, if it would be of any use to you. Mr. Cheong has made me a new one."

"You have been so good to me," Charlie said with a touch of emotion. "You have spoken fine words of me to the floor supervisor. I shall keep the jacket just as it is to remember you by."

"Don't be silly. Make some use of it. Get what cash you can. It's of good quality. It was expensive. And here is something more immediate for you." I handed him some paper notes in Hong Kong dollars.

Charlie's eyes almost became moist, and for a moment I thought he might embrace me.

Mr. Nichols entered urbanely with baggage men. Since it was much before the hour the plane was scheduled to fly, I think he came to speed the parting guests. Some important foreign dignitary was to be met on an incoming plane, and Mr. Ross's Rolls had to be there to meet him. Still, with the extra load of traffic following a two-day slowdown, it was much better to be on the safe side. Nick, as his friends called the porter, saw us down to the car, which was already purring at the curb. The old chauffeur was in attendance. The turbaned Sikh doorman held the door open. "But where is our luggage?" I demanded, balking to enter.

"All in the trunk," Nick said in a voice like oil on a troubled sea. In admiration for such smooth manipulation, I forebore to check the six pieces for myself, as I did everywhere else. I merely shook his hand gratefully, and left a banknote in it.

The old man at the wheel turned his benignly wrinkled face with the tender, all-knowing Chinese eyes like an accompanist awaiting the cue from a concert singer. I nodded. We were on our way to the vehicle ferry and we hoped we would soon be flying to Siem Reap and the temples at Angkor.

CAMBODIA

The Khmers and Angkor Thom

Although, in a gesture to appease the Chinese Communists, Cambodia had broken diplomatic relations with the United States in May, 1965, American tourist dollars were again welcomed in 1967. Visas could be obtained on arrival at the Phnom Penh airport with little trouble. But no American soldier or diplomat was permitted entry, and no South Korean or Chinese from Taiwan. Nor could an American journalist or writer secure a visa. I had been advised to disguise the fact that I was an author. I was prepared to declare my status as a retired university professor or gentleman farmer, though my kitchen-garden plot has less than half an acre. Before leaving Hong Kong I had secreted my written notes among my shirts so that evidence of my trade would not be obvious. Still, I felt some uneasiness that I might be tossed out of the country before seeing Angkor Wat.

As chance had it, the only delayed flight of our entire world circuit was that of Royal Air Cambodge from Hong Kong to Phnom Penh on October 20. If we did not arrive in time to change planes and reach Siem Reap in daylight, we would miss our connection and have to search out a hotel in the Cambodian capital, where there were only two decent ones—both, most probably, fully booked.

Because of late or canceled flights due to the typhoon, the Hong Kong airport was in a jabbering uproar. It seems that when a citizen of Hong Kong flies anywhere he is accompanied by all his near and distant relatives, who come to see him off. A host of such kinsmen and friends occupied almost all of the available waiting-room seats. I could get no satisfaction as to when our plane would arrive. It was scheduled to come from Phnom Penh and to return at 1:00 P.M. immediately after refueling. But instead of landing at Hong Kong, this particular plane, I was informed, had gone on to Canton in Red China and would eventually double back to Hong Kong.

Why had it changed destination and gone to Canton? The Chinese who managed Royal Air Cambodge shook their heads cryptically and indifferently at my query.

Finally, the aircraft turned up, four hours late, and we flew southwest over the South China Sea, Hainan, and South Vietnam. At dusk we could see the flashes of gunfire far below in South Vietnam, where the war was in progress. Though we had seemingly been racing the setting sun, I gave up the expectancy of reaching Siem Reap, in the Cambodian jungle, before night.

The one-class plane was full of "tours," American and French. Everybody was exhausted from the delay and uncertainty at Hong Kong. The first ten sections of seats were filled with twenty Cantonese Chinese of both sexes and varying ages. Whether they were emigrants or deportees we never understood. But they looked uniformly sad and exhausted emotionally. In the space directly behind the cockpit, the seats had been removed and small household gear of the "refugees" had been piled there, with green curtains to hide the stuff from view.

In the Phnom Penh airport, where I expected to face customs, no luggage except that of the Cantonese was removed from our plane. I sought out the airport's public relations officer, Kaing Pheng Siphar, whose name I had been given in correspondence by the manager of the World Travel Service of Bangkok. A short, wiry, personable fellow with light-brown skin, he had sculptured features and broad military shoulders. He proved to be the friend in need in a strange land. He took our passports, together with a small tourist fee in dollars, and, without my having to confront a single official, he swiftly attended to everything and brought the visaed passports back in about three minutes. Our relief was considerable. Mr. Siphar, the first Cambodian I had ever met, became one of my favorite persons in Asia then and forever.

The depressed arrivals from Canton were having their luggage examined with close attention. We were moved by the plight of one Chinese man who seemed to be about six feet two. It had taken him an unconscionably long time to get from the parked plane into the airport terminal. He hobbled with his arm about the shoulders of a supporting companion. Clutched in his right hand and held across his chest like a protective shield was the frame of an expensive tennis racket with the strings slashed out of the racket's heart and dangling. His rather handsome face was drawn with lines of suffering, as if each step caused him pain. To get him seated was a slow and obviously a hurting process, but not a groan escaped him. "That man has been tortured," I said to Thérèse. "And the affection with which he hugs that broken racket suggests that he was a first-class tennis player in the best club in Canton." Whoever tortured him must have tried to break him, as well as his racket, so that he could not play tennis again. Next to him sat a wide-eyed little Chinese girl holding a caged canary on her thin knees. She leaned down to murmur encouragement to the bird, upset by the night illumination of the airport. The uprooted Cantonese were our only glimpse of wartime tragedies in the Far East.

My new friend, Siphar, came to tell us that we were to proceed to Siem Reap on the very same plane that had brought us from Hong Kong.

"But how can we land on a little airstrip in the jungle at night?" I protested.

With quiet but triumphant reassurance, he said, "You couldn't have two months ago. But in September floodlights were installed on the Siem Reap field. We have made several night landings since. In a couple of years, Siem Reap will be ready for jets."

Soon we were off to cover the two hundred miles of jungle between the present capital and the ancient one of Angkor, where in the twelfth century the Khmers created one of the world's most illustrious civilizations and, according to their chroniclers, its kings ruled "a domain so vast that the sky barely sufficed to cover it."

At Siem Reap the windows of the brand-new ultramodern airport rose three stories. The blazing triangular sections of varicolored glass suggested that the aurora borealis had rocketed from Arctic regions to send up flares from the equatorial jungle. It was fantastic.

An ancient bus had been sent from the Auberge Royale des Temples to meet its patrons. One American couple besides ourselves, the John Sulzers of Locust Valley, Long Island, and twenty-odd French persons climbed aboard. The American "tours" had gone to the Grand Hotel in the town of Siem Reap, some five miles to the south. Our bags were not opened, merely stamped "passed" and sent on by truck to the "motel" where Peter O'Toole and his company had stayed while filming Conrad's *Lord Jim*.

The dirt road lay between cut-over fields, with shadowy forest at the far edges. As we proceeded directly east, the waning moon was rising behind five mountainlike peaks ahead. Suddenly we were aware that we were looking at the fabulous temple known as Angkor Wat. The nearer we approached, the more beautiful its stupendous outlines became, spreading out beyond the still water of its moat, which is as wide as a fair-sized river. This unexpected night view of the famed temple down a country road more than made up for all the inconvenience and apprehension of the journey from Hong Kong.

The way led directly to the broad stone causeway over the moat, which no motorcars desecrate. The bus made a right-angle turn onto a paved road, and at hardly more than a hundred yards we pulled into the palm-studded courtyard of the Auberge. A large bottle of Evian water stood on the table between our beds, and the air conditioner purred softly.

At nine the next morning the young guide the Ziffs had selected for us was awaiting us with a car and driver. Huot Samoeun's bright dark eyes bespoke his honesty and intelligence, his innate kindness and eagerness to be helpful. We knew at once with that instinct of seasoned travelers that we could have had no better person to show us the heritage of his ancestors.

We passed up a morning visit to Angkor Wat, for that temple should be approached in the afternoon, when the westering sun falls upon it. Driving slowly by, we merely took in its grave beauty as earnest of the afternoon visit. But its superb outlines, merely glimpsed, are deeply etched in the memory, as if in encaustic. We went straight on to ruins of the great city, capital of the Khmers, known as Angkor Thom, a mile to the north. The word "Angkor" simply means "great," so Angkor Wat is the Great Temple and Angkor Thom is the Great City.

Shortly before we reached Angkor Thom, to the left of the road rose the steep-stepped temple called Phnom Bakheng, guarded by two splendid stone lions. Far older than Angkor Wat, this mountain temple is built on the highest point of land in the area. Only the nimble and steady-headed should ascend the staircase, Huot told us, for the steps are ladderlike. But the temple has a splendid terrace atop it, on which its king-builder would stand at sunset and overlook the surrounding moats, canals, irrigation ditches, and houses of his subjects.

Huot Samoeun gave us the briefest outline of the history of his people. The race that produced the master builders of Angkor was formed slowly during the first six centuries of the Christian era by the fusion of the Khmer race groups. Indian traders had brought their culture to the land about the time of Jesus Christ, and had intermarried with the inhabitants. The civilization, which spread out around the middle Mekong River basin, became the cradle of the Kambujas, to whom the Cambodians owe their present name. "Khmer" is an ethnic term for "Cambodian," and still is proudly in use among some inhabitants, though the word "Cambodia" has been employed in various forms in European languages since the sixteenth century.

Everything of value borrowed from India, especially its religion and architecture, was assimilated by the Khmers and melded with native talents. By the beginning of the ninth century, the present province of Siem Reap had become the geographical center of the vast Khmer territories. There the rulers were to reside for six hundred years, enriching the landscape with sumptuous temple after sumptuous temple, until there were over one hundred impressive sanctuaries, "of which twelve were as extensive as the Great Temple at Luxor."

Of the long list of Khmer kings, only three need to be remembered by the foreign visitor. The first is Jayavarman II, who established Angkor as his capital in the ninth century and greatly expanded his empire. The second, Suryavarman II, built the incomparable Angkor Wat in the first half of the twelfth century. The third, Jayavarman VII, who took the throne in 1181, built the city of Angkor Thom, with its famous Bayon Temple.

Our driver had stopped the creeping car in the shade of a spreading mahogany tree, the last tree on the right just before one approaches the bridge that leads into Angkor Thom. The scene about us on both sides of the road was pastoral—soft, silky grasses, occasional trees, and here and there clumps of wild flowers. A sweet, countryside peace prevailed. One would hardly have suspected that not many yards ahead stood the ruins of the once teeming capital of a great nation. In the pause, as we savored the pleasant atmosphere enlivened with bird song, Huot Samoeun finished his brief outline of history.

Jayavarman II, who founded the early Angkor in the ninth century, inaugurated the cult of the god-king, that mystique which was partly responsible for the enormous prosperity of the Khmers and the conquering force of their armies. Temple building became a passion with this monarch and also with those who followed him. The twelfth century beheld the apotheosis of the Khmer genius. The power of King Suryavarman II extended then from the coasts of the China Sea to the shores of the Indian Ocean. It was he who erected Angkor Wat, the greatest architectural creation in all Asia. The building of Angkor Wat was loosely contemporary with those splendid French cathedrals of Notre-Dame de Paris and Chartres, but the Khmers, with unlimited slave labor, built faster than the devout Catholics. This "God-King who was protected by the Sun" died in 1150, to be followed by short-reigned usurping rulers who fell far short of his caliber. They kept the kingdom in turmoil and lost immense areas of territory.

But in 1181 the glory was restored when Jayavarman VII, the most fascinating personality among the Khmer monarchs, took the throne at the age of fifty. He had been a rightful inheritor, but, because he was a Buddhist convert and abhored bloodshed, he had remained in his monastery rather than fight with the greedy usurpers. However, when the Chams—eastern neighbors from what is now central Vietnam—invaded his country, sacked the capital, and chopped off the reigning king's head, Jayavarman was so outraged that he cast aside his monkish robes, emerged from pious retreat, took the throne, and commanded the army. He proved to have phenomenal gifts as a militarist. He chased out the invading Chams, conquered them on their soil, and made them his vassals. He extended his kingdom to its mightiest position in history.

Then in peace he began compulsive building activities. As if to honor the compassionate Buddha, he built 102 hospitals for the sick, 121 resthouses, and numerous roads for pilgrims and ordinary travelers. He improved the networks of vital irrigation systems throughout his kingdom and thus gave his people more abundance of food. After erecting several temples, he turned his attention to building his new capital, Angkor Thom. Jayavarman, the Buddhist, seemed to have gathered superhuman strength during his austere meditations. In any case, he developed a tremendous creative urge that seemed insatiable.

"In its years of glory," Huot said, "Angkor was really an immense series of towns spread out over some thirty kilometers east and west and twenty kilometers north and south. Double lanes of earth and water ran from each temple to the four cardinal points of the compass and led to other temples with moats or nearby lakes."

As tour buses from the Grand Hotel in Siem Reap drew up to park in the cleared space across the road from us, we walked on to the arching bridge over the greenish moat. Here, we were suddenly back in the twelfth century. The bridge was lined on each side with twenty-seven demonlike stone men, seven to ten feet high. On their laps and in their collective arms they held a gigantic naga, divine serpent, with its head facing south and ending in a tail more than a hundred feet away, virtually in the precincts of Angkor Thom. In ancient days, the broad moat was stocked with crocodiles to discourage sneak enemy attacks, just as the formidable giants and the monstrous stone snakes were set to inspire fear.

Before building his glittering capital city, Jayavarman completed sixteen kilometers of surrounding double stone walls pierced by five stately gates. The flanks of the massive gateway we entered were decorated with three-headed elephants, and the towers of the gateways were adorned on their four sides with Buddha-like faces.

"Angkor Thom is laid out as a square city, four kilometers to a side, with the Bayon Temple at its center," Huot explained. "It is believed that the Bayon was completed in twenty-one years—perhaps by 1210. Some archaeologists claim that the area within the walls of Angkor Thom was more spacious than any walled city of medieval Europe and that this area was extensive enough to contain Caesar's Rome. According to delvers into Cambodia's past, this walled enclosure was merely the royal and religious center, containing administrative offices of the court, the church, and the military. The simple folk lived in their stilted houses outside the enclosure along the river and as far south as the lake shores of Tonle Sap."

We made a right-angle turn to the left beyond some trees and there, across another stone causeway, rose the Bayon in all its bizarre immensity. High up in the soaring central tower of the three-tiered mass, an enormous face of Buddha smiled benignly, a blissful smile not of this world. We halted in our tracks. The impact was so forceful that it was hard to believe what we were actually seeing. But there the sanctuary abided in enduring stone. One wonders how those late-twelfth-century builders got the enormous blocks that form the features of the Blessed One raised to such a height without derrick and fitted so neatly together without cement that the face beams assuredly after almost eight centuries of tropical weather and importunate vegetation. The colossal face of Buddha is repeated on all four sides of the ornamental tower. This so-called tower of faces is the most astonishing innovation of Jayavarman VII. It soars above the pavilions, the galleries, the gables, and the other forty-nine towers in which 196 Buddha faces turn to all directions and produce a kind of spell in the beholder.

The temple's basic shape of a Greek cross is lost sight of in those forty-nine smaller towers, which upthrust 150 feet above the terrace platforms. Some say the faces portrayed are not really of Buddha, but actually of Jayavarman VII himself, because his statue in the Phnom Penh Museum possesses almost precisely the same physiognomy and expression. This so-called "smile of Bayon," however, has been proclaimed as "without doubt the supreme expression of Buddhist beatitude." The forgotten sculptor whose fingers feelingly caught this surpassing serenity of a man in a state of spiritual bliss must himself have had profound metaphysical intimations.

From the central sanctuary, circular in shape, radiate twelve chapels, all standing on a massive base. One treads the once sacred passages as through a labyrinth and might get lost without the guidance of a native. Though a patina of whitish-green moss overlays the dark-gray stone, producing an ineffable sense of age and a beauty of its own, I cannot say that the whole effect of the Bayon is appealing. Rather, it awes or overwhelms.

The history of the amazing Khmers is displayed in seemingly endless panoramas in long bas-reliefs, depicting the mundane glories of the Khmer kings, on the walls of Bayon's stretched-out galleries, its numerous courts and radiating chapels. Priests walk in processions, followed by dancing girls and musicians. The king holds council with his ministers; the queen gossips with her maids of honor. Archers shoot hosts of arrows into the air. Soldiers with swords and shields oppose each other in hand-to-hand clashes. Naval battles take place on the Tonle Sap between the Chams and Khmers. Someone has counted 11,000 sculptured figures of human beings and animals. Not only do royal armies set forth to conquer, but also the daily life of the humble is recorded in hundreds of different aspects. Men fish from boats, hunters stalk game in the forests, women husk rice or play with their children. Slaves labor in the stone quarries or make bricks. Monkeys swing with gay impudence among tree branches, elephants tread majestically, game-cocks leap at each other with merciless spurs seeking a vital spot, flights of strange birds cross the stone sky.

The panel that attracted us most was one of a Khmer family setting off to war, the father in front, bearing his spear and bow and quiver of arrows. The wife follows him at a respectful number of paces, carrying a baby in a sling on her back, a cooking pot, and supply of foodstuffs on her head. With her left hand she guides a toddling child. In her right, she aggressively bears a spear. "In those early days," Huot said, "wives often shared in their husbands' war ventures and even joined in the fighting if the battle got pressing. Children were taken along to make the warrior feel more at home in strange places."

I could not help but wonder at the final outcome for this little family starting off to war so purposefully. Like Keats before the Grecian urn, we would see no arrival, no return. The family had already been walking on the temple wall for almost eight centuries. The encroaching jungle had never halted their march, though for a time it had hid the figures from view. Now that the French had dug them out of dirt and roots and obliterating bushes, they were in such a sharp-edged state of preservation that they might continue on their patriotic way until time itself has a stop.

To the south of the Bayon we were shown the huge rectangular bathing pool with shallow tiers like a small stadium for spectators. The pool, Huot said, had been enjoyed not only by the royal family and distinguished guests but also by the thousand household slave girls.

A short distance from the temple to the north once stood the royal palace. It was built of wood, presumably because the Khmers had not the technique of the vast arch in stone, and the throne room and audience hall had to be far larger than any stone chamber that could be vaulted at the time. The mansions of dignitaries and the aristocracy had also been constructed of wood. Weather and termites have obliterated all trace of residences. But according to chronicles, the life lived in the gilded wooden palace was of unprecedented luxury. In front of the palace were laid out two plazas, known as the Terrace of the Leper King and the Terrace of the Elephants. They were so constructed that the court and the dignitaries could sit and watch athletic sports, circuses, and spectacles. What caught my special interest were the twelve Towers of the Cord Dancers, equidistant from each other and stretching out opposite the Bayon and the royal terraces. These square masonry towers served an unusual purpose. Their tops were starting and resting places for the tightrope walkers, whose art was a popular exhibition with the court. Cord dancing required great skill and supercoordination, for the ground was so far beneath the stretched ropes that a tumble would mean ruinous breakage if not immediate death.

Where Jayavarman's courtiers had once strolled on the terrace of the legendary Leper King, whose splotched statue stands on an embankment, modern concessionaires had set up little rolling wagons of bottled drinks. After the excitements of Bayon, I felt the need of refreshment, and, though the vendors seemed to desecrate the ruins, I was grateful for the cold Pepsi-Cola and glad to pay the equivalent of thirty cents for it.

Commaille, a French writer on architecture and decoration, declares that the Bayon is of a conception superior to Angkor Wat. He goes further to claim that "in a relatively restricted space the constructors of the Bayon have been able to enclose more marvels than in all the other Cambodian temples combined." Personally, I cannot agree. I much prefer the proportions of the larger Angkor Wat. To me, there is a dazzling too-muchness at the Bayon. But the multiple stone faces of Buddha in "the forest of towers" certainly create a compelling fascination.

"Buddha has by far the largest following of any of the great leaders in whose name religions grew," Huot reminded us. "In this world of permanent conflicts Buddhism satisfied man's longing for peace. Buddha's message is essentially and absolutely a peaceful one. In all world history there is not one instance where violence or torture has ever been employed in Buddha's name. Some historians attribute the final downfall of the Khmers to the practice of Buddhism. It made them soft, it is claimed, and took the fight out of them when they opposed aggressive invaders like the Siamese. However, they did withstand attacks from the Siamese for a hundred years."

The Khmers were anything but assiduous at keeping records.

Perhaps the most vivid account of the times following Jayavarman VII is that of a member of a Chinese mission sent by Kublai Khan's successor in 1296. His name was Chou Ta-kuan. He was a kind of commercial counselor who stayed a year in Angkor Thom and on his return to China wrote a long report for the Imperial Court on society in Kambuja. Although Jayavarman had been dead since 1220, court life was much the same in the closing decade of the thirteenth century.

Chou Ta-kuan recorded that the Bayon gleamed with gold leaf. A golden bridge was flanked by golden lions and faced with eight golden statues of the Buddha. About the many marvelous rooms within the palace he wrote only from hearsay, for he was not permitted to enter. The King, according to the Chinese observer, held two audiences a day. At appointed hours supplicating officials and private folk would seat themselves before a grilled window where the King was to appear. Music and conch blowing announced his formal approach. Then palace girls would raise a silken curtain and reveal the seated God-King. Petitioners would bow reverently until their foreheads touched the stone floor, and they could not raise their faces until the horns ceased blowing.

Conspicuous expenditure was in high evidence in Angkor Thom. Princes and state officials lived in elegant mansions with numerous slaves for servants. When nobles traveled through the streets they were borne in golden palanquins or walked under gold-handled umbrellas held by slaves. The Chinese visitor estimated the staff of palace girls at 5,000. Feast days were elaborate in their grandeur. Lords and their ladies arrived on richly caparisoned elephants or in horse-drawn chariots. Pyrotechnical displays followed dancing and wild-boar fights. Everywhere were gala festoons of lanterns and flowers.

As Lawrence Briggs wrote in his *Ancient Khmer Empire*, "The Khmers left the world no systems of administration, education or ethics like those of China; no literature, religions or systems of philosophy like those of India; but here Oriental architecture and decoration reached its culminating point." However, with the passing of the gifted Jayavarman VII, Khmer architectural achievement stopped. He had exhausted the nation's energies in his obsessive building.

No strong ruler came after him. His successors just barely de-

fended their capital from sporadic attacks by the neighboring Siamese, who finally completely overcame the Khmers in 1431, and
sacked and burned Angkor Thom. The Khmers fled south in 1432
and established three consecutive capitals, finally settling perma-
nently at Phnom Penh, two hundred miles from Angkor. The glory
of the Khmer civilization ended half a century before Columbus
discovered the New World.

After the Siamese had left devastation behind them and returned
to their homes laden with loot, the jungle began its insidious advance. In the next four centuries tropical vegetation pursued its
unimpeded depredations. By 1800 few recalled that Angkor had
ever been. When stories of a city buried in the jungle were repeated,
most hearers smiled skeptically or indifferently. Some peasants, returning to the northern shores of the great lake to plant crops,
would, in their game hunts through the forest, occasionally stumble
across half-buried shrines. A group of saffron-robed monks built
huts in the shadow of Angkor Wat, which obviously had had a
religious origin. But few credited the story of "jungle-smothered
sanctuaries created by ancient gods."

Then one day in 1861, following a shadowy path, an adventur-
some French naturalist and mining prospector named Henri Mouhot
beheld to his amazement the soaring towers of Angkor Wat. He
stood enchanted, much like those Spaniards who first stared upon
the Pacific "silent, upon a peak in Darien."

But Mouhot did not remain silent. He proclaimed his discovery
loud and bold, and eventually he cut his way from ruined temple
to ruined temple, making the most notable archaeological discoveries
in generations. When the French became protectors of Cambodia in
1863, they began to release the imprisoned splendors within a fifteen-
mile radius. Huot Samoeun assured us that his people would always
be grateful to France, not only for the lost temples, but also for the
stimulated economy through the world tourist trade that flows to
Angkor.

At the farthest end of the royal terraces, as if by some legerde-
main, our car was waiting. It had come in by a roundabout back
way. We rode about half a mile to a woodland path leading to the
ruined Ta Prohm. There we alighted and the car vanished, to meet
us later on another road farther to the east.

Jayavarman VII built the Ta Prohm before the more ambitious Bayon. This temple was dedicated to the memory of his parents and "conceived with love." The sheltering trees all about make mazes of cool shadows in the courtyard before the entrance. The one-story temple is built on ground level, but it spreads into scores of chambers, courtyards, corridors. Even the priests had difficulty in finding their way around in the complex, Huot told us. In neighboring vast wooden buildings, now gone without a trace, lived an enormous staff of priests and servitors.

Ta Prohm is distinctive from the scores of other Angkor temples in that it has been only slightly reclaimed from the smothering jungle. It stands almost as it did when Henri Mouhot stumbled upon it a hundred years ago. The walls and various corridors and chambers have been repaired just enough to forestall further deterioration and to make passage through the ruins safe. Bushes have been cleared from the corners of the rooms, but the trees have been left standing. "Don't be too casual about stepping on tree roots," Huot warned only half-jokingly. "A snake camouflaged as a root may occasionally stir and slither." I knew this to be true; for Fred Smith, editor of *The American Home* and a onetime student assistant of mine, had once almost stepped on what he thought was a thick root in Ta Prohm, when the cobra raised its hood and hissed. He had beat a retreat back to his guide. In Angkor, one should tread carefully, follow the guide's directions, and not explore wildly on his own.

Walls lean a bit, as in a fun house at a fair. Paving stones are up-heaved trickily. Here and there arches look ready to give up their struggle and drop before one passes under them. In corners, sleek, cream-colored trunks of silk-cotton trees rise like decorative columns and end in trembling green canopies high overhead. The trees have grown up from seeds lodged in pavement cracks. Side roots larger than boa constrictors shoot across chambers to find holes in an opposite wall and burrow into the rich soil outside. Huot said that the roots of the cotton trees suck mineral salts out of the masonry and so are called stone-eating trees. While some of the insidious vegetation acts as wedges to render walls apart, stout vines grip stones in a vise, as if determined to squeeze the substance from them.

The square supporting columns that have not fallen with the

weight of centuries boast capitals that are Doric-like in their simplicity. At the end of a side corridor the focal point today may be a whitish-yellow column of a "cheese" tree's trunk. It not only bars one's passage, but its exposed roots flow down the corridor to meet one like advancing serpents. Niches hold sculptured dancing girls with high ceremonial headdresses. Their skirts are modestly long, but the encircling belt begins about four inches below the navel, leaving the dancer bare and cool for her rhythmic movements in the torrid temperature of Kambuja.

We passed from a court to a chamber where a banyan tree had grown with reckless abandon. With the strength of an unshorn Samson, its probing roots had split walls and tumbled stone columns. Where floors had been thrown out of plumb, patches of wild flowers had possessed the mellow earth. High overhead, leafy branches formed a roof as of pale-green stained glass, and the noonday sunlight filtered into dappled gold on the pavement at one's feet. It was like traversing chapels of a ruined cathedral or wandering in a storybook palace with a haunting Poe atmosphere.

Despite potential dangers, Ta Prohm exudes an odd atmosphere of intimacy. Somehow the masses of fallen rocks and the pale chamois of tree trunks give the temple an aura of casual grace and appeal.

The French were wise not to restore Ta Prohm but to let the dynamic power of vegetation be revealed. Wandering through the ruins makes one realize the enormity of the restorative work of the French in the temples through acres of jungle.

We ended our zigzagging trail in a kind of enchantment. Stepping out of the back of this Khmer relic from about the year 1200, we came upon a narrow sandy road oozing dampness. The trees on either side intertwined in casual haphazardness. The woodsy smell was pleasant and evocative. "What does this make you think of?" I asked Thérèse. "A shady lane of my childhood—a peaceful Alabama cowpath." "Exactly," I said. "But those darting, chattering birds in the branches are parakeets, not mockingbirds. And we didn't have mole-colored monkeys swinging about overhead among the branches. Instead of Jersey milk cows, look, here comes a water buffalo. But the feeling *is* the same." In Japan and Hong Kong nothing whatever had reminded us of Alabama. Here in the Cambodian woods we were suddenly transported to rural scenes of our youth.

We moved out of the path of the plodding dun-colored buffalo and its keeper, a dark-skinned, broad-faced woman with a wide-brimmed straw hat. They were like those twelfth-century figures incised upon the stone panels of the Bayon. "Little has changed in the life of the Cambodian farmer through the ages," Huot observed. "The domesticated beasts are like members of the family. Though they drag the primitive plows, they are pets to lavish affection on. They sleep under the high stilted huts at night and are taken to the river to bathe, just as in the sixth century. They give milk and, when old, furnish meat and hides. Water buffaloes are a significant part of our economy. Most Cambodians are farmers. Rice, fish, and wood are chief items in this basic economy. These commodities we have in abundance, as well as mangoes and other tropical fruits. No one is hungry in Cambodia. And in this climate little clothing is needed. To put it another way, our peasants have about everything that Adam and Eve possessed in their famous garden."

After miles of tramping through Angkor Thom and Ta Prohm, we found our waiting car on a broad road an agreeable sight. As we drove along, the peace of the countryside seemed enhanced by the patient buffaloes being led to their midday rest. "Just like bygone centuries," Huot observed again, and, after a moment, added, "except for what's coming." Approaching was a yellow figure on wheels. It was a saffron-robed monk hitching a ride on the handlebars of a peasant's bike. His mien was humble with gratitude, while the owner of the bicycle smiled widely at the privilege of doing a kind deed for a holy man.

Soon we were passing at the back or eastern side of Angkor Wat. Its massive pile is guarded by the largest artificial moat in the world, a perfect rectangle, with waters 627 feet in width. Between the moat and the temple is a wall forming an inner rectangle a mile long on the longer sides. It was clarifying to have this circum-navigating drive around the immense structure before approaching it from the west in the afternoon.

At the Auberge we looked forward with keen pleasure to an appetizing lunch of French cuisine, followed by a refreshing siesta. Promptly at four, Huot Samoeun was again awaiting our pleasure.

"The Ultimate Expression of Khmer Culture"

I was first impressed by the words "Angkor Wat" in Bermuda during the Christmas holidays of 1931. The name was engraved on a narrow gold band around a square-headed, tapering walking stick of dark polished wood. This handsome stick belonged to my friend the late Stanley King, president of Amherst College, with whom we dined on New Year's Eve. It was a prized souvenir of the Kings' travels to some thirty exotic places, and had the names and dates of each visit inscribed on metal bands. I was peculiarly arrested by Angkor Wat, for I had never before known anyone who had actually been there. The Kings related the formidable difficulties of reaching the place in the 1920's, but they declared the effort had been more than worth the trouble, for they regarded Angkor Wat as the foremost of man's architectural creations. My strong desire to see the temple had been born then and there. The name "Angkor Wat" was the more deeply incised in my memory because a few hours later, in the early morning of New Year's Day, the exclusive guesthouse where the Kings were staying burned. They saved nothing but their bare lives. The walking stick commemorating their travels perished with their luggage. The incident came sharply into mind when we stopped at the entrance to the causeway.

As we took a long look at the structure, admiring its thrilling symmetry I recalled how Somerset Maugham in the 1930's had confessed that he was at a loss how to describe the ruins of Angkor. "I do not know how on earth I am going to set down in black and white such an account of them as will give even the most sensitive reader more than a confused and shadowy impression of this grandeur."

If the prospect staggered Maugham, one may imagine the feeling with which I approached this magnificent sanctuary. We had had a glimpse of Angkor Wat by moonlight and morning views from our passing car, and now, with the afternoon sun lengthening our shadows before us and illuminating the monumental spires, we started slowly across the broad causeway laid with great smoothly hewn stones. The balustrades were surmounted by stone nagas that extended more than a thousand feet, their threatening heads at the entrance to the west and their tails, guarded by two stone lions, ending at the terrace before the temple. I know of no more noble approach to any building anywhere. I thought of Chartres, with those tradesmen's shops pushing almost to the portals and mere alleys holding off the encroachment of petty dwellings. Here before the temple there was nothing but a lilied moat and then a green belt at the base of the moss-gray pile. Behind it all was a backdrop of cloudless azure.

Midway we stopped still to gaze upon the five soaring lotus-bud towers based in the more central portions of the temple. At the four outer corners rose turrets, which Huot said were once coated with gilt. Angkor Wat, unlike great European cathedrals, was not created for sheltering mass worshipers, but erected as a sanctuary for the gods and a repository for royal ashes. When the Khmer populace came to do homage to deity and king, they knelt in the forecourt. "The Khmers," Huot said, "built their version of the abode of the gods—to represent a kind of sacred mountain."

Angkor Wat was erected in honor of the Hindu god Vishnu, Huot told us. Most of the other Hindu temples within the fifteen-mile radius were built in the name of the powerful god Siva. But Suryavarman chose Vishnu, the "All-Pervasive," the "Protector of the World," because he is the most compassionate in the Hindu hierarchy. A few years later it was an easy transition when Jayavarman VII became a devout follower of the Lord Buddha.

To the right, in the ample verdant space before the temple's façade, were clumps of tall palm trees waving gently in the breeze. Down on the marshy green near the edge of the moat I counted forty white herons that were making shifting patterns on the grass. Here and there myna birds hopped and a few peacocks strutted.

We stood at the end of the causeway before Angkor Wat, looking up to the right and left, and like Maugham, knew forcibly that no words I might conjure up could give more than a shadowy impression of what we saw and felt. Hesitantly our Cambodian companion broke the silence by saying, "Although the spectacular Bayon came half a century later, Angkor Wat, I think, sir, is the ultimate expression of our Khmer culture." Enthralled, we could only murmur agreement.

Spreading far and rising high, the temple was obviously built with such splendid strength. As the Britisher Malcolm MacDonald says aptly, "No building on earth seems so sure of itself."

Actually, to be deeply impressed one does not even need to enter the temple, to trace the galleries, chambers, and open courtyards, or to climb the steep staircases that promise dizzying excitements. But the bas-reliefs are famous and should be noted. The shallow etched figures go on and on and on, as in an art gallery where the exhibits are never changed. The stone etchings have been extremely well preserved because they are under the cover of arcaded roofs. One long frieze adorning a gallery wall around the lower terraces reaches to a height of eight feet and stretches for more than half a mile. The faces and figures are cleanly cut. The expressions of emotions are patently evident. Even the details of hands and weaponry are sharp. For the most part, the subjects coursing the walls are derived from Indian epics, particularly the *Ramayana* and the less familiar *Mahabharata*. The latter, which tells a great tale of rivalries between two families, descendants of Prince Bharata, is a compilation of more than 100,000 couplets, eight times the length of the combined *Iliad* and *Odyssey*. Today we have little interest in the struggle of two rival families in northern India reputedly in the tenth century B.C., but we can admire the chisel skill of the Khmers.

The story of Rama, whose wife, Sita, was seized by a demon king and carried off to what is now Ceylon, is more interesting. The monkeys and bears who help Rama in the rescue are vividly animated. In two spots in the panorama Huot pointed out the face and figure of Suryavarman II himself, the temple's begetter. In one portrayal he was fighting valiantly to help Rama retrieve his wife; in another, he was regally holding court.

One chiseled subject is the churning of the Milk Ocean or Cosmic Sea in an attempt "to extract from its liquid the elixir of immortality," with snakes and demons enjoined in the struggle. Although it is somewhat bemusing, the creative imagination of the carvers is eminent.

Since museum trekking anywhere can soon become wearying, we stopped looking at the epic scenes on walls and took note of the "heavenly dancing girls" poised in courtyard niches. They had smiling, flattish but pretty Oriental faces and wore elaborate coiffures and quantities of jewelry, and, like the beauty we had noted at Ta Prohm, they were bare above the navel. The statues and bas-reliefs executed with such infinite pains by their creators attested to the accomplishments of the ancient Khmers but did little to enhance the impact of beauty and harmony of the vast sanctuary itself.

One cannot look upon beauty too long at a time without losing some sense of wonder; one needs an interval of something else for contrast. That was why the quarter-mile walk on the damp shady lane behind the Ta Prohm was a soothing respite, arranged by guides after crowded hours of looking. Now we had reached the saturation point of admiration and had no inclination to climb treacherous stairs for elevated views, however thrilling. Nor did we look forward to traversing the 1,260-foot-long causeway in the face of the sun. Huot had another pleasant surprise. Over by the cluster of yellow-roofed huts of resident monks he pointed to our car, awaiting us. The driver had come in over a back causeway.

"There is one thing I expected which I miss," I told our amiable guide as we left the temple by side stairs. "The thousands of bats and the stifling smell of bat's dung." Mississippi friends of ours, Frances and Pratt Thomas, on a world cruise in the 1950's had chartered a small dilapidated plane in Hong Kong and flown directly from there to Angkor. They said it was worth the price and the danger to life, but that they had been almost overcome by the stench of bats and disturbed by the flying clouds of them in the temple. Huot grinned, remembering the bats when he was a small lad. "All that was cleaned away several years ago," Huot said, "though a few may still be lurking about." But we did not see or smell a single bat in any part of the ruins.

It is a pleasant five-mile drive south to the little town of Siem Reap. There were shade trees lining the road and occasional middle-class villas, a modern school, and many small houses on stilts, with the water buffaloes comfortably tethered beneath. It was almost past teatime, but I asked for the Grand Hotel of which Maugham had written. A guidebook of three years earlier spoke of the Grand Hotel Bar Lounge as "an intriguing page from Somerset Maugham with huge fans lazily wafting air overhead." Today it seems completely lacking in atmosphere, and no fans turn. The bar lounge is, happily, air-conditioned, but it is all as varnished and commonplace as a small-town hotel in Kansas.

The waiter who served us tea and English biscuits was most polite, but he looked as though he had hardly ever served tea before in the afternoon. The *addition* was higher than it might have been at the Hassler in Rome. The whole place has had a face-lifting job within and without, and the Grand Hotel does a flourishing business with American tours. But we vastly preferred our Auberge Royal des Temples, within a gaze of Angkor Wat.

The front of the Grand faces on a pretty plaza with palm trees and flower beds. The principal streets of Siem Reap are paved, yet parts of it retain something of the flavor of native life in the days of the Khmers. Around the edges of the town the people still live in their primitive huts and pursue their daily life of rice husking, bread making, house repairing, and washing their clothes in the nearby river.

The central market place in Siem Reap, with its scattering of bazaars, is colorful and calls to mind market squares in Mexican towns. Prince Norodom Sihanouk, the prime minister, had a charming three-room house there, to which he retired occasionally from the strain of office in Phnom Penh. He had also built a pleasant villa for his widowed mother, the Queen.*

We stopped only once in our drive, to enter an inviting little one-room Buddhist shrine in a lovely garden. The pencil-thin caretaker within was not a saffron-robed monk but a mustached man in shirt and trousers. He was standing against a shadowy wall smoking a cigarette. The smoke mingled inoffensively enough with the smell of incense and, despite the cigarette, the atmosphere was harmonious

---

* In March, 1970, ironically, while Sihanouk was visiting Soviet officials in Moscow, the Cambodian assembly voted to strip him of his title and his powers. The Prince, though claiming neutrality, had allowed North Vietnamese and Viet Cong to use eastern stretches of his country as a sanctuary, staging area, and supply route for Communist troops. Conservative forces in Cambodia found the situation dangerous as well as insulting, and demanded that the alien soldiers leave. In a sudden command decision President Nixon sent U.S.A. troops across the Cambodian border to help clear out the sanctuaries and capture or destroy the enormous stockpiles of war materials and food supplies. As of May 25, the dramatic action was proving eminently successful.

and reverent. The surprised caretaker remained absolutely silent, as did we.

At dinner that evening in the French garden restaurant, which has three walls of glass, we were given a table for two with both chairs looking diagonally across the moat to Angkor Wat. The rising moon touched the scene with a silvery illumination. The five lotus-bud towers stood out like jewels above the well-proportioned mass and suggested a gigantic tiara in silhouette.

We lingered long over dinner while feasting our eyes on the moonlit temple. Everybody else was rushing across the causeway to a performance of dancing girls before the temple. But we had heard that the spectacle was rather amateurish, though the costumes were indeed gorgeous. We preferred to cherish the memory of Angkor Wat in undefiled beauty as we had seen it under the afternoon sun.

However, after dinner we strolled to the entrance of the causeway and took a long last look at the imperishable legacy of the ancestors of the present-day Cambodians. Recalling the opinion of the Stanley Kings, we could agree that if there is one supreme ultimate above all the monumental buildings of the world it must surely be Angkor Wat.

When we flew to Phnom Penh the next afternoon, to take an Air France jet to Bangkok, the pilot gave the passengers a bonus aerial view of Angkor Wat and glimpses of a dozen other temples we had not seen. The thrilling detour emphasized that what makes the glorious ruins of the Angkor region unique among the globe's wonders is the fact that such splendors in stone are set down in a remote Asian jungle.

At the Phnom Penh airport, on the veranda terrace of the restaurant, we had a long cooling drink with our charming new Long Island friends, Mary and John Sulzer. I was feeling a surge of gratitude at not having been detected as a writer, forbidden to Cambodia. Thérèse, still under the spell of Angkor, mused aloud. "I can only hope and pray that the war does not move into Cambodia. Angkor Wat might prove useful for storing explosives. The Parthenon was once—and it blew up!" With this sobering thought we walked out to the Air France jet. The thrill of Bangkok was only fifty-five minutes away.

THAILAND

Sweet Day to Do Nothing

In the vast and busy Don Muang Airport at Bangkok the customs men smilingly waved us through formalities without opening a bag. Instead of waiting for the limousine, we took a private car for the half-hour drive into the city. I sniffed the early-evening air speculatively, for I had read of the dreadful summer heat of Bangkok, where the atmosphere could be so humid that three cold showers a day afforded only spasmodic relief. This evening air on October 22 was pleasant and agreeable and mellifluous of green fields, for a soft breeze was stirring. We could relax on the long drive, because the many-laned highway was not crowded at the supper hour. Only in the last few minutes were we deeply immersed in modern traffic.

When we arrived under the portico of the fantastic Siam Intercontinental Hotel, with its steep roofs upturned at the edges pagoda-style, we were greeted by a lithe and handsome doorman, six feet two and in his early twenties. He was wearing a smartly tailored cream-colored uniform and that most ingratiating of all national smiles, the winning Thai smile. Naturally he had been chosen for his brisk good looks and his height, which was remarkable among the short-statured Thais. The ceiling of the lobby rose cathedral-high, for there were no rooms above it or above the bar or the various ground-floor restaurants. Two sides of the hotel lobby were lined with smart shops of various categories, with displays of antique bronzes, Thai silk dresses and cravats, jewelry, and everything in the way of drugs that one might use in England or the States. In this arcade, shopping could hardly have been easier for the tired traveler.

At the reception desk we were greeted by the youngish assistant manager, Peter Jentes, a golden-haired German, born and nurtured in the Black Forest. He had a fresh, out-of-doors smile that rivaled the Thai smile and a shy charm concealing his Teutonic efficiency.

In the mail handed me was a reassuring letter from Jay Long of the American Embassy reaffirming the cable to Tokyo that Their

Majesties would receive me on Tuesday at eleven. I noted the word
"Their"—so I was to see the Queen after all, even if Thérèse did
not accompany me. Mr. Long said that he would fetch me in an
embassy car in good time. And he enclosed two choice seats for the
Royal Barges Procession on the Chao Phraya River for the following
Friday. The omens boded well, as Jentes himself conducted us to
our room.

The two-tiered units of hotel rooms shot off into gardens at
angles, somewhat like the legs of a spider. We traversed arbors and
roofed walkways into a detached elongated building, down a thickly
carpeted corridor, and up an easy flight of double stairs, and finally
reached our door. There were no elevators. In the pleasantly air-
conditioned room we found white flowers and a bowl of golden
fruit. Before a great picture window were drawn curtains of heavy
Thai silk in subdued tones of rust and yellow. Everything was
fresh and new, for the hotel was not two years old.

The first sight of an alien city at morning from a hotel window is
always pregnant with expectancy. On awakening I drew back the
hangings and gazed upon green lawns and a commodious swimming
pool. Directly below our window the greensward was dotted with
yellow-beaked myna birds, their black backs glistening in the sun
like enamel. Beyond the hotel property limits stretched grassy fields
where fat white Peking ducks wandered delightedly, selecting succulent bugs for their breakfast. Some, already replete, were gliding
swanlike along a narrow stream, suggesting *Lohengrin* swans against
a painted opera backdrop seen from the top gallery. Those meadows,
I learned from the smiling waiter who brought our breakfast, were
the entailed property of the King's mother, and, blessedly, would
never be sold, so the hotel guests could ever soothe their strained
tourist eyes with perpetual greenery and flowers in season. And
here, cut off from city sounds by the soft purr of the air conditioner, we found it hard to realize that only a block away in front
of the hotel was a boulevard teeming with traffic.

We had arrived in Bangkok at a peculiarly fortunate time. Not
only was it the week of the Royal Barges Procession, but, according
to the Bangkok *Post* on this October 23, the nation was celebrating
Chulalongkorn Day, honoring the anniversary of the death of Siam's
greatest monarch, the Prince of *The King and I*. On this day, in
commemoration, wreaths were being placed before the equestrian

statue of the old sovereign, patriotic speeches were being made, schools were on holiday. The Royal Family and the entire nation honored its most famous king, who was not really so remote in history, for his thirty-nine-year-old grandson, Bhumibol, now wore the crown. The special edition of the English-language paper contained reams on Siam's history.

Significantly, as it turned out decades later, for making the world's moviegoers vividly aware of Siam, King Mongkut (Rama IV) in 1863 brought over a young British widow, Mrs. Anna H. Leonowens, to teach the English language and English manners to his eldest son, the heir apparent, Chulalongkorn, and others of his enormous brood of children. In 1944, Margaret Landon wrote her best-selling novel, *Anna and the King of Siam*, from Anna's two volumes of reminiscences. In two motion-picture versions Rex Harrison and Yul Brynner each presented the Eastern potentate in his own personalized style, with romantic trimmings. In any case, the real Anna had a great influence on the impressionable Prince during the four years she taught him, from the age of ten to fourteen. Both Mongkut and Chulalongkorn pleaded with her to stay on at court when she departed for England on July 1, 1867. The next year Mongkut died, and Chulalongkorn, spoken of even today as "Anna's pupil," was crowned on November 11, 1868.

Only fifteen when his illustrious father died, he had already been trained for the ruler's job by his sire, who had envisioned a more modern Siam and begun its Westernization by establishing diplomatic relations with several European nations and the United States. But since the young inheritor was not yet of age, a regency administered, while Chulalongkorn went into seclusion in a Buddhist monastery for five years. In that austere regime he meditated on the many things he might do for his people. Dynamic and vigorous by nature, when he emerged from the cloister he made the unprecedented gesture of traveling outside his own borders. He visited India and the Dutch East Indies to see for himself how other peoples in other lands lived.

With the inestimable advantage of national independence—the nation has never known European conquerors, as have India and Burma and most of Southeast Asia—Chulalongkorn steered his country into the stream of modern development. He sent the Crown Prince, Maha, and several of his more promising sons to England to complete their education. One bitter crisis faced him—in 1893—when France, ambitious for an empire equal to Britain's, endeavored to create an incident so that she might seize Siam as she had grabbed territory in Indochina and Cambodia. In July two French gunboats with cannon booming forced their way past the lower Siam forts up the Chao Phraya and anchored off the garden of the French legation in Bangkok. To save his country from a likely French oc-cupation, on Britain's advice, Chulalongkorn signed a treaty with-drawing all his troops from the east bank of the Mekong River. (Later the French forced him to cede the provinces of Battambang and Siem Reap to Cambodia, which only a quarter century earlier they had recognized as belonging to Siam.) It was a hard decision, but the King had spared his people bloodshed and a disruption of his progressive plans.

Against strong opposition from advisers, with a stroke of his royal quill Chulalongkorn abolished slavery, thereby releasing a great hu-man potential. He simplified the elaborate court etiquette. He estab-lished hospitals and public schools. He improved the army and the navy. He ordered a standard coinage and introduced postal and telegraph services. He interested himself in the sanitation, lighting, and policing of his capital city.

Britain was not only helpful to the King in curtailing the en-croachments of France, but also lent him a huge sum to build the first Siamese railway. In 1897 Chulalongkorn paid a visit to Europe and everywhere received royal attention. On August 19 in London Anna and her famous pupil had a touching and delightful afternoon together. On his return to Siam the King was able to accelerate his program of reforms and modernization and was still working dil-igently until his death on October 23, 1910. The significant effect of Chulalongkorn's foreign policy and reforms was to preserve Siam as an independent nation at a time when the rest of Southeast Asia was falling subject to Britain or France.

Two sons of Chulalongkorn in turn took the throne. The first was Oxford-educated Maha Vajiravudh. As Rama VI he joined the Allies against Germany in 1917, and thereby gained some valuable German shipping as spoils of war. Maha was a patron of the arts and a poet, and he translated some of Shakespeare's tragedies into Thai for stage production. His younger brother Prajadhipok became king in 1925. Partly because of the world-wide economic depression of 1930 to 1931 and the subsequent drop in the price of rice, Siam's principal export, a bloodless revolution occurred in June, 1932. It was led by a brilliant, ambitious young lawyer named Pridi Phanomyong. A constitutional monarchy was established. A national assembly of 156 members was created, half appointed by the government and half elected by popular vote. The dazzling absolute monarchy that reached far back into history dissolved overnight.

After three more years on the throne this second son of Chulalongkorn abdicated in 1935 because of a proposed curtailment of his power of veto. His ten-year-old nephew, Ananda Mahidol, who was attending a fashionable boys' school in Switzerland, was proclaimed king as Rama VIII. A Regency Council of three acted for him until he became of age. In June, 1939, the name of the country was officially changed to Thailand, "the land of the free," the better to break the lingering spell of the absolute monarchy. Some of the romance of the country went out with that evocative name "Siam," just as Bangkok's epithet of "Venice of the East" lost point as the main canals were filled and replaced by paved boulevards.

Political upheavals "at the summit" and various coups continued to occur. Changes were made in the constitution. But all the revolutions were typically Thai: that is, bloodless. In no wise was the internal peace upset or the advancing prosperity halted.

With the tragic accidental death of Ananda at twenty-two, when he had reigned for only six months, his brother Bhumibol Adulyadej acceded to the throne. Though the actual ruling power of the present King has been drastically shorn, as in most modern monarchies, an editorial in the Bangkok *Post* on this morning of October 23 ended with a significant sentence: "There is gratification in the knowledge the monarchy continues to be the sheet anchor of the nation's continued progress and stability."

The next day I would meet the Thai monarch.

A telephone call from Mr. Kusa Panyrachun's World Travel Service in the hotel lobby wanted to know our pleasure. A voice said that the Royal Compound with its complex of temples and *chedis* was closed on this particular Monday, because of the anniversary rites of Chulalongkorn, and would we like to do something else? I did not want a heavy day before my audience with King

Bhumibol the next day, so I said that we would see the best of the temples on Wednesday. Today I would relax, just wander about the hotel and gardens, and catch up on my Angkor notes.

I slipped on my bathing trunks and dressing gown, and went down to the inviting pool. International guests were stretched out in long chairs, sipping iced drinks and luxuriating in the autumn sunshine.

At the pool I met several American army officers. Bangkok was the favorite recreation city for fatigued soldiers recuperating from duties in Vietnam. Leaves were well regulated, I was told, so that no more than five hundred U.S. servicemen were in the capital at one time. I chanced to stretch out by a young redheaded artillery captain from a well-to-do New Orleans family.

"Of course you know," he said, "that Bangkok is a bachelor's paradise—with easy access to attractive girls, and not only in the notorious 'massage parlors.' But, besides, this fantastic city is like none other on earth. The Oriental splendors are linked with the latest modern comforts. The Thais themselves are the most amiable people I've ever known. They're satisfied with little and are not by nature competitive. Living in another Eden, they're relatively without ambition, unless they have been to college in the States. In a land of perpetual summer they have never experienced cold and have no heating problem. Brought up from babyhood in a warm and humid atmosphere, they do not even sweat as we foreigners do. Palm-leaf hats keep the sun's rays from the workers in the fields and on construction jobs. The need for clothes is minimal. Cotton is in year-round use, silk only for dress-up occasions. Silk is cheap, and many weave their own fabrics."

He seemed eager to talk about his new discovery. "Oh, yes, Thailand is the ideal spot for R and R. These happy-go-lucky Thais are themselves so relaxed—unless they are trying to board an over-filled bus—that the atmosphere seems permeated with an absence of strain. It is considered ill-mannered to lose one's cool or to cause another to lose face or equanimity. Annoyances are brushed aside. One keeps any unpleasantness strictly to himself. An American woman at a party who complains about the heat or the servants is not apt to be invited again. You see, the Thais are rather steadfast Buddhists. Self-control and tolerance come naturally to them. But don't believe that there is anything of the Puritan about them. They take to pleasures joyously, but in moderation. Where underprivileged youths in urban America form gangs and become ardent lawbreakers, Thai teen-agers often serve an apprenticeship as acolytes and novices in Bangkok's temples and practice the austerities."

He settled deep down in his long chair, lit a cigarette, and sighed contentedly. "A number of servicemen are so enamored of Bangkok that they say they want to live here as representatives of some big American firm. However, there's one big fly in the ointment."

I guessed it, and ventured, "The price of rents."

"Exactly. For a small apartment in the capital you have to pay $250 a month. And good ones are hard to find. Thailand, as you know, is the geopolitical heart of Southeast Asia, of all those countries that lie east of India and south of China. This crackling prosperity of the last five years has sent property prices skyrocketing, but construction is going on everywhere. Look at this hotel, at the large extension going on right over there—three hundred more rooms to be ready in a year."

"Can you still get servants?"

"Well, servants are incredibly cheap, but there aren't many experienced ones, and if you don't speak Thai there is a problem. Wages in general are so low, in fact, as to be scandalous. You see those women over there moving barrows of sticky earth to make a garden extension." I looked where he pointed and saw females in dirty sarongs and attractive lamp-shade hats doing heavy work. "What do you think they're paid for a day's work? The equivalent of seventy-five cents."

"You mean an hour."

"No, for an eight-hour day. Their husbands, those men working the tractors, get a dollar a day.* Since that isn't quite enough to support a family, even with commodities so cheap, the wives work to supplement the family budget."

As we watched the women rolling the heavy wheelbarrows on narrow planks, their sarongs spattered with mud, I remarked how strong they were and healthy-looking, and seemingly not at all put-upon. "Of course," the Captain said, "it's unfair for Americans to judge everything by our standards. The food these people eat is not only dirt-cheap, but they most likely raise their own.

---

* Wages have gone up substantially since 1967.

"Incidentally, another fly in the honeyed Bangkok ointment is the price of American or German beer. A bottle of Bud in the top bars costs about sixty cents. Let's have some." He called a boy and ordered two beers. "It's the freight and the tax, but I can't take their native beer. This country needs a first-rate brewery. Whiskey is high, too. You see, these Buddhists are supposed to be teetotalers like the Mohammedans. But where the Mohammedans were allowed four wives, the old Siamese kings sometimes took them by the dozens. Incidentally again, did you ever see more desirable and delectable bodies than those Thai girls in the coffeeshop? With those hip-clinging sarongs reaching just below the ankles, they make most of these miniskirted foreign dolls look dubious second choices."

The beer came, and we drank pleasurably as a breeze stirred and a blonde Swedish beauty in a white bikini leaped from the diving board into the cooling water.

After a moment the young officer said, "This is the place of places for *la dolce vita*—but without hard liquor or orgy." He glanced at his wristwatch and sat up straight. "I am about to miss a barber appointment," he said. "Will you excuse me? A Thai barber is like none other on earth."

I found that out for myself at half past five. We had luxuriated in *dolce far niente* all day, talking with Thais in the arcade shops and lunching in the coffeeshop, where several of the waitresses in their salmon- or yellow- or apricot-colored sarongs and scanty vests might each well have won the Miss Thailand title in a Miss Universe contest.

The barbershop in the Siam Intercontinental on the mezzanine next door to the Pan American Airways office was nothing extraordinary in appearance, a mere two-chair setup with first-class modern appliances. But its services were unique in my experience with barbershops from Finnish Lapland to plush Buenos Aires. When I was seated in the chair everything started out in orthodox fashion. The pleasant middle-aged barber, who knew only a few words of English, seemed to understand precisely how I wanted my hair cut. The bootblack, a hardy Thai boy of about twelve with a dash of Chinese blood in him, assumed before my nod that I wanted a shine and set to work assiduously. After finishing the left shoe, he deftly pushed the trouser leg up to the knee, yanked down my sock and began to massage my calf and ankle with practiced fingers.

My surprise, in staring down at him quizzically with a mild, what-the-hell, inquiring look, was met by a beguiling grin. His eyes seemed to say, "The joke is on you. Just relax." His ministrations almost immediately began to feel good, as he relieved the muscles still tensed by temple-hopping at Angkor. I was all but purring when he moved over to the right calf.

When the barber finished with the haircut and I indicated my satisfaction after surveying myself in the two mirrors, he began to knead the back of my neck and dig deep into my shoulders. Then he unbuttoned the three top buttons of my shirt and ran his fingers down along both sides of my spine. He massaged my upper arms to the elbow. Then, firmly grasping one arm, he brought it back first over my head and around across my chin until I crackled. He repeated the manipulation with the other arm. As the last smidgen of tension dissolved, I let out a contented sigh.

Then I sat up straight, on guard, as he brought under my amazed eyes a chisel and a tiny spoon and pincers and swabs of cotton dipped in peroxide. Instinctively, I said, "Oh, no!" "He only wants to clean your ears," a feminine voice called behind me. She was the manicurist, who was returning from the beauty parlor next door. "It's a Thai custom. In this humid climate ears should get an occasional thorough cleaning. It was a regular monthly service with barbers until recently the jealous doctors protested that legally only they were qualified for professional ear-cleaning. The barber must like you; he is offering you a special favor."

I regarded the chisel and the spoon obliquely and shook my head politely. I said that I had to change for dinner. Then I made up for my reluctance with triple-sized tips for the boy and the barber. Bowing my thanks like a Japanese for the extra courtesies, I left the barbershop in a state of euphoria. Before I reached our room I felt like kicking myself that I had not experienced a thorough ear-cleaning at least once in my life.

Another King and I

The quality of the hotel telephone operators was something as fresh in my experience as the Thai barber techniques. The girl who called me Tuesday morning at eight with a faint tinkle of the bell did not announce the time in the impersonal voice of custom. In the most dulcet tones imaginable, very softly, she murmured, "Dr. Strode—it's wake-up time." The voice was so inflected and melodious that her announcement sounded like song, as if she had been an angel chorister. The note on "wake-up" was high and lilting, and descended the scale on "time." She seemed loath to disturb my slumber but to suggest that like Pippa I would find on this lovely, lovely morning that all was right with the world.

I could hardly refrain from telling her that on this special day I was to be received by her King. While dressing, I began turning over in my mind what I knew about the man. An outstanding fact that struck Americans was that King Bhumibol had not been born in Siam but in Cambridge, Massachusetts (December 5, 1927). At the time, his princely father was studying medicine at Harvard. But the King had not learned to speak English in America, for his father had died when he was two and the widow had returned to Siam with him, his older brother, Ananda, and a sister. Then when the coup of 1932 abolished the absolute attributes of the monarchy, the perturbed mother fled with her little ones to Switzerland. There in Lausanne, in a rented villa, Bhumibol spent his childhood and was a day pupil at the Ecole Nouvelle de Chailly. It was in Switzerland that he learned to speak fluent English, and French and German as well. In his teens, Bhumibol, who had a keen sense of rhythm and a special talent for the clarinet and saxophone, became an American jazz enthusiast. And when he was old enough to get a driver's license he fancied fast sports cars.

Bhumibol's older brother, Ananda, who had been declared king at the age of ten when their uncle abdicated, continued his studies in Switzerland until he reached his majority and returned to Bangkok to be crowned. But Ananda's reign was one of the shortest in Siamese history; it ended tragically in six months. On June 9, 1946, the young King was found dead in his room with a bullet through his forehead. The revolver lying nearby was unquestionably his own. Suicide was spoken of—and murder was whispered. But undoubtedly it was an accident. So virtually everyone believes, though the mystery has never been cleared up. To the gay-hearted, jazz-loving Bhumibol it was a sad blow. He had never expected to sit on the throne of his grandfather. Kingship for him was something rather awful to face at eighteen. But the Regency in Thailand insisted that he complete his European education. After finishing his undergraduate studies he entered law school. He played less jazz, but he continued to drive fast. One day he had a smashup on a curving Swiss road. He was badly hurt and almost lost his left eye.

During his painful stay in the hospital, Sirikit, the lovely young daughter of the Thai ambassador to Great Britain, came to cheer him and to help with the nursing. Though she was his second cousin and herself the granddaughter of a queen, he had met her for the first time in Paris at an official reception when her father was ambassador to France. He was then fourteen, and he came close to falling in love. In the hospital he knew he was in love and wanted her for his consort. When he finished his law studies and returned to Bangkok, the royal wedding took place in April, 1950. In May came the gala coronation. Never was a union more popular with the Thai people. A daughter was born in 1951. Then on July 28, 1952, national rejoicing occurred when a son and heir to the throne was born. The Crown Prince was given the name of Vajiralongkorn, and in time he was sent to school in England, where he was now. Two other girls completed the family.

Most significantly, I knew that the King was a devout Buddhist, and that he had served his term in a monastery. I had read that he had shaved his head and humbly stood in the street with his rice bowl. Since I had planned nothing I was to say to His Majesty, it occurred to me that Buddhism in Thailand might be a lead.

Just before Mr. Long was to pick me up I posted a package at the special mail booth in the hotel lobby. The clerk was in his early twenties, inclined to chubbiness, with one of those Thai smiles that help make a stranger's day go right. After he had weighed the parcel and given me back my change, I said, "Tell me frankly, confidentially, what do the people think of their King?" Somewhat surprised, he looked at me steadily with his gentle eyes, then said feelingly, "We absolutely adore him." His conviction was of such simple intensity that I almost felt rebuked.

Stopping at the branch office of World Travel Service near the hotel entrance to make final arrangements about a guide and car for the next day, I noticed a large colored photograph of the King on some gala occasion. His Majesty was being borne on the Royal Golden Chair, elevated on poles by eight gold-helmeted bearers. A salmon-colored umbrella on a ten-foot extension shaded him. An oval feathered fan on an elongated handle ceremoniously cooled his head, a smaller one cooled his back. A great wide-brimmed black hat, with the left side curled up almost rakishly, further shielded him from the tropical sun, and round-lens dark glasses protected his eyes from the glare. Over his yellow court costume was worn a loose white silk coat with cloth-of-gold cuffs. An enormous eight-pointed star set with emeralds and rubies was pinned just below the heart, out of the way of other blazing decorations and two dangling necklaces studded with precious stones. His Majesty's silken court breeches stopped about three inches below his knees. The mauve silk stockings revealed surprisingly well-turned and sturdy legs in one so slight of build. On either side of him walked bemedaled dignitaries of state in white or red tunics according to their offices. Siamese kings once rode on proud imperial elephants, but this recent picture seemed to suggest holy processions in Catholic capitals, when the images of Jesus or regional saints make a street progress on honored shoulders through devout throngs.

I had read that a special charisma clung about the Thai Royal Family like a flattering mist. I knew that the illusive word "charisma" meant "grace," "favor," "gift," and was akin to the Greek *chairein* "to rejoice." Sirikit was reputed to be the most beautiful queen among the few still current; her only rival since Saroya of Iran had been set aside was the young Danish-born Anne Marie of Greece. I had seen many pictures of Queen Sirikit in Balmain frocks, as she was hailed year after year one of the "ten best-dressed women." Yet, to me, she looked more lovely in her native costume, with the body-clinging silken sarong reaching almost to the floor. Which would she wear this day: Paris or Thai?

As I awaited Mr. Long, I felt a pleasant anticipation at the imminent audience. I had known two other kings: the aging, scholarly, universally admired Gustaf VI Adolf of Sweden and the young, handsome, huge, athletic Constantine of Greece. I had admired them both for their qualities. But hedging them about was not that reputed charisma of Bhumibol and his Queen.

Someone offered me a copy of a morning paper. My first glance caught a small front-page item that made me frown. At eleven o'clock Her Majesty was receiving a special delegation of women journalists from Australia, and she was being televised for some prominent Australian channel. Eleven o'clock was the hour of my audience. Though Mr. Long distinctly wrote that *Their* Majesties would receive me, I recalled what Mrs. Johnson, the wife of our ambassador to Japan, had said to me: "If your wife does not accompany you, the Queen will not appear."

Mr. Long, a tall, amiable San Franciscan was here, and we were off to the Chancellery. In answer to some questions, Mr. Long explained: "The so-called Revolutionary party instituted the present government when it seized power in another bloodless coup on October 20, 1958. It purported to stabilize the national economy and to better the people's standard of living by developing the nation's natural resources."

I had read that the former premier, Sarit Thanarat, chief of the army, was noted for his progressive ideas, that he lived extravagantly, and, according to wild gossip, he kept a hundred mistresses, known as "minor wives."

"Well," said Mr. Long, "the present government is headed by Prime Minister Thanom Kittikachorn—since 1963. He is a contrast to his predecessor in his simple tastes. He scorns night life, and he has resigned from all his private businesses. Of course, the King is the nominal head of state, chief commander of the army, and head of the Buddhist church. But in reality an oligarchy of a few strong men—fourteen cabinet ministers—rules in Thailand.

"King Bhumibol's cherishing of one wife—his striking monogamy —pleases the Thais," Mr. Long went on. "His famous grandfather is reputed to have had a number of wives. The present royal couple are remarkably compatible. They share numerous interests. They took painting lessons together. They both enjoy sailing. They are continually engaged in dedicating schools, libraries, roads, bridges, dams. The great Bhumibol Dam, which holds back the waters of the Ping River and irrigates a million acres of rich farming lands in the central plain, was named for the King. The new dam is one of the best things that has happened to Thailand. The turbines in the five-hundred-foot-high seashell-shaped barrier have tripled the nation's electrical output since 1964. From the Bhumibol Dam is generated the power that keeps the blessed air conditioners running in your hotel and all over Bangkok.

"The King is naturally creative, with varied talents. A few years ago he built a thirteen-foot sailboat and steered it himself across the Gulf of Siam—a sixteen hours' sail. Sailing, after music, is his chief hobby. He has composed enough music for the Royal Band to put on an all-night concert of his works alone. He likes to join the band sometimes with his saxophone. In 1950, you may recall, Mike Todd used the King's 'Blue Night' in his Broadway production of *Peep Show*.

"By the way," he said, handing me a typewritten slip of paper, "as a footnote of possible interest, you might like to know that while Bangkok is the name popularly given to the capital, the Thais call it Krung Thep, City of Angels, an abbreviated form of the official name. Read the paper."

I read aloud the typewritten words:

Krung Thep Pra-maha-nakorn, Amorn-Ratanakosindra, Mahindra-Yudhya, Maha-Dilokpop, Noparatana-Rajdhani, Burirom, Udom-Vish-nukarn-Prasit. Roughly translated, this lengthy title means: The City of Gods, the Great City, the Residence of the Emerald Buddha, the Impregnable City of God Indr, the Grand Capital of the World Endowed with Nine Precious Gems, the Happy Abounding in Enormous Royal Palaces which Resemble the Heavenly Abode Wherein Dwell the Reincarnated Gods, a City Given by Indr and Built by Vishnukarn.

"The Thais do like long names—like the Welsh," I said, "as long as umbrellas."

"The King's full title is even longer than the city's name," Mr. Long said, as our car stopped at the Chancellery door.

I was received by the Minister, Illinois-born Norman B. Hannah, who said that he was going to accompany me to the Royal Palace and that we would go in the Ambassador's car. I noticed Mr. Hannah's smart bow tie of bronze-colored Thai silk. At the last hour I had decided against a bow tie as perhaps too informal and had bought a Thai silk cravat of black with discreet silver stripes to go with my thin black suit.

It was a beautiful, sun-splashed morning, not unpleasantly warm. While chatting I recalled the protocol of King Mongkut's era and inquired about current procedure. "Well," said Mr. Hannah with a grin, "you no longer have to prostrate yourself on the rug before His Majesty. But when the audience is over—he decides when—you back about six paces, until he turns his face away, and then you may turn and walk out."

He told me one other thing that I might bear in mind. "At the King's thirty-ninth birthday celebrations the past December, what pleased His Majesty more than all the manifestations of popular devotion and the flood of gifts was a cable from England announcing that his boy stood at the top of his class in mathematics. Incidentally, the Prince is preparing at Rugby before he enters a university."

We arrived at the gates of the Chitralada Palace a bit ahead of time and could drive slowly through the extensive landscaped gardens where drooping shower-of-gold trees were in luxuriant bloom. Bhumibol had built for himself a modern villa as his official residence. It was not extraordinary, but it was agreeable and attractive; some portions were embowered in bougainvillaea. He had eschewed his grandfather's pompous palace and used it only for housing foreign sovereigns and top V.I.P.'s. As the car stopped under the portico we were received by two Thai gentlemen in white uniforms decorated with medals. One was quite tall, slim, suave, and sophisticated, the King's private secretary. The other, an admiral, was stocky and slightly under medium height. I think the latter was chief of protocol. This first reception room was furnished in attractive polished bamboo. We chatted for a minute or so and remained standing. I noted the Admiral eying me sharply. He came up very close. At length he took hold of my left lapel and said, "I see that you have been knighted by the King of Sweden; that black rosette goes with the Royal Order of the North Star." I was really taken aback. "How on earth did you know that?" I said. The Admiral smiled blandly, his eyes narrowed like a detective's. "I was trained," he said, "at the Royal Naval School in Sweden."

At precisely eleven, we were ushered out into a corridor, then entered a large high-ceilinged drawing room. Renoirs graced one wall, and two full-length oil portraits hung on another, one of Chulalongkorn as an oldish man and one of Queen Sirikit in her fresh young beauty. Before a small davenport stood His Majesty in a black business suit. He was slight of build, about five feet six, and wearing thick-lensed horn-rimmed glasses. His black eyes were somber and penetrating. His mouth had a serious expression, almost sorrowful. His prominent ears stood out slightly from his head, as if on the alert to catch what was in the wind. I was struck by the contrast to my first meeting with the easy, radiantly smiling, physically magnificent young Constantine of Greece—in 1965. But through some intuitive chemistry I was instantly drawn to this grave young man. I was presented and bowed. Then somewhat to my surprise His Majesty advanced and extended his hand, and we shook hands. I had heard that once it was death to touch the person of Siamese royalty and that a nineteenth-century queen had been allowed to drown when her royal barge suffered a collision on the river and sank, for no one dared reach out a grasping hand to save her. Chairs arranged for me and the American Minister were set at a right angle to the monarch's settee. I was waved to the chair nearest His Majesty. In the movements of being seated I noted in the farthest corner photographers and a television setup in operation near the portrait of Queen Sirikit. In an ensuing pause I suddenly felt impelled to speak. "Your Majesty," I said, "in the two days I have been in your kingdom I have been greatly impressed by the gentleness and innate kindness of your people. I have the feeling that their amiability is due partly to the Thai custom of every man's spending some time in a Buddhist monastery."

The King eyed me responsively. His somber expression lightened. His lips almost curled in a smile. I saw that I had struck a good note. "I myself became a monk for a brief period." "I was aware of that," I confessed, "and your famous grandfather—on the wall there—lived a monastic life for five years." He saw that I had read some Siamese history. From here the audience went easily, without the slightest strain. His Majesty kept me in conversation for two hours.

When the photographers and television people silently folded their gear and departed through curtains in the far corner of the room, the hangings were not completely closed. A dark-faced figure appeared in the aperture and riveted his black eyes on me. At first

I thought it was some curious servant, but since he remained, a half-concealed fixture, throughout the audience, I believe that he was a security guard and most likely a deadly shot.

The King was speaking of the Communist infiltration. "A stranger enjoying the comforts of the luxury hotels or buying jewelry and silks in our modern shops is not faintly aware of the encroaching danger in the northeast. Thai-born Chinese, lured to Peiping and trained there in subversive methods and guerrilla warfare, sneak daily from Laos into our hinterland. They do everything they can to *retard* progress, and cry down the benefits of governmental services. A few hundred social workers, doctors, nurses, and teachers are murdered each year. The killers are hard to track down, because the simple villagers fear reprisals. Some Communist intruders are relentlessly shot by border police, though not officially. But the Mekong River, which divides Thailand from Laos, meanders for 550 miles. That makes border patrol as uncertain as it is hazardous. Although there are some 20,000 men of the U.S. Air Force based in northeast Thailand, the infiltration increases."

When I asked the King about birth control, which was assuming new positive aspects in Japan and India, his lips turned down wryly. "If the Thais practiced birth control," he said, "we should eventually all be Chinese. The Chinese are heavy breeders. They scorn birth-control practices and take joy in increasing their numbers." When I drove through the teeming Chinese section the next day, I could understand his apprehension.

"As for the Thais," he said, "we could feed a far greater population than we have now. We possess an ever-abundant food supply. Our people have never known hunger. As you know, we *export* foodstuffs. Rice is our chief commodity. More than 75 per cent of our cultivated land is planted in rice. The fine, long-stapled, non-glutinous quality of Thailand rice makes it eagerly sought in world markets. Our rice keeps some other nations alive. And we have several crops of fresh vegetables and fruits a year. We raise sugar cane, tapioca, peanuts, soybeans, coconuts, sweet potatoes, a top grade of pepper, and an overabundance of bananas. Our fishing fleet numbers almost 5,000 boats. So my people have plenty to eat, you may be sure. We are in a very different situation from poor India. When Marlon Brando was here recently he could talk of nothing but hunger in India, where he had just been. He was shattered. He seemed to want the United States to pour every cent of her foreign aid into feeding the destitute Indians. I could not comfort him by pointing out that India had always been stalked by hunger and that the unfortunate, half-alive wretches had always been a terrible drain on the nation. India has mighty need for birth control. Thailand doesn't."

We spoke of America's extraordinary faith in democracy and its seemingly naïve belief that the solution for backward nations was "one man, one vote." We agreed that some countries were by no means ready for democracy. The King pointed out the inherent danger from Communist or Chinese minorities if Thailand had immediate universal suffrage. Then he said quietly, with grave emphasis, "Sometimes, democracy can be the most cruel of dictators."

He shifted slightly in his seat. "I am happy to say, however, that we are now working on a constitution. We need one, and we have not had one since 1958, when the twenty-sixth bloodless coup since Chulalongkorn's reign occurred. It will be ready by midsummer of 1968."

I mentioned the enormous popularity of His Majesty and the Queen with his people. I said I had been told that almost every home in the land, to the humblest hut, had his picture hanging on the wall, and even the cells of monks.

"Oh, yes, we are rather constantly at work," he said, with a shrug. "We travel far—into the remote regions of the land. I often drive the jeep myself over roads that could hardly be called roads. People come from all about. On a recent trip in the far north, an old man had walked more than twenty miles to see the King. Half-exhausted, he crept up to the car to get a long look at me. He held out a parcel wrapped in a large leaf. 'After so far a journey, I thought Your Majesty would be hungry. So I brought you some lunch. I fixed one lunch for you and one for me.' He did not apologize for the food's simplicity, or grovel and say, 'I know it's not much, but it's all I had.' He just presented it with a dignified, man-to-man gesture, as if he knew I would be grateful. Mind you," King Bhumibol said, with an appreciative smile, "he did not offer me *both* lunches. He had no notion of giving up his lunch—even to me. And though a nice picnic basket had been prepared for me at the last town, I had to eat the old man's frugal fare." Mr. Hannah and I both chuckled.

"From time to time," the King went on, "the Queen and I must appear together in this part of the country and that. We have been to places so rough that to get to our destination my wife has had to walk five miles over rocky terrain in heavy rubber-soled sneakers. You see, we are the outward manifestation of the national unity." An acid note had crept into his voice. "We are very useful to the government."

I looked at the King questioningly as his tone changed. "But I have no power," he went on. "I see so much that should be done, which I *could* do. But I must do nothing direct. For instance, as a minimal example, if I am driving about Bangkok with my equerries and we pass a stagnant curve in a klong, I can say, 'That place stinks and should be cleaned up,' but I cannot order it done."

In the peculiar emphasis he put on the word "stinks," I knew that his enormous popularity did not make up to him for the loss of constructive ideas he might have put into operation if he had had more authority. Being elevated above political combat, King Bhumibol and the Queen set the standard of style and deportment and were in truth "the glass of fashion and the mould of form, the observed of all observers." And though in their roles they became idols of the people, for whom he had a passionate affection, the King found his position a bit galling.

I glanced across the room at the dominating portrait of Chulalongkorn, who had wielded an absolute power. I could wonder at what the old man would think of the turn of events in his grandson's time. And I could not help but reflect on the difference in the home life of this soft-spoken, serious-minded, troubled, monogamous king with that of his expansive grandsire and his great-grandsire, whose glittering palace buzzed with wives and concubines.

A slithering movement at my left caused me to glance down quickly. A middle-aged dark man in white was approaching the right side of the King on his knees with practiced speed. He was bearing a tall crystal glass in a gold filigree holder. He set it on the table at His Majesty's right elbow. It looked like orange juice. A moment later the cup bearer, still on his knees, slid two beakers onto the little table between Mr. Hannah and me. So one custom of ancient Siam was still extant. A serving man approached the King on his knees and to the side. His head must always be lower than the sovereign's. I smiled secretly to recall what a difficult time Anna had had trying to get her head lower than Mongkut's when he lay stretched on the floor reading.

Noting that I had glanced several times at Chulalongkorn's strong portrait, the King observed, "The world seems to admire only my grandfather. It wants to give him the entire credit for the so-called 'modernizing' of Siam. But it was my great-grandfather, Mongkut, Rama IV, who abandoned the policy of isolation and opened Siam to Western commerce and influence. He brought over European experts to help him reorganize government services for the good of his people. But he died in 1868 and had a comparatively short reign of seventeen years. Incidentally, in the quarter century before he acceded to the throne, my great-grandfather was a Buddhist priest. Chulalongkorn followed in his father's steps, and after his tutelage. Of course, he went much farther in reforms. He increased the pace. But, mind you, he had a reign of forty-two years in which to accomplish his ends."

"I almost believe that you admire your great-grandfather more than your world-famous grandfather," I ventured.

The King half smiled and made no protest of denial.

I felt quite thirsty, but His Majesty had not touched the inviting orange juice, and I presumed that by protocol I was not to sip until he did. But he was so amiable, so sincere, so engaging in his serious way, and I felt such a genuine rapport with him, that I made so bold as to touch the gold handle of the container and say, "May I?" Then I drank a good draft. The King politely took up his glass and sipped, and so, gratefully, did the American Minister.

The King questioned me about this special round-the-world trip of ours and then about my home. I told him that we lived in twenty acres of Alabama woods, in a kind of private bird sanctuary in a sort of Swedish modern house, with lots of glass, looking on dogwood trees. I said that in our long married life we had never possessed a radio or television to upset the peace, that our music came from bird song: wood thrushes, cardinals, mockingbirds. I said that I wrote my books in longhand on a wooden lapboard in a studio away from the house, and that my wife did the typing. He looked at me oddly, with something like a momentary wistfulness.

I finished off the beaker of orange juice. Then, as I bespoke my admiration for the stunning portrait of Queen Sirikit on the wall I suddenly realized that I did not grieve too much that I had missed the exquisite lady. While I had longed to meet the lovely beauty, who was regarded as a virtual work of art in herself, the conversation would have taken a different turn if the Queen had been present. Doubtless the audience would have been terminated much sooner. His Majesty had been very frank with me, and underlying all the talk the burden on his heart was perceptible. What would happen to his beloved country in the next few years? Cambodia, Laos, and Burma, which surrounded Thailand on the east, north, and west, were already half Communist in sympathy or policy. Red China with its might was actually not much more than one hundred miles away from the Thai frontier at one place—the distance of Richmond from Washington. What would happen when the American forces were pulled out of South Vietnam? That was King Bhumibol's night-and-day concern.

As a last cheering word, I said, "A German naturalist expressed what I already feel for Your Majesty's country. 'Anyone who has breathed the air of Thailand, who has savored its sweetness and bitterness and silvery enchantment, will dream of the day he can return.' "

The King looked pleased and moved to the edge of his settee. "The Thais set high value on what they call *chai yen*," he said. "It means 'cool heart,' and is a synonym for equanimity. My people endeavor under all situations to maintain a tranquil atmosphere in the world of business and in their own families. But—in these dangerous days—well, it isn't so easy."

Mr. Hannah and I moved forward in our chairs. The King rose. We stood. Out of the corner of my eye I noted the black-eyed dark figure, still a fixture between the draperies.

When I expressed profound gratitude to His Majesty for granting me this audience, I think he divined my sincere sympathy for his problems. He stepped forward and took my hand warmly. A friendly smile lighted his face. I had started to back away when an impulse struck me. I moved up close to him—hoping the man in the corner would not shoot—and said somewhat hesitantly, "May I be so very bold as to beg Your Majesty for a photograph of yourself and your lovely Queen?" He was taken by surprise, but seemed in no wise displeased. "In my studio in Alabama," I added quickly, "I have inscribed photographs of the King of Sweden and the King of Greece—and if I could have photographs of Your Majesties, I would be happy indeed." The King nodded something like assent, though I did not hear exactly what he said, and I again began backing away. In the first reception room we made our adieus to those of the royal staff who were waiting to see us off. The Ambassador's car was at the door. "I see why his people love him," I said to the tall private secretary. "Incidentally, His Majesty is going to send me photographs. I am staying at the Siam Intercontinental." A clock struck one.

"He kept you two hours," Mr. Hannah said as we drove away. I glanced at him. "I hope I did not wear you completely out. I got a bit carried away. I liked him, and he was so easy to talk to."

"Some of the talk was illuminating to me," Mr. Hannah said. But I had a feeling that he was not altogether pleased that I had been in such agreement with the King's ideas and had doubted democracy as a cure-all. We stopped by his club, where he was late for a luncheon engagement. Then he instructed the chauffeur to take me to my hotel.

That evening I half expected that the photographs might be delivered to my room. But none came then or during the next five days of our Bangkok sojourn. Perhaps His Majesty's consent had merely been Oriental politeness. A Thai can hardly bear to say no. As we circled the rest of the globe I lost all hope of receiving the royal photographs. And then, shortly after New Year's Day, the photographs arrived at my home in Alabama, forwarded from the Thai Embassy in Washington. The King had not forgotten.

I had expected black-and-white photographs and was considerably surprised by the colored photographs that arrived in two oblong boxes of deep-blue Thai silk. The sterling-silver frames, delicately chased with stylized ornamentation and bearing medallions in white enamel and gold with different emblems for the King and for the Queen, were backed by polished teakwood. The photograph of the King was signed in a strong masculine hand, with the signature underscored. I was deeply touched by His Majesty's gracious generosity.

Siamese Phantasmagoria

At nine the next morning a telephone call from the tourist office in the lobby said that a car and a guide were waiting to take us to the best of the temples, of which there were three hundred in Bangkok. Then he added, "I saw you on TV last night with our King." "Really? I would have looked myself in the lobby," I said, "if I had known it was to be." But I was feeling grateful that the Intercontinental had no TV set in any of the bedrooms to disturb the pastoral peace.

In the lobby a bright-eyed, slim young man presented himself to us. I was instantly struck by two long, wiry hairs that curled out from a small flat mole on the left cheek of his dark face. I had seen one other such blemish only three days before on an oldish Cambodian porter at the Siem Reap airport. Was it a fetish or superstition of some kind that nurtured and retained these twin two-inch-long hairs? Later, when I knew the guide better and had discerned that he was something of a flirt, he confessed that he kept the two hairs as a talisman to draw the attention of girls. And he had another physical idiosyncrasy, which he demonstrated: he could twitch his left eyebrow, as some people can wriggle their ears. A number of Thais had this peculiarity, he said, and that was the reason that the eyebrows as well as the head hair of young monks were shaved —so that they would not be tempted to flirt. The twitching eyebrow was supposed to carry a more potent charge than any winking of one eye.

Our young guide, who had been to college, was as knowledgeable and informative as he was engaging. He talked agreeably and volubly. As we drove out of the spacious grounds of the Siam Intercontinental into the stream of traffic, he reminded us of the amazing change in Joseph Conrad's Bangkok. "Less than twenty years ago," he said, twisting about in his front seat and facing backward, "Bangkok possessed great canals with lotus flowers. Now they have become six-lane boulevards. Once, stilted houses and poled boats were silhouetted in the water. Today this ceaseless motor cavalcade, as you see, is reflected in the glassy fronts of modernistic business structures. Hardly a decade ago mango orchards flourished and water buffaloes grazed where today there are paved streets and housing developments."

"Tell me a bit about your ancient history," I suggested.

He accepted the challenge with pleasure. "The Thais came originally out of southeast China below the Yangtze River valley. In the latter part of the seventh century they founded the smallish independent kingdom of Nanchao. Invading hordes of Kublai Khan in 1250 presumably caused a mass migration southward to our present home, known for centuries as Siam. In the fertile Chao Phraya River valley we became the dominant race. There were various periods in our early history, and several capitals. Finally, in 1350, the capital was established at Ayudhya, fifty-five miles north of the present Bangkok. That's the main thing you need to know. In 1431 Siam's King Boromaraja II captured the fabulous city of Angkor in Cambodia and caused the Khmers to abandon their capital and move far south to Phnom Penh.

"Altogether, thirty-three kings ruled in Ayudhya during 417 years. Then a surprise invasion of Burmese from the west came in 1767. The beautiful capital was sacked and burned. Most of its citizens were massacred. The king was lost in the holocaust. The survivors fled south, and fifty-five miles downriver they established a new capital at Thonburi, just across the water from this present Bangkok. The Siamese had been driven from their templed city, just as they had driven the Khmers from Angkor three centuries before. But after a few years the top surviving general, Phra Chao Tak Sin, half-Chinese, half-Siamese, rallied his forces. He returned to Ayudhya, routed the Burmese, and sent them scurrying to their own boundaries. But Ayudhya was never again to be the capital. In the Khmer style of architecture, the new leader built the magnificent temple at Thonburi called Wat Arun, the Temple of the Dawn. Then, strangely, he became raving mad and was assassinated. Another strong man arose, a young general named Chao Phya Chakri. He assumed the crown as Rama I. In 1782 he removed the capital from Thonburi to the east bank of the river at Bangkok, and began building the fantastic temples that men cross the ocean to see. The dynasty Chakri established exists today. My King Bhumibol is a direct descendant, known as Rama IX." He paused and looked at us intently to see if we were still interested. Then he quickly finished off his history digest.

"The first Europeans to appear in old Siam and at Ayudhya were those great seafarers the Portuguese, who arrived in the sixteenth century. In the next century came the Dutch, followed shortly by the British and finally the French, who briefly secured a mighty influence on the Siamese king. Louis XIV at Versailles was led to believe that the Siamese might be converted to Catholicism. In 1687 Louis sent a group of Jesuit missionaries, well supported, as most godly missions were, by troops and warships. The arrival of the foreign squadron and the establishment of two French garrisons caused alarm. Since the contemporary king of Siam lay mortally ill, a leader of an anti-alien faction seized the throne and demanded an immediate French evacuation. Then they ousted all other Europeans. From 1688, the Thais, distrusting all white men, became strictly isolationist, like the Japanese, and remained so for a century and a half.

"Rama III was the last of the Siam kings to obstruct all Western influence. Mongkut, his half brother, who succeeded him as Rama IV in 1851, saw no advantage in the isolationist policy. He signed a treaty of commerce and friendship with Great Britain in 1855, and soon made other treaties with the United States and many Continental governments. He was undertaking a kind of modernization when he suddenly died. Then in 1868 came Chulalongkorn."

A pretty young Thai woman driver (in a brand-new Chevrolet) came dangerously close to hitting our car; she apologized by waving disarmingly and flashing a dimpled smile. The guide shrugged. "My people," he said, "are as delighted with their new motor vehicles as ten-year-old American boys used to be with toy electric trains before the space age. These last few years Thai girls have learned to drive with grace, if with dubious skill. They envied those independent female secretaries from the embassies who drove like men —and when prosperity hit us, we bought cars like mad."

I commented on several Mercedes in transit. "Yes," he said, "the Mercedes-Benz is the special status symbol here. The change in aspect and tempo in these last dozen years has been phenomenal. Of course, prosperity has been accelerated by aid from the United

States in the way of loans and subsidies offered Thailand—to make
a good show window for the rest of the Southeast. Thanks to the
U.S.O.M., Thailand's industrial growth has been tremendous since
the United States has had soldiers fighting for the freedom of South
Vietnam. And to further prosperity and help Thailand forestall the
Red menace, the U.S.A. is kindly employing a few thousand servicemen to help us construct strategic paved roads and some ordinary
roads of convenience to link villages in the hinterland. We greatly
need America's know-how and construction tools."

The young man went on talking, still twisted about in his seat as
we pushed on through the modern business districts. "Rarely does
a capital city stand for the entire country as Bangkok does. You
might even say Bangkok is Thailand. Its population is now beyond
two million. Only one other Thai city can boast of as many as
100,000 people. So Bangkok is the cultural center of the nation, as
well as the administrative head. Here we have five of the country's
six universities and several other special institutes of higher learning.
Bangkok has libraries, museums, the Thai National Theater, and
twenty-five daily newspapers—two in English. Yes, altogether
twenty-five—far more than New York, I am told. Bangkok, as you
know, is the headquarters of the Southeast Asia Treaty Organization—SEATO. As you may already know, we have the most modern
airport, and it serves over twenty international airlines. Bangkok is
the nucleus of a state railway founded in 1888, which today operates
almost 2,500 miles of railroad. As a center for international shipping,
the river port of Bangkok is able to handle vessels up to 10,000
tons. In 1965 outgoing ships carried more than three million tons
of export cargo, from rice and teak to silk fabrics and jewelry."

He spoke with frank pride, and he had his facts and figures at the
tip of his tongue. "Well, here we are!" We had reached the vast
complex of temples, where tiered pagodas and fanciful spires pointed
golden fingers at the intense blue sky.

As we left the car, I thought of Samuel Johnson's plain dictum
of two centuries ago: "The use of travelling is to regulate imagination by reality, and instead of thinking how things *may be*, to see
them as they are."

When you step through carved gateways flanked by gigantic
guardians in stone into one of the temple gardens with its sacred
trees and grotesque sculpted beasts, you are in a stranger world than

ever Alice slipped into. Here in these fantastic acres, wandering among these gifts of history like a pilgrim in Xanadu, you are so bedazzled by the unfamiliar forms and the embellishments of Siamese architecture that it is not easy to distinguish between imagination and a reality that you can actually touch with the palm of your hand. You seem to be straying in a dream realm, and you give yourself up to the spell and end by not recalling anything too clearly. Here even down-to-earth Dr. Johnson might have been bemused as well as enchanted.

Though the general scene of palaces, temples, chapels, pagodas, and spiraling *chedis*, those repositories of the ashes of dead kings, looked older than from the time of Marco Polo, our guide reminded us that Bangkok was about as young as Washington, D.C. It did not become the capital of Siam until late in the eighteenth century. The Grand Palace was begun by King Rama I in 1782. The Chapel Royal of the Emerald Buddha was constructed about the same time.

To many a traveler the colorful Grand Palace is one of the most spectacularly beautiful structures in the world. Its gleaming white walls emphasize the surrounding dazzling colors—bright orange, yellow, sky-blue, and the deep violet of the roofs. The near pagodas have twisted spires of gold encrusted with glass that rise at unexpected places dramatically. The glittering Kandharasdr Pavilion, decorated with broken pieces of colorful pottery, was built by King Mongkut. And in the nearby Pantheon, or Shrine of Kings, stands his statue, along with all the Siamese monarchs since 1782.

Within the Royal Palace the golden Niello Throne in the audience hall is an exquisite piece of elaborate Thai craftsmanship. In another room is the ceremonial altar, where Their Majesties today pay homage to the presiding Buddhist priest. The elaborate dressing room of bygone kings with the gilded mirrors, golden bowls and utensils, offers a show of elegance, set off by peach-colored silk walls.

Our guide indicated a door from which the boy Chulalongkorn, whom he often referred to as "Anna's pupil," peeped at the Englishwoman when she first arrived.

In the elaborate audience hall of Amarindra, the locale of state ceremonies, the most striking object is the great nine-tiered umbrella of white silk with silver trimming that rises above the golden throne almost to the red-beamed roof. The walls are of luminous blue tile in variegated designs. One may imagine King Mongkut presiding there in majestic solemnity, where his word was absolute law to the Siamese nation. But it was less easy to imagine how he kept in order his numerous wives scheming for advancement and how he policed his quantity of children, who had inherited some of his own animal spirits.

One object in the open courtyard that is most easily remembered is the platform contraption of red lacquer posts surmounted by gold pointed crowns at the edge of the white marble balustrades of the building in which the coronation ceremony takes place. "Here is the station where our King mounts his elephant in traditional cere-monials without having to be hoisted," the guide explained.

Perhaps the most impressive attraction of the Royal Compound is the Temple of the Emerald Buddha (Wat Phra Keo). The front façade is a creation of Oriental luster, of gold and multicolored mosaics, with three pairs of entrance stairs in fanciful tile, each guarded by colossal lions in black marble with snarling jaws agape. Nine ornate columns reputedly represent the major planets. The great lacquered doors are decorated with mother-of-pearl inlay. The famous Emerald Buddha is not really emerald at all, but pol-ished green jasper. The beautiful statuette, which is believed to be of Ceylon origin, is only twenty inches high. Its full figure is never revealed, for it is partially clothed in costumes of precious metals that are changed three times a year to accord with the three sea-sons: cool, hot, and rainy. Its elevation on an altar of tier after tier of pure gold is strikingly imposing, giving it importance and dignity. The very serenity of the figurine causes the viewers to tread lightly in their stocking feet through the vast hall.

Large statues of Buddha abound around the wall. On murals within and bas-reliefs on outside walls are depicted episodes of the Blessed One's life. Also, there are sculptured scenes from the Indian classic the *Ramayana*. In the courtyards rise nagas, serpents in stone, fancifully painted, and numerous mythological beasts in bronze. From here and there come the tinkling of wind bells touched by the breeze. It is very pleasant to submit to the allurement of this never-never land.

But the lingering spell was jarred when we stood before a "new" palace Chulalongkorn had built for himself at the turn of the century after his triumphant tour of Europe. He took a little here, a little there from all that he had admired architecturally, and he had had various elements mingled in an enormous building. Partly neoclassic, mixed with Versailles, it calls to mind the Opéra in Paris or some baroque Grand Hotel somewhere. Though it is grand, it is unsympathetic, and looks strikingly out of place among Siamese temples and the delicate needle spires of the *chedis.*

"My present King absolutely refused to live in such a place," the guide said. "He built himself the villa or small palace you saw yesterday."

We moved on to another wat, whose elementary school was in session; it was not completely alfresco, for it had a high roof, but was without outside walls. The pupils were so engaged in stealing smiling glances at tourists that I wondered how they could profit by their lessons. Personally, I was disappointed in this Temple of the Reclining Buddha (Wat Po), though the stretched-out figure, which measures more than 150 feet, is internationally famous. Because of the great square stone pillars that support the roof and surround the figure, one sees the image in sections. The only unobstructed view is of the mother-of-pearl soles of his feet at the farthest end of the building. Yet this temple is most popular with tourists. Natives, too, seem partial to this reclining colossus. We saw them buying square inches of very thin gold leaf and pasting them votively on smaller images lighted by a thousand candles.

I remarked upon the devout expressions on the faces of men who knelt and offered the wispy squares of gold, and our guide said in a low voice, "My people take their religion seriously. But," he added, as we went down the temple stairs to retrieve our shoes, "they wear it lightly. Ours is a soft, kindly manifestation of Buddhism, like that of Ceylon—not like Japan's Zen. My people try to live it in their daily life, and it gentles them. We have no church rules to gauge outward behavior. We are too happy-hearted for that, too pleasure-loving. There is no Catholic fear of a burning hell after death, though Thais still think that evil spirits have to be guarded against in this life. My people do not proselyte. And, frankly, if I may say so, we are rarely impressed by missionaries of any sect, however tolerant and sanitary they may be." His smile was beguiling.

We stopped at a vendor's stand in the forecourt where souvenirs and excellent temple rubbings were sold. I bought several of the latter, of stylized horses in groupings of threes, in rusty red, antique green, and black. On strong fibrous paper, the distinctive rubbings weighed next to nothing, and could be rolled up to take home for unusual presents.

Around us here and there monks in their thin saffron robes went about their duties. Some taught in the compound school; some recited sutras and performed ceremonies. All, we noted, had had their eyebrows shaved. Our guide claimed that there were more priests and monks and acolytes per capita in Thailand than in any other country. "Incidentally," he said, "my people drink little or no alcohol, and some forgo meat entirely, like the high Brahmin caste in India."

As we returned to our waiting car, the young man talked of strict daily routine in the monasteries. The monks rise at five and go into the temple for lengthy prayers. Once the signal for the new day's beginning was a cannon shot from the Royal Palace. Now at each monastery a man enters the bell tower and strikes the clapperless bell with a heavy gnarled root of bamboo. At eleven o'clock the monks assemble for breakfast—their only meal of the day. Their food comes partly from offerings of the grateful, who leave bowls and baskets of this and that at the gates. However, because there are thousands of priests in the city wats, many sally forth in the morning with their rice bowls. They never beg for food—the empty bowl does the begging. They merely stand before a house until someone comes out and fills the bowl with rice and fish and vegetables or whatever is available. No one resents feeding these mendicants, for he feels he is gaining rewards in the next incarnation.

"Of course, you know," our guide said, "that these monks take the vow of poverty along with that of chastity. They possess nothing but a yellow robe, sandals, a rice bowl, and a blue sunshade, which is their only luxury, but a necessity under our sun because of their shaven heads. You have seen the monks riding on the handlebars of someone's bicycle. Though they often have errands to do, no monk owns a bicycle, and he must 'hitch a ride,' as Americans say."

I reminded him that Buddha himself had one other personal possession: a toothpick.

"Yes, that is right," he said with a grin. "Our monks do, too."

Then, looking almost serious, he said, "You know, my people do not worship Buddha as God. He is merely the highest embodiment of the enlightened man. And truly ardent Buddhists strive to emulate his compassion. Perhaps this is why our crime rate is so low. In any case, the three pillars of Buddhism—tolerance, sympathy, and love—are they not really the keystone of all the world's worthwhile religions?"

The magic we had reveled in began to be dispelled when we got enmeshed in the traffic and the human jam of the Chinese quarter. This Sampheng, or "Chinese City," was once called the economic heart of Bangkok. The Thais by nature have little enough interest in trade, for which the Chinese have sharp talents. Shops and booths crowd each other with goods from all over the world spilling out onto the sidewalks, which are almost as thick with human beings as Broadway on New Year's Eve. The slow-moving mass makes jabbering uproar while tram bells clang warnings, automobiles sound horns brazenly and ceaselessly, motor bikes roar and weave dangerously through dubious openings, half-naked children scream delightedly at play along the gutters, and dignified Indian women glide with sedate gravity among the sea of yellow faces and Chinese costumes, the hems of their saris draggletailed in the muck and the dust. Many foreign tourists head straight for the Chinese markets to shop and haggle for bargains. But we only longed to get clear of the milling throng, the cacophony of blaring loud-speakers, and the shrill human hubbub. I had requested this glimpse of the Chinese quarter and I was glad to have seen it once, though I had not expected the snail's pace that seemed essential if we were to live another day.

When our guide divined that Thérèse was a bit shaken by our progress through the roaring clutter of the Chinese quarter, he reminded us gently that an American walking alone after dark in Bangkok was ten times safer than in Washington, D.C., or, for that matter, in most American cities.

"My people have a problem here with our Chinese population," the young man said. "They are very clever and persistent, the Chinese, and they get rich. They are the big businessmen and the little shopkeepers, the chief money-changers and restaurant proprietors. They cleverly get around a law that forbids Chinese to own property in Thailand. Many of the well-to-do Chinese simply bided

their time, after the law was put in effect, and then began to court
the daughters of Thai property owners; after marriage, when the
girls inherited properties, the Chinese husbands had control of
them. Now many of the handsome mansions you will see in the
residential areas are owned by Chinese or their Thai-Chinese sons.
The big trouble is that our government officials are concerned about
the ultimate loyalty of these Chinese. Many are suspected of being
secret agents of Peiping or Hanoi. Though the Thais' motto is
'live and let live,' there is little social mixing between the two
races in Bangkok, and the Chinese are not admitted to the best
clubs. Certain Japanese, however, are welcome."

Through the excitement-crammed hours I had had to wear a
jacket and tie, as everyone does in the Royal Palace Compound,
and though it had not been unpleasantly hot, I was relieved to
freshen up in our air-conditioned hotel room. It was soothing to
look out our window again on the calm reality of green lawns and
the far meadow, where the white ducks clustered contentedly under a shade tree by the stream like patriarchs of old in their tents
at noonday.

There were only two other temples—out of the special three
hundred—on the Bangkok side of the river that we strongly desired
to visit: the Marble Temple (Wat Benchamaborpitr) and Wat
Trimitr, with its five-and-a-half-ton golden Buddha. After a good
luncheon and welcome siesta we decided to visit these two straight
off.

The splendid Marble Temple is to me the most harmonious. It
sits alone, uncrowded, serene in a landscaped garden. It is the last
of the royal monastery temples built in Bangkok. Its construction
was ordered by King Chulalongkorn in 1899. Some experts deem
it the finest example of modern Thai architectural style in the
country. This handsome building of satiny white Carrara marble is
surmounted by varitiered roofs of golden Chinese tiles. It is pleasingly spectacular, from a distance and from close up. The ends of
the multiple roof sections are upturned and crowned with celestial
serpents, demigods of rain. All through the East one is reminded
that an enormous cobra once crawled up behind the Lord Buddha
and, instead of giving him the sting of death, raised itself on its
coil and spread its hood over the Holy One's head to protect him

from the rain. So roofs in Thailand make use of the holy-snake motif as protection against evil spirits. The temple windows of rich stained glass are set in gilt frames. Slender stylized lions sculptured from white marble guard the main entrance.

In the elegant interior a replica of a splendid early fourteenth-century Buddha sits surrounded by gold-stenciled tapestry. Crossbeams are of black lacquer and gold leaf. Chulalongkorn spared no expense, and though he could not or would not remove the Emerald Buddha to grace his new temple, he did have the ancient royal pavilion of the Wat Phra Keo brought to the Marble Temple grounds as a domicile for the chief priest. It had once been the residence of the young king himself when he was a monk for five years at the Temple of the Emerald Buddha. An interesting feature of the splendid inner courtyard is a collection of fifty-two bronze Buddhas brought from various Eastern countries and set up along the walls of the cloisters.

Our guide pointed out two huge turtles that were laboriously climbing up the slanting rock-facing of the klong, which ran along the west side of the garden. From the temple's boat landing, where monks take canoes to beg their daily fare, naked boys were diving into the klong and cavorting happily in the very shadow of the wat.

Though we had not particularly admired any of the arcaded statues in the courtyard of the Marble Temple, we were mightily impressed by the Buddha of Wat Trimitr. In a poor neighborhood, crowded by an elementary school in the temple complex, stands a small, narrow recent structure without style. But it houses a real treasure.

The image was brought to Wat Trimitr from an abandoned temple on land sold to the East Asiatic Company as part of a project to expand Bangkok port facilities. Because of its size and weight it was very difficult to remove. And since there was then no building large enough to contain it, it was placed under a temporary shelter in the monastery yard until May 25, 1953, when the new building was ready. While it was being transferred by cranes it crashed to the ground. That very night a torrential thunderstorm raged over Bangkok. The next day the abbot inspected the image and, finding it splattered with mud, he set about to clean it himself. Through cracks in the old plaster made by the fall and the downpour, he saw glittering metal. Calling upon monks to assist, he removed all the plaster and found the whole Buddha image covered with gold.

Later it was discovered that the piece had been carved and cast in gold during the Sukhothai period (1238–1378), when the old capital before Ayudhya lay far to the north. To deceive foreign invaders it had been heavily coated with plaster, and in the following generations the precious metal was forgotten.

Today one reaches the image by steep stairs leading to the shrine. Though not well placed, this largest gold statue in the world is magnificent. The representation of Buddha is lean, broad-shouldered, and narrow-waisted. He sits cross-legged in the "Calling-the-Earth-to-Witness" pose, with the left palm upturned in his lap and the long-fingered right hand hanging over his left leg halfway between the ankle and the knee. He has a longish face with a brooding mouth; this is the only example I recall in the East where Buddha's lips did not hold the suggestion of one elevated to enlightenment and bliss. The sad, compassionate eyes of this image, with an anxious frown between them, bespeak the Blessed One's concern for all creatures who must endure their coming hither into this phenomenon called life.

If the gleaming image is not of solid gold, it certainly looks as if it were. But the statue cries out for a more worthy setting, far from the swarms of energetic school children and the monks' rude dormitories. It needs a chaste temple, bare of embellishments, containing nothing but this superb golden image.

As we descended the shrine stairs I felt that my decades of desire to see this fabulous city of Bangkok had now become a reality. Yet those glittering, twisted towers and tiered roofs, those fanciful concoctions of white marble, gilt, tile, and colorful porcelain shards that rose like dream fancies, still seemed a bit incredible. I would like to have heard Dr. Johnson speak after such a day.

Mystery of the Thai Silk King

People were still speculating about the baffling case of Jim Thompson, the most notable and popular American in Thailand in this century. On a holiday in the Cameron Highlands of Malaya on March 27, 1967 he had mysteriously disappeared from his host's patio terrace during the siesta hour. One of the most extensive searches for a missing person ever conducted had ensued, with large rewards offered. But in late October not the faintest authentic clue had turned up. Captain James H. W. Thompson, scion of Delaware textile executives, a man of impeccable antecedents and a Princetonian, had arrived in Thailand two days after V-J Day on a mission for the Office of Strategic Services. He had fallen in love with Bangkok and the Thais and since 1946 he had made it his permanent home, though he had maintained his American citizenship. At the time of his arrival, the United States was still quite chummy with its Communist allies, and Thompson naturally got to know many prominent Communists, including agents of Ho Chi Minh of North Vietnam.

A few years after the Pacific war's peace settlement, Thompson became internationally famous as the "founder of the Thai silk industry," though the Siamese had been raising silkworms and weaving and dyeing silk fabrics for centuries. The genial American foresaw the export possibilities and took sample lengths of glimmering silk to an old family friend in New York, Edna Woolman Chase, editor of *Vogue*. The lady went into ecstasies over the exquisite stuffs. When Thompson returned to Thailand he began arrangements for what eventually turned out to be a multimillion-dollar affair. Thai cottage industries became big business.

At first, Thompson had only to cross a wooden bridge from his Bangkok house across a klong to the thatched huts where silk was woven. He offered higher wages than had ever been known for silk weaving. Eventually he created thousands of jobs for the underprivileged. He thus became an American benefactor of Thailand, before the United States government initiated lavish loans for internal improvements through U.S.O.M. Accepted gratefully, Thompson was both admired and loved. In disposition he was as kindly disposed as the gentle Thais themselves. He became a legend in his own time, like that English governess Anna late in the nineteenth century.

Thompson built himself a fascinating home in a garden on a klong by assembling seven old Siamese houses purchased in various regions and joining them together conveniently. From all over the land he collected antiques: furniture, carvings, artifacts, images in bronze and in stone. The museum pieces were placed about his house with artistic discrimination so that each showed off to advantage. Eventually, as a charitable gesture, to garner money for the Blind Institute, he opened his house on Mondays and Thursdays to the public. Volunteers, à la Junior League, from the American Embassy, the Consulate, and various missions acted as hostesses. So Thompson proved to be a philanthropist as well as an employer of entire families. Few foreign tourists with as much as four days allotted for Bangkok fail to spend an hour or so visiting Jim Thompson's place.

Thérèse and I had earmarked Thursday morning, October 26, for our visit to this "must" attraction. The approach to Thompson's house is not impressive. We drove down a lane between shrubs and then into a forecourt. Some twenty cars were parked. Because of the high tropical planting, it is impossible to get a clear view of the long house from the front. Some of the roofs face forward and some are in profile. All are tiled in peaked Siamese style, with representations of protective snakes on the ridge ends. The main entrance has narrow double doors of intricately carved teakwood—not to be compared, of course, with the bronze "Gates of Paradise" of the Baptistery in Florence, but beautiful in their antique native artistry.

Some nine American ladies were on duty as guides. The girl from Pennsylvania who looked after us told us that the main section of the house, which contains the drawing room on the upper story, was the finest. It was originally built about 1800 in Ban Krut, the silk weavers' village just across the klong from Thompson's place.

It had belonged to the most prosperous of the clan, and had been purchased from the great-grandson of the original owner, himself now a very old man.

Teak is the material used for wall panels, ceilings, columns, floors, and roof timbers, but the entrance-hall floor is laid with Italian marble, and the bathrooms are done in Siamese marble. The terraces, garden walls, and paths are made of seventeenth-century brick brought from ruined Ayudhya. The green tiles of the parapet are antique Chinese tile, which arrived as ballast on the returning boats that had carried rice to China. Down at the edge of the klong is the *salanam*, or boat landing; it has a protective steep roof and is constructed from ancient Siamese columns and pediments.

In every room of the house there are priceless objects to catch the imagination. Most of them were collected in various regions of Thailand, but some originated in Burma, Cambodia, China, and the island of Bali. There are twin bridal lamps from Japan. The very oldest treasure is a headless Buddha of green sandstone, perfectly placed as the focal point at the far end of the entrance hall, standing apart among tropical plants. It is from the early Dvaravati period (sixth to tenth century), the post-Gupta era in India.

Admiringly we traversed the rooms in which the American bachelor Jim Thompson (once divorced) made his home in an exotic museum. In the center of the rectangular high-ceilinged drawing room is a royal bed about a foot and a half high. On very hot nights the master would sleep here, where he could catch the breeze from four directions. In his quarter century as a citizen of Thailand, Thompson had become thoroughly acclimated to humid heat. Unlike most Americans, he scorned air conditioning; only his guest room was air-conditioned.

In the guest room in a northeast wing, where one can view both the garden and the klong, the weavers' village across the water is ever in panoramic view. Movements of daily routine formed a kaleidoscope of quickly changing patterns. Brown youngsters in their healthy nakedness were diving into the water. Some climbed out along an enormous overhanging tree branch and had the thrill of plummeting down with whopping splashes. Two youngsters pushed, pulled, and cajoled a little brother no more than three years old up and out onto the tree branch and then loosened his hands and let him drop into the klong, where other squealing kids were there to make a sport of his feat and take him back safely to land, dazed and sputtering, but too triumphant to bawl.

Here in these cottages bordering the klong and in scores in the back area live the silk weavers whom Thompson employed for his international trade. But where is the main factory located, I wanted to know. There is no main factory, I was told. His weavers and dyers are scattered throughout the country, in private houses shaded by mulberry trees.

"In encouraging cottage industries, Mr. Thompson did for Thailand what Mahatma Gandhi sought to do for my country," said a vibrant voice behind me.

I turned and saw a luxuriantly beautiful young Indian woman in a black chiffon sari. She had enormous dark eyes and classic features. I got in conversation with her. She was not only lovely, but also highly intelligent. She was from New Delhi, where her husband was one of the editors of a leading daily. She was now in Bangkok gathering material for some articles. I told her that my wife and I were flying to New Delhi on the next Sunday. She said that, alas, she would not have returned when we arrived, but that she would be there before we flew to Rome on November 15. She wrote her husband's name and their house address in my notebook and asked me to telephone him. She said that we would be invited to dinner.

It was surprising to make friends so easily with a Hindu woman in Jim Thompson's guest room. If she had been from Georgia or Mississippi, acquaintanceship could hardly have been more easy. This was a change indeed in Indian mores, for women had been out of purdah or its equivalent for barely a generation. Her natural cordiality and sophistication were inspiriting on the eve of our visit to the mysterious subcontinent with its mighty problems.

The animate beauty had all but surpassed for me the centuries-old art in cold stone. And out on a corner of a gallery that gave on a tangled garden I found another of nature's little masterpieces. In a huge floor-to-ceiling cage of heavy meshed wire, about six by six in width, perched a white cockatoo with superb tail feathers. He, too, was beautiful and regal. He sat high on a lopped-off branch of a dead tree that was fixed to the floor. At first he scorned my admiring attentions, staring distantly across the klong, like a sailor standing watch on the sea. But as I continued to murmur compliments he slowly turned his head and looked down at me with melancholy golden eyes. When I continued to talk to him, he cocked his head and regarded me quizzically, as if with a ray of hope. Then slowly he stepped from the end of his perch and began descending the wire netting, using his scimitarlike curving beak as well as his talons to climb down. He came as close to my face as he could, with intense, questioning eyes. Was he asking, "Where is Jim? Why does he stay away so long?" Hearing my man's voice among all those feminine voices of the ubiquitous guides, did he think for a moment that I *was* Thompson? Or was he merely seeking masculine consolation? In any case, a bond was formed, as I continued to speak to him sympathetically. When Thérèse found me and came up to the cage she understood the situation instantly. "This must be Mr. Thompson's pet cockatoo. I remember pictures of him with a white cockatoo on his shoulder. Birds, like all animals, can feel inexpressible grief." She was as moved as I. It was hard to leave the handsome fellow. When I said good-by, his eyes followed me with odd yearning until we rounded the alcove corner.

"Did that white cockatoo mean something special to Jim Thompson?" I asked a guide by the staircase. "When Mr. Thompson was home, they were inseparable," she said. "The cockatoo lived on his shoulder." I neglected to ask the bird's name, but two months after our return to the States, because his melancholy image still haunted me, I wrote to Mr. Sheffield, the assistant director of the Thai Silk Company. "Mr. Thompson called him Cocky," came the reply.

Two days later, on Saturday, October 28, we entertained at luncheon Connie Mangskau, the person in Thailand who knew Jim Thompson best and was with him when he disappeared. Mrs. Mangskau, born of an English father and a Thai mother, was the widow of a Norwegian. She was the proprietor of Monogram, an antique shop with branches in the arcades of the Erawan Hotel and the Siam Intercontinental. I had bought a small bronze torso of Buddha and a beautifully modeled hand of Buddha, both from the seventeenth-century. I purposed to keep them on my studio desk to remind me of serenity. When Mrs. Mangskau learned that I was gathering material for a book on Eastern travel, she accepted our invitation for lunch. She was an impressive, olive-skinned woman in her forties with fine large eyes and assured poise, the kind of person who seems to know prominent people around the world.

She told us the story of Jim Thompson, whom she had chanced to meet the very first day he arrived in Bangkok at the end of World War II. He had requested her advice then and through the years that followed. "Jim," she said, "was an idealist and creative; he had vision, but really little practical business sense. He saw the world possibilities of Thai silk, and at the beginning he was not averse to hawking silk himself to tourists in the lobby of the Oriental Hotel. The industry he founded on $700 capital eventually came to do a million-and-a-half-dollar business a year. And as other independent companies sprang up—almost 150 now—silk became a major Thailand export.

"We were close friends through the years," she continued, "and this past Easter we went to spend the holidays with our friends Dr. and Mrs. T. G. Ling at their summer bungalow in the Cameron Highlands in Malaya. Romantically called Moonlight Cottage, it lies at 5,500 feet above sea level. The place is about 140 miles north of the Malay capital, Kuala Lumpur. The Lings' main home is in Singapore. He is Chinese; she is English. When Jim and I arrived at the Bangkok airport to fly to Penang, the officials asked for his income tax receipt. I had brought mine along, since all Thai natives must produce tax receipts before emplaning for a foreign country —even for a weekend. Jim looked vague. He was very careless about details of business. He left all accounting to others in his office. He felt sure the tax had been paid, but he couldn't produce any receipt. The airport official said he couldn't fly without it. The plane was ready to go. I said, 'Look here, you all know me, everybody in Bangkok knows me. I will sign something saying that I am responsible for Thompson and for any part of an unpaid income tax.' They were reluctant, but finally they let me sign a paper, and we flew to Penang.

"The next morning we set out by hired car for Moonlight Cottage. Jim had previously arranged and paid for the taxi in advance. At a town garage along the way our Malay driver got out and said he could go no farther, but that his brother would take us on. I thought this very strange. And as soon as the purported brother

Shrine gateway,
Toshogu Mausoleum,
Nikko

Mount Fuji in winter

Aerial view of Horyuji Temple, Nara

Katsura Imperial Villa, Kyoto

A Chinese junk in Hong Kong Harbor

The fishing village of Aberdeen

Ruins of Angkor Thom

Temple of Angkor Wat

Her Majesty Queen Sirikit
of Thailand

His Majesty King Bhumibol
of Thailand in traditional
ceremonial costume

Chedis in the
Royal Compound,
Bangkok

Two of the thirty-seven golden barges in the Royal Barges Procession
on the Chao Phraya River

The Taj Mahal, Agra

The Hawa Mahal,
or Palace of
the Winds, Jaipur

Palace at Amber

Chandni Chowk,
the main plaza
of Old Delhi

took the wheel, two men emerged from the shadows. They squeezed into the front seat with the new driver, who said the men were only going to a village along the way. Jim did not protest. He's an amiable soul. But I didn't like it a bit. I said, 'Look here, Jim, are you going to stand for this? This is your car, which you have paid for, and we don't know these strangers.' So Jim demanded that they get out, which they did. After passing miles of tea plantations, without further incident, we arrived at the Lings'.

"That afternoon, Jim and Dr. Ling took a long walk in the jungle. The next day was Easter Sunday. After a picnic lunch on Gunong Brinchang at 6,000 feet we returned to the bungalow about two-thirty. It was siesta time, and we all started to our separate rooms. I went on to mine and presumed that Jim went to his. But at the last moment he told his hosts that he would stretch out for a while in a long chair on the patio. Jim has never been heard from since."

Connie Mangskau took a couple of bites of food. Then she continued. "At teatime, when I came out of my room I noticed that Jim's door was slightly ajar, and I presumed that he was still resting. When tea was served somebody went to fetch him. He was not there. On the terrace by the long chair lay his jacket and his cigarettes. We thought that he might have gone for another walk in the jungle. He liked jungles and had a keen jungle sense. On one of our former visits to the Lings, Jim had been stung by hornets about half a mile from the bungalow, and he had mentioned on the plane that he might want to return to the spot and look about. When dusk came we began to be concerned. It was utterly unlike Jim to leave his cigarettes, and in the Highlands it becomes quite cool when the sun goes down. He knew that well, and he would not have left his jacket if he had planned a long walk. We began to fear that he had had an accident. Mrs. Ling suggested that a tiger might have attacked him. The servants declared they had seen no stranger in the area. But both the Lings recalled that they had heard the chair scraping on the patio stones, and Dr. Ling said he heard footsteps pass his window about three-thirty and had supposed that Jim was going for a walk. Ling went down to the village and made inquiries. Nothing. That night he called for the Malay police. They came and rounded up a party of jungle abo-

rigines. They all searched the near jungle with lights until 2:00
A.M. Not the faintest success.

"The next day a full hunt began. Experts and hundreds of ama-
teurs, including Malayian Boy Scouts, joined in. Miles of jungle
were thoroughly searched. The latest devices in American electronics were brought to the Highlands. An aerial tower was set up on
a water tank near the bungalow. It threw a radar communications
net within a ten-mile radius. Some men were equipped with walkie-
talkie field telephones and loud-hailers. Many were armed. If an
animal had eaten Jim there would have been bones and shoes left.
Nothing!

"There were only indefinite clues. A cook at the Lutheran Mission cottage farther down the slope said that she had seen a white
man pass near her kitchen window in midafternoon. She said that
he stood on a nearby plateau for about half an hour and then suddenly disappeared. Another person declared that he had seen a car
with three men moving slowly up toward the Ling place. Still another claimed that he had seen a cavalcade of five cars going up
the hill and then had noted its return about the time of Jim's disappearance. Since traffic was a great rarity in the region and the
Lings' cottage lay in a most isolated spot, this was highly unusual.
The immediate theory was that Jim had been kidnaped for ransom."

Mrs. Mangskau paused and took another bite of food.

A thought occurred to me: "The men might have stopped the
car at a distance from the Lings', and then crept up and taken
him at gunpoint, so that he did not dare cry out."

"That is certainly possible," she said. I did not voice a further
thought that Thompson may have *expected* someone to meet him
on secret-service business, and then had been double-crossed and
kidnaped.

"How did the Malay police respond?" I asked.

"The Malay police were co-operative," she said without empha-
sis. "Helicopters were provided by the military. British soldiers
from a convalescent hospital joined in the search. Brigadier General
Edwin Black, an old friend of Jim's, who commanded the United
States support troops in Thailand, flew down. The Thai Silk Com-
pany offered a reward of 20,000 Malay dollars, and then raised it.
I stayed on for a week and finally returned to my business in
Bangkok, daily expecting news. The official search, which got in-

ternational headlines, lasted ten days. There was never a demand for ransom.

"Malay jungle witch doctors, called *bomohs*, began offering absurd solutions. Then a well-known clairvoyant from Holland, Peter Hurkos, was brought over to the scene by Mrs. James Douglas, Jim's younger sister—her husband, you know, was a former Secretary of the Air Force. Hurkos, a onetime house painter, had taken a tumble from a ladder, which, he claimed, had resulted in remarkable extrasensory perceptions, and, in truth, he had had some surprising success in divination. The Dutchman first went to Jim's house in Bangkok to get the 'feel' of things. There he said he had ominous sensations, and in the dining room around the table he became quite agitated. 'Thompson has been playing with hot fire,' he exclaimed, 'associating with the wrong people.' He asked for photos of Jim to take to Moonlight Cottage in Malaya."

I did not mention that Thérèse told me on Thursday evening that she had had a queer sensation in Thompson's dining room that odd intrigues had gone on around the table. We were later told that all C.I.A. men went straight to Thompson's house on arrival in Bangkok and generally dined with him.

Connie Mangskau went on: "At the Lings' house, Hurkos' pretty girl assistant took down on a tape recorder the clairvoyant's reactions when he went into a kind of trance. He put one hand on Jim's photo and the other on a map of Southeast Asia and began speaking. Briefly, he said, he saw Jim sitting alone on the terrace. A man whom Jim had known, named Bebe or Preebie, presumably a Thai, came up. They shook hands and then walked down the road together. About half a mile from the Lings' the man put a handkerchief over Jim's face, which put him to sleep. Then a truck with several men came and took the unconscious Jim to an obscure airstrip and flew him to a village in Cambodia, where he was still a live captive. With a finger he indicated the geography of the village.

"In Bangkok, when the story was printed, many immediately thought that Preebie might be the lawyer Pridi Phanomyong, who had brought about the bloodless coup that made him prime minister. Some years later, after a new coup ousted him, he fled to Red China, and as far as anyone knows Pridi is still living there uneasily.

"With diplomatic relations nonexistent between Thailand and

Cambodia and between the United States and Cambodia, the United States did not feel inclined to make a forced search. But, oddly, a respected Thai monk reputed to be clairvoyant reached the same conclusion as the Dutchman. He said Jim was alive in a Cambodian village and indicated about the same spot on the map. However, his story differed from Hurkos' in that he saw Jim taken by four men to Cambodia in a boat." Mrs. Mangskau picked at her salad.

"The mysterious case got fresh sensational headlines last month," she went on, "when Jim's elder sister Katherine was bludgeoned to death in her house in a fashionable suburb of Philadelphia. You know that she was the divorced wife of a son of the illustrious Major General Leonard Wood, hero of the Spanish-American War. It was seemingly a savage revenge killing. Nothing was taken from the house, though some of her private papers had been rifled. Her family declared that she had not an enemy in the world and that she lived almost in seclusion, indulging her hobbies of gardening and occasional fox hunting. Her divorced husband had died in 1950. The case, without clues, was unsolved. Mrs. Wood was one who had firmly believed that Jim was alive. They say she expected him to appear for dinner on Labor Day, because he often visited her about that time. But four days before Labor Day her maid arrived in the morning to find the lady beaten to death. The whining dogs who slept in the room with her gave no indication of having been drugged. Hurkos declared that Jim's kidnapers had murdered Mrs. Wood to force him to denounce American military presence in Thailand—and in Vietnam. And that if he did not talk, other deaths might follow. Now it is whispered that Mrs. Douglas, Jim's favorite sister, is in terror of her own life."

"Do you believe Thompson is alive?" I asked.

Mrs. Mangskau looked at me steadily, and said, "Yes, I do." Then she began to eat again.

Did her reply come from mere wishful thinking? Being something of an incorrigible optimist, I was inclined to think he was alive, too. But Thérèse had no more hope than the forlorn cockatoo.

A bellboy came up to the table to say that the car with Mrs. Mangskau's friends was waiting for her. She was going for a short weekend house party at one of the Thai beach resorts on the Gulf of Siam, where the King and Queen were enjoying their sailboat.

She begged to excuse herself from dessert. She promised to let me know by cable the moment there was any definite news of Thompson. I have had several letters from Connie Mangskau since, but the fate of the Thai Silk King remains as stark a mystery as his strange disappearance from a terrace in Malaya on Easter Sunday in 1967.

Facts from a Happy Economist

Thérèse needed a new cotton dress besides those she had brought along. We were told the smartest frocks could be found at an establishment named Design Thai. One afternoon Thérèse waited in the lobby while I stopped at the cashier's window to change money. As I pocketed the Thai notes a soft voice behind me said, "Dr. Strode?" I turned, and there was Wattanee, a lovely Thai girl who had got her master's degree in business administration at the University of Alabama about five years earlier. We had entertained her at tea in our woodland home. Thérèse had been delighted to find that Wattanee was a Buddhist. She was a pretty girl with a light complexion and she was unusually tall and willowy for a Thai. An aura of quiet serenity clung about her. She had been born in the north of Thailand, some hours by train from Bangkok. At the University she had made a top scholastic record, and was now teaching accounting in Chulalongkorn University.

Here she stood in a soft white dress with a baby girl about a year old in her arms. Behind her was her husband, holding a two-and-a-half-year-old girl. The husband's name was Umphon Phanachet. He had received his doctorate in economics at Cornell. He was a handsome chap, bursting with good health and high spirits. Like his wife, he came from the north, and, like her, he was quite light-complexioned. Though his eyes were large, there was something faintly Chinese about his face, yet his countenance was the opposite of "inscrutable." He taught economics at the University, and he also had an important position with U.S.O.M.

"Where is Mrs. Strode?" Wattanee asked. "We have come to take you for a drive. Our regular nurse is sick, so we had to bring the children."

I made the proper compliments about the bright-eyed little girls, as the cashier behind the cage spoke warmly in Thai to Wattanee. "Do you know each other?" I asked. "I taught him accounting," Wattanee said. "In fact," she added modestly, "I taught most of the accountants of the Intercontinental."

We found Thérèse looking at a bronze temple bird in the Monogram shop. She was more than happy to see Wattanee again, and I noted that she, too, was instantly charmed by Umphon. The Phanachets' well-being became the more conspicuous when they led us out to the parking lot to a month-old white Mercedes-Benz, where a substitute nurse had been left sitting. "Instead of a drive now," I said, "please take us first to Design Thai and help Thérèse get a cotton dress." When we arrived at the shop we left the baby with the nurse and Umphon carried the older girl in with us. An English-born woman assistant came to wait on us. Thérèse said we wanted to see the best tens. Almost instantly I spied just the thing on the rack: a stylized splashing white print on a blackish-blue background. Thérèse tried it on. It was a perfect fit, and had distinct style. The Phanachets agreed enthusiastically. "And I can wear it without a girdle," Thérèse said with relief. Girdles are anathema in humid climates. I paid the $16.50. At Saks' or Bergdorf's it would have cost at least eighty-five dollars. Thérèse was to wear the dress nine days later when we were entertained by the Maharani of Jaipur. The successful shopping expedition had consumed hardly a quarter hour.

Because it was teatime, I suggested that I take them to tea at the nearby Rama Hotel, where we could really talk. The Rama, a Hilton hotel, was one of Bangkok's top three luxury hotels, along with the Siam Intercontinental and the Erawan. I wanted to look it over. This time we left both babies in the parked car with the nurse.

During the conversation Wattanee said that they had hoped to have us to dinner in their home, but that her cook, as well as the regular nurse, was sick, and would we dine with them at the brand-new President Hotel, which they would like to try? Could it be on Friday evening? Because early on Saturday they had to drive far north to a funeral ceremony of Umphon's father. When I conventionally expressed sympathy, Wattanee said, "Oh, he has been dead for six months, but it is the custom to hold the ritual later, when the ashes are stowed in a final resting place. I am wearing white now because white is the color of mourning in Thailand."

We spoke of many things, of how the Thais are slow to anger and have no urge to fight, but make valiant fighters when they have to. Umphon admitted it was prudent to shoot Communists who sneaked across the northeast borders with subversive intent. Bullfights and fox hunting are repellent to the Thai nature. "But," said Umphon, "our boxing matches are sometimes quite fierce in their way, though it is the extraordinary skill and alertness that are admired. It is *de rigueur* for the opponents to use knees, feet, and elbows, as well as their fists, to attack and defend." Then, with a grin, he interpolated: according to the Thai boxing rules, "biting, hair pulling, and spitting are strictly forbidden." Besides their colored trunks, combatants are permitted to wear on their upper arms amulets of superstitious value to protect them from cuts and serious bruises. "Bangkok has two large stadiums for the matches, at which the reaction of the betting spectators is as interesting as the swift acrobatic movements in the ring."

I also learned that the Thais' other fighting proclivities are confined to kite fighting and matches between cocks, crickets, and tiny fish, the two latter events being sharply curtailed as to spectator space. "Thais," Umphon said, "enjoy the betting more than they do the contest."

"Bangkok has its Royal Sports Club, with race track, tennis courts, a golf course, an enormous swimming pool, and all the luxurious facilities of a country club, with bars, restaurants, reading rooms, and library. Foreigners with good credentials are welcomed to the club's amenities. Would you like a card?"

I shook my head. "I can have country clubs at home, thank you. Here I am interested in the exotic."

"Swimming and yachting are sports especially relished by water-conditioned Thais," Umphon said. "In Bangkok, as you know, our citizens swim from babyhood. King Bhumibol is one of our most enthusiastic yachtsmen. He races next Saturday."

"I regret that you are not going to our ancient city Chiangmai," Wattanee said. "It's an easy two-hour plane flight to the north. Four new hotels have been built there in recent years and the craft villages that surround the city are quite interesting. We are looking forward to a new airport large enough to accommodate jets. The University of Chiangmai, which opened its doors in 1964 to students, is attractive."

"Yes," I said, "I've seen colored pictures of the men's dormitories. They look ultramodern and positively posh. But we pack suitcases and go through airports just as seldom as possible. We are out here only for the whipping cream of the East. Bangkok is too fascinating to move to lesser excitements this time."

"Has anything in Bangkok disappointed your expectancy?" Umphon asked.

"Yes," I said, on quick reflection. "I have seen no Siamese cats and not one elephant on the street."

Umphon laughed. "But we have one white elephant here in the zoo, the property of His Majesty. In the northern provinces work elephants still drag the great teakwood logs from the forest better than any machine yet devised. However, the number of elephants, which are used as draft beasts, is decreasing annually. Ours are the gently disposed kind, like those of India. Less than 2,000 are employed in forestry work, and now only a very, very few of the females act as protective nursemaids for small children."

I found Umphon extremely knowledgeable in answering specific questions. He was the kind of economist who had facts and figures ready.

I learned that besides the 76 per cent of all cultivated land being planted in rice, in southern Thailand a million acres are planted in rubber, generally on smallish private estates. Annual production of rubber today has risen to 200,000 metric tons. Sugar cane is raised on some 400,000 acres, but almost all of the sugar is consumed locally. Corn or maize is rising in export importance; Japan buys most of it. Tobacco and cotton are cultivated in the less fertile lands of the north. "As in your South," Umphon said, "our cotton is pestered by insects.

"North Thailand is rich in forests," he went on. "Some 35,000 square miles contain valuable teak. Just after World War II teak production rose to 200,000 cubic meters annually. Other forest products include bamboo and rattan, charcoal, and various gums and resins. The high quality of our lac has caught the attention of foreign buyers. Do you know what lac is? Its name comes from a Sanskrit word; it's a resinous substance formed on native trees by a variety of scale insect. When this is scraped off, melted, strained, and allowed to reharden, it forms a fine shellac.

"As to livestock raising, it has become increasingly important. Some five and a half million head of cattle were reckoned in 1966 and about the same number of pigs. The water-buffalo population, used for draft and also for food, goes beyond the seven-million figure. The water buffaloes, which for centuries have been domesticated, are invaluable labor-saving devices and much beloved. Unhappily, Thais as yet know little about dairy cattle, but we are beginning."

"Then where do you get your milk?" I asked.

"Right now many persons make use of Foremost Dairies products imported frozen from the States." Again he smiled his genial smile. "As for mining, it is not of great importance except tin, which is found chiefly in the southern peninsula. The tin mines are generally operated by British and Australian companies, and tungsten is mined along with the tin. Our industry has far to go. At present it is chiefly the processing of agricultural commodities and building materials. But we have quantities of sawmills, sugar mills, yarn mills, and factories for making glass and plywood."

"What of your export-import ratio?"

"Thailand generally exports more than she imports, but this past year imports ran above exports. Japan ranks first in providing imported products. The United States and the United Kingdom follow, second and third. Though the government budget is slightly exceeded by annual expenditures, Thailand is, on the whole, in very good shape economically. In 1965 her gold and silver reserves amounted to approximately 550 million dollars."

As Umphon talked, soft-voiced, clear, assured, engaging, I thought all the more that he would make a worthy representative of his people to some foreign government. Charm plus a doctorate in economics would stand him in good stead in some future useful mission for his country.

I asked Umphon if he had done his allotted time in a monastery. "Not yet," he said reflectively. "I am waiting now until the children are older. It is not a thing to be done lightly. I thought of doing it as soon as I finished Cornell. But then Wattanee returned, and I couldn't postpone marriage." His buoyant smile returned with a flash. Then he momentarily became grave again. "Thailand faces an uncertain immediate future. And even too much prosperity can create problems. I hope my retreat may give me something that can sustain me, whatever may occur."

After tea we drove for half an hour through the quieter streets bordered by little canals, past the university where the Phanachets taught, past municipal playgrounds and hospitals of various categories, which our hosts proudly identified for us.

It was heart-warming to see the content of this responsible young intellectual couple, so obviously in love, greatly admiring each other's qualities, and prosperous beyond their expectations. Though both were practicing Buddhists, Umphon was joyously extroverted, Wattanee serenely introverted. All they needed to perfect their situation was a boy child.

Late that afternoon, immediately after our return to the hotel, we were treated to a "matinee" of Thai dancing by the second assistant hotel manager, a young Frenchman, whose speech was almost as soft as a Thai's. The performance took place on the green lawn, where chairs were arranged along a section of rooms. Everybody but ourselves seemed to have a camera for colored shots. There were representatives of *Life*, various American women's periodicals, and several foreign journals, and some twoscore amateur photographers.

The Frenchman explained to us that Thai dancing indubitably has its roots in India, reaching back perhaps to the sixth century. There were ten performers, male and female, who danced in several short classic ballets. After each dance the mistress of ceremonies called out over a loud-speaker, "And now for close-ups, please!" and most of the audience surged down upon the lawn and snapped stills. Personally, I regret to report, we could not stir up much enthusiasm for the "world-renowned" Thai dancing, though the rich and ornate costumes were eye-catching indeed. Some consisted of baggy silk pantaloons with bejeweled tight-fitting jackets, colorful scarves and sashes, and fascinating peaked helmets studded with semiprecious gems. Two of the girls were extremely pretty, and all of them used their hands with exquisite grace. The men seemed amateurish, without much style or skill. It was not because I had a distaste for male dancers per se; Nijinski had been one of my youthful admirations, and I can be stirred today by Nureyev and Denmark's Bruhn. To me, the boys were simply short on talent. They seemed to lack that professionalism of the Noh and Kabuki dancers in

Japan, in which I took only a faint interest. The group was not to be compared to an Indian troupe I had once seen at Covent Garden. A special interlude gave us a distinct shock. While the dancers were changing into more elaborate costumes, a stunning-looking young woman came out on the platform that surrounded the refreshment stand, grasped the mike, and without accompaniment burst into a wild native love chant of ancient vintage. I couldn't believe my ears, for I had grown so accustomed to the mellifluous soft tones of Thai voices. Both the Chinese and Japanese can do gratingly offensive things with their vocal chords. But in her screeching this delicately built Thai woman made the most hideous sounds I have ever heard from a human throat. A man from *The New Yorker*, who sat next to me, shivered and said, "She sounds like a wildcat bitch in heat." I could not gainsay him. And I began to wonder if some Thais still retained in their cosmos an atavistic savage streak, going back to the fifteenth century, when Siamese warriors scared the daylights out of Cambodians at Angkor and sent them fleeing two hundred miles south.

When the three-quarter-hour performance was over, we politely endeavored to conceal our lack of ardor, but our host divined our disappointment and said that we would enjoy Thai dancing much more if we saw it in the Silpakora Theater. Perhaps I was being unfair about the dancing; for, as Thérèse reminded me, this matinee was really arranged for foreign photographers. At least we could sincerely praise the fascinating costumes, which were superb in their way. The costumes were evolved from that same unique genius that had dreamed up and executed those fabulous Siamese temples we had marveled at on Wednesday.

Thirty-seven Golden Barges

On Friday, October 27, came the Royal Barges Procession, probably the most colorful pageant in the world today. The ceremony is called Tod Kathin, the day on which the monks receive their new

saffron robes for the year's wear. The custom is followed throughout Thailand. But what draws tourists to Bangkok at this particular
period is the flotilla of thirty-seven golden barges oared down the
river to the Temple of the Dawn at Thonburi. Though King
Bhumibol gives gifts throughout the year to wats in various parts
of the land, this particular festival of carrying boatloads of yellow
robes to Wat Arun is spectacularly symbolic of the royal favor.

On the previous Wednesday afternoon at four-thirty the religious
part of the ceremony had started, when the King, accompanied by a
retinue of court dignitaries and high-ranking officials, proceeded
from Chitralada Palace to begin the first Kathin functions. A front-
page news photo in Thursday's paper had shown His Majesty in
the uniform of the Supreme Commander of the Royal Thai Navy—
a white tunic with dark trousers and a white admiral's cap—accepting a stack of neatly folded robes from a kneeling gentleman of the
court before the Marble Temple. The King bore his charitable
burden ceremoniously into the main part of the temple and presented
the robes to the high priest. The service, the paper said, took about
three quarters of an hour. And then the King had performed the
same ritual on Thursday at other temples. But this Friday marked
the climax, with the water pageant.

The city was in a state of festive excitement. All tickets to spectator seats had been sold. We had an early lunch, for the World
Travel Service buses that left from the Siam Intercontinental were
scheduled for one o'clock departure. Our particular bus, in which
every seat was filled, was of such odd and ancient vintage that we
could not imagine in what country it had been manufactured. I had
certainly never seen its kind in the United States even in my childhood. It was a long ride out of Bangkok and over a river bridge
north of the city into suburbs and then south again for a few bumpy
miles through tortuous village streets, awash with dogs and children.
Finally we pulled into a vast compound where thousands of cars
and buses were parked. We made our way slowly through the
throng, which seemed as dense as that of a Rose Bowl football game.
But there was no shoving, no haste. The removable bleacherlike
grandstand extended for the equivalent of several city blocks. It was
only eight tiers high, and we found our seats without difficulty in
the third row of what seemed to be the "friends-of-foreign-
embassies" section. Blessedly, these seats were among the few that

had backs to them. The grandstand, set up about twenty feet from the riverbank, could accommodate only a small portion of the spectators. Many had engaged seats in berthed boats and sampans up or down river. The "swank set" and most of the diplomatic corps crowded the galleries and terraces of various clubs on the Bangkok side. Queen Sirikit, with her ladies, was seated on the balcony of the Royal Naval Officers' Club on our side of the river at some distance from the north end of the grandstand. Three miles of standing human beings on both sides of the Chao Phraya were there in festival expectancy to witness an ancient wonder in the modern world.

We had a goodly wait before us, for our bus had left betimes to negotiate safely amid the mad traffic of the day. We watched the panorama of the gaily dressed spectators arriving. At the near end of the grandstand and far beyond, all the way to the Temple of the Dawn, Thais were standing thirty deep, and I wondered how those in the back would ever get a glimpse of the barges. During the wait we were "entertained" by masked dancers and papier-mâché demons, acrobats and antic children doing tricks on the broad concrete walkway between the grandstand and the green grass of the riverbank. It was all quite amateurish and reminded us of the sidewalks of New Orleans at Mardi Gras. However, behind the grandstand, on an improvised stage, students from the National School of Dance put on their own posturing show, and on a high dais exhibitions of Thai sword fighting were in progress. At one of the crowded concession stands, where I finally managed to get a Pepsi-Cola, I ran into Frank James of St. Louis. We watched the sword fights for a few minutes and then rejoined our respective wives with opened bottles in hand for them.

During my absence, a Swedish engineer had occupied the seat next to mine. Thérèse and he had already got into conversation. He was a frank Nordic, husky as a Viking, with thick blond hair. I told him that I knew his country well, admired it greatly, and had written a book about it. He had recently returned to Thailand from special construction work in India, and he had seen the Royal Barges Procession three years before. I said that we were leaving for New Delhi on Sunday night and that I was apprehensive that the sight of the gruesome poverty we had read so much about might be difficult for Thérèse to bear. I also mentioned we had been warned by Americans of "Delhi belly"—acute dysentery—and had some other health anxieties about India. The Swede was uncommonly reassuring. He had worked in several parts of India and had never been plagued with the ills of the flesh of which so many complained. He declared that he was not even apprehensive in the villages of Thailand, where his supervisory job sometimes took him.

He leaned across me and said to Thérèse, "I know how you must feel about India's poverty. Coming from Sweden, which is aseptically clean, as you know, and where there are no slums whatever, I was appalled at first. I was moved by the rags and skinniness of people, the bony cows wandering at loose ends, the dust of the road in which people squatted, and the dirty sidewalks, where some sprawled for night sleep and siesta. At first I turned my head away. Then I gradually looked closer into the faces, and I came to realize that there were more smiles in India than in my Sweden. Those people, who by our standards should have been excessively miserable, did not really seem to be so. They could live, like Gandhi, on a glass of goat's milk a day and one banana, with a dab of rice or a bit of wheat bread. Flies and dust did not faze them. Watch a group at noonday squatting under a roadside shade tree and see if they aren't happy enough. If you stay in New Delhi and avoid the adjoining Old Delhi, your wife won't see anything to distress her. Remember—more smiles in India than in Sweden!"

There was a palpable stirring in the multitude. The Swede with his far-seeing blue eyes looked up the river. "The first barges are in sight," he said, as the costumed entertainers began to scurry away. "There will be thirty-seven barges in all. Note the stunning precision of the rowing. The oarsmen have been practicing all year for this hour."

Two widely spaced, long and narrow barges, painted gold, appeared together. They were rowed by men in bright red with red helmet headdresses. They would stroke the water with their gilded oars and then raise them aloft as in salute, pause for a moment, and again in perfect unison make the next stroke. As the first two boats passed the grandstand, we could marvel at the superb synchronization. In the entire procession of thirty-seven we were not to see a single rower make a slip. We could hear clearly the thump and clack as the rhythm keeper in each boat struck a wooden paddle on a block of wood in the hull.

The barges now came single-file; these were longer and more

elaborate in their carvings and richer in gold leaf. Finally, preceding His Majesty's by two, came what was known as the "King's auxiliary barge." So the Swede told us. "It is ninety-three feet long," he said, "longer than many suburban lots. It is called the Ekachaihurnhao. It was built in the time of King Rama I in the late eighteenth century. If you count, you will see that its crew is composed of thirty-four oarsmen."

Climactically the best was saved for the end. The next-to-last barge, preceding the King's, was the Anantanakraj, with an elaborate, heavily carved figurehead of a seven-headed serpent at the bow. "That boat is tremendously important," said the Swede, "because in the pavilion amidships are stacked the Kathin robes for the monks. The barge itself is 129 feet long and has for a crew fifty-four oarsmen, two steersmen, two officers, one flagman, one rhythm keeper, two songsters, and twenty ceremonial drummers."

"The drummers, I presume, are announcing the approach of the King."

He nodded. "And there he comes, in the most splendid of them all. His barge is some 135 feet long and ten feet wide, and, you see, the swan-head prow rises almost as tall as a three-story building. His Majesty's barge is called the Supannahongs. '*Hongs*' is the Thai word for 'swan.' "

The crest of the golden swan did seem to rise three stories above the water. The flagman at the bow or lower neck of the swan, where it joined the hull, would have to use a fireman's ladder to reach the top. Like a casual necklace a great loop of amethyst silk hung about the neck and dipped to the water. The swan reared its head so high that its long golden beak pointed at the sky. Its jeweled eyes of sapphires seemed to proclaim, "I bear a precious burden." It was remarkable that a barge of such size should have such consummate grace.

Like a good and precise chorus the Swede remarked, "This crew numbers fifty. But there is only one songster—why, I do not know. The songster you hear is chanting to the cadence of the oarsmen's strokes. And, incidentally, there are seven canopy bearers, for the King when he goes ashore."

In the pavilion, with its peaked roof of crimson and gold silk, sat King Bhumibol, as if enthroned. He wore the full-dress uniform of the commander in chief of the Royal Navy. His black glasses protected his sensitive eyes from the watery glare at midafternoon. Though a pleasant breeze stirred, His Majesty was being fanned by long-handled fans in the traditional manner, in the days when no King of Siam moved in the streets without his fanners.

I thought of Cleopatra's barge upon the River Cydnus when she captured the heart of Marc Antony. I recalled the line of Enobarbus about "the divers-color'd fans." I quoted aloud:

> "The barge she sat in, like a burnish'd throne
> Burn'd on the water; the poop was beaten gold."

But these Thai oars were also the color of gold, and not of silver like Cleopatra's. Though a serious male monarch sat here in state in A.D. 1967, his show of thirty-seven golden barges far surpassed in spectacle the enchantress's triumphant barge in 40 B.C. And though "the city cast her people out" to behold Egypt's Queen on the river, today hundreds of thousands beheld the King of Thailand, including spectators from all over the globe.

It took perhaps half an hour for the entire procession to pass the grandstand. Down-river, at the landing of the Temple of the Dawn, out of our range of vision, His Majesty descended from his barge, where Prime Minister Thanom Kittikachorn and the Cabinet were waiting to receive him. At the main building an official presented the saffron robes to the King, which he carried inside the temple to complete the religious ceremony.

We chatted with the Swede until the procession returned up the river. In coming down, the rowers had had a tail wind to assist them; in fact, they had to feather their oars to hold the barges back. "The normal speed of the King's barge," said the engineer, "is eleven and a half feet per paddle stroke. Now, facing a head wind, the oarsmen have to row the harder."

We enjoyed a second full view of the passing barges and again admired the grace of the golden vessels. We marveled once more at the splendid synchronization of the oarsmen. The Siamese seemed all the more an extraordinary race with unique creative gifts to have devised such a spectacle and put it into smooth-as-cream operation. Inordinate lovers of festivals of all kinds, the Thai populace had been given something as original as it was eye-filling, with components of religion and royalty. The best of the Mardi Gras celebrations in New Orleans and Rio de Janeiro were tinsel-tawdry beside this spectacle. Even the water fetes in enchanting Venice seemed lackluster in comparison. Perhaps only in the grandeur of Imperial Rome, when a conquering hero returned with his chariots and legions and the spoils of battle, followed by thousands of miserable captives, might such extraordinary display be paralleled. But the difference was striking, for here the hero of the occasion was no boastful warrior in armor, but a slender monarch of undoubted religious bent, whose heart's desire was to keep his people happy and free.

Yet with the Red menace all but surrounding him, how often in the future, I wondered, would one be able to behold such a glamorous exhibition. In the leveling processes of so-called democracy spreading around the world, perhaps a cry would be raised not only against any conspicuous expenditure that was nonmilitary, but against rank as well as royalty. Every aristocratic tradition might soon be gone with the wind, and there would be little left "remarkable beneath the visiting moon."

Floating Markets and Fragrant Tokens

The primitive and age-old aspect of Bangkok lies in what might be called the culture of the klongs. Though in the main thoroughfares boulevards have superseded waterways and motorcars have replaced canoes, the maze of canals intersecting the old city continues to function. The Thais are naturally adept at poling their craft, often chanting rhythmically as they glide over the water. Foreign visitors remember feelingly the early-morning tour to the floating markets below Thonburi, the former capital across the Chao Phraya from Bangkok. When Princess Saroya of Iran had a single day's pause in Bangkok on her way somewhere, during our Bangkok sojourn, she chose the floating-markets trip.

We had left that "absolutely must" attraction for our last sight-

seeing in Bangkok. At eight o'clock on Saturday a launch was waiting for us on a dock near the Oriental Hotel with a steersman and
his boy assistant. With the same bright guide we had before, we
headed across the river toward the right bank and then turned downstream amidst small fishing boats and ocean-going freighters. Trains
of open barges, lashed together, descended the Chao Phraya, laden
with exports of teakwood, rice, corn, copra, jute, pottery jars, and
"forbidden" opium, the one money crop of primitive tribes in the
far north. Regular household routine proceeded in the junks: meals
were being cooked, babies' diapers were being changed, potted
plants in tins were being watered, as families sailed to the Gulf of
Siam.

Eventually we turned off into a shaded klong to course through a
pristine jungle, impenetrable with palms, gigantic ferns, and looping
vines. Trees here and there were decorated with wild orchids of a
hundred species. (There are 750 varieties in Thailand.) Tropical
birds in brilliant plumage darted across the walls of variegated
green. Some birds were poised on branches, silent. Occasionally one
sang sweetly. Others merely chattered after their kind.

Except for the mechanical motor attached to our craft, we might
have been cruising in primeval days near the dawn of history.
Though this region was only a few miles from the sophisticated
Eastern capital, it was like proceeding through the dark heart of
Conrad's Africa. Each bend and curve of the klong presented a
fresh and fascinating vista, occasionally studded with white waterfowl making a frieze for a Japanese screen.

On either side of the klong the fecund jungle swooped down upon
us, stayed only by the water. Though the sun shone with tropical
brilliance, my eyes could not penetrate "the eternal twilight of the
trackless woods." I felt my blood pulsing with excitement, as if I
were exploring a world where no man had ever passed—though perhaps a motor launch had preceded us by no more than five minutes.
We had purposely set out late to avoid the seven o'clock crush.

Then suddenly in the midst of the rank vegetation loomed a man-
made hut on stilts, which almost seemed an anachronism. The little
clearing, with a sweet-potato patch handy, and bananas, oranges, and
coconuts, brought one back to the reality of contemporary existence.
Even with an occasional rude habitation, however, this water journey through canyons of lush forest was as remote from anything in

Europe as was the glittering Siamese architecture of the Royal Compound.

As we approached the so-designated floating markets, sampans, scows, junks, and dugout canoes jostled each other gently. Piled lemons and green vegetables might fill one canoe, bananas and oranges another. One could buy cooking utensils and ceramicware, as well as ready-made cotton dresses and butcher meat. Our guide told us that the butchers are invariably Chinese, because the Thais' religion frowns on killing any living thing, except to protect one's life. The vendors in the boats were more often women than men, reminding us of those handsome female stallkeepers in Tehuantepec. More oddly, it was the men who knelt on the wooden stoops over the washtub or rinsed the clothes in the canal from the bottom step of their pile-supported huts.

A boatman delivering mail bumped a floating restaurant, where spicy Thai odors mingled with the morning freshness. "Ice boats" sold ice by the cake or shaved. Some canoes offered only the Thai straw hats shaped like lamp shades. Yellow-robed monks with their begging bowls paddled on their morning rounds of collecting food for the day's one meal.

Around ten-thirty, suddenly feeling a hunger pang, I asked the boatman to slow down and I beckoned to a woman in a banana skiff. She was wearing a fetching straw hat and she had traces of beauty. In a few deft paddle strokes she brought her craft alongside. I picked out a stem with six bananas. She weighed them on her scales, and said, "Two bahts." I paid her the equivalent of ten cents. As our boats separated, I thought of the floating gardens of Xochimilco and of the female vendors of fruits and flowers there in their swift canoes. No one on our launch wanted a banana but myself. Its flavor was first-rate, and I devoured it with relish, well aware of the dictum: in the tropics eat only fruit that can be peeled.

Intimate family life on the banks of the canals was lived unselfconsciously, as if the natives were oblivious of the fascinated foreign gazers. Naked boys leaped from porch steps for their morning dip. Some kids were answering the call of nature. A woman stooped over to brush her teeth in the contaminated water. One housewife dipped a bunch of spinach in the klong to freshen it. Another threw out table scraps. The klong water is highly polluted with all sorts of deadly bacteria, but through generations the Thais have built up an immunity and apparently can swallow the liquid with impunity. Foreigners are ever enjoined to drink only bottled water or soft drinks or the purified water that is served in all first-class hotels.

A police boat arrived to help disentangle a traffic jam, caused partly by a big motor launch full of American tourists stopping at a curio shop where the guide would get a commission. We passed some small factories making teakwood furniture, then a sawmill in operation, kilns for baking earthen jars, and a workshop for fabricating coffins, where little girls were busy painting flower designs in gay colors on the sides and the lid.

As our launch approached nearer to the great river again, country villas of the bourgeoisie appeared, half-smothered in purple bougainvillaea. Their owners preferred to commute to their city jobs by boat rather than live in town apartments, our guide told us. Television antennae rose above each roof. In the gardens close to a corner of the dwellings, fanciful "spirit houses" stood on pedestals or poles five to seven feet high. "Almost invariably," our guide said, "a Thai home has its spirit house in which 'Chao Ti,' the ruler of the plot of ground, lives. Some are quite elaborate and constructed of carved marble. Before each little house is a small table, on which daily offerings are laid for the presiding spirit—tidbits, fruit, flowers, candles, incense sticks. Naturally, strangers exclaim over the quaint 'birdhouses.' But the birds know that these ornamental affairs are not for them."

Occasionally the edge of the klong was lined with small shops, with a Buddhist temple complex rising in the back. In former times, our guide said, the temple grounds extended in lovely gardens down to the water, but now, with dirt so valuable, the monks have had to sell off their waterfront property for shops or villas. Those half-hidden old temples in the background looked charming and inviting, but also as if they had not been treated with the respect they deserved.

The canal broadened, and we sighted the outlet into the busy river. I thought of the over-all impression of our two hours' meandering through jungle and floating markets. These klong-reared people seemed happy, with a pervasive simplicity and wantlessness, as our Japanese friend Mr. Kubo had found. They do not suffer from headaches and ulcers due to strain. And that overvalued word "progress," which politicians flaunt incessantly, means little to them.

Though all children are required to go to school now, these klong people of the Thonburi region seem to exemplify Thomas Gray's gem, "Where ignorance is bliss, 'tis folly to be wise."

Once again we were out into the broad Chao Phraya, where sampans spread rust-colored sails. Two sturdy Norwegian freighters were passing each other, one coming, one going. Our boatman steered for the great Temple of the Dawn. This Wat Arun has the most commanding situation of all the temples in the land. Standing on a rise of ground back from the river, it is one of the world's most striking temples. Four magnificent *prangs* (spires), seemingly made of porcelain and surrounding a towering central spire about twenty stories high, reflect the noonday sun in a spectacular way. "When the Burmese attacked and destroyed the ancient capital of Ayudhya," the guide was saying, "those who escaped fled south, and General Phra Chao Tak Sin founded a new capital here at Thonburi. One of his first acts was to erect this decorative wat to catch the first light of dawn and to impress the ships that passed all day long. It was a tremendous effort for a broken nation. It was done with a swiftness that was phenomenal." Then he added with his engaging smile, "In those days everybody worked with a will and helped each other."

While he was talking, our boatman, aided by his boy helper, was maneuvering patiently but skillfully to get us to the landing stage. Scores of small market boats laden with fruit and flowers and green vegetables occupied the water surface cheek by jowl with tourist launches attempting to reach the steps. Finally we scraped against the landing, and five boys in their early teens reached out competitive hands to assist us out of the boat. When we had touched terra firma, flaring arguments arose as to which had helped us up the steps. So I gave some change to each of them, the larger coins to the least clamorous. Then they dashed back to their stations to assist others in disembarking.

"You will note that this temple follows the Khmer style of the twelfth and thirteenth centuries at Angkor," the guide said, as we ascended the path from the river. "Just as do those ruined wats at Ayudhya. King Rama I developed what is known as typical Siamese architecture when the capital was moved across the river to Bangkok."

Besides flowering shrubs, the way to the temple was lined with flimsy kiosks, offering all kinds of tourist lure and gimcracks. The tributary walkways were thick with sight-seers: American, British, German, French, Thai pilgrims from upcountry, and visiting yellow-robed monks.

Close up one can see that the towering spires that sparkle like jewels from a distance are made of broken pieces of colorful pottery and sea shells embedded in the stucco. On one side of the very tall central *prang* several daring Americans and Europeans were climbing the extremely narrow steps on an outside wall to reach the top for the famed panoramic view of Bangkok. It made one almost sick with dizziness to watch their perilous progress, without benefit of mountain ice stick or rope.

Along the paths of the back compound, stone images of the Buddha were ranged, a few with their heads off and lying like sacrificial offerings at their feet. "Even here," our guide said, "we have some vandal pranksters." On the walls, in bas-relief, the life of Buddha was depicted from his birth to his enlightenment and passage into nirvana. In one unusual piece of sculpture the Moon-God rode a milk-white steed.

While the devout prayed within the temple a lively business in baubles went on outside. I myself was happy to buy some rather distinctive temple rubbings. The price asked at Wat Arun was half that asked before the Temple of the Reclining Buddha.

During my trading I lost track of our guide. I began to hunt among the kiosks. "Perhaps he is praying in the temple," Thérèse suggested. But I found him near some giggling girls, and I suspected that he had been twitching his left eyebrow at them.

Since it was past noon, we declined the invitation to visit the hangars that house the thirty-odd royal barges. We had seen the barges in flashing action the day before in resplendent pageantry; we did not want to spoil that thrilling memory by gazing on them inert. So it was "Home, James!" We zigzagged among two-way water traffic across the river. After bidding a grateful, paper-money farewell to the steersman and his boy, we found our World Service car awaiting us in the Oriental Hotel parking lot, all efficiency.

The klong trip through the Thailand jungle and the visit to the floating market had been another memorable experience, to rank, in its way, with a thrilling flight over the snow-peaked Andes in 1935, though nothing could have been more different.

We were loath to leave colorful Bangkok, which had surpassed our high expectations. Joseph Conrad's favored city had for us been aureoled with glamour. The myths were external realities. The fabulous was real, yet still fabulous. Though modernity, with its rectangular concrete and glass structures, had inched forward and obstructed many fine views, the old treasures were still there behind the new-age walls.

While Bangkok was fast losing point as the "Venice of the East," it could still be called the City of Two Thousand Pagodas. And, unlike Japan, where fires periodically made disasters of fine wooden temples and palaces, Bangkok's pagodas and *chedis*, with their needle-topped towers of golden stucco, stayed as they were. By night, the luminous spires of the Buddhist temples seem to float over the active city like "reminders of a higher law." The Thais' chosen brand of Buddhism, the gentle Hinayana or Little Vehicle, seeped into the people's blood stream and took possession of their minds. Multitudes still kneel in the temples and pay homage to the Buddha who taught them the special virtues of loving-kindness and a calm heart.

When our bags were all packed early Sunday evening, we took a long look out of our window beyond the garden to the meadows where the ducks roamed free in their green domain. A young Thai from the front office came up and asked if we would like him to accompany us to the complicated airport, since few there spoke English. He would arrange the checking of our luggage and see us to the proper waiting room.

We made our adieus to the office force in the lobby, and our Thai friend attended to the loading of the bags. As we were getting into the car the young Frenchman rushed out. "Oh, are you leaving for the airport so soon? But a young lady wants to say good-by." He flew back into the hotel and then came out immediately, followed by a graceful Thai girl in a cream-colored sarong, bearing, not garlands, but two thick ropes of pale flowers intricately wrought in patterned designs. When she hung them about our necks they reached to the waist.

Though in Hawaii encircling leis of loosely strung large flowers are more or less routine, these ropes of patterned tiny blossoms, divided at ten-inch intervals by jewel-like clusters of topaz-colored and amethyst blossoms, are distinctly rare. I did not have time to ask the origin of the custom or the names of the flowers, but I did exclaim, "Why these garlands are works of art!" What patience, what hours of labor to weave hundreds of blossoms for a moment's tender gesture! Was it a show of appreciation for our obvious appreciation of their land and their people? In any case, it was the fragrant token of a new love affair with an exotic land.

INDIA

Madame Pandit and Nehru's Museum

For our sojourn in India we had decided to concentrate on three cities: New Delhi, Agra, and Jaipur. Owing to our restricted schedule we regretfully had to miss seeing Kashmir, at the foot of the Himalayas. It was the tag end of the season for Kashmir: airplanes would shortly make their last run. We hesitated to risk an appalling experience of some friends who had been hemmed in at Shrinigar by an unexpectedly early snowstorm.

From the comparative roomy quiet of the first-class compartment of a BOAC plane we emerged into the soft Indian night and a swarm of brown-faced humanity. A tiny woman wearing a dark-purple sari approached, bowed, and seized my small blue bag. She insisted on carrying it into the air terminal. When I demurred, because she was both unknown to me and frail-looking, she announced herself with dignity as a "ground hostess."

A hitch in immigration formalities ensued, because the stewardess had neglected to have us fill out the proper landing papers. By the time this task was done and the checked luggage passed customs, without being opened, we turned to meet the Mercury Travel Service representative, Prem Kajla, at the barrier. The ground hostess was now nowhere to be seen, nor was my blue bag, which contained my toilet articles, certain preventive drugs, and my notes of the journey. In a gathering panic I left Thérèse with Mr. Kajla and elbowed my way back through the crowd to find the vanished lady. As I started off in consternation to look for her, I stumbled over an object; there on the floor, amid scores of milling walkers, sat my bag. The hostess had apparently got impatient and abandoned it. It was gratifying to be able to bear witness that thieving in Delhi was certainly not rampant.

Mr. Kajla, who had large soft brown eyes and a most soothing manner, told us that his immediate boss at Mercury Travel was Rita Dar, Nehru's niece and Madame Pandit's youngest daughter. Only a month before we left home, Ruth Shaver, who happened to be the godmother of Mrs. Dar's little girl, had written of my desire to meet Madame Pandit, Nehru's sister. Word had come that the lady would be happy to see us if she were in Delhi. "Is Madame Pandit here now?" I asked.

"She is, but she's about to fly to New York to accept some international award for her work in Indian birth control."

I explained to Kajla that we did not intend to "see" Delhi now. Our first objective in India was a visit to the Taj Mahal. We wanted a chauffeured car to take us to Agra the day after tomorrow, Tuesday, October 31, which was my birthday.

The white Imperial Hotel spreads out under tall trees in a walled garden near the city's business center. A floor chief and three porters accompanied us to our second-floor "room," which turned out to be four. "Mrs. Dar thought you might like Shirley MacLaine's corner suite," said Mr. Kajla. "The movie star was here recently." The huge living room was attractive in gay flowered chintz. There was an equally large glassed-in sun porch; a dressing room with washbowls, a bureau, and mirrors; and a small bedroom just barely large enough to contain the two beds and a wardrobe. The tub and the toilet were in two separate compartments. It seemed an odd arrangement of space, but this was India, and, though first-class, the Imperial was not a new hotel.

After mineral water and fruit were brought up, we were left alone in pervading quiet like that of the country. No dance music was reverberating, no noise came from a bar. "Of course," I reminded Thérèse, "bars are uncommon in India." Good Hindus and Muslims do not indulge in alcoholic beverages. "Night life" is said to be virtually nonexistent.

After a deep sleep we awoke to the soft cooing of white fantailed pigeons under our window. Flocks of them were strutting about a green lawn under palm trees, protected against intruders and perilous flight by a high wire fence entwined with crimson bougainvillaea.

An English breakfast of tea, toast, marmalade, bacon, and three-minute eggs was served on our sun veranda, where the dappled light filtered through unfamiliar tree branches. Though the British had been gone for two decades, ghosts of the English way of life seemed to hover discreetly in the atmosphere. The soft murmurings of the pigeons were the only conspicuous morning sounds.

I telephoned Rita Dar at her Mercury office in the hotel and asked her to lunch with us at twelve-thirty. She had a lilting voice, somewhat high-pitched but charming. Her English had been perfected when Madame Pandit was India's High Commissioner to Great Britain. She said that at lunch we could talk over our travel arrangements and about the meeting with her mother, who was even now packing for New York.

I had always thought of India in connection with outstanding personages who in diverse ways had made an impression on the world. Besides Gandhi and Nehru, the persons varied greatly—from the Lord Buddha, who was said to have revealed mystic truth almost six centuries before Christ, to the nineteenth-century Ramakrishna, one of the most remarkable Indian saints of modern times. India meant to me Rabindranath Tagore, the handsome, white-bearded Bengali aristocrat, whose mystic poetry won him a Nobel Prize in 1913, and who had worked persistently for international understanding and peace. India brought to mind Robert Clive, the eighteenth-century Shropshire lad who came out to Madras at the age of eighteen, and who later, as both statesman and soldier, became one of the chief wielders of British power in India.

Of the very early Indian rulers before the Mughals came, only Asoka, the powerful emperor of the third century B.C., had caught my interest. He was the grandson of the man who defeated the Greeks established in Indian outposts under Alexander the Great. Eventually revolted by the horrors of a war in which he killed 100,000 men, Asoka became a Buddhist convert, suppressed the royal hunt, and stressed the sanctity of all animal life. He sent the first Buddhist missionaries to Ceylon and Southeast Asia. Under his humane rule there was a splendid flowering of art and architecture in India, with some flavor of Greek influence.

A telephone call from Rita Dar broke into my thinking. Since we were leaving for Agra the next day and her mother was flying to the States, she had asked her to join us for lunch, if we could postpone the time until one o'clock. "A blessed happy chance!" I said. We agreed to meet in the corridor just outside the Imperial dining room.

Since Nehru was dead, the person we most desired to meet in India was his sister, Madame Pandit, who had brought good will to India from her varied ambassadorial posts in two hemispheres. Vijaya Lakshmi Pandit had been her country's emissary not only to Britain but also to the United States, the Soviet Union, Spain, and Mexico, winning friends and understanding for her nation in the alien lands to which she was accredited. And because of her own qualities and her enormous prestige as Jawaharlal Nehru's sister, she had served as president of the United Nations General Assembly in 1953–1954. Now in her late sixties, she was a potent member of India's Parliament.

I had read Anne Guthrie's life of Madame Pandit, *Madame Ambassador*. I knew that the lady had been born at Allahabad in northern India on August 18, 1900, under the magnetic sign of Leo. On the day of her birth the heavens had opened and the rains came after a devastating drought in which hordes had died from famine. The baby's ayah declared that the birth, coming precisely with the rains, was a signal of good fortune, and that this first Nehru daughter would be a blessing to India.

Even today many enlightened Indians do not scorn astrology. Jawaharlal Nehru's wedding date had been carefully chosen by astrologers, and so had his sister's, when she married the handsome poet-scholar-lawyer Ranjit Pandit on May 10, 1921.

Because he had married into the outstanding political Nehru family, Pandit was made to suffer severely for his civil-disobedience activities. "I long," he once wrote from a fetid prison cell, "to sense the abiding peace and beauty of the forests, which are unaware of the agonies and convulsions of a continent." For his last penalty he had been locked in the dread Bareilly Central Jail, where the atmosphere was polluted by foul factory smoke. Shortly after his final release, for "health reasons," he succumbed, in January, 1944. Neither his brother-in-law nor Gandhi could attend his funeral, for they were still held in separate prisons. Because the two older girls had been sent to England, only the youngest daughter, eleven-year-old Rita, was then at home to comfort her mother.

Rita was now married to Autar Dar, a rising young government official shortly to be made ambassador to Lebanon. She maintained a governess for her two children so that she could continue working for Mercury Travel Service, where she was next highest in command.

We met the lovely slender young woman with sparkling black eyes outside the Imperial dining room. We recognized each other instantly. She was coming down the corridor briskly, holding out her hand and saying, "My mother will be here shortly."

As Rita Dar was greeting Thérèse and they were speaking of mutual friends, I turned to see Madame Pandit far down the hall, approaching with a radiant smile. I have always been keenly aware of smiles that come from a deep-seated loving-kindness. It was that beautiful smile of Madame Pandit's which had won over multitudes, at home and abroad. She was so obviously a personage of distinction. She was now wearing a gray sari that set off her wavy gray hair. I bent over her hand in the diplomatic manner to which she was accustomed in Europe, but my gesture had all the sincerity of instant captivation.

"I hope you don't mind my coming so unceremoniously to join you at lunch," she said. "But otherwise we might have missed each other entirely."

"But this luck is too good to be true," I said. "To meet with Nehru's sister at our very first luncheon in India!"

When menus were brought, Madame Pandit spied pomfret on the fish list. "Pomfret is absolutely the finest fish in India," she said. "It is flown here fresh from Bombay. I'll have the pomfret." We all took pomfret. The waiter returned to announce regretfully that there was no more pomfret. "Then I shall have the chicken," Madame Pandit said. "They do an excellent sauce for it here." We all took the chicken. Of course, I had offered them sherry or a cocktail. But being of the Brahmin caste—and Kashmiri Brahmins, at that—they did not drink anything stronger than mineral water. When I had suggested the steak with Béarnaise sauce, their fleeting smiles reminded me that Brahmins do not eat the flesh of cows.

After speaking first of her own distinguished accomplishments, I asked Madame Pandit to talk about her dead husband, who had impressed me as a kind of beau ideal among Indians. "How did you meet?" I asked.

"Gandhi's secretary, who had been with my husband at Oxford, sent me a brochure Ranjit had written. I was deeply impressed. The

secretary told Ranjit of my admiration. It was a whirlwind court-
ship. He appeared at our home in Allahabad one day, the next he
proposed, and the third day I said yes.

"For the wedding outfit my mother planned a sari of pale-pink
brocade. Gandhi, who had written that he would be delighted to
come to the wedding, assumed I would be married in khadi, the
rough homespun cloth of the peasants. My mother insisted on
'elegant brocade.' My father finally agreed with Gandhi. If a family
prominent in the independence movement, like the Nehrus, married
their daughter off in rich silks, what would the newspapers say,
when khadi had been 'adopted' by the Congress party members to
stimulate home industries? The British, you know, had forbidden us
to have our own textile mills, to force us to buy Manchester cloth.
Our household was in a state. The khadi sent to the dyers was too
coarse to take dyes evenly; it was streaked and awful-looking. I
wrote to Gandhi in despair. No answer came, and the wedding date
was almost upon us. Finally one morning a package arrived for me
addressed in Gandhi's well-known handwriting. It contained six
yards of fine-textured khadi with a card from Gandhi's wife, which
said, 'Spun by Kasturba Gandhi, with her love.' The cloth was sent
posthaste to the dyers, and I married in golden orange like the
sunrise."

Thérèse told Madame Pandit that our long-time admiration for
her brother began in Bermuda in 1932, when we had read Nehru's
Letters from a Father to His Daughter, written in prison for his
little girl Indira, now the prime minister. "But I know almost nothing about India's very early history," I confessed.

"It is largely dim to us, too," said Madame Pandit. "We did not preserve records carefully like the Egyptians and the Chinese. But the
earliest recorded exports from India relate to the year 975 B.C., when
Hiram, King of the Phoenicians, sent a fleet of ships to buy ivories
and peacocks for decorating the temple of Solomon. And you know
that Solomon ruled in the tenth century B.C. The Roman historian
Pliny, who wrote in the first century A.D. under Nero, tells that
Rome made annual purchases from India amounting to the equivalent
of two million dollars."

When the splendor-loving Mughals conquered northern India in
the sixteenth century, she remarked, they greatly enriched India's
tradition of crafts. They brought their opulent talents for creating

carpets and shawls, brocades, enameled brass, blue pottery, and stone inlay. Under the British, handicraft wares went into sad decline. "But now again," said Madame Pandit, "Indian handmade products are exported to a hundred foreign countries. Trends in the value of handicraft exports are at present most encouraging. Handicraft items, including jewelry with precious and semiprecious stones, have reached fourth place in India's export trades. Encouraging cottage industries is one of my chief missions."

"In this new socialistic democracy, what is the general attitude toward the caste system?" I queried.

"Gandhi, as you know, struggled hard to abolish the caste system in India. He was so touched by the degraded position of the so-called untouchables that he bestowed on them the title of Children of God. Somewhat in the manner of Jesus washing his disciples' feet, Gandhi publicly cleaned latrines. But untouchables still remain in great numbers to dig ditches and clean toilets. Yet no longer do their fellow folk feel polluted if the shadow of an untouchable chances to fall upon them. Today these unfortunates enjoy full constitutional rights. But although they have the vote, it will apparently be some time before they are out of the class of 'second-class citizen,' to use a current American phrase."

"Are the people still aware of who the Brahmins are?"

"Just as Virginians are conscious of first families and blue bloods. The Brahmins, originally the priests and interpreters of the sacred scriptures, are generally regarded as the top of the social castes, but the second class, called the Kshatriyas—originally, 'the warriors'— are almost as top-drawer. The nobles and the onetime temporal rulers, the rajahs, as well as military officers, belong to this caste. The merchant class—the businessmen and the artisans—come in the third caste. Democracy naturally involves continual change, and the caste system will completely dissolve with time. Now that we are free, we shall have our political squabbles and fierce loyalties to this or that individual politician or idea. We have far to go, yes, indeed." Madame Pandit paused. "But please remember," she added almost appealingly, "we have had freedom for barely twenty years."

We touched on advances in education and that staggering problem called family planning. In regard to the birth rate, Madame Pandit said, with an odd God-save-the-mark smile, "Someone has called the population explosion in India the arithmetic of desperation. With only 2.4 per cent of the globe's land area, India supports 14 per cent of its people. India has a larger population than the continents of Africa and South America combined. Now, in 1967, babies are being born at the rate of 55,000 a day. With United States aid, birth-prevention clinics have been established all over India. The number has grown from one in 1948 to almost 12,000 in 1966. Many of us work hard, make speeches. We are well received. Contraceptives are free. Good results have followed. We can only hope. . . . Now let's talk about what you should see in Agra and Jaipur."

I said that we were to see the Taj Mahal on my birthday, the next day, October 31, and that we would stay in Agra for three days. I mentioned that we expected to be received in Jaipur by the Maharani. I had talked that morning with John W. Shirley of the American Embassy about the appointment, and he thought it had been properly arranged.

"The Maharani is not very happy just now," Madame Pandit said, with a soupçon of wryness. "Parliament is thinking of cutting off the $240,000 tax-free allowances that the maharajas have been receiving annually since their lands were divided among the people. There will be a big to-do about this when Parliament reconvenes."

"Do you suppose that I might see your niece the Prime Minister? Thérèse and I have such a tremendous admiration for her father that I would like to meet the daughter."

Madame Pandit pondered. "Indira is a terribly busy woman. She's in Moscow just now, as you may have seen in the papers. She's continually traveling about India. And Parliament opens shortly. I just don't quite know what to say."

"Shall I invite her for dinner with the Strodes?" Rita impulsively volunteered.

"You know that Indira never accepts social engagements of any kind," said her mother.

"Still . . ." said Rita, "I shall try."

"May I beg a very special favor of you, Madame Pandit?" I ventured. "Could you yourself accompany me to your brother's house, Teen Murti, which is now a museum? Such a visit would be a most treasured remembrance."

In a flash she thought of tasks that had to be done before she flew to New York, but then she suggested, "Later this afternoon? Say, at five?"

"That would be a little short of marvelous. Where may I pick you up?"

"We had better go separately. I have some appointments. I'll meet you at Teen Murti. Present yourself to the curator. I'll tell him you are coming." Madame Pandit rose from the table. "And now, I'm afraid, I must fly."

"And I must go back to work," said Rita Dar. We all got up.

"I hope you will find much to like and remember in our strange, struggling land," Madame Pandit said to Thérèse in pressing her hand.

Arriving ten minutes early at Nehru's museum I was received by the youngish scholarly curator in his office, where bookshelves rose to the ceiling. He was still collecting and collating documents and manuscripts, he said. The museum, he observed, would not be declared absolutely complete for some time. Though, of course, millions of people had gone through it already. The building, spread out like a small palace on imposing grounds, had been the official home of the Prime Minister for the last seventeen years of his life. The modest Shastri, who followed Nehru as prime minister, had extremely simple tastes, and he declined to live in a place so grand. So did Indira Gandhi, who maintained her residence in a moderate-sized villa owned by the government. It was fitting that the house Nehru occupied during his long primacy had been turned into a museum as his perpetual memorial. Some of the rooms were exactly as they had looked when Nehru had lived in them up to his death in 1964, with his personal possessions scattered about.

As the curator and I talked, Madame Pandit appeared in the doorway in a black-and-silver sari, beautiful in her elegant simplicity and smiling her incomparable smile. Before going through the house we went out into the vast rose garden. "My brother had two hobbies," Madame Pandit said, "children and roses." There were countless varieties of rosebushes in acres of designated beds, but now at this season they were only in early bud. "In December," Madame Pandit said, "they will be in their glory."

She showed me where Nehru had lain in state under a wide, small-leafed tree, which the curator identified as a *chorisia spectabilis*. For three days mourners by the hundreds of thousands passed his bier. Then his body was taken to the banks of the Jamuna River and put upon the funeral pyre, a half mile north of the spot where Gandhi's remains had been reduced to ashes and scattered in the Ganges. But Nehru's ashes, Madame Pandit said, were taken up in an airplane and pinches of his dust were sifted on various hills and mountaintops and in valleys in far-flung regions of India, as well as in the sacred river.

"My brother relaxed here working among his rosebushes," Madame Pandit observed. "He almost always wore a rosebud pinned to his jacket—pink, yellow, or red—from the conservatory, if none were in bloom in the open."

Within the great house where Nehru had had his private life, I was impressed by the numerous statuettes of Buddha. This puzzled me, because Nehru confessed himself to be a nonbeliever, and the devout Gandhi could never "bring him round." But there sat replicas of the benign Buddha in various known attitudes, in this room and that— in sandalwood, in ancient bronze, and in ceramic—on the desk in Nehru's study, on a bookshelf in his library, in the drawing room. When I expressed surprise, Madame Pandit told me that her brother admired Buddha above all men who had ever lived in this world. "He put the images about," she said, "to remind him of serenity."

I told her of my amazement in finding in a place of honor on the desk of Muñoz Marin, when he was governor of Puerto Rico, a four-inch ivory statuette of Gandhi. In answer to my questioning glance he had said simply, "To keep me in mind of humility."

In Bangkok a few days before I had bought a seventeenth-century six-inch head and half-torso of Buddha in bronze and a reposeful hand in green bronze mounted on wood that had reputedly come from some small statue of the Buddha. In the Indian Art Emporium in the Imperial Hotel arcade only that day, I had purchased an eighteenth-century ivory image of a seated Buddha, in the teaching pose and with a spiked halo, mounted on a dark teakwood base. I said that I had spontaneously decided to get some Buddha statuettes for my studio and our house to remind me of serenity, before I knew of her brother's predilection.

Nehru's presence seemed to hover in his bedroom; it was as if he had just left it earlier that morning for Parliament. By his bedside table, beside a Buddha figurine, was his gold pocket watch, stopped at the run-down hour after its last winding. The watch lay on a

white note pad on which Nehru had written these words of Robert
Frost, whose poetry he admired:

> The woods are lovely, dark, and deep,
> But I have promises to keep,
> And miles to go before I sleep.

Madame Pandit tenderly recited the verse aloud. As we left the bedroom, she said softly, "My brother himself had the compassion of
the Buddha."

I had often wondered, I said, why the Indians practiced Hinduism,
with its many conflicting good and evil gods, rather than Buddhism,
which extolled the One Spirit. "Gandhi," Madame Pandit said, skirt-
ing the question, "declared that the essential part of the teaching of
the Buddha forms an integral part of Hinduism. Gandhi maintained
that Buddha was himself saturated with the best that was in Hinduism. He gave the religion a new life and new interpretation. But Hinduism owes an eternal debt to the great teacher."

Along corridors under glass frames were cardboard rectangular
placards in large English print and in Hindi of significant sayings
from Nehru's speeches. He was known for his eloquent oratory,
which swayed the masses. Madame Pandit repeated some of the gems
aloud to me in her beautifully modulated voice.

We entered a room walled with standing glass cases, containing
native costumes from various lands. They had been presented to
Nehru on official and unofficial foreign visits. They were all cut to
his size: apparel from Russia, Saudi Arabia, Afghanistan, Greece,
Argentina, and many other countries. "My brother liked fancy-dress
parties in which he could appear as something other than himself
and throw off the strains of office," Madame Pandit explained in-
dulgently. "Favorite among the garments were this cossack outfit
here and that sheik regalia over there. He liked fun. He was really
very human."

When I left the museum that housed oddments of Nehru's life, I
carried away an intimate impression of the man behind the world
figure.

As I saw Madame Pandit into her car I said, "I can never tell you
how much I appreciate your kindness in showing me your brother's
home. And thank you particularly for reading aloud those inspiring

lines from his public speeches. I wish that I might have heard him."

Madame Pandit smiled an odd smile and said, "You may yet." She reached over and took up a large flat package. "Because tomorrow is your birthday, I have brought you a little present."

"I am touched," I said, regarding the package questioningly.

"It is something I think you will like—a long-playing record of my brother's best speeches. And because I have a birthday gift for you, I have also brought a trifling remembrance for your wife." She handed me a small rectangular box.

"You are too too kind!" I exclaimed. "I cannot thank you enough. A birthday present for me, in India! And from you!"

We wished each other happy journeys—hers to New York and mine to the Taj Mahal. She drove away. Her radiant smile seemed to linger in the courtyard of Teen Murti.

Back in our sitting room I handed Thérèse her package. "Look!" She held up an evening bag of black silk with stylized designs in silver threads. It was a fine handicraft work of India. "I think," she said, " 'endearing' is the word for Madame Pandit."

The Road to Agra

At breakfast on Tuesday, October 31, I glanced at the weather report in an English-language newspaper. "Fine" was the paper's word for it; the temperature would reach a high of 85° and a low of 58°. It boded well for the drive to Agra.

Three waiters had brought our simple breakfast. Seven servitors came to the room to see us off: the floor steward, the two men who "did" our rooms, the two porters for our bags, and then, grinning, in the shadow of the corridor were two very dark fellows I had not seen before. "And who are you?" I said pleasantly, in some surprise. "I do the bathroom," one said. "I do the toilet," said the other. I first tipped the floor steward, who accepted with the slightest inclination of his head, then the two room boys, who gave little bows, and then the bath and toilet chaps, who bent considerably lower. The cortege saw us to the elevator, where we exchanged bows.

At the hotel entrance an old black Cadillac was awaiting us, guarded by a huge, genial Sikh with a clean white turban and so much beard that he wore a cosmetic net like a hammock to keep it from flowing down to his navel. He introduced himself as Bhupinder Singh, our driver and guide. I learned that every Sikh is surnamed Singh, which means "lion," and that according to their religion no Sikh may cut a hair from any part of his body. Bhupinder later told us that the strength of Sikhs, who were reported to be ferocious fighters, lay in their hair—"like Samson's."

The courtyard temperature stood at a perfect 76°. The air was autumn-fresh and very dry. When I said I doubted if we would need air conditioning at all, the driver said, "There will be dust where the road is being mended in many places." We settled back in roomy comfort as we took the road to Agra. We were exhilarated at the thought that the Taj Mahal was our real destination. Within a few hours we would have realized another "ultimate" in travel.

There is nothing remarkable to see on the leisurely three-hour 120-mile drive to Agra. The land is flat. There is no town; only scattered hamlets are to be seen. Disdainful camels and patient white bullocks, women in saris and men in dirty dhotis along the way give it the flavor of India. In the fields men plow with primitive implements; occasionally a co-operative tractor looms on the horizon. The huts seem to be made of wattle. A long, low building with mud walls is a schoolhouse. A bus lumbers shakily from the opposite direction. No private car passes us from behind. We saw two poultry farms that had been initiated by the Peace Corps. "Quite successful," the driver tells us. "The eggs give Indians much-needed proteins."

Under clusters of sheltering roadside trees, groups of men sit at ease, enjoying desultory gossip and ignoring whatever dust swirls about them. Some are stretched out flat on the ground taking a morning snooze. As the Swede at the Royal Barges Procession in Bangkok had said, they looked contented merely to laze. "India," I remarked to Thérèse, "seems a land of more obvious *dolce far niente* than Italy."

When a man came down the road leading a trained bear by a chain leash, some of the reclining figures sat up with mild interest.

Noting men drawing water from a strange slender contraption, I
asked the driver to identify it. "That is a tube well. They are being
sunk all over India. Tube wells are the peasants' new salvation. The
government helps the people install them."

Sensing that I was quite amenable to talk, the Sikh went on
volubly. "Perhaps you know that 80 per cent of India's population
is rural—only seven of our cities have a population of a million.
But you probably don't know that a movement is under way that
with some exaggeration may be called an agricultural revolution
from the top. Agriculture used to be looked down on and its workers
considered the lowest of the low. Suddenly agriculture is becoming
fashionable. Gentlemen farmers drawn from the higher castes may
be found within driving distance of every large town. Some see
themselves as patriots acting in the national interest to help free
India from dependence on foreign food imports. At the same time,
many have found that farming can be highly profitable."

The gentlemen farmers are experimenting with new strains of
wheat and corn—all kinds of hybrids, he went on to explain. They
are buying tractors, and many are personally supervising planting
and cultivation. Only a very few, however, really live on the land.
They drive out from their city villas. This new class of farmer in
India is made up of retired army officers, superannuated civil servants, city merchants needing to diversify their holdings, and law-
yers desiring more outdoor life. However, some are mere specula-
tors, who find agriculture a profitable investment, since there is no
agricultural income tax. "Who can say how far the new farmers
will succeed?" he continued. "But certainly they are increasing
foodstuff production, and their humbler neighbors are learning the
necessity of fertilizers and pesticides. Our cities, it is prophesied,
will some day be ringed with poultry farms, fruit orchards, and
truck gardens."

Bhupinder Singh changed the subject abruptly. "Look at those
white cranes at the edge of that pond," he remarked, "bowing to
each other just like Japanese." And so they were.

"What are those hogs doing, grazing on grass like sheep?" I
asked. "I never saw hogs crop grass before."

"Domesticated boars. They have been trained to enjoy munching
grass."

A Goodyear Tire & Rubber sign stood out against the blue

sky, the first touch of the States I had seen on the road. "Yes, Goodyear tires are made here now." Then a familiar Esso sign flashed by. "But filling stations are hard to come by. We chauffeurs generally fill up at Delhi and Agra."

"What about comfort stations?" I asked. "I've heard that they are virtually nonexistent in India. A man at the American Embassy told me yesterday over the phone that you just have to take to the bushes—if you can find a bush."

The Sikh chuckled. "Almost every day the newspapers complain that India can't attract many tourists until it has more rest rooms. But nothing is done. However, I have a surprise for you up ahead."

Thérèse was relieved that we had seen no one on the road or in the fields who looked downtrodden or hungry, though most of the people we saw were stylishly thin. The Swede in Bangkok had said there were more smiles proportionately in India than in Sweden, though the Indians were not as naturally a smiling race as the Thais. "You Sikhs seem happier and smile more than the Hindus," I ventured.

"Ah, the Sikhs leave it to God," Bhupinder said with conviction. "The Sikh will do and then think. Good Sikhs don't worry. Worrying makes people weak. And it will all come out as God wills. We believe in education and health measures, and we practice our religion."

A BOAC sign proclaimed the virtues of its international air service. Although most likely few who actually lived between Delhi and Agra had ever been in an airplane, foreign tourists passed this way in busloads, morning and evening. "Do you know what the Indians say BOAC stands for?" Bhupinder asked. " 'Better on a Camel,' " I responded properly. "Some say," he added, "it means 'Bring Over American Cash.' " We both laughed.

We drove into a mass of enveloping dust where the road was being repaired. Bhupinder Singh said, "Soon, a little farther on, I shall give you a break, to stretch your legs."

At length, on the left, we came to a stout fence with gates. It looked like an oasis in a desert; there were mango trees, a flower garden, and an idyllic-looking cottage. A sad-faced attendant of about thirty approached, perplexed and wondering. The Sikh got out, said something in Hindi to the man, and opened the door of the car for us. We stepped out under a tree that reminded me of a

mimosa. "It is a neem tree," said Bhupinder. "We get toothpaste
and toothbrushes from it, and a fine soap for skin diseases."

"Look, what a lovely parrot!" Thérèse exclaimed. Half the size
of the parrots we knew and of the softest chartreuse green, it was
feeding its young in a nest in the neem tree, clinging like a bluebird
at the opening of a hole. Parrots love neem trees, we were told,
because the wood is soft and easy to peck out.

Some tiny birds I had never seen before were darting into two
pendent arrangements made of grass and twigs and shaped like
pineapples or small punching bags. The birds looked like finches.
"They are called weaverbirds," the Sikh said. "Their habitat is
India and Africa. I don't think you'll find them in your country or
Europe."

"Look," Thérèse said, "there are fifteen or more of those nests
hanging to tree branches, but all except two are gaping open at
the bottom."

"When the babies are old enough to fly, the parents merely tear
out the bottom and the little ones plunge down as through a trap
door and instinctively spread their wings and learn in a split second
that they can fly."

Motioning toward the cottage, Bhupinder said, "Would you care
to refresh yourselves? This place is really a rest station for federal
highway engineers. It is not open to the public." The caretaker
resignedly led the way. Inside, it was dusky cool. A double bed
was covered with an India print. It looked as though it had been
arranged for siestas. There were neat toilet facilities, but no running
water and no string to pull. Beside a bowl and pitcher of water
were stacked clean towels. Thérèse and I made ourselves comfortable. We gathered from Bhupinder Singh that after we were
gone the keeper would take a bucket of water and in that way
flush the toilet.

When we returned to the car, the Sikh, as if performing a magic
trick, revealed a narrow rectangular icebox inside the trunk and
offered us a choice of Pepsi- or Coca-Cola. I took a bottle to the
caretaker, who accepted it almost as if he shouldn't. We drank
standing in the shade of the neem tree, watching the parrot feed
its young in the nest.

The Sikh declined to drink. "This is Wednesday, my fast day,"
he explained, with a beaming smile. "I must eat nothing and drink

nothing! It is not only a religious observance, but also a health measure. By fasting once a week I am kept cleaned inside, and I hold my weight down. See, my belly is flat and firm." He reached for my hand and pressed it to his middle. It was flat, and the muscles were rock-hard. A big and burly specimen, he reminded me of Ernest Hemingway with a flat belly.

"Do you mean," I asked in some astonishment, "that you can go on all day and drive to Agra and back to Delhi without a bite of food to sustain you, or a drop of water?"

"Sikhs learn to discipline themselves," he replied simply.

I walked up to the unsmiling caretaker, thanked him, and pressed some money into his hand. I asked Bhupinder Singh to express our compliments on the care he gave the place. He obviously loved the flowers, which were well watered. The Sikh spoke in Hindi. There was the barest flicker of pleasure at the compliment. "Life has been a disappointment to him," Thérèse said to me. The man showed us the way through another gate beyond the flower beds. He opened the gate for us, inclined his head, and almost smiled. "He seemed rather glad to get rid of us," I said. "It's good the engineers did not drive up and catch us there. But I am glad Sikhs act first and think later."

Refreshed, we enjoyed the rest of the ride as if we were just starting out. There was still nothing noteworthy to be seen until we were five miles from Agra. Then on the left there was Akbar's tomb at Sikandra, with its high imposing arched gateway of red sandstone inlaid with white marble. Akbar, who was one of the great Mughal emperors, died in 1605. Four three-storied minarets of white marble rose at the corners. "The tomb itself," said Bhupinder Singh, "is laid in a vast garden of 150 acres, where red monkeys roam, as well as herds of black buck and deer."

After the general impression of emptiness along the road, now, past the tomb of Akbar and only a few miles from Agra, we ran into "traffic" that increased steadily. But automobiles were sparse, and most of them were apparently near the end of their useful lives. The traffic was made up of human beings on foot, bicycles, and donkeys, bullocks, and camels. "Going into the city for the festival tomorrow night—the celebration of Dewali, on November 1," Bhupinder explained. "There will be fireworks and millions of candles burning. The most wretched hut in the poorest quarter will have a light in a window, or in the doorway if there is no window. It is the Indian celebration to the Goddess of Prosperity."

Bhupinder swerved to dodge a herd of goats. I asked when Agra was founded. "Little is known of the early history of Agra. Scholars say that the present city was the far southeastern outpost of the early Aryan settlers and was called Arya Grah, abode of the Aryans. It is supposed to have been early occupied by the Rajputs, that ruling caste and military power of northern India. An invading Afghan made it the seat of his government in 1501. Babar defeated him and founded the great Mughal dynasty in 1526. He spent most of his four short years in India in Agra and laid out famous gardens along the banks of the Jamuna River. His grandson Akbar, whose monument we just passed, chose Agra for his capital. He built the fabulous Red Fort, which you will see."

When we entered Agra I became more surprised and disappointed. It was a sprawling city, crowded and busy, with occasional factories belching smoke. I had somehow expected a more pastoral town, of about 50,000, grown up around its supreme attraction, the Taj Mahal. Bhupinder Singh quickly disabused me with statistics. "The population now stands around 600,000. Agra is an important communications center, a railway junction, and a commercial center. Cotton is ginned and pressed here. There is carpet weaving, tanning, and shoemaking. It is an educational center, too—with seven accredited colleges, including schools of medicine and engineering. It has large military and air force installations."

Sidewalks became more crowded with passers-by, many of them servicemen from the cantonments. Thérèse was silent and dismayed. She had expected a replica in miniature of the spacious boulevards of New Delhi. But, finally, at the far southeastern end of the city, we passed along parks and suburban villas and at last reached the Clark's Shiraz Hotel, set in a pleasant garden. The snake was here, too, right at the entrance gates: a huge python longer than the man who was holding it up by its sluggish neck and leering at us hopefully, inviting us to throw him a rupee. "Poor thing," Thérèse said, her sympathy going out to the tranquilized serpent. The Sikh waved a sharp, imperious negative at the snake charmer, and we drove into the hotel grounds. In the well-kept, spreading lawn a swimming pool was shaded on one terrace by neem trees. Long chairs were stretched out, inviting visitors to enjoy sun or shade.

But most guests were at luncheon now. It was a blessed dispensation to find another hotel laid in a country setting, away from the hubbub of trade. Chartreuse-colored parrots, like the one we had seen at the engineers' rest house, graced the dark-green tree branches, not singly or in pairs, but by the dozens.

At the lobby desk the pleasant clerk said, "Mrs. Dar called from Delhi. You have a room that faces the Taj."

"And may I introduce you to our Mercury representatives here?" Bhupinder Singh asked, indicating the first stand in the arcade of shops. "These men will take good care of you." The three Hindus in the travel booth were the Agarwall brothers, who had a strong family resemblance. They looked small beside the burly Sikh. We thanked Bhupinder warmly for his courtesy and good driving and for his interesting information along the way. He had given us fresh slants on India and we would remember his compelling personality.

Our seventh-floor room was attractive, with all the comforts. I walked straight to the long window. And there it was, with its dome and minarets shimmering like some lapidary jewel carved out of pearl. That incomparable dome of the Taj Mahal and the four graceful minarets were set off by the intense blue silk screen of the sky. We stood in rapt admiration. But I was again wrong in my imaginings. I had expected the hotel to face the Taj from a pleasant walking distance of some three or four blocks. It was a good mile away.

The Taj Mahal

The amiable plump uncle of the three brothers in the travel bureau was waiting to drive us to the Taj. While his nephews were carefully correct in their Western-style clothes, he himself wore a carelessly looped dhoti. All smiles and cordiality, he spoke little English, but he had provided a friend who spoke it well. A light-skinned man of about sixty emerged with quiet dignity. He had an unusual name for an Indian: Salvadore Elyas. It had been given him by the Catholics, he said. He himself belonged to that faith and lived in the city at a Roman Catholic mission adjoining the old cathedral. I did not ask if he had been a foundling.

"I thought I might be helpful," he said. "I am a teacher at the mission school. I shall not go inside the grounds of the Taj with you," he added tactfully. "That is for you to see alone. But I may give you bits of reminder information."

The road from the hotel to the Taj was winding, tree-shaded, and pleasant, made characteristically Indian by the yoked bullocks, laden donkeys, and white cows, wandering daft but imperious. As we came to a full stop for one especially inconsiderate cow, the Catholic Elyas, who has not the Hindu respect for cows, said, "We have a little jingle about the deference paid to the poor creatures:

> " 'The train was on the railway track;
> A cow was passing by.
> The train jumped off the railway track
> To let the cow go by.' "

We laughed and then listened attentively to our guide. "Shah Jahan, who built the Taj Mahal, was the great-great-grandson of the conquering Babar and the fifth of the Mughal rulers. But he was half Indian, for his mother was a Rajput princess. Because of his dedication to building, he is the most important to the world at large. He ruled for thirty years, contemporaneous in part with Louis XIV of France. He died in 1666, and became known in Indian history as the Great Mughal.

"But by no means did Shah Jahan have a completely good name. He was supposed to have got rid of three brothers who might have interfered with his succession. And the common people suffered dreadfully to maintain the extravagance of his court and the vast army required to keep the populace in subjection.

"Mumtaz Mahal was nineteen when she became the second wife of the Prince, who in 1627 took the throne as Shah Jahan, 'King of the World.' Though he had other wives, as was the custom, she was the favorite. Gifted with rare wisdom, she became his chief adviser and the keeper of the royal seal. On occasions, she even rode by his side into battle.

"The adored wife bore him fourteen children—the Mohammedans

consider sixteen legal. With the last child she died. One evening, when far gone in pregnancy, she was playing cards with her husband. Suddenly she turned pale, and the cards dropped from her fingers. 'My baby cried aloud within me!' she exclaimed. 'It is an evil sign, and I shall die.'

"When she was brought to childbed she was so sure of dying that she got her husband to promise, as a testimony of the love she had borne him for eighteen married years, that he would erect over her remains the most beautiful mausoleum the world had ever beheld. Then she died, as she had prophesied. Distracted with grief and feeling guilty that he had caused her to bear so many children, the Emperor straightway began planning her monument."

Salvadore told the story well and continued relating specific information. Shah Jahan called up 20,000 laborers and artisans from India, the Mohammedan countries, and China. Flower carvers in marble came from Bukhara, master masons from Qandahr, the foremost designer of domes from Constantinople, a pinnacle maker from Samarkand, and Persians who could inlay marble with semiprecious stones.

A two-mile ramp, sloping gently upward, was set up to carry building material to the dome. Marble was brought from Makrana, sandstone from Sikri. From the mines of Persia and Afghanistan, as well as India, came semiprecious jewels by the bushel. Someone has said that the Mughals built like Titans and finished like goldsmiths. For twelve years men labored to execute the inspired design of the gifted architect Ustad Isa of Shiraz.* And then another ten years were spent in building tombs and mosques, for balance, at respectful distances.

On the south bank of the Jamuna River, the mausoleum stands on a 312-foot-square plinth of marble twenty-three feet high. Above all, supported on a drum, is the most beautiful bulbous dome ever conceived. Salvadore turned about to face us. "The dome," he said, "is almost as large as that of St. Peter's in Rome, which, as you know, Michelangelo designed. Its designer was a Turk from Istanbul named Ismail Khan. I have not seen St. Peter's, but people tell me that that

---

* Some scholars say Shah Jahan selected the design by Ustad Isa Khan Effendi, a Turkish-blooded Indian already in his employ. A recently discovered epigraph in Persian gives the credit to a noted architect from Lahore named Ustad Ahmen.

dome is not so beautiful as the one of the Taj. Will you tell me later what you think?"

When we drove into a vast square with parked cars and buses and moving people, I noticed ornamental buildings of red sandstone, which I asked him to identify. They were tombs of various wives, we were told, and of members of the royal household. A flight of stone stairs led to the artists' colony called Mumtazabad—a village in itself—where dwell descendants of those seventeenth-century artisans who worked on the Taj.

Our slow-moving car finally stopped directly before the three-storied gateway leading into the Taj Mahal garden. The uncle procured entrance tickets at a kiosk. We approached the massive gateway of marble and sandstone that rose to a height of a hundred feet. Like a graceful festoon of vines above the gateway was a quotation from the Koran carved in Arabic script. The huge doors studded with knobs were wrought from eight different metals. Lord Curzon, at the turn of the century, presented the enormous metal lamp that hangs suspended from the vault.

Some years ago a distinguished world traveler remarked, "To those who have not already seen it, I will say, 'Go to India. The Taj alone is worth the journey.'" There it stood, at the far end of a long reflecting pool, white and sublime. At the four corners of the terrace platform three-storied minarets of beautiful proportions thrust themselves straight toward the heavens. The heart skips some beats as one stands in motionless tribute, in wonder that anything of such perfection could have been created by man. The first sight of the Taj Mahal stirs the senses in an ineffably sensuous way.

Thérèse and I sat down on a stone bench against the inside red wall and gazed far across the spreading Persian garden. The luminous white marble became touched by the pink of first sundown. A roseate glory seemed to emanate from the building. Ruskin's phrase of "frozen music" for architecture came to mind. And I thought, too, of those lines of Sir Edwin Arnold, who had been fascinated by India, its culture, and its literature. Of the Taj Mahal he had written: "Not Architecture as all others are. But the proud passion of an Emperor's love, wrought in living stone, which gleams and soars with body of beauty, shining soul and thought." Though the world's most famous monument is in India, it is hardly Indian at all.

It is Persian, with a Turkish dome. But never in any age, in Turkey or in Persia, was anything more perfect.

After a half hour of enriching our eyes at a distance, we went down the steps and started up the right-hand walk by the elongated pool, bordered by slender clipped yews. The reflection of the dome was washed in pale rose. Feeling somewhat like pilgrims, we walked slowly along the marble walkway and ascended the steps to a platform, where two kneeling men reached for our feet and tied enormous brown canvas moccasins over our shoes. We paused to observe the intricate *pietra dura* on the face of the great arch, the marble inlay of semiprecious stones. Inside the mausoleum we were each handed a marigold by an attendant. We moved behind the exquisite perforated marble screen to the sarcophagi of Mumtaz Mahal and her lover-husband. The tiered marble of the tomb was inlaid with pale colored flower designs and stylized Persian patterns. As eerie light filtered through the double screen of perforated marble onto the sarcophagi, one became conscious of a lack of symmetry. The Empress's tomb was directly under the center of the great dome. Her husband's was to one side. But Shah Jahan had not planned to rest eternally beside his wife. He had intended to build a monument for himself in black marble across the river and to join the two tombs by a white-and-black marble bridge. At least the story goes so.

We declined the invitation to descend the steep steps to the crypt directly beneath, where, on the ground garden level, repose the remains in tombs identical to those we had just seen. Wandering around the outside terraces, we looked now to east and to west at the great flanking buildings of red sandstone: a mosque to the west, a balancing structure to the east. High walls enclosed the forty-two acres of patterned garden. At first almost resenting the red buildings, though they were good in themselves, we came to see that by contrast they brought out the essential white purity of the Taj. On the back of the wide terrace we saw the Jamuna River meandering below. Originating in Himalayan snows, it had passed Delhi and the Gandhi monument and now lapped at the ground on which stood the tomb of the historic lovers.

First dusk was approaching when we returned down the walk alongside the pool, stopping now and again for yet other enchanted glances. A medley of sweet evening odors rose about us from the garden. Parrots fluttered overhead in groups on their way to roost, their movements punctuating the evening calm. There were a few other stragglers besides ourselves, but we were hardly conscious of them. We took a final lingering look at the bulbous dome that now almost seemed to float in the air. I reflected that while Gandhi and Nehru had done tremendous service to the Indians by securing freedom and instituting social reforms, Shah Jahan was benefactor to the world with his architectural jewel.

Our men were looking out for us in the plaza. The teacher-guide raised his eyebrows questioningly. "Yes," I said. "The dome surpasses that of Michelangelo's in Rome." And I quoted aloud for his benefit: "The Taj Mahal alone is worth a journey around the world."

The next day, as we started off after tea, Salvadore Elyas said, "Perhaps the Tomb of Itimad-ud-Daulah is the second 'must' in India after the Taj. Nehru was a great admirer of this monument. Some say he even went so far as to prefer its smaller perfection to the greater glory of the Taj. At any rate, he called it an 'exquisite jewel box.' I hope we are lucky with the bridge. It is narrow. The traffic over it must always be one-way. If we don't hit it just right, we may have to remain in line for a quarter hour."

To reach the river bridge more quickly, we traversed crooked streets and alleys through some crowded poor quarter, where cooking was in process on the sidewalks. Men stretched out on the pavements used the outside walls of houses like the backs of chaise longues, now and then drawing their toes in from a passing car or a straying cow. Poverty rose to the surface here and revealed its grimy face. The saris and the dhotis were mostly smutty. But children, unaware of their communal pauperism, played happily, with or without benefit of loincloths, jumping in and out of a public well. Rude neighborhood shops lined some of the dingy blocks. Citizens were purchasing their meager necessaries and stopping to exchange brief pleasantries.

As we approached the high bridge over the Jamuna, the Taj loomed to the right above the trees in all its white majesty. Down below on the sandy shore were spread thousands of colored garments and white squares of cloth, as if a whole village had gone to bathe in the river. But this turned out to be a business affair of professional laundresses, who would collect their rough dried work before nightfall and return to their cramped dwelling places with mountainous bundles on their heads, to begin the job of ironing. Three camels, led by their dismounted drivers, came down the rim of the river to drink.

We missed by three car lengths our chance to cross the bridge, and, because the far greater traffic was going into the city for Dewali's festival of lights, we were immobilized for almost half an hour. So we were unlucky; but, on the other hand, lucky, too. For sitting in the comfort of a closed air-conditioned car we watched all India go by, hardly a yard from our faces. Past us went a host of bicycles and a mob of plodding pedestrians, a few old men assisting themselves with patriarchal staffs. One tall fellow marched as if to a ceremonial, carrying an armful of tuberoses. Enterprising laundresses, who had already gathered up their clothes, stalked with stately mien, bearing prodigious bundles high on their heads. Fruit carts clattered by. Then came a shepherd herding nine sheep. Three ancient automobiles passed, with Mohammedan women veiled to the eyes. And after them came one of those two-wheeled carts so prevalent in India, with two seats for holding three persons each. But this cart was perilously overflowing with ten people, including children. A half-naked hermit, with wild flowing gray hair, a matted beard, and mad eyes, passed in state, as one conscious of his exalted position, though on a hitched ride in a wheezing jeep. He looked as if he had not eaten in a week or bathed in his entire life, but he still had an air of occult authority. Camels passed with their noses in the air, as though disgusted with the scent of the general atmosphere. In all the vehicular, human, and animal movement, however, there was a certain order and patience. Then suddenly, dodging in and out, in a kind of distraught flurry to get ahead, came scurrying a white cow. When possible, she charged forward, not caring what she bumped into. She grazed a laundrywoman with such jolting impact that the vast bundle was almost dislodged from the woman's head. Pedestrians gave way. Bicycle bells rang out warningly to halt her headlong rush, but they only agitated her the more. I looked at her closely. I had not seen such a frantic expression in any human eyes in India.

"What on earth is the matter with that cow?" I asked. "Has she got the running fits?"

Salvadore Elyas laughed. "She miscalculated, that's all. She got to the bridge too late. She had not expected this unprecedented traffic of Dewali. She fears she will get no supper, for it's just past milking time. You see, the owners of cows turn them loose after their morning milking to forage all day for what grass they can pick along the roadside or what they can scrounge from garbage. But to get their evening meal—however small—they must be home in time for the milking. The cow knows the rules. She dallied too long over some weedy tidbits across the river—and then, caught in this traffic jam, she becomes distracted and tries to beat the game. She probably won't get any supper tonight, but you may bet she'll be back home in time tomorrow."

The traffic policeman changed the signal, and we went over the bridge. Rickety booths with candies and cakes had been set up to entice travelers before they entered the city. But the shocking-pink confections dotted with flies looked anything but appetizing. We passed a settlement where other boys were frolicking in a public well, which overflowed from a gushing stream like an artesian well. At last we came to the entrance gateway of the mausoleum. The car was parked, and we proceeded on foot.

Elyas told us the story: Itimad-ud-Daulah was the father of one of Emperor Jahangir's wives, the one called Nur Jahan—"Light of the World." He was a Persian, who had risen to an important post in Akbar's court. Jahangir as a prince had fallen in love with the girl, but before he had declared himself, her father had married her to an Afghan nobleman. As soon as Jahangir ascended the throne he conspired to have the Afghan murdered so that he could marry the widow—like David in the Old Testament. It took six years for him to persuade the young woman to become his empress. Then he raised her father to the topmost rank among his ministers. She, dutiful daughter, doting on her parents, persuaded her husband to let her build this mausoleum for them. It was completed in 1628. Perhaps never in all the chronicles were a monarch's in-laws so honored. This Nur Jahan was the aunt of Mumtaz Mahal.

"So these that lie entombed here were the grandparents of Mumtaz Mahal," I said. "And if this tomb had not been built at the direction of Mumtaz Mahal's aunt, the Taj might not have been conceived?"

"Precisely. And Mumtaz Mahal wanted it surpassed in her own monument. You can see how potent Mughal women of the seventeenth century were at commanding the devotion of their husbands."

We entered through an imposing red gateway and beheld in the spacious garden a mausoleum of white-and-cream-colored marble, squarish in design, with four octagonal minarets at the corners, each topped by domed pavilions. In the center of the roof rose a large square pavilion with pierced marble windows. Broad double walkways of pink marble led to the tomb across green lawns. The Moorish arches, the pierced marble, the pastel mosaics could be discerned from a distance, and the whole monument grew more lovely the nearer we approached. It was both elegant and serene.

Glancing up, I saw ranged along the top of the marble balustrade a delegation of white doves. Their soft beauty added a breathing embellishment to the seventeenth-century masterwork. Three birds were perched on the twisted black pinnacles of three of the four domed towers. We removed our shoes, pulled on airplane slippers, and entered the monument.

"I suppose," said Elyas, "that hundreds of people have separately declared that this monument looks like a music box made of mother-of-pearl. The inset matched arches have a peculiar grace and beauty, I think. You may observe in the carvings the recurrent themes of cypress trees and wine jugs, both masculine symbols. The pierced-marble screens here that enclose replicas of the tombs below are much appreciated by art connoisseurs. Note the fluting of flowers around the tombs, with the inlay of multicolored stones."

We moved up aloft to the airy pavilion, where we got a fine view of the river and of Agra on the opposite side. When we came down and out upon the front terrace again, a troop of small monkeys, the color of moles, was skittering gaily along the top of the garden wall and in and out of the neighboring trees. Suddenly a misty green cloud moved swiftly across the garden as if borne by a strong wind.

"Parrots!" Thérèse exclaimed delightedly.

"Alas, those parrots are a pest," Salvadore Elyas said, smiling wryly. "They despoil the mangoes and other fruits. Decorative but destructive, they serve no useful purpose. Now, on the other hand, the monkeys do have an economic value. Caught alive, they can be sold for two dollars apiece."

"To zoos?"

"For medical purposes—to the Rockefeller Institute and biological laboratories for experiments and testing serums."

"Poor little monkeys." Thérèse sighed.

"But, madam, they do help to support some near-destitute families and they serve a sacrificial purpose in making life more healthy for the human race."

We turned for a last look at the monument in the light of late afternoon. It was as Nehru had said, like an exquisite jewel box.

At the bridge this time we were fortunate and caught it just right. Though it was barely dusk, lights were on in most of the houses and candles were burning in windows. In the hotel garden, bellboys and busboys were rushing about purposefully, stopping here and there to light the oil wicks of canisters stuck into the ground. Across the upper terrace on the hotel's façade little lamps had been placed at intervals. Some were flaming, but most were out. The lawn was wet. "They've had a shower here," the driver observed, "while we were across the river."

On entering the lobby we were almost overcome by a heavy spicy scent. All the boutiques in the arcade were burning incense in their bid for a year's prosperity. Lights blazed, and boxes of sweets were being delivered by messengers. It is the custom on Dewali evening for friends to send each other candy made from very special recipes. Even businessmen send each other fancy sweetmeats. Everyone appeared to be in buoyant mood, full of contagious good will and bright hope.

In a men's shop, called Moghul Treasure, where I stopped to pick up a black-and-white raw-silk sports coat I had bought that morning, two full boxes of sweets were now held out open to me, one by the Hindu proprietor, the other by his assistant, who had sold me the jacket. He was a tall, slim young man who wore a neat auburn beard like that in Renaissance representations of Jesus Christ. He had a warm voice, a beautiful half-smile, and strangely compassionate eyes. I declined the sweets. Then, noting the disappointed expression on both faces, I said, "They do look delicious. May we save them until after dinner?" I selected a piece from each proffered box.

Starting away, I said to the shop assistant, "But surely you aren't Indian."

"I was born in India. My father was English, my mother Greek." He had an upper-class English accent.

"He lives with my family now," the Hindu said. "He is the light of our house. My two children adore him."

To cover his embarrassment the young man handed me his printed card: Rudy Denis Mahoney.

The proprietor courteously accompanied us to the elevators. "Rudy had a most unhappy childhood. His father gave up the Greek wife and took an Indian one. At six he was sent to an English boarding school here in India. You can't imagine how good he is! But he's a good salesman, too, for tourists instinctively trust him." He bade us good night, and we wished him a year of overflowing prosperity.

"So much in India is unexpected," Thérèse remarked. "And such infinite variety!"

"Well," I said, "today at the bridge you really beheld India as it is."

"Yes," she agreed. "And I'm glad I did—once. But I can't go to see the frolicking in the city tonight with all those crowds."

From the picture window of our room we saw the haze of illumination in downtown Agra and noted the oil lamps flickering erratically along the hotel terrace ledge below, around the swimming pool, up and down the driveway. Shadowy figures were busily trying to keep wicks aflame. A wind had sprung up, and the lights, already dampened by the shower, were being blown out.

"I hope," I said, "this putting out of lights does not presage a restricted prosperity."

"Hardly—with this hotel erecting a huge new wing."

We had noticed the seven-story construction in progress when we arrived. The fifth floor had already been reached, and some forty-odd workers, half of them women, were mixing concrete, carrying concrete, pouring concrete, and spreading it. The men, bare to the waist but hatted, wore dirty dhotis that were little more than looped rags. The women, even at construction work, wore the traditional saris, and the hems of their garments brushed the wet concrete with indifferent swishes.

I nibbled at a candy, not waiting until after dinner. "It's delicious;

just what, I don't know: dates, almonds, pistachios, mixed with some creamy substance. Let's go down to the bar and celebrate Dewali with a drink." I began putting on a fresh shirt. The first red-and-yellow rockets burst forth across the backdrop of the heavens, momentarily blotting out the stars and illuminating the Taj. They disintegrated into a million sparks, and a faint roar of delight reached us from the direction of the city.

"I'm not going into Agra tonight either," I decided. "Remember, we were almost crushed to death once in broad daylight, at Mardi Gras in New Orleans. And to mingle with a million celebrating Indians at night . . ." After dinner we watched the fireworks from the roof garden of the hotel.

In the morning I awoke temporarily at daybreak and crept to the window to see if the Taj Mahal was in view. Its transcendent beauty was faintly veiled with mist. Satisfied, I went back to sleep. At eight-thirty the Taj was shimmering in resplendent sunlight.

The Taj Mahal is so sublime that every other noted building in India may seem an anticlimax. Yet the stupendous Red Fort, built by Shah Jahan's grandfather Akbar, is something also to be seen. Its formidable outer wall is a mile and a half in circumference and a hundred feet high. Within, there is ample space for grand parades and elephant fights, as well as for a military barracks. It took Akbar eight years to build it (1565–1573), and it was later embellished by other emperors, especially Shah Jahan, who had marble palaces and mosques erected within the walls. While Akbar was content to build massively of red sandstone, his grandson preferred to work with choice marbles.

Of the scores of points of interest inside the protecting walls, four stand out particularly. One is the huge cauldron, twenty-five feet in circumference and five feet high, hewn out of a single rock. For what purpose it was used, unless for a king's bath, no one knows. Another specialty is the underground chambers for siestas, beneath the so-called Grape Arbor, a salvation in the punishing midday heat of an Indian summer.

For his private pleasure palace Shah Jahan built the lovely Khar Mahal of white, pale-blue, and pink-veined marble, with some unusual windows made of translucent alabaster slabs. Window screens of pierced marble grace and ventilate inner chambers, where decorations with inlays of red carnelian are to be admired. But completely gone are the stairway of solid silver and also the throne of pure gold, with its royal canopy supported by twelve bejeweled pillars, that originally embellished the palace.

When Shah Jahan completed his palace within the Red Fort in 1637, a scroll, which may be seen today, proclaimed, "If there is a paradise on earth, it is this, it is this, it is this!" In his life of war, lush ease, and fantasy, the Emperor did not dream that this palace was eventually to be his jail. He spent the last eight years of his life here, a prisoner of his son. Aurangzeb had led a palace revolution, declaring his sire deranged by his mania for building, a judgment in which some high officials strongly concurred. The usurping emperor maintained that he moved only to save the country from utter depletion because of his father's heedless extravagances. But he did not subject Shah Jahan to any dungeon-bread-and-water incarceration. He tethered him among soft silken beds and the seventeenth-century opulence of an Eastern court. From a columned terrace or an octagonal tower the beauty-loving monarch was privileged to look upon his beloved's tomb from dawn to dusk and by moonlight and starlight. The aging Emperor died, propped up with cushions, gazing at his masterpiece. His death, on January 22, 1666, marked the beginning of the end of the glamorous, if oppressive, rule of the Mughals in India. Their imperial sway lasted hardly half a century after Shah Jahan's passing, and then it broke up in civil strife and a kind of loose feudalism.

During the decades following the departure or absorption of the Mughals, both the Red Fort and the Taj Mahal were allowed to deteriorate. Thieves chipped out semiprecious stones from the *pietra dura*. Petty vandals made depredations. Fortunately India's viceroy from 1899 to 1905 was Lord Curzon, who had a passion for keeping up and restoring historic buildings. It was his appreciation of the Taj Mahal that inspired the restorative work that preserved it.

In the late afternoon we went to have a farewell look at the Taj, to fix its beauty more deeply in remembrance. I had read in a book that morning that Shah Jahan gave to his architects and builders the touchstone: "It is to be as beautiful as Mumtaz Mahal was beautiful, as delicate as she was delicate." And he further commissioned them to make it "in the image and the soul of her beauty." His orders had been almost mystically carried out. Though the construction work may have been grueling and even life-destroying, the result appears as pure a labor of love as the Chartres Cathedral is claimed to be, where thousands offered their labor and skills freely to the glory of the Virgin. A transcendental quality emanates from the Taj's glowing surfaces, re-emphasized by the ninety-nine names of God inset in Arabic over the soaring entrance. The four minarets are constant reminders that the religion of Mohammed exhorts the faithful to frequent prayer. Not only is a man's love for a woman immortalized, but Allah is praised as if in a ceaseless paean of adoration.

The Taj Mahal should be viewed when few human beings are in evidence. Because of the crowds, it is not always so desirable to see it by moonlight. For during the times of the full moon, cavalcades arrive from the far corners of India to mingle thickly with the foreign tourists disgorged from buses.

On this first afternoon after the climax of Dewali, throngs of Indian visitors had not yet returned to their homes. Families sat in groups about the lawns eating from paper containers. Children romped unawed in the shadow of the Taj, as if it had been no more than an elephant slightly different from the one in their town. Plump and nubile Mohammedan girls, with black chiffon veils that left their eyes uncovered, glanced about in a deceitfully demure manner, and one switched her derrière provocatively, as if to dislodge a horsefly. But two different groups of three lovely Hindu girls came down the walkways in elegant pastel saris with fully revealed faces of high breeding and marked beauty. They stood out like rare blossoms, to remind one of the oft-discounted value of cherishing and cultivation. Thérèse and I sat apart on a stone bench set against the red entrance wall and gazed over the people until finally we were hardly aware of them.

Although on this afternoon no rose illumination came from a sunset, as the shadows of slender trees and clipped shrubs lengthened in the approaching twilight, the Taj took on an aura of enchantment. When we finally rose to go, the words of Prospero re-echoed: "Our revels now are ended. . . . We are such stuff as dreams are made on." Pausing for a last backward glance in the arch of the vast entrance gateway directly under Curzon's hanging lamp, I felt that Keats, above all the poets, even Shakespeare, should have seen the Taj Mahal. He might have caught its essence and its history in verse as deathless as his "Ode to a Grecian Urn."

To Jaipur

The morning of November 3, we left by car for Jaipur well attended. Because the eldest of the Agarwall brothers, Ram, spoke little English, brother number three, Prakash, was also sent with us, while the second brother, Shyam, kept the travel-bureau office. The brothers had surprises in store for us. At a spot where we stopped to pick up some Pepsi-Colas in ice, they brought forth a friend who they announced spoke excellent English and for a lark would like to go along and practice it on us. He was slim, graceful, ingratiating, and a Mohammedan. His dancing gray eyes and wavy light-brown hair proclaimed him of some different blood from his black-eyed comrades. But it was his left hand that caught my special attention. His ostentatiously manicured nails on that hand were excessively long and pointed. "But why?" I asked with direct curiosity. He regarded me with a beguiling smile and said frankly, "To show the world that I do no manual labor, not even handicraft work."

I never learned precisely what he did do, but I think he held some governmental clerkship. I knew that he was no secretary, however, for with those nails he could not possibly have manipulated a typewriter. He mentioned that his wife had a good job, and that they had no children and did not purpose to produce any, the present world being in such an upturned state. Prakash said that he had two kids, but that there would be no more. Ram, who was doing the initial driving, confessed somewhat sheepishly that he had six before he had thought much about the matter, but would have "absolutely none in the future." The new idea of birth control was obviously taking some hold in India.

The two Hindus seemed quite fond of their long-nailed friend, sitting between them in the front seat. Hindus and Mohammedans, who had been maiming and slaughtering each other with ferocity only twenty years before, were coexisting in cordial amity now. The car pulled up before a house with a tan stucco façade in a street where all the houses were attached and a common stoop barely a yard deep ran the length of the block. "What is this stop for?" I asked, impatient to be on the way. "Our family wants to see you, and we would like you to meet our family."

A goodly proportioned, medium-stout, and rather handsome man in his late fifties appeared with genial dignity in the doorway. He was wearing a fawn-colored Nehru jacket and a fresh white dhoti. "This is our father," said one of the brothers, as we got out and shook hands. The father had the air of a man of some municipal consequence. We were ushered inside.

There, in a corner of the patiolike living room, grew a tree, its trunk a yard in circumference around the base, its top branches in the full sunlight, far above the second story. Light from the morning sky filtered upon the paved floor of the patio, brightening potted plants and small shrubs. A fire was glowing in the huge fireplace that took up half the space of the left wall and was large enough to roast a whole sheep or calf. The smiling mother paused in her pot-stirring to be presented. Three pretty wives of the brothers and the wife of the uncle and some unmarried sisters hovered nearby. Two of the women, not considering themselves properly dressed for visitors, fled away in giggles. Four youngsters were seated on the hearth eating their breakfast out of plates held in their hands. Hearing sibilant whispers, I glanced up. A row of six kneeling children peered down at us with friendly curiosity through the grilled balustrade of the second story, where a gallery ran outside the sleeping quarters.

"How many families live here?" I asked politely.

"Five, and all but our youngest unmarried brother have children."

Congeniality seemed to pervade the patriarchal atmosphere. This was obviously a prosperous middle-class family. All the school-age children, we were told, were being taught English. One chubby youngster of about seven, the last born of the amiable uncle, voluntarily gave us a "taste of his quality." He took a stance, pointed at the sky, and began to recite in English "Twinkle, twinkle, little star." At the line "How I wonder what you are," he dropped his cheek to his right upraised palm and rolled his enormous liquid eyes upward, pondering philosophically. When he finished, I called "Bravo!" and gave him a congratulatory handshake. After bows were exchanged, we got back into the car. Driving away I observed, "With eleven children under one roof, I become a bit dubious about India's crusade for family planning." All three in the front laughed, and shrugged.

Some thirty-five miles from Agra we turned off the Jaipur road and drove south for about a mile and a half to a place of rare interest. Suddenly we were beholding thousands of water birds— flapping, soaring, grounding, diving, or just basking in the early November sun. We had entered the Keoladeo Ghana Bird Sanctuary, which draws thousands of tourists who come on wildlife sight-seeing expeditions.

Once, all these acres were the private property of the Maharaja of Bharatpur, and this had been his famous duck-shooting preserve, where the ruler of the former princely state entertained his foreign guests. When the Maharaja realized that with the new independence most of his land was to be taken from him, he made a regal gesture and presented his preserve to the government as a perpetual wild-bird sanctuary.

The swampy region is a prime breeding spot for waterfowl. We saw, in prodigious quantities, open-billed storks and painted storks, ibises, spoonbills, gray herons and blue herons, numerous varieties of wild duck, three species of exquisite white egrets, and several spectacular kinds of cranes. Some birds were diving in the shallow lake for food. Deep-water waders seemed to delight in mere wading. Great birds perched lazily on stumps or dead tree branches. Obviously, these square miles where the atmosphere had not reverberated with gunfire now for several years was a bird paradise.

Ornithologists have long known that species of birds who enjoy the brisk mountain air of Switzerland in summer come to winter in India. "Migratory birds," remarked the Mohammedan, "are the world's most privileged travelers. Like the rich, they are in the best places at the proper seasons. This winter-resort sanctuary might be compared to the Riviera or Palm Beach."

Presently I observed a strange group of brownish-black snakes swimming near the shore with erect heads a foot and a half above the water.

"But *are* they snakes?"

The men laughed. "They are snake birds or darters."

"But where are their bodies? They look like periscopes."

"They do look like periscopes," Prakash agreed. "Their submarined bodies are beneath the surface. The anhinga—for that is his proper name—like the grebe, is able to cut down the air he stores and so reduce his buoyancy until his body submerges and only his long neck with the small head and spearlike bill appears above the water."

The slender necks, especially when curved into a serpentine S, looked startlingly like snakes cutting through the water and ready to strike. Dipping below the surface and sighting prey—a small fish or a water snake—the darter skewers his victim with his lethal lance. Then he flips his booty into the air, catches it deftly and swallows it, his neck bulging as the dinner goes down. He can only swallow when his neck is vertical, we were told. One darter brought his victim to the shore's edge and pounded it insensible against a rock before gobbling. On land the snake bird, about thirty-four inches high, is ugly and awkward-looking. The only attractive feature about him is the wing tips splashed with silver streaks.

When I marveled that there was enough food to supply this vast congregation of bird life, Ram walked a few feet from the car to the edge of the swamp and stooped down. He brought back an enormous snail, larger than a golf ball, somewhat smaller than a baseball. He cracked the calciferous shell for our inspection and exposed the succulent mollusk. "The snail and the frog," said the Mohammedan, "are really the basis of the economy here, and both breed profusely in these sloughs."

A thrilling flight of white egrets, clothed in their lilylike purity, lighted in the near water. Dipping their golden slippers into the grayish liquid, they began to wade in search of a meal.

"In the drier parts of the sanctuary," volunteered Prakash, "many interesting animals roam in herds, like the black buck and slate-blue antelope we call nilgai. There are also spotted deer, and cheetahs and wild hogs and a few hyenas. Three-day bird-and-animal-watching parties are sent down here by Mercury Travel Service from Delhi. Two overnight guesthouses are provided, one called Forest Lodge and the other the Bharatpur Guest House. The roads are open all year—unless real floods come in the rainy season." "But none of the regular tourist buses makes a stop here," the Mohammedan said. "They spend their time at Fatehpur Sikri, India's Pompeii."

We had purposely passed up this old capital of the Emperor Akbar, once more populous than Agra, twenty-two miles to the southwest. The guidebooks give its attractions high rating. But after the last look at the Taj we had no desire to see any more buildings until we reached Jaipur. "Anyhow," the Mohammedan said, "Fatehpur Sikri is merely a collection of deserted palaces, mosques, and mansions, set on a hilly eminence in the midst of a vast expanse of khaki." Then he remarked, "I suppose you know that 'khaki' is taken from the Persian word for 'dust.' And dust is a baneful thing here. Never come this way from April to August if you can help it," he added with a grin. "You might choke."

When we drove away from the sanctuary the brothers exchanged slanting smiles at our visible delight in the waterfowl, just as though they had shown us their own private preserve. We settled back in our seats, for there was nothing more remarkable to observe in the flat landscape on the road to fabled Jaipur.

Our attention was called to the fact that we had entered the state called Rajasthan. "You will find," said the Mohammedan, "the order of things in Jaipur very very different today from what you would have found a few years ago, before we got our independence and were repartitioned. But Jaipur, called the pink city, is to me still the most romantic city in India."

"Keep on talking," I encouraged our volunteer guide. "The best thing I know about Rajasthan is that the white marble of the Taj Mahal came from its Makrana mines."

"It is still rich in white marble, but far richer in pink sandstone. It also possesses quantities of gypsum and salt, and some deposits of silver-lead zinc. Among its principal manufactures are glass, textiles, and sugar refining. It makes agricultural tools and implements. It is quite famous for its cottage handicrafts, which turn out superior pottery, handwoven goods, and 'tie and dye' fabrics. For hammered brassware it is unsurpassed."

The Rajputs in Rajasthan were originally a martial people of feudal chiefs and landlords. Now the princely houses of Jaipur, Udaipur, and Jodhpur and some lesser ones have been stripped of their temporal power. Their territories have been combined into one constituent state of the new Republic of India. Rajasthan today has an area of almost 132,152 square miles, and is the second largest state of India. It is six times the area of England, and its total population numbers twenty million. There is plenty of breathing space, but in the west lies the bleak Thar Desert, which borders West Pakistan. The desert makes for red dust, and sometimes the hot summer winds blow the dust as far as Delhi, two hundred miles away.

In the eleventh century one of the Kachhwa Rajputs, who claimed descent from Kush, son of the Lord Rama, hero of the Indian epic the *Ramayana*, founded the kingdom of Amber. His ancient capital was seven miles north of the present Jaipur. When the conquering Babar established the Mughal dynasty in India, he was fought fiercely by the Hindu ruler. But when his grandson, Akbar the Great, offered friendship, Man Singh, the then princely ruler, accepted it. Man Singh proved such a brilliant soldier that he rose to be the commander in chief of the Mughal army.

Jai Singh II, Man Singh's grandson, who built Jaipur, was a lad of thirteen when he ascended the throne of Amber. Born in 1699, he was the most gifted of all the rulers. Besides being a statesman and a superior soldier, he had a passion for building and for astronomy. He designed huge observatories—which still exist in prime condition—not only in Jaipur but also in Delhi, Varanasi, and other places. In the midst of the general turmoil of the times he pursued science and art. Because of his bright wit, the Mughal emperor Aurangzeb called him Sawai—prodigy—and this word is incorporated in the title that the princely house of Jaipur bears today.

Before building his new capital of Jaipur, Sawai Jai Singh pored over plans of outstanding European cities and studied ancient Hindu treatises on architecture. Jaipur, founded in November, 1727, is still considered a model of town planning. The city was originally laid out in six great rectangular blocks, separated by boulevards 111 feet wide, running east and west. Intersecting them are three principal roads running north and south, with open squares at the crossings. The old city is surrounded by a stone wall nine feet thick and twenty feet high, pierced by eight gateways. The Maharaja personally supervised the building of Jaipur. He would come down almost daily from Amber on the hill to criticize or praise the work in progress.

In 1818 the British took Jaipur "under their protection." During the fierce Indian mutiny of 1857–1858 the Maharaja of Jaipur, grandfather of the present head, kept his people loyal to Britain and profited greatly by his fealty. The present Maharaja Sawai Man Singh, direct descendant of the astronomer-king, was given full ruling power by the British in 1931. But he was forced to merge his state in the union of Rajasthan on March 20, 1949, and a civilian governor was appointed to administer it.

On the formation of the new Rajasthan, the Maharaja surrendered not only his temporal power, but also most of his vast landholdings, to the new central government. In exchange, he was permitted to keep his personal property and a couple of his palaces and granted a large annual tax-free pension of $400,000.

"The cream-colored Rambagh Palace at Jaipur is now operating as a hotel," the Mohammedan observed. "The illustrious Prince of Jaipur has become an innkeeper."

"Like the young Aga Khan in Sardinia," I interjected. "With the Aga Khan it is a hobby."

"With the Maharaja of Jaipur it is a profitable business. The hotel is fully booked. . . . Ah, this changing world!" The Mohammedan gave a profound sigh, and followed it with a mischievous grin.

Entering Jaipur through an eastern gate in the crenelated pink wall was like venturing into the pages of *The Arabian Nights' Entertainments.* Elephants, camels, and white bullocks added to the impression, as we passed façades of mingled Mughal and Hindu architecture: mysterious latticed galleries, pierced marble balconies, twisted Moorish columns. The general tone was pink, from the pinkish sandstone to stucco painted a deep powder-pink. Prideful old men wore their snowy beards in a distinctive styling, parted in the middle and brushed upward to meet their twirling upturned mustaches. Their wide turbans of red or yellow cotton, resembling oversized icepacks, made them the more colorful. Some wore patriarchal gowns of richly printed stuff. A few of the women wore wide swirling skirts and jangling silver beads instead of the ubiquitous saris.

"Except for the addition of a few automobiles," the Mohammedan observed, "some streets are much as they were in the eighteenth century. And yet Jaipur today is oddly different. That great stucco barracks you see to the right there once housed the four hundred personal bodyguards of the present Maharaja—no man under six feet. A few years ago, on passing this way, you would have heard the rattle of knives and forks and the clink of glasses. What you hear today is the tap-tapping of hundreds of typewriters, and perhaps by more women's fingers than men's. The old residency of the royal guards has become a governmental agency. The harem, too, is dissolved. The concubines are dispersed. Some have been married off to army officers—quite happily, we hear."

The landscaped grounds of the Rambagh Palace outside the old city walls constitute a seventh of the municipal area, where the population now reaches 450,000. We entered one of the Rambagh's seven gates and drove past the enormous enclosed swimming pool, with its arched glass roof. So as not to desecrate the formal terraces, green lawns, balustrades, and garden stairs of the palace's noble front, hotel clientele enter by a side porte-cochère. Our bedroom opened to long verandas on both sides. On one, French doors gave upon an irrigated fruit orchard; the other looked over and down into a sunken formal flower garden in a great rectangular court. Our room was as large as a good-sized suite. The old-fashioned bathroom was larger than some first-class hotel rooms. A welcome window air conditioner was throbbing dutifully.

All three of our escorts from Agra accompanied us into our room to make sure we were satisfied. They set various small bags and parcels on the blue-velvet davenport. A clean-cut, personable room boy directed the two porters where to place our suitcases. "Distilled water is iced in the thermos," he said, "and a tray of fruit is on the table there in the corner. My name is Gopal Das. For whatever you want you have only to ring for me."

Before we could bid good-by to the trio from Agra, our telephone rang. It was the private secretary of the Maharani of Jaipur. Her Highness, he said, would be pleased to receive my wife and me the next morning at eleven.

I had wanted to meet the lady not merely because she was a world-famed beauty, but also because she was now a hard-working public servant. With her "comedown" in royal mode of living, she had not been content to sit sadly and reminisce over the "death of kings." She had sharpened her wits, studied the crying needs of her people, and entered a political career. She had stood for the Indian Parliament on a Conservative ticket, and when the elections came she won by the largest majority ever known in socialistic India.

When Maheshwar Singh, the Mercury Travel representative in Jaipur, came to call to arrange our sight-seeing, he filled in some information about Her Highness. He was an olive-skinned man in his early thirties and reminded us of an intelligent-looking Rudolph Valentino; he had dark-green eyes and a wisp of Continental mustache. "When the Maharani went out campaigning," he said, "she proved herself eloquent and a shrewd politician. She drew enormous crowds. Except for the topmost among upper classes in Jaipur, few had ever laid eyes upon her. Of course, they knew she was *there*. But she was a kind of legend, like her beauty. When the masses saw her, they were captivated. She talked sense. She had practical ideas. She went out into the byways in jeeps or any old car through clouds of dust and in monsoon rains. If she had had to get to a political rally by bullock cart, she would have done it. For all her feminine appeal, she is tough. She just won't cancel a scheduled appearance. Her husband was amazed at her political acumen. Now, as you know, he is India's ambassador to Spain, and she goes to stay with him in Madrid when Parliament is not in session. Parliament opens next week. That is why she is here now. You are fortunate to catch her.

"Incidentally," he added, "the present lady is the Maharaja's third wife. She was born Gaytri Devi in the small princely state of Cooch Behar. Her father was a maharaja, but one in comparatively meager circumstances. Her mother, however, was an extremely clever woman. She got all three of her daughters married to important maharajas."

When I expressed concern about our flight reservations for Delhi on November 6, because they had been made in Tuscaloosa, Alabama, the previous May, Singh reassured me. "Don't worry!" he said soothingly. "I shall attend to everything, believe me. Don't worry," he repeated with a respectful grin that was something like a mild reproof. The word "worry" was inflected as if he had been educated at Oxford, though I do not think he had ever attended any college.

On questioning him, we learned that his name was unusual in that both the first and the family name meant "lion," though he was no Sikh, and that he was born under the zodiacal sign of Leo, the lion. While he was generously endowed with that magnetism reputed to go with Leo natives, there was a faint hint of cynicism now and again at one corner of his mouth when he smiled. But he had an air of absolute certitude about him. After he had gone I said, "Now we may relax. With that charming fellow we don't have to worry about anything."

A car would be at the hotel to take us to the Rajmahal Palace at 10:45 A.M. on the morrow.

The Maharani of Jaipur

By ten o'clock the November morning was so pleasantly warm that for our visit to the Maharani Thérèse put on the smart sleeveless cotton print she had bought in Bangkok. A taxi took us to the Maharani's present resident palace, called the Rajmahal, where her husband and she have lived since 1957. It was smaller than many mansions in Newport. This one had no need for four hundred tall guards. There was only one entrance gate.

From a long, low building facing the palace a man came down the veranda steps to ask us courteously to step into the office. There we were identified, apparently for security reasons. Another Indian then conducted us across the dusty unpaved court to the palace entrance, where we were received by a third man.

We passed along a corridor where artistic groupings of antique swords, spears, and burnished shields made arresting wall decorations, and I recalled a colored picture of this corridor in *Holiday* Magazine. Through a screened door off an intersecting hallway we were ushered into a paneled library with a long picture window that gave upon a columned arcade and a flower garden. Bookshelves lined three sides of the room. My eye ran along the varied titles. They were well chosen, the authors ranging from T. S. Eliot, Aldous Huxley, and Keynes to Faulkner, in English. Proust, Malraux, and others were in French. Various Indian authors were in Hindi and Sanskrit. Deep comfortable chairs had standing reading lamps beside them. A beige davenport was backed by the picture window. There was a fireplace for winter evenings. The room had a lived-in, intimate, and cozy feeling, like a library in an English manor house. It was quite a contrast to the satin-and-velvet gilded parlors at the Rambagh.

An unliveried servant appeared and indicated a long table with bottles of Scotch, gin, and sherry, an ice bucket, and an array of glasses. We were urged to partake of something. We took sherry. Ceremoniously but perfunctorily the old servant served us, unsmiling, as if once he had served princes, but since the Maharani had gone into politics . . .

On a nearby table I noticed a framed photograph of Jack and Jacqueline Kennedy, as a laughing, youthful couple, shown mounting some stairs. In the inscription Jacqueline thanked the Maharani for her hospitality in Jaipur and expressed the hope that someday she might also bring her husband to India. Nearby was a doubly signed photograph of Queen Elizabeth and her consort. And then on another small table, as if in a special niche to itself, was a full-length photo of the dashing Philip alone, looking his most handsome and inscribed in memory of tiger-hunting hospitality. A fourth silver-framed photograph on another table was of Princess Beatrix, heir presumptive to the throne of the Netherlands.

A youngish attractive Indian entered to announce that the Maharani would be here in just a moment. "She has been slightly ill —a touch of flu—and she must leave for a speaking engagement in another town at three." Then he remarked, "I know that you are a writer and—many things about you."

"Really," I said. "How is that?"

"Well, you see, I was with the Maharani in Madrid in September when your letter was forwarded from here. She was staying with her ambassador husband." He smiled engagingly. "And then we 'looked you up,' as it were. . . . Will you excuse me for a moment?"

I turned to observe the oil portrait of the Maharani that hung on the wall facing the picture window. She was undoubtedly beautiful, but it was not an entirely sympathetic portrait. The artist had given a petulant touch to the mouth. I had seen dozens of photographs in American and European magazines in which she far surpassed this oil.

The young man was back almost immediately to say the Maharani was coming now. As he spoke, she glided along the arcade outside the window, something like a pink cloud, and then appeared in the doorway. She seemed about five feet two, just Thérèse's height. She was wearing a pink chiffon sari of the shade of a Pink Perfection camellia. It seemed peculiarly appropriate for the Pink City of Jaipur. Instead of throwing the end of the sari over her left shoulder in the usual manner, she wore it draped lightly like a mantilla over her wavy shoulder-length brown hair. I caught my breath at her beauty. The international magazines were not wrong; perhaps she was the most beautiful woman in the world. But her delicacy of feature surprised me. Her magnolia complexion was lovely, although she seemed pale from her illness. She used no face rouge or eye shadow, only some powder and an unaccented lipstick. And she wore no jewelry: no necklace, earrings, ring, or bracelet. Her only jewels were on her soft gold-colored sandals, which were studded discreetly with sapphires and pink pearls.

"I am so sorry to keep you waiting, but I am getting ready to go to a political rally, where I must speak this afternoon." Her voice was well-modulated, gentle, and low, but faintly hoarse from her cold. "I received your letter in Spain, but I could not answer because you had already left Alabama for Japan by the time I had it."

She moved with natural grace toward the davenport and sat down, with her back to the light. I glanced at Thérèse and saw that she, too, was charmed. We took the two armchairs at right angles to the davenport. I offered to get the Maharani a glass of sherry. She hesitated, and then decided that she would take nothing.

We spoke first of our mutual delight in Spain and particularly in those incomparable towns Toledo and Segovia. She had a genuine admiration for Franco and the way he had managed to raise the country's economy and uplift the proletariat without destroying the aristocracy. Thérèse and I were to spend a week in late November in southern Italy, at Ravello above Amalfi, and were to see again the Grecian temples at Paestum, below Salerno. The Maharani had recently been to Paestum on a September vacation with her husband and had been deeply moved by the beauty and antiquity of the temples. In Ravello we were booked to stay at the same delightful little hotel, the Palumbo, where the Maharani had been a guest. "You will be enchanted with the view of the Gulf of Salerno," she said.

In answer to my query about her native home, the Maharani said, "Cooch Behar was a tiny province, hardly 1,200 square miles —at the foot of the Himalayas, east of Nepal and south of Sikkim, in a far northeastern corner of India. My father was the ruler there. From early days to 1950 it was a so-called 'princely state.' Then, with the repartition, it was merged with West Bengal. The town of Cooch Behar itself is quite pretty, with well-laid-out parks and artificial lakes. The district abounds in foliage and flowers, and in the forest black bear and tiger roam, and rhinoceros as well. Because we had so many rivers and plenteous rainfall on loamy soil, we raised good crops of rice and jute, tobacco and sugar cane. Here half of Rajasthan, as you must know, is desert. We need irrigation terribly. The desert soil is fertile enough if we only had water. The Socialists faithfully promised to provide the people with irrigation. But they haven't done it!" The last words came out as an accusation with a slightly biting emphasis. "In Parliament I plead for water for the people. A little is being done, but we need so very much more!"

"Is your Conservative party gaining strength in the Parliament?" I asked. "What is its Indian name?"

"The Swatantra or Freedom party. It was founded by conservative independents only in 1959. And already it is the largest opposition party. Its support for private enterprise has won it wide publicity—and popularity."

"It seems to me that India needs to encourage private enterprise," I said, "to make an effort to attract foreign capital, instead of offering obstacles."

"You are so right," the Maharani agreed. "The government of

India—that is, mainly the Congress or Socialist party—allows foreign private investments, but the potential investors face such frustrating delays and unattractive terms that they back away."

The Maharani touched on her special interest in crop rotation, sanitation, elementary education, and family-planning clinics. Then she spoke particularly of her efforts to stir the rural people out of an understandable lethargy to try to better their own lot. "At last," she said, "the government gave in to granting foreign firms an entry into India's chemical-fertilizer market. We need fertilizer desperately, but the Socialists fear for foreigners to own businesses. However, a change has come, and improvement in agriculture is already manifest. Massive additions of chemical fertilizer is what India needs—perhaps above all else. Our farmers plant 320 million acres annually, about the same amount as your farmers, but our return is hardly 40 per cent of your yield. Indian farmers have been using only about one-thirteenth as much fertilizer per acre as Americans do. Now we have the great hope that sometime in the 1970's we can lift the output of cereals from 400,000 tons a year to 2,500,000."

Changing the subject from India's needs and hopes, she asked me about my writing methods. She, too, was interested in writing, she said. I told her that I wrote with a soft pencil, on an old sixty-five-cent plywood lapboard.

"You don't type?"

"My beloved wife types my manuscripts—sometimes four drafts."

The Maharani regarded Thérèse with keen interest. "I have tried to type, but I am just no good at it." With an impulsive movement she reached for Thérèse's nearest hand. "Let me see your hands," she said. "Ah, I see! You keep your fingernails short." She glanced at her own long white nails, somewhat wistfully, as if in a sudden quandary as to whether to sacrifice them or not. I doubted if she ever would, because they were so much a part of the charming movement of her hands.

"You have so many male secretaries about you to do your typing," I said, consoling, "why should you?"

"Still . . ." she murmured. The word trailed away and we spoke of other things. She was highly conversant with what was going on in the world at large, even in our southern part of the United States. She confessed that for all the American prosperity, she did not see how we were to solve our problems of riots, crime, and racial differences. We confessed we did not either. However, we agreed that "restlessness" seemed world-wide.

I commented on the two photographs of Prince Philip. "Yes, he came to stay with us twice, once with the Queen and once by himself, when my husband and I took him on a tiger hunt." Her dark eyes lighted with warm recollection.

That part of her sari draped with apparent casualness over her lustrous hair dropped to her shoulders. With a deft movement of utter grace she rearranged it. This was the second time it had happened. Was it a practiced gesture? It was beguilingly feminine. I appreciated the grace, "art or hap."

Once, when she coughed—it was obvious that she had still not completely recovered from the flu—I again offered her sherry. She shook her head, and asked instead for water, which I gave her.

It was surprising to feel so at ease and "at home" with the Maharani. She had a quality that inspired a man's protectiveness. It was difficult to reconcile this exquisite fragile beauty with the statement "But she is tough!," which we were to hear about her three times in India. I could rejoice that she had the stamina and the courage to undergird her soft glamour.

Her dark eyes lit up brightly again as she spoke of her son, who was at college in England. She had a much older stepson, the Maharaja's heir, now a colonel in the army, who, on a brief leave, was staying at the Rambagh and had dined with her the previous evening. Now he was practicing polo on the Rambagh field. In the new democratic government, however, neither son would ever be legally entitled "Maharaja." Princely titles may soon be completely obsolete in India.

"How do you like the hotel?" the Maharani asked.

We told her that we were delighted: with its architecture, the service, the gentleman manager, and particularly with our attentive room boy. "Though you are relieved of a terrific responsibility as chatelaine of such a huge outlay," I said, "it must have been a wrench to leave that beautiful place."

"I was very comfortable there," she confessed. "I loved my own apartments and was a little sad to give it all up. But my husband felt that it was too great an expense to keep—for our residence. You know there are seven gates to the estate, which had to be guarded night and day. He owned this place where we are now, so he did a deal of restoration and modernization, and here we are. And the Rambagh is an operative hotel."

"Well," I said, "your lovely old palace is a magnet to bring tourists to Jaipur. It has its economic, as well as aesthetic, value for Rajasthan."

"I may hope so," she said, with a faint sigh.

The young secretary appeared to say that some delegation was awaiting the Maharani in an anteroom. We rose to go. "Perhaps I really should see them now," she said. "For we leave just after luncheon for a two hours' drive to the political meeting."

"But," I said, as she coughed slightly, "are you quite well enough to go? Flu can be extremely weakening. Shouldn't you call it off, and rest? You're always elected to Parliament by what we call a landslide."

She smiled at my spontaneous solicitude. "I'm afraid I really must. It has been arranged for weeks. The meeting is largely about new schools, and we are so backward in education. You see, people are expecting me."

People were expecting her. It was a call of duty. She had to be tough with herself.

"If you would like to attend a session of Parliament in New Delhi," she offered, "I should be most happy to send you tickets. My house phone number is listed. It's very easy. Telephone or write. I'll walk with you to the front." We went down the corridor together to the door of the anteroom, where a small delegation awaited her. There we made our adieus, and she glided into a semidark room. An equerry escorted us across the dusty courtyard to our waiting taxi.

"Well?" I questioned Thérèse as we drove away.

"Yes!" she answered, instantly responsive.

"*Is* she the most beautiful woman in the world?"

"I've never seen one more beautiful. And she is highly intelligent and grace itself and full of appeal and—yes, sweetness."

I had been prepared to be captivated by the lady. I was delighted to have my wife's appraisal to back up my impression.

"Do you think she's happier in her new role of active public servant, instead of a wax doll in regal luxury?"

"Let's say she's made the adjustment gracefully."

Driving back to the hotel, I reflected that much of the resurgent advance of India could be attributed to the franchise for women. Again and again we were to note the stimulating effect of women only recently emerged from centuries of suppression taking important roles in politics and municipal affairs. Madame Pandit, who had been more or less India's ambassador to the world when most needed, had set the pace. And Indira Gandhi, Nehru's tireless, dedicated daughter, was now holding the most arduous premiership of any nation. The traditional Indian notion that females existed chiefly for men's dalliance and for breeding was fast dissolving, even in remote regions of the subcontinent.

When a tenderly brought-up girl who became a maharani could speak words of hope and specific reform to rural throngs from bullock cart, if necessary, in lieu of a platform, Indian women who had accepted a pain-ridden life resignedly took fresh heart and began to reassess their stultifying attitudes.

City Palace and Amber

That afternoon Singh, head of the travel bureau, sent us his most appropriate guide. He was a retired schoolteacher of sixty-four named G. S. Mathur. India retires its teachers early to spread the jobs. After forty years of teaching, Mr. Mathur's pension was twenty dollars a month. He supplemented the pittance by acting as a guide. Small, wiry, neat, almost dapper in his well-brushed old clothes, he had a courtly manner that was both alert and ingratiating. His English was good, his information was pat, and some of his opinions were original and even acid. We liked him at once.

Mr. Mathur told us that as Max Lerner departed the pink city, he exclaimed, "I have seen Jaipur, and now I can die!" "Of course, that extravagance was for the local press," Mr. Mathur said. "But the Russian-born American did declare, perhaps sincerely, that he linked Jaipur with Venice and Paris as one of the three most beautiful cities in the world." Though without either flowing or tidal water, Jaipur has a very special flavor and personality. It has the dreamlike quality of some legendary tale.

By all odds the most arresting building of the City Palace complex is the Hawa Mahal or Palace of the Winds. Its fanciful façade is smack on the main street and rises five stories high in a modified pyramidal shape. The whole front is a mass of semioctagonal overhanging balconies with perforated screens for windows, curvilinear roofs, and half domes. The balconies, with decorative finials at the apexes, rise one above the other. The general effect is light and airy and suggests a confectioner's masterpiece in pinkish-brown sugar. The Hawa Mahal was built in 1799 for the ladies of the court to watch, unseen, the royal processions that passed below. This wide street before it is called the Procession Road. From the City Palace within the royal compound a covered passage leads to the Hawa Mahal, which has no living quarters. "The elaborate façade," Mr. Mathur explained, "is an attestation to Jaipur's construction skill, for the balconies adhere to walls only eight inches thick. Breezes blowing through the perforated screens give the building its name, Palace of the Winds. It was once the favorite of the concubines. They could stand or sit anywhere in the tiers of balconies, like opera boxes, and secretly watch the world go by. Now only the ghosts of the harem ladies appear at those mysterious apertures."

The whole effect is alluring, hinting at the quintessence of amorous delights suggested in *Arabian Nights*. "I doubt if Xanadu had anything to equal this," I remarked.

Though full of riches, the rest of the elaborate City Palace complex behind pink masonry walls seemed somewhat anticlimactic after the Hawa Mahal. The many courts are reached through series of imposing portals. One of its principal structures, the Maharah Mahal, was built as late as 1900. Its exterior is embellished with upper galleries of lacelike marble balustrades and columns. Since 1950 no royal retainers dwell there; today it houses a Textiles and Costumes Museum. Here one sees beautiful woven textiles and magnificent embroidered costumes worn by former princes. One particularly memorable robe is of heavy black silk studded with pearls and emeralds.

A gateway flanked by two marble elephants leads to enormous

brass doors and into a court, in the center of which is the Hall of Private Audience. The open pavilion on a raised platform is graced by a double row of marble columns supporting engrailed arches. In former times the hall was used for royal coronations and state banquets. The Chandra Mahal, which is seven stories high and towers above the other buildings, is cream-colored and a pleasant contrast to so much pink. Within, our guide pointed out the ivory inlay of doors, the gold work on the ceilings, and the rooms with mirrored walls. He told us that the reception and banquet halls had been refurbished for Jacqueline Kennedy's visit to Jaipur while her husband was President of the United States.

As we walked about, our schoolteacher would say unobtrusively, "Notice the curvilinear cornices and the grace of the slender tapering columns." Some buildings contain art treasures, oil portraits and miniatures of maharajas and maharanis, and rare manuscripts in Sanskrit, Persian, and Arabic. Included are works on astronomy and mathematics by Sawai Jai Singh, the builder of Jaipur. A splendid collection of old arms and armor—more than 2,000 pieces—is on exhibit, including the eleven-pound sword of Akbar's Rajput general. Most impressive of everything within doors is the magnificent collection of Oriental rugs. They fill an enormous hall. Some are suspended from the high ceiling like wall decorations. Other specimens, sixty feet long, are spread on the vast floor. In color and design they were the most beautiful we had ever seen. But we did not want to tarry in a museum. So Mr. Mathur led us out into the Persian garden adorned with intricate geometrical flower beds, water channels, and a forest of fountains. "When Mrs. Kennedy was here," he said, "they had the fountains flowing."

Suddenly bells clanged, and citizens came rushing from all directions for evening service at the temple at the far end of the garden. "That," said Mr. Mathur, "is the temple of Govindji, guardian deity of the maharajas of Jaipur. The idol was saved from the destructive fury of the Mughal Aurangzeb's hatred of Hindu sacred relics. Sawai Jai Singh brought it from Mathura and set it up here in his new capital in 1734."

Standing near the center of the garden amid the lush foliage and flower fragrance, we surveyed the varied buildings that had been erected to house a royal court. "Until the repartition, this whole

City Palace compound belonged to the present maharaja. Now it is owned by the municipality. Perhaps the guardian deity lost her protective potency."

"Perhaps," I said, "Govindji blessed this last maharaja by relieving him of the responsibility of taking care of all this."

When we started to leave the garden we were almost knocked into by a well-dressed, swarthy stout man rushing belatedly to the evening temple service. The man had no neck. An expression of sour distaste passed over our schoolteacher's face. "Never trust a man without a neck," he half hissed. "They are cun-ning-g-g—" The word hummed with conviction and warning. "They may cheat you if they get a chance."

I recalled those four "little no-neck monsters" in *Cat on a Hot Tin Roof*, the repulsive children Elizabeth Taylor so abominated.

"I will have no business dealing with a man without a neck, one whose head rises straight from his shoulders," Mr. Mathur declared.

"I must confess," I said, "that I've always found men and women without necks singularly unattractive. But I didn't know they were supposed to be rascals."

"But indeed! And look out for the fellow who has a cast in his eye, an eye that doesn't focus level with the other. By inclination he is tricky, though he generally manages to keep within the law." He took a deep breath, and then added, "And a one-eyed man is the worst of all. At least I have found it so in India."

The spread-out complex known as the City Palace is so intricate and so filled with a multiplicity of treasure that it seems perhaps more confusing than imposing. But we did not once tire of the sharp observations of our philosophical guide. What one remembers best is the unforgettable fantastic façade of Hawa Mahal as seen from the street. This exciting and original architectural triumph is a prime reason for so many renowned travelers to declare that Jaipur is their favorite city in all India.

Our schoolteacher guide awaited us at half past nine the next morning with all his spry affability. The only difference about him was a green felt bag, which he carried by its drawn string. It was almost identical with the green bags Harvard students carry their books in. But it did not bulge as if with books. I wondered, but asked no questions.

We took the road to Amber, the long-abandoned capital, at Jaipur's northeast gate. For approximately seven miles the rose-colored granite road climbs gently toward the gateway of the palace compound. On both sides of the approach to Amber are patches of forests, then gardens, temples, and cenotaphs of various maharanis of Jaipur. Farther back from the main road stands the sacrificial stone column commemorating the "horse sacrifice" performed by Sawai Jai Singh, the last ruler to live at Amber and the builder of Jaipur. On high ridges all about rise defensive ramparts and terraces, with watchtowers slowly crumbling into ruin, made picturesque by the patina of centuries.

As we neared the deserted city the sun bathed it in a warm radiance. At the foot of a hill groups of patient elephants were waiting to convey tourists on their fancy howdahs up to the palace. The elephants were all females, past the age of young-bearing. They had had their faces and trunks bizarrely painted, like old dowagers made up for a gala ball. Some of them were rouged a brighter pink than the houses in Jaipur. Others were splashed with varicolored curlicues. They all looked like gently disposed old biddies. Instead of being loosed to unexciting, skimpy pastures, they were earning their keep by toting admiring tourists and posing a dozen times a day for snapshots to prove the elephant ride to folks back home.

We, who had said positively, "No elephant ride," entered modestly through the arched gateway in a Chevrolet. The great court before the high palace is surrounded by buildings that were once barracks and royal stables. Amber is a fine specimen of old Rajput architecture, built in the early 1600's. Within the palace one gets a first general impression of vast triple-arched Moorish windows and walls of colored mosaic in stylized patterns. Beyond an open marble court and approached by a ramp is a small temple of Kali. Behind a silver-plated door, surrounded by delicately carved marble work, is enshrined the image of the Hindu goddess in black marble, brought here long ago from Bengal.

"On his last stay in India," our cicerone informed us, "before he returned to his ambassadorial post in Spain, the Maharaja of Jaipur came to make his devotions to the goddess. It was quite a court ceremony."

"But surely the Maharaja doesn't believe in such a conception as Kali," I said.

"Who can say? He is a Hindu. Would you care to enter?"

Though I had a strong aversion to this double-dealing Kali, we were prepared to take off shoes, despite the damp floor. But when the guide said, "You will have to take off your belt too, and, Madam, you must leave your alligator handbag outside," we demurred.

"But why my belt and her handbag?"

"They are made from unclean animal hides and would offend the goddess."

So we gave a cold shoulder to Kali and moved on to the princely apartments. Access to them was through an ornamental gateway with fresco paintings. The upper portion was known as the Temple of the Blessed Wives, and from behind carved marble screens the ladies, unseen, could observe the happenings in the court below. "But once they passed the portal," Mr. Mathur stopped to say, "the pretty girls became prisoners—nothing more—pris-on-ers for life." He hissed the s's and rolled the r's of the word "prisoners" with eloquent condemnatory effect. "For all the surrounding splendors," he added in a melancholy tone, "it must have been a most monotonous existence, and often there were so many ladies that one's turn came only once a year."

Now that harems had vanished with other regal perquisites all over India, I wanted to know how the princes managed their amours. Mr. Mathur rolled his eyes slightly upward and to the left. "Dancing girls and the like—scattered in apartments in the cities. It is far less expensive. In former times, if a prince took a girl to his bed for a single night, he was responsible for her keep for life. Today, it is more like 'protection' in Paris, say, or on Park Avenue in New York."

We traversed rooms with such names as "Temple of Victory" and "Hall of Pleasure." One wall of the latter boasted a marble cascade connected with a channel where running water once cooled the torrid atmosphere. The cascade was fed from a tank on the roof.

We moved about the complex of chambers, up ramps, along closed corridors, down flights of stone stairs, and out upon a hanging balcony; it was much like a maze deliberately fashioned for courtly intrigue. When our schoolteacher wanted us to admire an especially intricate inlay of ivory he pulled open his green felt bag and with a magicianlike gesture presented a magnifying glass to Thérèse. Then he would bring forth from the bag binoculars with which we could survey the distant battlements and even the very narrow steps that led steeply to the watchtowers.

We came at length to a unique reception room where the walls were lined with a million glittering tiny mirrors closely embedded in the plaster. The ceilings, too, were masses of small mirrors and spangles. We were told that this room was the most famous of its kind in the world. Other apartments, rich in marble carving, were grouped around an ornamental garden. Two oblong chambers, surrounded by a veranda and arcades, were adorned with alabaster panels inlaid with delicately hued glass.

By a winding ramp we reached a roof terrace that adjoined some of the women's quarters. Here we had a superb panoramic view of hill crests and the once formidable fortifications. The Indian sky was a luminous azure with a few patches of drifting clouds, which were reflected far down in the blue lake below. The romantic old capital of Amber, set on a majestic elevation in a basin surrounded by hills, possessed natural scenic beauty denied to flattish Delhi, Agra, and Jaipur itself.

Struck with a sudden thought, I said, "I have noted the cooling cascades and the channels for running water, but what of plumbing arrangements for the ladies who lived high up on this topmost story?" Mr. Mathur smiled out of the corner of his mouth and cast a glance to see that Thérèse had paused indoors to look closely at some mosaic. He spread his hand in a gesture to include the whole wide terrace. "The ladies squatted here," he said *sotto voce*, "day or night. Menials were the modern conveniences and cleaned up after them at various intervals." "Well," I observed, "they certainly had an inspiring view for it—in full sun or by moonlight."

When we returned to Jaipur, the main square called Bari Champat was stirring with strollers and jaywalking shoppers, as heedless of motorcars as were the camels and the wandering cows. In the center of the square the stalls of flower sellers added color and scent to the shifting scene.

Because we had seen enough for a morning, we said no to inspecting the famous Observatory of Sawai Jai Singh or visiting the Jaipur Museum. The museum, which lies south of the walled city, was built by the grandfather of the present maharaja to commemorate the 1876 visit of Edward, Prince of Wales, who laid the cornerstone. Created in the Indo-Saracenic style of marble and sandstone with pink balustrades and kiosks, the museum took ten years to complete. We accepted Mr. Mathur's word for the fine collection of ivory carvings, the rare specimens of illuminated manuscripts and, particularly, more treatises of Sawai Jai Singh on astronomy.

So the guide directed the chauffeur to drive us through a colorful street where varied handicraft work was pursued in open-faced shops and even on the sidewalks. I was well aware of the old custom of buses halting at shops where the driver got a commission on sales. But we consented to stop at a noted place that had been making enameled brassware for almost a century. "This establishment," we were told, "has the accolade of the *National Geographic*. It is owned and operated by Mohammedans. Blessedly, at the repartitioning we did not kill our Mohammedans in Jaipur, as some states did. We value our Mohammedans highly because of their industry and workmanship. They seem more energetic than our Hindus." I did not bring up the young Mohammedan with the inch-long fingernails on his left hand; naturally, there are exceptions to rules.

We entered the display rooms through a driveway and courtyard where boys and men were squatting or kneeling on the paving stones, industriously hammering and chiseling brass artifacts. One lad, looking no more than ten years old, who was sitting nearest to the sidewalk, caught my special interest by his intense concentration in struggling for perfection. The proprietor within was a portly man of dignified and impressive appearance. From under a display case he brought forth a dog-eared copy of the *National Geographic* of several years past and opened it to the illustrated pages that dilated on his wares and reputation.

We praised various platters with intricate designs in pastel-shaded enamels. I ended by buying a chased brass ashtray with a small white tiger reposing in the center, as well as two useful heavy bar utensils in the form of a "key to the city," with bottle opener, ice cracker, and corkscrew concealed within. They were both hand-inlaid, one with pale-pink enamel and the other with pale-blue. They were sturdy, handsome, original, and a bargain.

Back in the driveway I paused beside the intent boy who was bent over his chisel and hammer with such absorption that he did not even look up to see to whom the shoes and trouser legs belonged. When I dropped a two-rupee note into his lap, he glanced up, startled, his eyes widened with question. I gave the lad a pat on his capped head, and merely said, "Because you are such an earnest worker." To Mr. Mathur I observed, "You keep your Indian boys off the street and out of mischief by giving them employment."

"They seem the happier to be employed," he said, "and to help with the family income."

"Think It Over"

Following siesta hour, Major Rawat Singh, the director of our delightful hotel, sent over one of the old palace guards to show us the former apartments of the Maharaja and the Maharani, which had been left almost intact. The man was six feet three and excessively thin, with a profile resembling that of the mummy of the great Rameses. But he walked with the air of one who had been of consequence, and he carried the silver keys with an almost ceremonial air. The adjoining suites on the second floor afforded veranda views of the front terraces and the charming wings of the palace, with the domed kiosks at each end of the upper story.

The apartments were as spacious and luxurious as expected, and were furnished in most excellent taste, but more in the continental European than Indian tradition. The Maharaja's suite had a definite masculine flavor, with much leather and wood and dull-orange and olive colors. The Maharani's adjoining apartment was regally feminine, with turquoise walls, rich cream-colored carpets, and crystal chandeliers. Her bathroom was the *pièce de résistance:* all pale-yellow marble, with a great sunken bath and fixtures of gold. No queen could have desired more. And the suite looked as comfortable as it was elegant. In case the air conditioner's electricity suffered a shutdown, a three-bladed ceiling fan of ivory was still in place.

"Are these rooms ever let to guests?" I asked.

"Occasionally. The Maharaja's suite is booked for tomorrow—an English gentleman of title."

At tea we had the long veranda outside the white-and-gold cocktail lounge exclusively to ourselves until we were joined by Maheshwar Singh, the travel-bureau manager. He had stopped by to get our impressions of Amber and to say that he himself was fetching us at 10:00 A.M. the next day to put us on the Delhi plane. Singh was married, he told us, and had a three-year-old daughter, of whom he was inordinately fond.

I questioned him about the frequency of the surname Singh. I said I knew that all Sikhs were named Singh, but there were so many other Indians bearing the name.

"Right," he said. "We have a common saying in India: 'All Sikhs are Singhs, but all Singhs are not Sikhs.' "

Referring to our visit to the Maharani in her present palace and her former elegant apartments in the Rambagh, directly above the place where we now sat drinking tea, I said, "We are struck by the social change in India in two decades."

Singh smiled noncommittally. "If you had known the Nizam of Hyderabad before the British pulled out, you'd have seen a more dramatic reversal in fortune. Once worth two billion dollars in lands, jewels, and art treasures, with an annual personal income of seven million, he ended his days scuffing about in carpet slippers and wearing a battered old red fez. In his heyday he used his 150-piece solid-gold table service at dinners in the grand manner. Later he wrote his invitations on scraps of paper torn from personal letters."

I had a special interest in this Nizam of Hyderabad because my friend and college mate Oliver Cromwell Carmichael, from Good Water, Alabama, had lived in one of his palaces as tutor to the royal princes. While getting his degree in anthropology at Oxford—he was a Rhodes Scholar—he had taken a year out to accept a tutorial post with the Nizam, who acceded to the throne of Hyderabad in 1911. Carmichael, who later became head of the Carnegie Corporation in New York and afterward president of the University of Alabama, succeeded to a place that had been held by E. M. Forster. While tutoring in India, Forster had got material for his famous *A Passage to India* (published in 1924).

Both Forster and Carmichael had enjoyed their exotic sojourns in India, though the latter had found a few practices hard to take. I recalled his vivid recital of a special ceremony in the palace courtyard. A sacrificial goat was slaughtered in a strikingly original way.

The designated man killed him by biting off the live goat's head, round and round in a bloody circle until the head was severed. The youthful Carmichael had almost disgraced himself by being sick in the princely presence. He had saved himself by half closing his eyes and thinking of "a host of golden daffodils."

Descended from the last of the Mughal viceroys, Singh told us, the Nizam of Hyderabad had ruled over a state about the size of Italy and some eighteen million people. Although the province was overwhelmingly Hindu, the Nizam was a strict Mohammedan. He was determined not to become a part of the new Indian Republic, but to head a separate kingdom. The government finally sent in troops. For his recalcitrance the Nizam had almost all of his property confiscated. The old man sulked until he died in 1967.

"He was a tiny man," Singh went on, "only five feet three, and he weighed about one hundred pounds. He had a thrifty streak in him and bemoaned the upkeep of three wives, forty-odd concubines, two hundred children, and three hundred servants. After independence, just before the Indian army took possession of his land, it was reported that he flew planeloads of accumulated gold and treasure to Mohammedan Karachi and created there the Nizam State Bank to hold it. Finally, in his last years, he lived in one sparsely furnished room, ate like a bird, and darned his own socks. The new socialistic taxes had left him destitute, he wailed. His confiscated white marble palace in New Delhi is now used to house foreign V.I.P.'s."

As we finished tea, returning sight-seers began stretching out in the long chairs on the grass terrace to rest their feet, while others sought the cool bar. Singh strolled with us down into the far garden to see the covered swimming pool the Maharaja had built in 1945. The main door was locked, but at the end of a lane of flowering shrubs we entered through a side door. While hotel guests were welcome to swim there, the place was now empty. It was enormous, with a vast arched roof of glass and numerous diving boards and trapezes. Alcoves and open rooms held chairs and couches for relaxation. Marble was in such plentitude that I thought of Imperial Rome and the relics of Hadrian's Villa at Tivoli.

"What a place this could be for training of Olympic champions," Singh observed. "I doubt if there's a finer enclosed pool in the world. So the international guests have declared. And when there were no guests, the concubines did greatly enjoy the pool. But the

Maharaja had his pool for only a dozen years before he moved to his present residence for economy. No one dreamed the break-up in the old order would come so swiftly."

Returning to the hotel we passed two paunchy Indians holding hands as they strolled a garden path. Talking earnestly, they seemed oblivious of passers-by. On the hotel verandas for two nights I had observed two different pairs of middle-aged men swinging clasped hands as they walked. In my global travels among sophisticates and primitives I had never before noted such a practice.

"Isn't that rather odd?" I asked.

"Think nothing of it," Singh said. "It means nothing. You see they are middle-aged or older. Indians are sentimental. Perhaps it's like Frenchmen kissing on both cheeks. The custom may go back to the days when women were rarely to be seen, and marriages were arranged. Now that girls have jobs side by side with boys you don't see young men swinging hands."

As we parted at the hotel terrace steps Singh remarked that the United States was far more important to India than politics or pride could often tolerate. "The bonds that tie us to the U.S.A. constrict as well as succor," he said. "Even in relatively good crop years we still count on grants of American wheat to feed our hungry peoples. If American aid is withheld, our economy suffers a terrible blow. An Indian columnist wrote recently, 'Economic planning which gets completely disrupted when assistance by one country is withheld cannot be regarded as sound.'

"But," he added, with a wide smile, "things are looking up for us. And, on the whole, Indians do not worry greatly and they have a sense of humor. A sense of humor is almost as conducive to serenity as a meditative religion. Nothing deflates self-pity like the consciousness of the insignificance of the individual in the broad perspective of humanity. We are a complicated people, but some Indians know that laughter is a potent remedy for the ills of self-tenderness. . . . Tomorrow at ten. Don't worry!"

The next morning just before my big suitcase was snapped a messenger from the Maharani arrived. She had sent us a large handsome photograph of herself inscribed in a distinguished hand, "Sincerely, Gaytri Devi." It was a glamorous portrait in which she wore evening dress with a magnificent three-strand necklace of pearls and pendant earrings of pearls and diamonds. But we liked better her beauty unadorned, as we had seen her, in a sari without any jewels except on her sandals.

At the airport our friend attended to everything. When the plane arrived he guided us through a private gate and came with us into the plane to say au revoir. In parting he handed me a copy of that morning's English-language daily, the New Delhi *Indian Express.* "See the editorial page," he said with a slightly cynical expression. Then he smiled a warm good-by smile and, with a last admonitory "Don't worry!," he was gone. I had found India's papers dull, for the emphasis was heavily on local politics. Pages and pages of petty wranglings and bickerings in various states clogged the sheets, along with accusations and counteraccusations, and hints of corruption. Little enough interesting foreign news appeared. While the plane's engines warmed up, I turned to the editorial page. In large print across two columns, under the headline "Think It Over," was a quotation from Thomas Carlyle: "If a country finds itself wretched, sure enough that country has been misguided."

Heritage from Britain

When we arrived at the Oberoi Intercontinental Hotel in New Delhi, with its city conveniences and country charms, we decided to settle down for a relaxing eight days' stay. Far out on Wellesley Road at the southeastern edge of the city, it was like a resort hotel in the best sense of the word. On three sides it was surrounded by green stretches of an expansive golf links.

In the center of the Oberoi lobby, at what was designated the "hospitality desk," presided an extremely pretty, fair-complexioned Parsi widow named Freny Nallaseth. She had wisely been selected by the manager for her sparkling charm to give information and friendly advice. She helped to set the tone of the place instantly. Beautifully groomed, she apparently owned quite an array of exquisite saris, for she changed her costume three times a day and we do not remember ever seeing the same sari twice. Mrs. Nallaseth had been her late husband's sometime hostess when he was director of the government-owned Asoka Hotel. We were later to see her album with pictures of herself taken with scores of world-known figures, from Nehru to Philip, Duke of Edinburgh.

From our seventh-floor bedroom we looked down upon the Oberoi's ultra-up-to-date swimming pool and the terraces set with long chairs for taking the sun. Down to the left was an open-air restaurant, gay with striped umbrellas. Far beyond the green acres of the golf club stretched the buildings of the city, set not upon a hill but on a gentle incline that led to the crowning old Viceroy's Palace.

We lunched under a white-and-orange canopy at the edge of an elevated flower garden, with pomfret as the main dish. Around four o'clock we called on the manager of the hotel, with whom I had had some pleasant correspondence. We were fortunate; he was instantly available. Though he had a good English name, William Land, I detected a slight foreign accent. He was an American citizen, all right, but he had been born in Freiburg, Germany, and trained there in hotel management. He had once been assistant manager of the Roosevelt Hotel, where I often stayed when in New York. He was lithe, lean, and sun-browned, blond and blue-eyed, and good-looking. Mr. Land offered us tea in the hotel's Oriental coffee shop, which was divided from the main dining room by a great aviary of tropical birds, from brilliantly colored macaws to tiny pure-white birds as small as field sparrows. There was fascinating kaleidoscopic movement beyond the wall of plate glass.

"Alas, this is Monday," Land said, "so I cannot give you toast or even bread and butter. By government edict, as you see on this printed card, no bread can be served on Mondays from 3:00 P.M. until midnight, and on Thursdays and Saturdays no rice at any hour. The law is enforced all over India—to conserve for the starving."

As we emerged from the coffee shop, Land noted two men carrying a large cabinet through the lobby. He flew to intercept and question the bearers. "By whose orders?" I heard him demand. The reply apparently satisfied him. "I have to have my eye on everything," he said, returning with an apologetic smile. "We have been running at virtual capacity ever since the day we opened. And there are ten thousand details. We're having a world convention of textile manufacturers here later in the week—Swedes, Japanese, South

Africans, representatives from all over the globe—and there are banquets to arrange and much to see to, as you may imagine."

Land's private secretary, a lovely highborn Indian girl named Aruna, who had acquired a Cambridge University education, came to fetch him. He was wanted for a long-distance call from Milan. In parting, Land said with charming reassurance, "I think you will be very pleased with New Delhi. I love this city."

Land's straight back disappeared briskly around a corner.

We took a cab with a turbaned Sikh driver to see those spacious boulevards for which New Delhi is noted. We began at the eastern edge of the city at the India Gate, a memorial to the Indian soldiers killed in World War I, and drove west up Rajpath. Lined with double rows of trees and handsome buildings set in green lawns on either side, Rajpath is broader than any thoroughfare I can think of in England or the United States. Because of the scarcity of cars in India we could drive at a leisurely pace.

"This," said Thérèse delightedly, "is what I expected in Vienna on the way to the Schoenbrun. But instead I got a jam-crammed street, tram tracks, and thousands of horn-tooting automobiles."

"This," I said, "is something like the Champs Elysées minus Paris traffic. The British left India a rare heritage."

The Sikh driver turned to regard me with a grin. "That is what we like to hear, sir. For we Indians say that this *is* our Champs Elysées. And we are aware that the British gave it to us." He waved to right and left. "All this fifty years ago was just fields and sorry huts and anything but Elysian, I assure you.

"In 1911, the year I was born," he went on, "at the royal durbar on the northern outskirts of Old Delhi, King George announced that the capital would be transferred from Calcutta, in the east, to Delhi, nearer the geographical center. It took some time to decide precisely where the new capital was to be laid out. Eventually the site was chosen right here, adjoining Old Delhi. It included miserable villages, which were razed and the inhabitants resettled."

Sikh chauffeurs, as I had found, were often as well informed as professional guides. The original site of New Delhi, the driver told us, covered about ten square miles, and the city was planned for residence by no more than 70,000 persons. Most of the important buildings were completed by 1930. The formal inauguration occurred on February 8, 1931. Today the New Delhi area embraces some thirty-three square miles. Two top British architects were commissioned to design the focal parts of the metropolis. Sir Edwin Lutyens conceived and built the Viceroy's Palace, and Sir Herbert Baker built the two blocks of the Central Secretariat and the colonnaded circular Parliament House with its round reflecting pool. These buildings combined harmoniously Roman classical architecture with Indian details.

At what was once called the Viceroy's Palace but is now the President's House, we could only peer through tall grilled gates somewhat resembling those of Buckingham Palace. "With permission you may visit the building," the driver said. "The gardens are laid out in Persian style, with pools and fountains. From December to March the flowers are quite spectacular."

We turned around to retrace our route down the south side of the boulevard. "From here to India Gate," the driver said, "a great pageant takes place annually on Republic Day, January 26. It is our most elaborate celebration. The lanes and walks are packed with people from all over India. Every tree is alive with urchins. The slow-footed elephants are adorned with golden masks and ceremonial pink paint. Before the grandstands erected for the notables prance Naga warriors and other strange tribal folk. Red-skirted men do the Bangra dance. Chosen chaps and beautiful young women from the great diversity that is India march with pride. Overhead, in formation, Indian Air Force planes trail columns of varicolored smoke that fills the sky with horizontal rainbows. The Freedom celebrations last a full week. Then military taps is sounded. The end of January is perhaps the best of all times to visit Delhi—if you can endure crowds. And then you will undoubtedly need a topcoat."

The driver called our attention to special buildings along the way, but I recall little specific detail besides the balcony and windows of Indira Gandhi's office, where climactic decisions of policy are resolved. To be prime minister of the Republic of India at this time, I thought, must be the most arduous and unenviable political position in the world. Suddenly a small inner voice whispered that I was not going to be able to pay my respects to Nehru's daughter. But the occurrence that actually did thwart an arranged meeting the following week was something the most fantastic ESP could not have presaged.

"In former days," the driver was saying, "the British would move the seat of government to cool Simla when the heat came. But now, with air conditioning, the work goes right on in New Delhi. The flowering trees, the blue jacarandas, the golden laburnums, and a host of shrubs, bloom in the hot months. With air conditioning in trains and hotels we now have tourists the year round."

As we turned north on Janpath and headed for Connaught Place, it occurred to us forcefully that it was the trees lining the boulevards and residential districts that gave India's capital its special glory. Trees often formed overlapping arches at the center of the less wide streets, just as in, say, Montgomery, Alabama. I had noted the rich green of certain spreading small-leafed trees, but I could not identify the species.

"They are berry trees," the driver informed us. "The Indians called them Jamun berries. Their botanical name is *Eugenia jambolina*. Forty years ago the British, in their wisdom, decided to plant throughout New Delhi trees that would provide nutriment as well as shade." We learned that the sweet berries that ripen in late summer are considered a delicacy by Indians. The government had to make regulations. Technically, the government owns the trees and leases them to special berry pickers—peasants who pay a few rupees a tree. A rural family will sometimes contract for a whole block of a given street. When word comes that the berries are about ripe, the peasants rush in from the country and set up housekeeping in lean-to shelters. They guard their crop and chase away climbing children as well as crows and parrots. Only the contractors may shake the trees and collect the fruit. Of course, those that fall to the pavement before the shaking may be had by any passer-by. But once the berries are gathered into great baskets they belong completely to the berry-picking contractors. If the government had no control, the trees might be debranched by the mob.

"I think the British did some mighty good things for India," I ventured.

"You are so right, sir. And here we are at Connaught Circus, our handsome shopping center. The English left us this, too."

The word "circus" recalled London's Piccadilly, but, architecturally, New Delhi's Connaught Place is more harmonious and pleasing. At the center of the encircled area is the green Nehru Park with its berry trees. The buildings are uniformly two stories high with round-columned porticoes and round-columned balconies. They reminded us of the Regency residences in Bath, and seemed designed by the British to take the curse off commercialism. Here international and local banks flourished, along with travel bureaus, airline offices, and smart shops. There was only one disfiguring effect: some Indian business firms had put up such boldly painted banners advertising their wares that these diminished the charm of the hundreds of cream-colored columns. But, happily, no supermarket was in evidence to sour the harmony of this attractive circus.

Driving down Parliament Street and eventually into Wellesley Road, we had noticed Curzon Street, Lady Harding Road, and Dalhousie Road. The British names gave off pleasant reminders that England had served India some good turns by leaving traces of its culture, which Nehru had so greatly enjoyed when he was a student at Cambridge.

On the way back to the hotel, we passed a standing statue of King George V under a graceful marble canopy suggesting the spread cobra's hood that once protected the Lord Buddha from the rain. We swung by the handsome white marble palace that before independence had belonged to the Nizam of Hyderabad. It filled an entire block, but it had been built after my friend Carmichael's tutorial sojourn in the southern central province of Hyderabad.

Our stimulating drive along New Delhi's tree-shaded streets helped us to understand why so many aliens insist that New Delhi exerts a subtle hold on the human heart.

Tiger Burning Bright

Shortly before we left Alabama to course the globe, when it became clear that we could not have our scheduled week in Egypt because of the restrictions against Americans after the Six-Day War, I had asked Ruth Shaver what we might best do with an unexpected "free" week.

"Stay in New Delhi," she had said. "You can relax there. It is a lovely modern city with spacious boulevards and shade trees. Delhi's historical monuments hold endless fascination."

"What is your favorite of all attractions in the twin cities?" I asked.

Without hesitation she declared, "The white tigers in the zoo." And so it was to prove for us. We had never seen a white tiger. They were phenomena native to India and extremely rare even there.

We called our favorite Sikh driver, M. K. Singh, and gave up an afternoon to the expansive zoological gardens, which maintain all specimens of the rich Asian animal and bird kingdom. Because of the great distances to be traversed, pony traps and a few elephants are available for hire to sight-seers. But we chose tramping on foot instead, and headed through circuitous walks directly to the chief objectives—the white tigers.

A pleasant space of a quarter acre with green grass, outcropping rock, an artificial brook, and some shade trees on a slight incline was the fenced domain of the first white tiger we beheld. He had strolled down the slope to look in and sniff at the cage of his mate and two baby cubs to see that they were all right, and he was now returning up the incline to his favorite rock for taking the sun. We watched him approach with majestic grace the outcropping rock near the fence where we stood transfixed in admiration. He was a beautiful beast, some fourteen feet in length and weighing perhaps five hundred pounds, the Sikh said. He stood about five feet at the shoulder. His fur was a uniform rich white with black transverse stripes laid on with superlative artistry. He was regal, noble, and exciting.

Blake's tribute to the tiger breed came floating into mind.

> Tiger! Tiger! burning bright
> In the forests of the night
> What immortal hand or eye
> Could frame thy fearful symmetry?

And the poet had seen only the orange-striped beasts.

The tiger came nearer with a rhythmic liquid motion and paused at the irregular slab of rock hardly ten feet from us.

"You are undoubtedly the handsomest creature in the world," I said aloud. "No lion or any other beast is comparable."

He cocked his short black ears to get the tone of tribute in my voice and regarded me for a moment with his ice-green eyes. He knew that he was esteemed, and that he excited wonder. "It's like beholding another Taj Mahal," I said to Thérèse. Then, speaking directly to the tiger, I said, "You're as superb and surpassing in your way as the Taj."

He accepted the compliment with a show of indifference, and looked away. Then he stretched his great length on the low rock. Couchant, he made a sublime sculptural figure. I recalled the tribute Isak Dinesen paid to the live lions who made an African monument to Dennis Finch-Hatton, the Etonian white hunter, buried in the Ngong Hills of Kenya. She had reflected that Lord Nelson in Trafalgar Square had only bronze lions for his monument. And now I fancifully thought of this grand white tiger as making a living monument to the millions who had died in the preserving of India, before Alexander the Great and after, and during the invasions of Mughals and the taking over by Britain.

The cat began the commonplace ritual of licking his massive paw and washing his face. We were lost in delight until our gentle guide asked, "Would you like to see the new white cub now?"

Going around the green enclosure, we came to the door of a wooden structure that contained the cage of the white tiger's yellow wife and cubs. Our guide said something to the attendant and he opened the door just wide enough for us to squeeze through. We came up close to the cage. The two cubs were old enough to sit up and regard the strange new world with wide-open eyes. One of them was of the usual tiger color, the other was lustrous white with black stripes. The white one sat in front of the other on the straw, as if he realized that he was something special. His mother, lying to the side, seemed to think so, too. "Cute" might be the simplest word for him, but his youthful dignity made him far more than that. One might be thrilled to have him for a pet if he stayed forever a cub. He never took his light-aquamarine eyes off us. We were odd creatures to him, but he was not in the least unfriendly, just speculative about our admiration. His little brother or sister had the look of knowing that the rare one was the beauty of the family, and seemed content to stay in the background while he occupied the place of honor. The mother, preening with pride, relaxed before our gaze.

And then the attendant, apparently to please us, rushed up to the cage, yelled, bared his teeth, and flapped his arms to stir the mother to some snarling action. "Oh, don't!" cried Thérèse. "Don't!" "No," I commanded sharply, "stop it!" The attendant, surprised at our reaction, seeing that he had made a wrong gesture, desisted. But, strangely, the lioness had not been the least affected by his performance. After all, she knew him well, he fed her the rich hunks of raw meat, and she had doubtless witnessed such mankind foolishness before.

We reluctantly left the little house with the nursery cage and went to see our Sikh's particular favorite, a four-year-old. On the way the Sikh told us some facts about white tigers. "In the forests of Rewa," he said, "only nine white tigers had ever been seen before 1951, and then a white male cub was captured. At maturity he was mated to a normally colored tiger. The first litter was normal. But when one of these orange females was eventually bred to her white sire, she dropped a litter of four white cubs. It almost seemed that a new race of cats had come into being."

Singh went on to explain that the small city of Rewa was formerly capital of the hilly princely state of Rewa. Because the town has no rail connection, it is remote, now incorporated into Vindhya Pradesh, although it lies only some seventy miles southeast from Allahabad, Nehru's birthplace. When the 120-room pink-marble palace of the Maharaja had to be abandoned because he could no longer afford its upkeep, it became a breeding place for white tigers. The beasts sleep by day in what used to be the boudoirs of the harem, and by night they roam among the arcades and fountains of the palace courtyard. They are cared for by a governmental agency.*

Singh stopped and said, "Here we are at the home of my favorite white tiger, and, see, he is out playing with his keeper."

A crowd of about twenty, half of them children, had gathered near the high fence of iron bars that enclosed the tiger's "garden." His cage-house was in a corner. The Indians politely made way for us to have a close look. This white beast was also huge and hand-

---

* Outside of India, a white tiger may be seen in only three zoos: in Bristol, England; in Miami, Florida; and in Washington, D.C. Recently in Washington the female Mohini gave birth to two white cubs. The Indian government has nationalized its white tigers, and no more may be exported. According to the Associated Press, there are only thirty-four white Bengal tigers in the world.

some, though not quite as large and magnificent as the first one we had seen. And this fellow was minus the great swinging tail. He had only a stub, like a Manx cat. Outside the cage stood his mild-looking guard and feeder, a grin on his mustached face as he stuck his foot between the bars. The great cat sprang at it with zest, put its teeth around the shoe, and held it teasingly and caressingly. After some moments the man removed his foot and made the slightest bow as if he had just extricated his head from a circus lion's mouth. Then he would stick his foot and ankle farther into the enclosure between other bars, and the animal would make gleeful grabs. This happy tiger was like a child playing. He would make a miniature leap of about four feet and look quite proud of himself. In the forest he might have leaped twenty feet with ease. He did not seem to realize that he was full-grown.

"How do they capture these tigers?" Thérèse wanted to know.

Our guide asked the keeper, who replied that they dug deep pits in forests where the rare beast had been reported seen. Thérèse, who is ever on the alert to detect man's cruelty to animals, said, "I knew they hurt them. Look, that must be how he lost his tail—in the trap."

The guide asked the attendant if the tiger had lost his tail when captured in the pit.

The man broke into a broad grin, and then laughed. "Oh, no," he replied. "This particular cat was born in captivity. His yellow mother was so proud to have a white cub that she licked him vigorously with love every day. And once, in an excess of passionate affection, she bit off his tail."

We all laughed. "Not man's careless inhumanity," I said to Thérèse, "excessive mother love."

"The tiger mother died while the cub was quite young," our driver explained, "and this male attendant became like his parent. That is why the animal is so gentle and so playful."

The tiger, with a simulated great effort, would make his short leaps of joy and then come up to the bars and put his face against them, as if desiring praise for an extraordinary feat.

"What a play pet!" I exclaimed. "I would like to get in there and have a romp with him. Might I just stroke him?"

The Sikh looked dubious. "I'm afraid I wouldn't advise it," he said. So I had to forgo the tactile pleasure of stroking the rich white fur. We finally left this triumphant freak of nature, carrying away a stirring memory, for though we observed scores upon scores of other well-arranged cages of various animals, the sensation of the glorious mutants virtually blotted out the remembrance of other specimens. In my lexicon, Delhi's white tigers were an ultimate, like the Taj Mahal.

Old Delhi

For me, personally, in retrospect, the star attractions in New Delhi, besides the spacious tree-lined avenues, the magnificent white tigers, and the Nehru museum, are Gandhi's black cenotaph, Stone's American Embassy, and the Birla back garden where the Mahatma was assassinated. These choices may seem unorthodox to tour guides and to the Delhians themselves, particularly the last three, which I had not yet seen when I asked to be shown Old Delhi. I am fully aware of the fine monuments the Mughals left in Delhi, but having beheld their architectural triumphs at Agra, and also the fanciful Rajput creations of Amber and Jaipur, I felt that I had done my major sight-seeing before we returned to Delhi. However, I took a car with our Sikh driver, M. K. Singh, for a look at the old city.

After so much zoo-trekking the previous afternoon, Thérèse decided to enjoy the quiet luxury of the Oberoi. She did not mind passing up Old Delhi with its swarming hordes. Some 500,000 Hindu refugees had poured in immediately after the partition of Pakistan, and many persons were still seeping into the capital, supposedly for bigger relief handouts.

The two Delhis together, divided by only a wide street and a long sports field, had a population of 3,057,000 in 1967. It was somewhat hard to realize that the combined Delhis held a quarter million more people than Paris.

According to scholars, the precise origins of Delhi are so remote in history that there is much speculation. The place was apparently first called Indraprastha, and in an ancient epic, the *Mahabharata*, it was described as situated "on a great mound on the west bank of the Jamuna." In the eleventh century A.D. a Rajput chieftain built a tank, a dam, and an amphitheater, which are still in good enough condition to be visited by tourists. The last important Hindu ruler, Prithvi Raga, who ascended the throne in 1170, died defending his capital from Mohammedan invaders in 1192. In 1526 Babar, descendant of Tamerlane, came conquering and proclaimed himself emperor of all Hindustan. While he maintained his capital at Agra, Humayun, his succeeding son, preferred Delhi for the capital. But during the reign of Humayun's famous son, Akbar, Agra again regained pre-eminence. Akbar's still more renowned grandson, Shah Jahan, who was crowned at Agra in 1628, was really the creator of the present Old Delhi. He made it his capital and the center of the Mughal Empire at the height of its glory and power.

The British East India Company established itself firmly in the eighteenth century. In 1804, the English, under General Gerard Lake, took command of Delhi. Thereafter India was to be ruled loosely by Great Britain. At a great durbar at Delhi on New Year's Day, 1877, Queen Victoria, through Disraeli's shrewd maneuvering, was proclaimed Empress of India. With the advent of railways, Delhi became a prosperous commercial city. In 1911 Delhi was designated the capital of all India, and India remained under British dominance until independence in 1947. From 1192, then, until 1947, the Indians were not really masters of their own country.

One is told that the Red Fort in Old Delhi must not be missed. It was built by that same remarkable Shah Jahan who built the Taj Mahál. To enclose his capital city he erected a stout wall some 7,000 feet in length, with twenty-seven towers and fourteen gates. Only a few traces of the picturesque originals are left. But the Red Fort stands almost as it was and occupies acres of ground. The exterior is impressive. Red sandstone walls rise seventy feet high. It was constructed on an even grander scale than his grandsire's mighty Red Fort in Agra, which had preceded it by a century. I had read of its marble pavilions and palaces and the Pearl Mosque within the walls, and the fabulous Peacock Throne studded with precious stones and valued in its own time at twelve million pounds. The throne had been appropriated by Nadir Shah of Persia, who sacked Delhi in 1739. It was carried off to Teheran with caravans of treasure, including the Koh-i-noor diamond, which was said to have weighed 790 carats when found. The ultimate destiny of the Peacock Throne remains a mystery, though the famous diamond is today among the British crown jewels.

I had thought to look in at the Red Fort, but when our car arrived within sight of the main entrance, the square was so congested with everyday ambulating humanity that I hesitated. Before I could open the door to reconnoiter, a haggard woman with dark-brown leathery skin and clothed in conglomerate rags pushed her wrinkled face against the window on my side of the front seat. She was holding a pitifully scrawny infant in the crook of her left arm. Indicating the baby with burning eyes and a jerk of her head, she raised her cupped right palm in supplication. I had been warned by Indians not to give anything to a street beggar unless I was willing to provoke a stampede. But I could not possibly deny this desperate woman. I was impelled to roll down the car window and give her some money. As she murmured thanks, other figures in the jam started closing in. "Drive on," I said, and I departed the Red Fort without entering its gates and without much regret, for it had been sacked of its most resplendent glories in the eighteenth century.

A short drive away from the fort's formidable walls rises the enormous mosque called Jama Masjid. Set on a rocky eminence, it was begun in 1650 by Shah Jahan and finished six years later. Even Hindus declare this mosque to be the noblest in the East, as well as the largest. I did not leave the car, but I shall never forget the sight of gray-bearded old men, encrusted with dirt, their pilgrim staffs beside them, sunning themselves on the broad steps that go up to the mosque from the street.

We turned back into the teeming Chandni Chowk, the main plaza with three- and four-story buildings adorned at the roof corners with graceful belvederes and gazebos covered with gold leaf. For the general tourist this section is a "must" attraction. Foreigners seek antiques and jewelry and new handicraft wares here today in what is sometimes called Silver Street and was once reputed to be the richest street in the world. Our car had to creep because of the mass of pedestrians, bell-tinkling bicycles, and bicycle taxis. "This Chandni Chowk," the Sikh reminded me, "was the very heart of the seventeenth-century capital decreed by Shah Jahan and called by him Shahjahanbad." For the adventurous tourists who do not mind crushing crowds, there is the fun and excitement of seeking and haggling.

"Many lovely old mansions," the driver said, "are hidden down alleyways behind bazaars that are not overly clean. The houses have graceful balconies outside and inner courtyards where fountains play. Within are handsomely carved doors and rare chandeliers. Some of the aristocratic old families still live in their inherited dwellings, though many have built modern villas in New Delhi."

Before we left Old Delhi, we passed St. James Episcopal Church, built by Colonel James Skinner, a famous cavalryman, long before the new capital was conceived. We paused briefly below Asoka's Pillar, a towering piece of solid wrought iron. The pillar, which resembles an elongated tapering phallic symbol, is said to have been already 1,500 years old when it was brought to Delhi to adorn a ruler's palace. After all the centuries of rain and wind it has remained unrusted, which attests to the remarkable metallurgical ingenuity of ancient India. A contemporary record describes the special carriage with forty-two wheels designed to move the pillar: a stout rope was attached to each wheel and two hundred men pulled on each rope. It took the strength of more than 8,000 men to bring the pillar to Delhi, but the account does not say by what means it was erected atop its stony foundation.

M. K. Singh was eager to have me see his favorite Sikh temple. It, too, is situated on an eminence and is approached through an upward-sloping courtyard and then by broad steps. Halfway up the incline on the right we stopped at a large one-room museum. The walls were covered with paintings depicting dramatic moments in the history of Sikhism: victories over persecuting enemies, and tortures and executions of Sikh leaders. There was a large painting of the benevolent, white-bearded Nanak (1469–1539), who founded the Sikh religion at the end of the fifteenth century. The son of a Hindu revenue official of a Punjab village near Lahore, he was preoccupied with spiritual matters from an early age. Living in a region of northwest India where Muslims and Hindus were continually in controversy, he founded a monotheistic sect that purposed to coalesce the purest teachings of Hinduism and Mohammedanism in one religion, proclaiming the brotherhood of all men in the sight of God. Rejecting many of the cherished practices of Hinduism,

Nanak accepted the Islamic rule of prohibiting idols of any kind. He opposed the prevailing Hindu caste system. He repudiated meaningless rites like bathing in "holy" rivers or making offerings to the dead. He decreed against alcoholic beverages and smoking as injurious to health. He advocated married life as ideal within normal human society. There were to be no priests but, rather, teachers or gurus who would read from holy writings in the temples.

Savage persecutions turned the Sikhs from pacifists into a militant sect. They proved to be valiant warriors, with little fear of death. Paradise was promised as a reward to those who died in the Sikh cause. Today Sikhs are known as India's most formidable fighters.

In 1699 Guru Govind Singh introduced a ritual of baptism at which Sikhs were given five signs marking them off from Hindus and Moslems. One of these, the prohibition of cutting off hair and beard, marked Sikhs as noticeably different from their fellows. Their joint drinking from one bowl of baptismal nectar denied any caste system. At the religious initiation at puberty henceforth every Sikh boy was to add the suffix Singh (lion) to his name.

The last really outstanding Sikh leader, Ranjit Singh, became chief at the age of twelve. In 1822 he employed officers of Napoleon's disbanded troops to train and modernize his army. But eventually the British annexed the Punjab, and after the Indian mutiny of 1857 many Sikhs were recruited into the British army. Partly because of the Sikh observance of keeping their hair and beard unshorn, the Sikhs have kept their separate identity. Their beards and wound turbans are their cachet. They believe strongly in education; the proportion of literacy among Sikhs in India is higher than among other sects. Though the Sikhs are shrewd in business, they also make excellent mechanics and good husbandmen, and in Delhi most of the taxi drivers are Sikhs.

Since I wanted to look in at the temple, I removed my shoes and left them on the window ledge of the museum, feeling slightly dubious, but being earnestly reassured by my driver. Ascending the temple stairs I noted a great water trough where the devout in double queues were washing their feet. At a marble basin of running water others were cleansing their mouths. Again I was reassured by Singh: as an alien I might enter the sanctuary unpurified.

The interior of the temple was notable for its simplicity, its lack of ornamentation. A layman guru was reading precepts from the

Adi Granth, the book of Nanak and his successors. The rapt expressions on the faces of the standing and kneeling worshipers made their religion seem meaningful.

"What is he saying?" I asked in a semiwhisper.

Singh answered *sotto voce:* " 'As the fish out of water, so is the infidel dying of thirst.' And now: 'The ignorant fools take stones and worship them. O man, how shall the stone which itself sinketh carry you across?' "

After I retrieved my shoes, I paused to observe a frail white-haired old lady in a flowing white sari making her devotions on her knees at the street level of the incline before the temple. The delicacy and distinction of her features marked her good breeding. Her sari was of excellent material; she must have been well-to-do. She was praying with wide-open eyes, as if someone's very life depended on her silent intercession. I had not witnessed such humble devotion anywhere in the East. Only once before in my life had I remarked such miracle-seeking ardor: in a tall, red-headed, well-dressed young man who was kneeling in wide-eyed supplication before the Virgin's shrine at Lourdes. That sight had never faded in my memory, nor would this of the elderly Indian lady, who was not abashed to kneel in the street before the Sikh temple.

"Nanak's working faith," Singh explained, "proclaimed insistently 'the majesty and unity of God, the comparative insignificance of prophets, the fleeting vanity of worldly life, and the need to approach God in awe and love.' "

As we drove away from the temple precincts, I had an even greater respect for the virile, no-nonsense religion inaugurated by the inspired and gentle Nanak. I have the feeling that, because Sikhs possess a healthy sense of the dignity of labor and by shrewd investments have acquired some influence in India's commerce, free India's progress may be helped by this sturdy small minority among so many Hindus.

At the end of our leisurely four-hour morning tour, Singh drove me far to the south to see the Qutb Minar, the extraordinary rose-colored "victory" tower that rises in five graduated stories like a minaret to a height of 236 feet. At appropriate intervals are four projecting lacy balconies. This tower is deservedly considered one of the most beautiful in the world. More than two hundred years old, it adjoins a ruined mosque, much in the manner of an Italian cathedral bell tower. As a last attraction of the enriching morning, I was shown the tomb of Humayun, second emperor of the Mughal dynasty. It was built in 1565 by his dynamic widow. A splendid specimen of Persian-style architecture, it is set in an extensive walled garden. Constructed of rose-colored sandstone and inlaid with white marble, it has pleasingly harmonious proportions. Significantly, its great white marble dome gave Shah Jahan inspiration for the dome of the Taj Mahal. And so, as in Agra, the beauties of Old Delhi are Persian and Mohammedan, rather than Indian and Hindu.

Rajghat and the Place of Assassination

Not far from the Delhi Gate, on the western bank of the Jamuna River, is the Rajghat, where Gandhi was cremated. It is a hallowed place of pilgrimage. From the street entrance gate a long broad concrete walkway slopes east and upward. A wide belt of green lawn extends a mile or more to the north. At the top of a grassy embankment steps lead down to a flat area, about the size of a foot-ball field, surrounded by arched masonry walls. A few young trees have been strategically placed. In the center four elongated upended slabs of white marble enclose the cremation site. There in the center the black marble *samadk* marks the spot of Gandhi's burning. The cenotaph looks to be ten feet long and four feet high. It seemed to us altogether a most fitting monument, chaste and elegant. Garlands of marigolds lay on the polished black top and some marigolds were scattered on a low black marble seat. Three Indian men in Western dress stood at the foot of the tomb and four women in saris knelt at one side. The Jamuna flowed placidly in the near distance.

"Shall we descend?" our driver asked. "We shall have to remove our shoes."

Thérèse and I opted to stay where we were and pay our respects to the Mahatma from the ridge of the embankment. A lone Indian in a dhoti went slowly down the stairs carrying his sandals. Under the bright Indian sun, with so few persons about, the memorial, for all its classic beauty, looked rather stark. I thought of the millions who had traveled from far and near to the actual cremation, when Gandhi's eldest son had put the torch to the pyre. Every road into Delhi had been clogged with hordes of humanity. The railroads had broken down with the enormity of the masses. In the excitement of ecstatic grief, women and children, and men as well, had been trampled to death.

"I know that Gandhi's ashes were dropped into the sacred Ganges," I said, "but, still, he looks a bit lonely in this vast field."

"For two miles all this land will eventually be a memorial deer park," Singh said, pointing to the north, where a half mile or more away was the memorial to Nehru, above the site of his cremation. It was then in the process of being completed, and tents for the workers with their gear surrounded it. Beyond Nehru's monument, a half mile still farther north, a cenotaph would be erected to honor Prime Minister Shastri.

"But for deer you will need trees," Thérèse protested. "The summer sun would kill them if they had no protection."

"Thousands of fast-growing trees are to be planted," Singh said. "On this coming November 14, Nehru's birthday, thousands of schoolchildren will plant trees. Indira Gandhi will herself lift the first shovel of earth. This deer park will eventually become one of Delhi's chief tourist attractions."

We thought of the delight the thousand tame deer at Nara had given through the centuries, and tried to envision what this place would be like after the trees gave shade and spotted deer dotted the landscape.

But it saddened Thérèse to feel that Gandhi seemed somewhat forgotten only two decades after his death. When we had spoken of him to persons under thirty, they listened politely, if a bit vaguely, but had no responsive comment. Independence was now merely taken for granted in India. Besides members of the Nehru family, only one Indian we had met had voluntarily mentioned Gandhi, and that was the schoolteacher guide in Jaipur, who, prefacing some remark, had twice said, "Our father has told us. . . ." Yet even though the Mahatma's fame seemed fast dimming in this new era, his "great soul," the schoolteacher had said, "would surely be an immortal flame in world history."

"Late this afternoon," I said to Singh, "we shall want you to take us to the site of the assassination—you know, in Birla's back garden. The shooting, you recall, occurred shortly after five." Singh, who had been born in Malaysia and had only been in Delhi for a dozen years, looked surprised and puzzled. In all his twelve years of chauffeuring in Delhi, no one, native or alien, had made such a request, and he himself had never seen the place. I explained further that Ghanashyam Das Birla, whom he knew as one of India's richest men and greatest philanthropists, was devoted to Gandhi, and that Gandhi was his house guest at the time of the assassination.

Our driver had to stop twice to ask the way to the Birla back garden. Finally, he turned into a narrow unpaved street that wound behind the place. It was hardly more than an alley with shade trees. As we crept along slowly, our presence in the neighborhood seemed to excite considerable curiosity. Eventually we arrived at the back gates, which were open. We left the car and walked the wide path down which the masses of the faithful had gone to attend Gandhi's last afternoon prayer service on January 30, 1948.

Tall slender trees lined one side of the way, and eight-foot-high shrubbery bordered the side that backed the lawn garden. A smiling dhoti-clad Indian in attendance was more than ready to offer explanations, though he apparently spoke not a word of English. Singh had to gather what he could pick out in Hindi. About a dozen poor persons with a few children straggled in our wake and listened attentively. The guardian pointed out the foot-high platform from which the Mahatma conducted the services. Then he moved a few feet to the exact spot in which the assassin had crouched in his leafy ambush diagonally behind Gandhi. Imitating the murderer, the man sprang out and, aiming his finger at the imaginary Gandhi's right side, he barked, "Bang-bang-bang." The fanatic had sent three revolver shots into Gandhi's rib cage and then had fled through the shrubbery.

Having read Vincent Sheean's vivid eyewitness account—he was among the crowd kneeling before the saintly little man—I could re-create the scene with fair ease. On the very morning of the assassination Gandhi had received the American writer in one of the Birla parlors, which the philanthropist had offered the Mahatma for his private audiences. About a fortnight before, Sheean had had a strange presentiment of Gandhi's death, and in the middle of the night he had awakened his neighbor, Ted Patrick, editor of *Holiday*, to tell him that he had to fly to India to see his guru alive, for he was shortly to be murdered. Patrick had related the odd story to me and told me that he had had to soothe Sheean's second-sight excitement by playing classical records in the early-morning hours. Sheean did fly to India. He had had an inspiring talk with Gandhi, and then witnessed at the five o'clock service what he had previsioned and dreaded.

With the Hindu word "Rama" (God) on his lips, Gandhi had sunk to his knees and then dropped unconscious to the platform before the horrified devotees.

The guardian made a sweeping gesture toward the arcaded summerhouse—about an oblique twelve yards from the platform—and indicated that the dying Mahatma was borne there and laid on the floor. We followed him into the summerhouse, trailed by the poor people. Here we were joined by a well-dressed Indian gentleman who was as interested as we were in the details. This latecomer understood Hindi and spoke good English. He would listen attentively to the caretaker and then translate for us.

"Gandhi breathed his last right there on the floor before a doctor could reach him. That long dark stain on the stones behind the corded barrier is Gandhi's blood, which Birla and others do not want washed away. There is one significant change. The once-white plaster walls are now covered with the murals you see depicting Gandhi's life story. It shows him married at the age of twelve to a twelve-year-old girl, by whom later he had three children, before he took the vow of chastity. There he is studying law in London. And here in South Africa he is being rudely put off a train because he insisted on sitting in a first-class carriage for which he held a first-class ticket. He was told only white people could ride first class."

We followed Gandhi's pictured biography around the three walls, to his first imprisonment for civil disobedience and his first meeting with Nehru, who became his second-in-command in the struggle for India's independence.

Gandhi left prison for the last time on May 6, 1944. With the

European war over and Churchill defeated by the Labour party in 1946, the new British Prime Minister, Clement Attlee, was quite willing to grant India independence. But Gandhi was to suffer heartbreak when the Mohammedan leader M. A. Jinnah demanded and got a separation of the predominant Mohammedan sections of India into West and East Pakistan. Not only had Gandhi's hope of unity been dashed, but on August 16, 1946, bloody riots broke out in Calcutta between Mohammedans and Hindus. Gandhi, deeply depressed, called the partition "a spiritual tragedy" and considered that his thirty-two years of dedicated work had come to an inglorious end. But the tragedy had just commenced. As Muslims began slipping out of Hindu territory and Hindus began flocking in from the two Pakistans, killings and atrocities mounted. On Independence Day, August 15, 1947, in Calcutta, the despairing Gandhi, who was struggling to stop fresh bloody riots, issued a statement to the press. He announced his last fast, one to the death, unless communal slaughters ceased. His threat had a potent effect. Killings stopped, and Gandhi returned to Delhi on September 9 and began holding peace prayer meetings at which he bemoaned the animosity and inhumanity of Indians to Indians. He declared it was the duty of both governments to protect all minority peoples. A peace committee in Delhi signed a pact promising the protection of life, property, and religion of the Muslim minority. Gandhi was to fast no more. But a few extremists were bitter beyond words that the Muslims who remained in India should be spared, and one young fanatic determined to kill the Indian leader.

It was sad to contemplate that for all his inspiring leadership, political and spiritual, little had turned out according to the pattern of Gandhi's idealistic thinking. Though India had her freedom, his great struggle to establish the need for peace in the consciousnesses of his people had come to seeming naught. He whose steps had been followed by millions, to get his darshan of gentle serenity, had actually thought that he might change human nature. But he had seen a vicious cruelty among compatriots and neighbors, a rampant hatred between Indians more intense than any animosity displayed toward the British. And depressing to Gandhi was his gathering realization that he had failed to instill in the villagers a contentment with the simple life, in which they spun and wove their own cloth.

For their salvation he had hoped that the masses would not take on bourgeois cravings, which led to bourgeois vices. But with independence his people quietly began putting aside their little spinning wheels and began to look covetously at motorcars.

Before leaving the pavilion, I felt impelled to stoop and reach my left hand under the cord and with my fingertips touch lightly the dark stain made by Gandhi's blood.

Stone's Embassy and an Alfresco Luncheon

Rita Dar had arranged a small dinner at her home on November 10 for us to meet Indira Gandhi, who had promised to come. I had jokingly told Rita that it would be superperfect if she could also invite the young Aga Khan, who was in India at the time. From boyhood he was a friend of the Nehrus. He accepted, she told us, when she said she was having no more than eight at dinner, for he disliked large parties.

I had looked forward to this engagement with keen anticipation. And then Rita's aunt, Nehru's youngest sister, Mrs. Krishna Hutheesingh died unexpectedly in England on November 9. She was visiting Indian friends there at the time and reading page proof of her new book on the Nehru family. According to the paper, her body was being flown to Bombay for cremation. On November 10, the very day of the scheduled dinner, she was cremated at the electric crematorium in Bombay, with all the family connections attending the funeral, and the Aga Khan as well. So, by this strange unlikely chance, we did not get to meet India's Prime Minister.

However, we did get to know our Ambassador to India, Chester Bowles, to whom our mutual friend Senator Lister Hill had written a letter.

Ambassador and Mrs. Bowles invited us for lunch at 1:15 P.M. John W. Shirley, my special contact at the Embassy, telephoned to say that he was to take us to their home and he would be glad to show us the Chancellery before the luncheon. We were eager to see at close range this work of Edward Durrell Stone, which had been extensively pictured in world magazines. I was interested in the fact that the famous architect, who had done notable buildings in such varied places as Lima, Beirut, Brussels, Palo Alto, and New York, had been born in Fayetteville, Arkansas, and was graduated from the University of Arkansas before he studied at M.I.T. Planning the Embassy complex had begun in the early 1950's, when a twenty-eight-acre site in the diplomatic enclave was allocated by the Indian government to the U.S.A. Stone had studied ancient Indian architecture for inspiration before designing his strikingly original embassy. The cornerstone was laid in September, 1956, and the building was opened formally in January, 1958, with Prime Minister Nehru in attendance.

To complete the feeling of serenity that Indians impart to a monument by having it reflected in water, Stone had placed in front of his building a round reflecting pool, 139 feet in diameter, with four narrow curving jets of water aiming at a central jet that shoots straight into the air.

As our taxi circled the fountain pool, we were instantly impressed by the harmony of the color of the Chancellery—white, green, gray, and gold—its pierced stone walls, and the fifty slim gold-colored columns that support the overhanging flat roof. The dramatic entrance to the building is at the top of a flight of Markana marble stairs and a podium paved in squares of stones from the River Ganges. Behind a suspended Great Seal of the United States, engraved in gold on a round disk of thickest plate glass, lofty glass portals rise, two stories high. An open reception hall leads directly into an enclosed water garden. The ceiling is a silvery screen of aluminum mesh that filters a honeycomb of light and shade over the whole area.

Mr. Shirley met us as we entered. Born in Europe, he had the attractive qualities of a sophisticated cosmopolite with a desire to make mundane living as pleasant as possible.

"In designing this building," Shirley said, "Stone sought to capture the spirit of the best old architecture in India and blend it with modern Western concepts. When he visited Agra he was so enraptured by the Taj Mahal that he instantly determined to incorporate some of its superb simplicity into his final design. The first practical problem to be solved was that of automobiles, which in a hot climate should be shaded, and, also, because the idea of a monumental building rising out of a sea of multicolored, fin-tailed cars revolted him. So he placed his structure on a platform—like the Taj—with a parking garage underneath. To shade the floor-to-ceiling windows from the sun, he used mosaic grille for exterior walls. The cost of pierced marble like that of the Taj would have been prohibitive in these times. The grillework was fabricated on the site, molded into square tiles, and polished by hand. Because it diminishes the fierce rays of the sun effectively, air-conditioning expense is reduced by 30 per cent. To resist further the Delhi summer heat, the roof structure—a flat rectangular canopy a foot and a half above the second-floor ceiling—projects fourteen feet beyond the face of the building on all sides. But to give both the illusion and reality of coolness, Stone created this water garden in the center of the building instead of designing a courtyard."

In the long rectangular water garden, groups of minor fountains bubble, with the highest stream shooting almost to the roof. Clusters of circular islands grow exotic tropical trees that expand into fanciful shapes. Whenever one goes out of any of the ninety offices of the two floors, he steps onto an arcaded passage around the water garden.

Stone's harmonious and exciting creation is judged by many to be the most attractive modern building in Asia. Marked by dignity and stateliness, as well as originality, this structure was praised by other great architects, such as the Finnish-born Eero Saarinen and Frank Lloyd Wright, who proclaimed it "one of the finest buildings in the last hundred years."

At a right angle to the Chancellery stands Roosevelt House, the official residence of the ambassador. It is wrapped in mosaic grillework, with a row of pencil-thin columns. In the state salon that forms the central hall, the full height of two stories is retained, and a graceful curving staircase ascends to a walkway between the two separated halves of the upper story, which has seven bedrooms. The walls of the salon are lined with pierced stone, and the back wall is of glass curtained with a translucent white Indian fabric.

"Why don't the Bowleses live here?" I wanted to know.

"It's just too utterly inconvenient as a *home*," Shirley said, with emphasis. "Somehow it is almost impossible for daily living. No ambassador has liked it. So it is used to house V.I.P.'s. Richard

Nixon was among the last we entertained here. It does make an impressive guesthouse."*

Shirley had the Ambassador's chauffeur drive us to 17 Ratendone Road, about a mile nearer to the center of New Delhi. There the Bowleses resided in a comfortable, homelike villa. The beautiful rugs Mrs. Bowles had had especially woven on Indian looms were the most striking features of the furnishings. We were ushered through the house and a book-lined den, to be received on the back veranda, which gave on a lovely garden. Dorothy Bowles, who, like her husband, is a sincere lover of India and the Indians, was wearing a brown-and-white-checked sari of serviceable native stuff, one Gandhi would have approved of.

November 13 was as perfect as one of those rare June days in the Bowleses' native New England. The garden was lushly green, and the birds were full of song. Thérèse instantly spied on the lawn a perky little bird she did not recognize. It was black and white and brown, with a pert red topknot. Several of its kind were flitting and hopping about the grass, industriously picking off insects. "It is called a hoopoe," said Mrs. Bowles, pleased that we had noticed it. "I, too, am very partial to them, and they seem to like our place. They are very friendly, not at all shy. They have lunch with us every day."

We spoke of the fascinating water-bird sanctuary on the road to Jaipur. Mrs. Bowles had been there, too, and to many other sanctuaries in India to observe birds. "It is my experience, though," she said, "that if you stay in New Delhi you may see, sooner or later, specimens of all varieties of birds right here in the zoo."

We lunched on the lawn under a shade tree and began with Gimlets. The Ambassador had had some recent indisposition and could not join us in a drink. I regarded him carefully. He was,

* In his delightful and witty *Ambassador's Journal,* John Kenneth Galbraith, who was the first ambassador to live in Roosevelt House, wrote on March 27, 1961: "Towards the end of the afternoon I went over the plans for the new Embassy Residence. . . . It is most interesting, and possibly a trifle too grand in its big state rooms. It will be a little like living on a balcony overlooking the main concourse of Grand Central Station." A footnote to this opinion after the Galbraith family had actually resided there reads: "This indeed proved to be the case."

first of all, an essentially kind man, and very astute. He had been regarded in Washington as an incorrigible optimist.

When President John F. Kennedy appointed Chester Bowles as our ambassador to India, he publicly declared, "No American has a deeper understanding of India and Asia than Governor Bowles. A decade ago he was a pioneer in creating bonds of understanding between India and the United States." Bowles had previously been ambassador to India from 1951 to 1953, and was a lifetime student of world affairs. This Springfield, Massachusetts, native, born in 1901 and educated at Choate and Yale, told me that he was the first of a staunch Republican family to become a Democrat.

"How come the change?" I asked.

"The sufferings of the Depression," he answered simply.

After holding various high positions in Washington under Franklin Roosevelt, Bowles became governor of Connecticut. In the Kennedy administration he became the President's roving ambassador, his special adviser on Asian, African, and Latin-American affairs. He and his wife had traveled continually for a time and delved wholeheartedly into the problems of the underprivileged.

Now Mr. Bowles was obviously happy to be in India again. Its need was great, and he felt needed. He nudged the Washington administration for all possible aid to India, and the Indians regarded him confidently as their best friend.

During luncheon I asked about the Communist party in India. The Ambassador said that indeed there was a Communist party. "By 1957 the Communists had thirty-one seats in Parliament. But the Chinese aggression of 1962 caused them to lose considerable face as well as some seats. Since 1965 they have been split into two enemy factions: pro-Soviet Russia and pro-China. They are spottily distributed, but their greatest strength is in the far-southern province of Kerala."

"The Conservative party is now the second most powerful in India," Shirley said. "Your friend the Maharani of Jaipur is one of the most effective leaders, and very able she is. The Conservatives' advocacy of private enterprise is gaining them many votes."

I asked how much aid altogether the United States had given India since independence.

Shirley answered that question. "Well, altogether, in free grants and loans, we have helped independent India to the tune of about eight billion dollars. Telling assistance has been given to such a wide variety of projects as the building of dams and mills, smallpox eradication, crop production, craftsmen training, dairy development, and higher education. Electric power has increased ninefold in kilowatts since 1948. Almost twice as many acres are now under irrigation as there were in 1948.

"Some of the millions who live in rural villages are really progressing. Others, it must be confessed, are cultivating their fields in the traditional methods of the last millennia."

I said that we had remarked villages on the road to Agra and Jaipur and that the general impression we got was that the people seemed fairly contented with their lot; but, of course, we had been on well-traveled roads. "Ah, yes!" Mr. Bowles said, "we are doing what we can to inspire the Indians to want to rise above their poverty."

Thérèse turned slightly in her chair. "What is that delicious scent?"

Both the Bowleses smiled, and Shirley and I sniffed with interest. Unnoticed, the butler had set incense sticks here and there behind us in the grass. Now they were wafting a delicately exotic Eastern odor.

"In lieu of the flowers that won't be in bloom for another two weeks," the Ambassador explained. "In December the garden will be a blaze of color, and we lunch amid fresh flower fragrance."

"I should think that you could have blossoms now at a perfect season like this," I said.

The Ambassador smiled again. "We could, if they were watered. But somehow at this time of year the gardeners just disappear. I can't say why. They will be back in December, which is the height of the blooming season in Delhi and lasts until the heat comes in April. It's the Indian's way."

The hoopoes were hopping nearer and nearer to the luncheon table.

"May I?" Thérèse asked the hostess, holding some cake crumbs between her finger and thumb.

"By all means. They would be disappointed if they didn't get a few bits."

"I have read," I said to the Ambassador, "that a most successful campaign has been waged in eradicating malaria."

"In 1948, in the first year of independence," he explained, "over eighty-five million cases of malaria were recorded. As late as 1953 more than 800,000 persons died of the fever that year. This past year fewer than 100,000 cases were reported, and there were no deaths whatever. The Indian government's massive drive against malaria is one of the world's most successful ventures in the field of public health. And most of the insecticides, drugs, and what not have been financed by dollar grants from the U.S.A."

"The supply of physicians and the number of hospital beds have doubled in the last dozen years," Dorothy Bowles added.

While coffee was being served, I ventured to bring up the number-one question. "Is the birth-control movement going to win out?"

"Well, India is desperately trying. The government has spent some fifty million dollars annually on the program. A government plant is producing 15,000 plastic loops a day to help in the struggle. Family-planning programs are being broadcast on all thirty-three stations of All-India Radio. The daily newspapers disseminate massive amounts of information on the importance and necessity of birth control. Field Publicity Mobile Vans show films in the backwoods. Various states are erecting signs and billboards presenting the case for family planning. Because so many of the people are illiterate, the recognizance symbol, the Red Triangle, identifies the location of family-planning facilities in the towns."

"Sterilization is gaining favor with men who already have three children," Shirley interjected. "In some states direct cash payments are made to men who are willing to undergo a vasectomy [removal of the sperm duct]. An original incentive program is now under way in Madras. A man who has been sterilized persuades as many of his acquaintances as he can convince that the slight operation is a good thing, and the state pays him a bonus of ten rupees for each recruit. Last year this novel arrangement produced 230,000 sterilizations. It is becoming the thing to do." He smiled and added, "In certain Bombay textile mills, surgeries have been installed where male workers may get a free vasectomy. And the men are paid full wages for the period of recuperation. Bombay has about the lowest birth rate of any state."

"As you know," Dorothy Bowles said, putting in the last word on the discussion, "child marriage ceased years ago. At present in

India the minimum legal age for marriage for women is fifteen and for men, eighteen. But a radical proposal is now being considered to raise these minimums by law to twenty-one and twenty-five. Doubtless a compromise between the two will become the law."

When we finally rose from the table, the Ambassador reminded us that India had embarked on an agricultural revolution that would have been difficult to visualize only a few years before.

"New high-yield strains of rice and hardy dwarf wheat developed in Mexico are two keys to India's 'green revolution.' With intensive field aid from the Ford Foundation, farmers have planted some twenty million acres in the Mexican wheat, and first reports indicate phenomenal success. It is now estimated that next year's wheat crop will surpass India's previous record harvest by 25 per cent.* Former arid brown regions from here to the Himalayas are green because of diesel and electric pumps used in irrigation. One day India expects to be quite independent of the fickle monsoon rains."

It had been a most pleasant and cheering luncheon in what could be called "heavenly" weather. I had learned much.

"India, as you know, is the world's largest democracy," the Ambassador said with an optimistic smile, walking with us back through the house to the front door, "and it is on trial to prove that self-sufficiency can be achieved without resort to totalitarian disciplines. That is why India's success is vital to the United States."

"Despite your mountainous problems," I said, as if India were the Bowleses' own country and responsibility, "this land obviously has a stimulating present, as well as a marvelously fascinating past."

"And her future, I believe," the Ambassador said, "will be full of interest for mankind."

While the car was drawing up, I said to the Ambassador with a grin, "I recall that twenty-odd years ago you wrote a book called *Tomorrow Without Fear*. Could it be that your well-known optimism has infected India?"

He returned a kindly, almost deprecating smile in silent reply, and waved us an affable good-by.

* The 1968 crop topped India's previous record by 35 per cent—more than four million tons.

Farewell, Delhi

After luncheon with the Bowleses, where the future of India seemed to take on a slightly rosy glow, our own immediate future was rent by an unexpected disappointment. When we reached the hotel we learned that our Wednesday flight to Rome on Air-India had been canceled. The pilots were on strike. The preceding May, I had carefully arranged for this one and only weekly daytime flight from Delhi to Rome. Leaving at the civilized hour of nine, it would have got us to Rome at three in the afternoon with only one stop—at Teheran. With the Middle East still in muttering crisis following the Six-Day War, it had not seemed a happy time to visit Iran, but I had looked forward to glimpsing Teheran from the air, enjoying an hour's stopover, and perhaps picking up a pound of Iranian caviar to take to Rome for snacks.

I hustled to the Air-India office in the hotel arcade, where an exquisitely saried and beautiful young princess presided, the twenty-two-year-old daughter of a "comedown" maharaja. I told her teasingly that my faith in India was shattered, and that I had counted on trailing the Indian atmosphere with me clear to Rome. Shaking her head regretfully, she was prepared to change our reservations to any of five other lines. But all other flights to Rome were nighttime affairs. As I pondered, a page called me to the telephone. The call was from Prem Kajla, our special guardian. He had already reserved seats for Wednesday night on Lufthansa, "the next best thing." Lufthansa departed in the evening at nine—a twelve-hour flight in darkness instead of a nine-hour daylight flight. Stops in Karachi and Dhahran, Saudi Arabia, were to be made, and one other he did not recall just then.

"Just so that third stop isn't Cairo!" I insisted. Egyptians were still actively hostile to Americans. But Cairo *was* the third stop. However, we felt lucky to be guaranteed first-class seats on Lufthansa. I crossed my fingers against being routed out into the Egyptian night at 3:00 A.M. for questioning or incarceration.

On Wednesday we had a farewell luncheon with Rita Dar and her husband, who was going to Lebanon as ambassador. Then we began saying au revoir to numerous friends in the hotel. Taking last looks from our bedroom windows at "cowdust" hour, just before sunset, we realized how much we had delighted in our New Delhi sojourn. A misty haze always hung over the city in late afternoons and gave this tree-luxuriant green capital the semblance of a Corot landscape. We could rejoice that there were no skyscrapers to break the harmony of the silhouette. Only our hotel, far out at the edge of the city limits, rose high.

We were glad we had postponed our visit to India until just the right time for us, when there were first-class air-conditioned hotels. We had not missed the characteristic old colorful punkahs pulled to flap away flies and cool the air. We had been glad to avoid the once ubiquitous sight of tired people suffering from malnutrition and "mostly squatting on their heels over fires of cow dung." India was still fascinating in countless manifestations, and we had liked the gentle people, from top Brahmins to taxi drivers and room boys.

On the surface, India had been the picturesque land we had expected. But the Indians of today were not a conglomeration of mystic dreamers and driven devotees of sex, as some older writers had portrayed them. I doubted if a copy of the *Kama-sutra* would be found in many homes. Indians actually seem less sex-conscious than the French or the Japanese—or English and Americans, for that matter. One does not see young couples embracing in the parks and plazas. Indian films, I was told, do not show kissing. The married men I had met in both high and low circles seemed good, steady husbands who loved their wives and children. Wives were supposed to be faithful, and husbands discreet and circumspect. Indian women were generally treated with great respect.

Observing women closely—in hotel positions, in commerce and public office, in banks and boutiques—I concluded that with the rending of the restricting curtains the emergence of women had been about as dramatic as Nora's slamming the door on her Norwegian doll's house in 1879. Customs that had grown up through centuries vanished. But this mixing into male affairs had in nowise diluted the Indian woman's appealing femininity. Apparently 95 per cent still wore the becoming sari.

Kajla accompanied us to the airport, saw that our tickets were in order, and attended to the luggage checking.

The lobby was thick with squatting, sitting, or recumbent figures. At first I thought that these dark-skinned denizens might be meeting friends. Kajla explained that they were merely "night occupants." Some of them had walked the miles from Delhi to be under a roof with space. Families were grouped about blankets like camping gypsies. Several smiled back at us as though pleased at having been clever enough to secure such a pleasant night's lodging.

Well, at least these poor could lie down for the night. We would be sitting up, and paying over $1,000 for the privilege, but we were grateful that we would not have to scramble for "economy" seats among the troupe of gigantic Rumanian wrestlers who had just completed a week of exhibition matches. We clasped Kajla's hand and passed on down a corridor into a waiting room for outgoing passengers. An electric sign announced that the Lufthansa flight was on time. The plane was even then landing. Again we were lucky, for some other airline flights were hours late.

Soon we were in our seats, enjoying an excellent dinner with plenteous high-grade champagne. A delicious feeling of well-being suffused us. We did not bother to look out at Karachi. But at Dhahran, in Saudi Arabia, the starlit desert cast a spell, as Arabs in white burnooses, looking like sheiks, strolled past our plane. We went to the open door and out onto the platform of the stairs to admire Edward Durrell Stone's beautiful airport. Its arches and columns were brilliantly outlined from the blaze of lights within. The midnight desert air was fresh and cool. The sight of this stunning modern structure set down in square miles of pale golden sand almost made up for our missing a daytime flight.

We slept peacefully until the landing at Cairo. None of the debarking passengers in either class was allowed to stir from his seat until a short, greasy-faced, roly-poly man had sprayed the cabin air against alien germs and insects. Under lowered lids I feigned sleep until the disinfector and a black-mustached official had finished casting suspicious glances at all the passengers and departed.

When scented hot washcloths were offered us we knew that we were approaching Rome's Leonardo da Vinci Airport. We set our watches back three hours and made ready for breakfast.

At the entrance to the airport luck sent us headlong into a Lufthansa man in uniform, who, with his heroic build and handsome face, looked ideal for playing a modern-dress version of Siegfried. Because the Lufthansa office in Delhi had radioed Rome to have us met by one of their representatives, I took this man for him. But he was the top manager of the airport facilities and was here at 6:00 A.M. on a Roman November day only for some very special reason. However, with a charming urbanity he saw us through immigration and customs. As I shook the German's hand in gratitude, first dawn came.

When we arrived at the Eden Hotel on tree-lined Via Ludovici the increasing light glinted from the golden leaves that still clung to the autumn branches. Although it was the sixteenth of November, the weather promised to match the aureate quality of the trees. The first time I had visited Rome in the 1920's it had seemed like an alien land. Now, after the exotic East, the Imperial City was as familiar as home.

Acknowledgments

Since a convenient itinerary and good hotels are of significant importance in the success and pleasure of foreign travel, I flew to New York for personal consultations. A long-time friend, Miss Marguerite Allen, Vice-President of Robert F. Warner, Inc., Distinguished Hotels, advised me according to my desires for hotels with garden or harbor views, and she made reservations for me in Japan, Hong Kong, and Italy. Mr. H. Ishida, manager of the Japan Travel Bureau International, assisted me perceptively with scheduling our time in Japan according to the places we wanted to visit. At the Government of India Tourist Office, Mr. A. K. Guha and Mr. Eustace Pereira gave me needful information about travel in India. Thardy Travel Bureau in Tuscaloosa, Alabama, booked our passage on ocean liners and our airplane flights throughout Asia and to Rome.

I am uncommonly indebted to Senator Lister Hill and Mr. William B. McComber, Jr., Assistant Secretary of State, in arranging an audience with His Majesty King Bhumibol of Thailand.

By good chance, while we were making our plans, we entertained in succession in our home three men who had recently made trips similar to our proposed journey. These three each gave us freely of the fruit of their personal experiences in the Far East. I am indebted to Mr. Fred R. Smith, then a senior editor of *Sports Illustrated* and now editor of *American Home;* to English-born Viscount Edwin Samuel, currently teaching at Jerusalem University in Israel; and to retired Admiral Charles R. (Cat) Brown, who ended his distinguished naval career as Deputy Commander of NATO.

Among the many Japanese who showed us courtesies and to whom we are grateful are: Mrs. Takakichi Aso, daughter of Prime Minister Shigeru Yoshida; Mr. Shimichiro Kudo, publisher of the Manichi newspaper complex, and Mrs. Kudo; Mr. John Ishizaki, managing editor of *This is Japan* magazine of the *Asahi Shimbun* chain; and Mrs. Mitsuko Shimomura, an assistant editor.

We are indeed grateful to Mr. Seymour Ziff, who asked various industrialists to look after us during our first days in Tokyo. Chief among those who made us feel welcome are Mr. K. Endo, President, and Mr. T. Kubo, General Manager of the Tokyo Electron Laboratories.

On crossing the Pacific on the *President Cleveland* to the Orient we had the good fortune to meet Mr. Albert Swing, head of U.S.O.M. in Thailand, and his stunning Swedish wife, who entertained us at their home in Bangkok and were most helpful with data and suggestions.

Mr. Harvey S. Olson of the Olson Travel Organization, Chicago, and author of the reliable *Olson's Guide to the Orient* was uncommonly kind in sending me special advice by letters, though I was doing no "business" whatever with him.

In Hong Kong Mr. Ronald McLaren, Director of the Government Information Services, gave most generously of his time, furnished specific data, and drove us all about the island. To Mr. T. V. P. Ross, British manager of The Mandarin, and to his Chinese public-relations chief, Miss Kai-Yin Lo, we are indebted for numerous thoughtful attentions.

In Thailand we were shown courtesies by Mr. Norman B. Hannah, and by Mr. Jay Long of the United States Embassy. Dr. Umphom and Wattanee Phanachet, husband and wife professors at Chulalongkorn University, entertained us in Bangkok and gave significant help. Mr. Kusa Panyrachun, American-educated Director of the World Travel Service, Ltd., based in Bangkok, assisted us signally by correspondence even before we reached Thailand to make use of his facilities.

I am more than profoundly grateful to His Majesty King Bhumibol of Thailand for his graciousness in receiving me at Chitralada Palace.

I am indebted to Madame Vijaya Lakshmi Pandit and her daughter Mrs. Rita Dar for numerous thoughtful courtesies in New Delhi, and to Ambassador Chester Bowles, who entertained us at luncheon.

Mr. William Land, manager of the Oberoi Intercontinental Hotel of New Delhi, and the Parsi hostess Mrs. Freny Nallaseth went far beyond the line of duty in doing us favors.

In Jaipur the Maharani entertained my wife and me at a private meeting in the library of her palace. Major Rawat Singh, manager of the Rambagh Palace Hotel in Jaipur, extended us personal hospitality. And Mr. Maheshwar Singh, local manager of Mercury Travel Service, was not only extra attentive but also became a personal friend.

I am grateful to Mr. Wade H. Coleman, Jr., Professor of Romance Languages at the University of Alabama, for reading my sections on India and Thailand with an editorial eye. And to Nagasaki-born Miss Emiko Sakurai, lecturer on Oriental Literature at the George Mason branch of the University of Virginia, for reading the section on Japan.

To Mr. Buford Boone, Pulitzer Prize-winning editor of the Tuscaloosa *News,* and to Dr. Paul Garner, Dean of the School of Commerce, University of Alabama, who have both traveled extensively in the Far East, I am indebted for their good counsel. And I thank Mr. Frank F. Stallworth for his assistance in typing the manuscript.

As a striking evidence of serendipity, Mr. David H. Engel, noted landscape gardener, gave me help and checked my descriptions of Buddhist temple gardens in Kyoto, where he had lived and studied for four years. Mr. Engel is the author of *Japanese Gardens for Today,* a copy of which had been presented to my wife in Tokyo. After our return to Alabama I gave a copy to my friend Mr. Jack Warner, President of the Gulf States Paper Corporation. Mr. Warner was so impressed that he engaged Mr. Engel to design a Japanese garden for his new three-and-a-half-million-dollar administration building, created in Japanese-style architecture. I am indebted to Jack Warner for bringing David Engel to Tuscaloosa and to our home, and to Mr. Engel for his authoritative advice.

Above all others I am grateful to my wife, Thérèse, for her several typings of my handwritten text, her indispensable criticism, her prod to my memory, and her valiant patience.

M